Chocolate

Protein Shake

Thank you very much for purchasing *Haikyu!!* volume 39! I wonder, is there a name for that phenomenon when you buy your favorite flavor of protein shake in bulk only to suddenly realize you're tired of that flavor?

HARUICHI FURUDATE began his manga career when he was 25 years old with the one-shot *Ousama Kid (King Kid)*, which won an honorable mention for the 14th Jump Treasure Newcomer Manga Prize. His first series, *Kiben Gakuha, Yotsuya Sensei no Kaidan [Philosophy School, Yotsuya Sensei's Ghost Stories]*, was serialized in Weekly Shonen Jump in 2010. In 2012, he began serializing *Haikyu!!* in Weekly Shonen Jump, where it became his most popular work to date.

HAIKYU!!

VOLUME 39

SHONEN JUMP Manga Edition

Story and Art by

HARUICHI FURUDATE

Translation ■ **ADRIENNE BECK**
Touch-Up Art & Lettering ■ **ERIKA TERRIQUEZ**
Design ■ **JULIAN [JR] ROBINSON**
Editor ■ **MARLENE FIRST**

Printed in the U.S.A.

Published by VIZ Media, LLC
P.O. Box 77010
San Francisco, CA 94107

10 9 8 7 6 5 4 3 2 1
First printing, July 2020

VIZ MEDIA
viz.com

ratings.viz.com RATED T TEEN

PARENTAL ADVISORY
HAIKYU!! is rated T for Teen and is recommended for ages 13 and up for mild language.

SHONEN JUMP
shonenjump.com

HARUICHI
FURUDATE

LITTLE GIANTS

39

Karasuno High School Volleyball Club

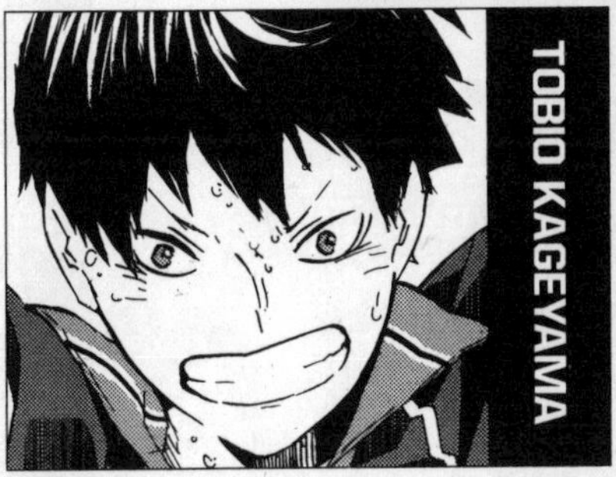
TOBIO KAGEYAMA

1ST YEAR / SETTER

His instincts and athletic talent are so good that he's like a "king" who rules the court. Demanding and egocentric.

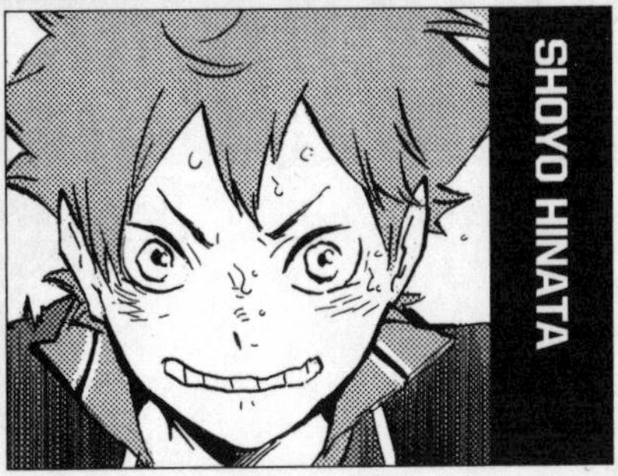
SHOYO HINATA

1ST YEAR / MIDDLE BLOCKER

Even though he doesn't have the best body type for volleyball, he is super athletic. Gets nervous easily.

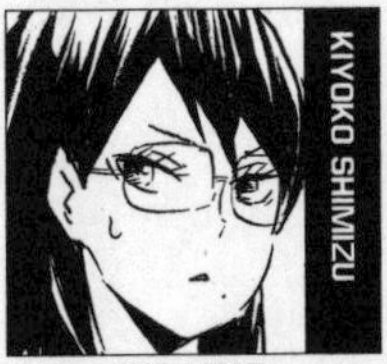
KIYOKO SHIMIZU

3RD YEAR
MANAGER

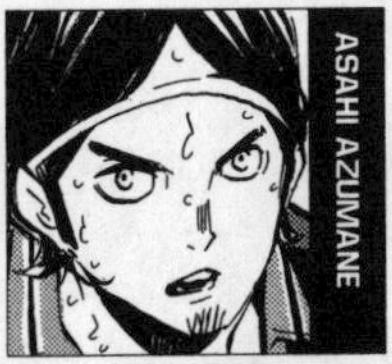
ASAHI AZUMANE

3RD YEAR
WING SPIKER

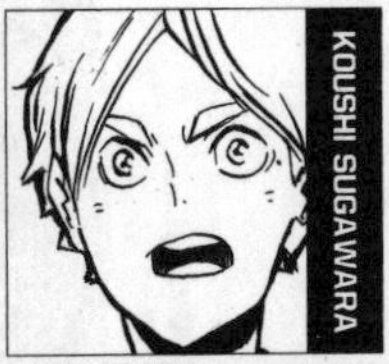
KOUSHI SUGAWARA

3RD YEAR (VICE CAPTAIN)
SETTER

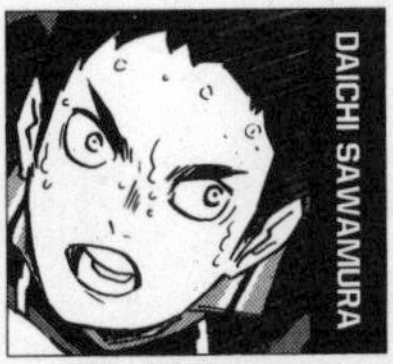
DAICHI SAWAMURA

3RD YEAR (CAPTAIN)
WING SPIKER

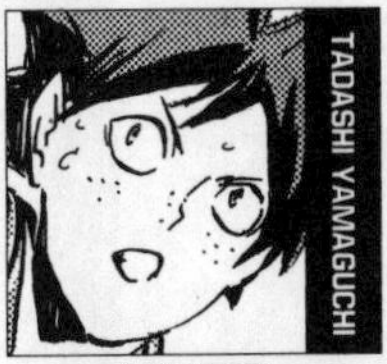
TADASHI YAMAGUCHI

1ST YEAR
MIDDLE BLOCKER

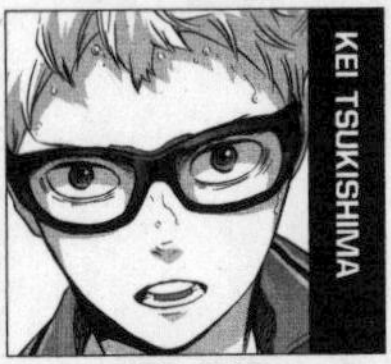
KEI TSUKISHIMA

1ST YEAR
MIDDLE BLOCKER

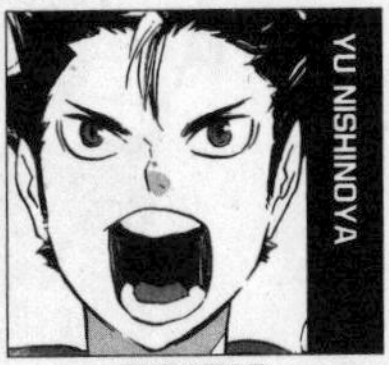
YU NISHINOYA

2ND YEAR
LIBERO

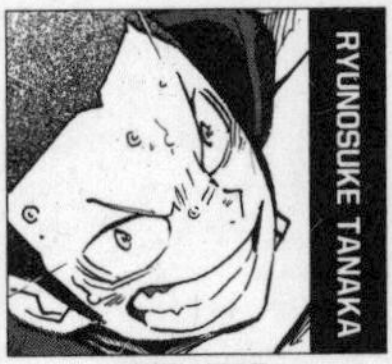
RYUNOSUKE TANAKA

2ND YEAR
WING SPIKER

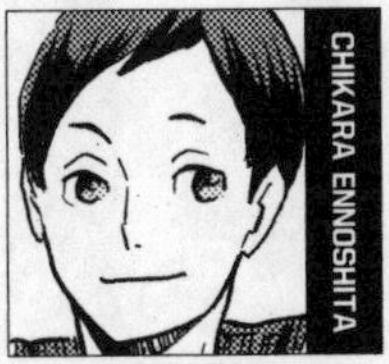
CHIKARA ENNOSHITA

2ND YEAR
WING SPIKER

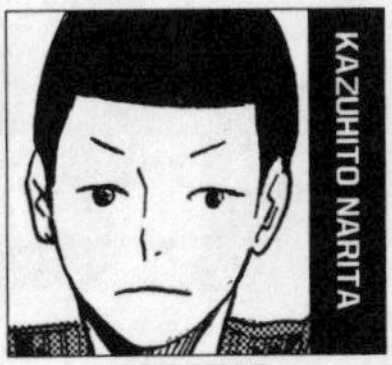
KAZUHITO NARITA

2ND YEAR
MIDDLE BLOCKER

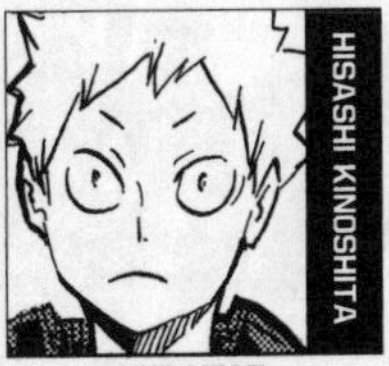
HISASHI KINOSHITA

2ND YEAR
WING SPIKER

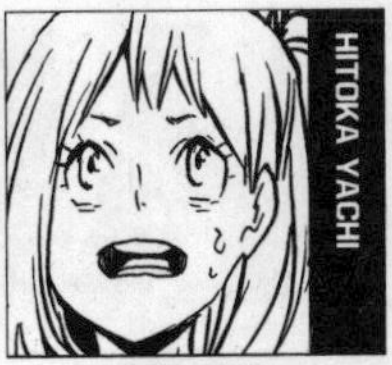
HITOKA YACHI

1ST YEAR
MANAGER

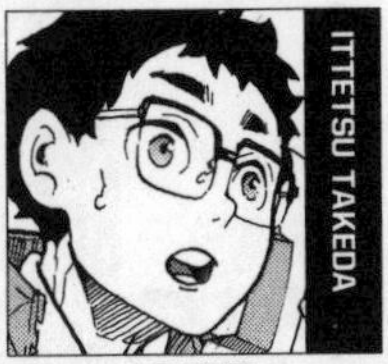
ITTETSU TAKEDA

ADVISER

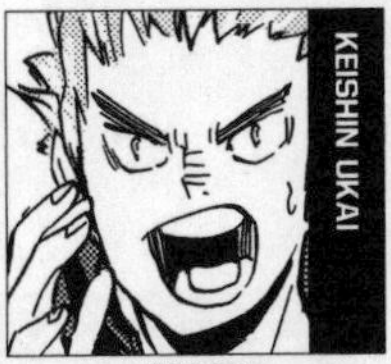
KEISHIN UKAI

COACH

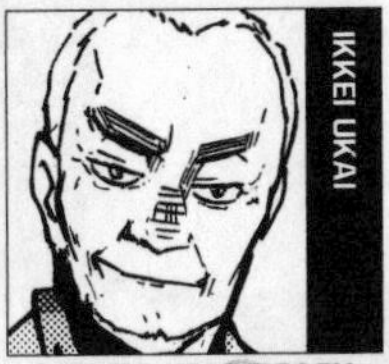
IKKEI UKAI

FORMER HEAD COACH

CHARACTERS

NATIONAL SPRING TOURNAMENT ARC

Kamomedai High School Volleyball Club

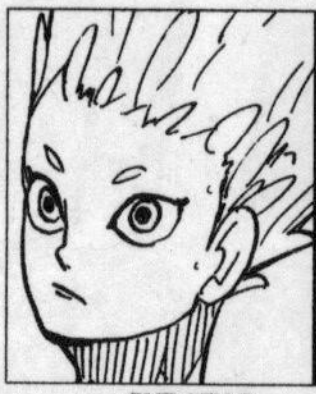
KORAI HOSHIUMI
2ND YEAR
WING SPIKER

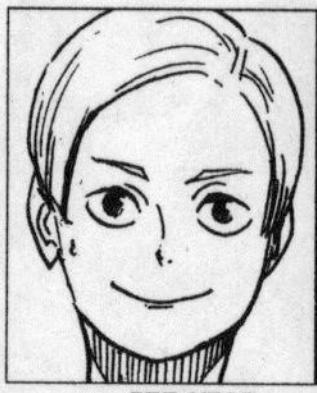
KEIICHIRO KANBAYASHI
3RD YEAR
LIBERO

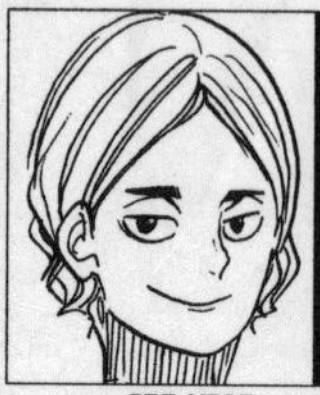
IZURU NOZAWA
3RD YEAR
WING SPIKER

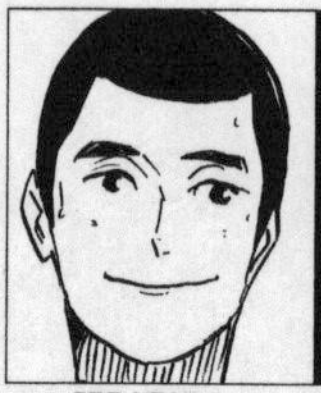
AIKICHI SUWA
3RD YEAR (CAPTAIN)
SETTER

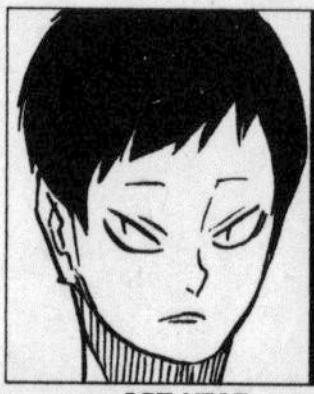
KAZUYOSHI BESSHO
1ST YEAR
MIDDLE BLOCKER

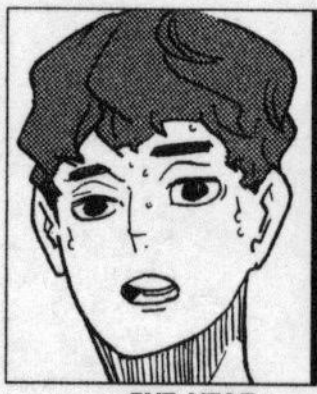
SACHIRO HIRUGAMI
2ND YEAR
MIDDLE BLOCKER

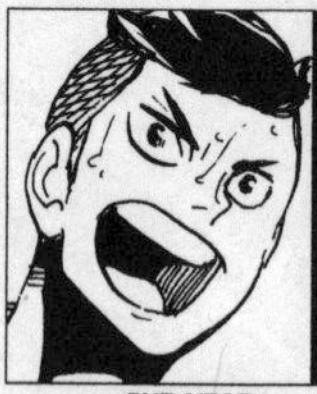
GAO HAKUBA
2ND YEAR
WING SPIKER

Nekoma Volleyball Club

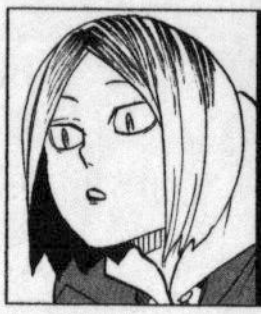
KENMA KOZUME

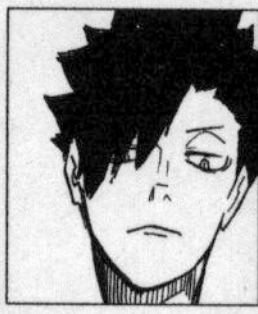
TETSURO KUROO

Karasuno Cheering Section

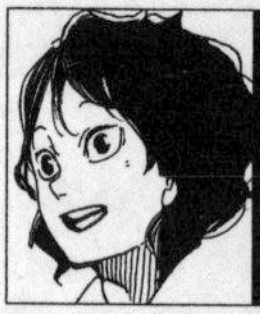
TENMA UDAI

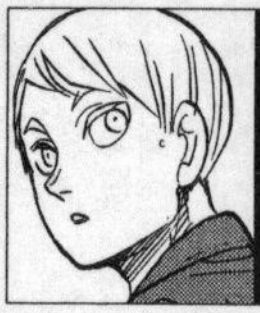
KITERU TSUKISHIMA

Ever since he saw the legendary player known as "the Little Giant" compete at the national volleyball finals, Shoyo Hinata has been aiming to be the best volleyball player ever! He decides to join the volleyball club at his middle school and gets to play in an official tournament during his third year. His team is crushed by a team led by volleyball prodigy Tobio Kageyama, also known as "the King of the Court." Swearing revenge on Kageyama, Hinata graduates middle school and enters Karasuno High School, the school where the Little Giant played. However, upon joining the club, he finds out that Kageyama is there too! The two of them bicker constantly, but they bring out the best in each other's talents and become a powerful combo. It's day 3 of the Spring Tournament, and Fukurodani is squaring off against Mujinazaka in the quarterfinals. Akaashi does poorly in the first set and gets benched. But after some self-reflection, he comes to the realization that the best he can do when playing with star players is to do what he always does. Returning to the game, Akaashi answers the expectations of an even-more-demanding-than-usual Bokuto, and although Kiryu—also influenced by Bokuto's enthusiasm—is playing at an incredibly high level, Fukurodani still gets the win. Meanwhile, Karasuno has begun its quarterfinal match against Kamomedai. Only a few plays in, and with the original Little Giant, Tenma Udai, watching in the stands, Hinata and Kageyama's freak quick gets stuffed by Kamomedai's Hirugami!

HAIKYU!!

39 LITTLE GIANTS

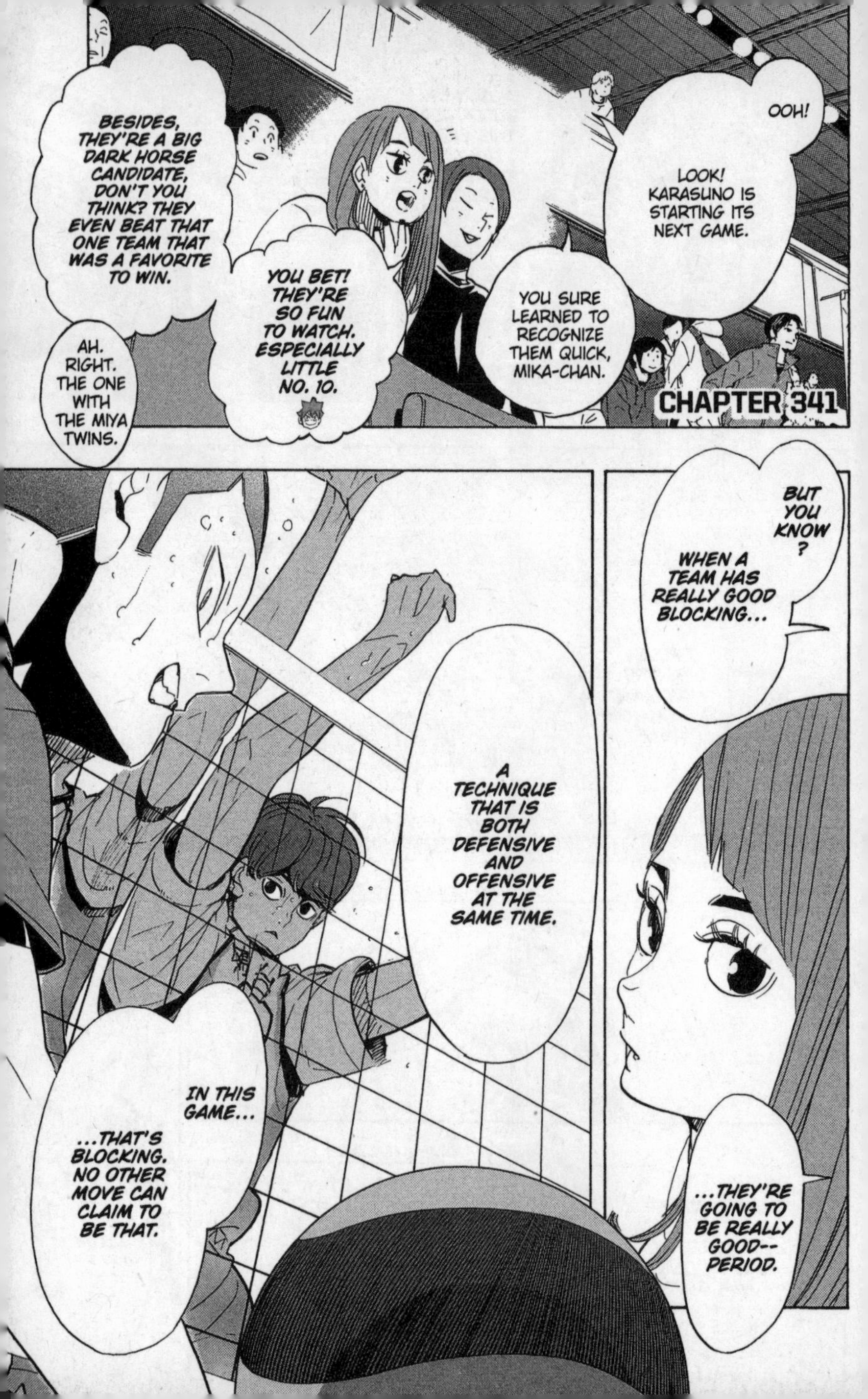
OOH!
LOOK! KARASUNO IS STARTING ITS NEXT GAME.
CHAPTER 341
YOU SURE LEARNED TO RECOGNIZE THEM QUICK, MIKA-CHAN.
YOU BET! THEY'RE SO FUN TO WATCH. ESPECIALLY LITTLE NO. 10.
BESIDES, THEY'RE A BIG DARK HORSE CANDIDATE, DON'T YOU THINK? THEY EVEN BEAT THAT ONE TEAM THAT WAS A FAVORITE TO WIN.
AH. RIGHT. THE ONE WITH THE MIYA TWINS.
BUT YOU KNOW?
WHEN A TEAM HAS REALLY GOOD BLOCKING...
...THEY'RE GOING TO BE REALLY GOOD--PERIOD.
A TECHNIQUE THAT IS BOTH DEFENSIVE AND OFFENSIVE AT THE SAME TIME.
IN THIS GAME...
...THAT'S BLOCKING. NO OTHER MOVE CAN CLAIM TO BE THAT.

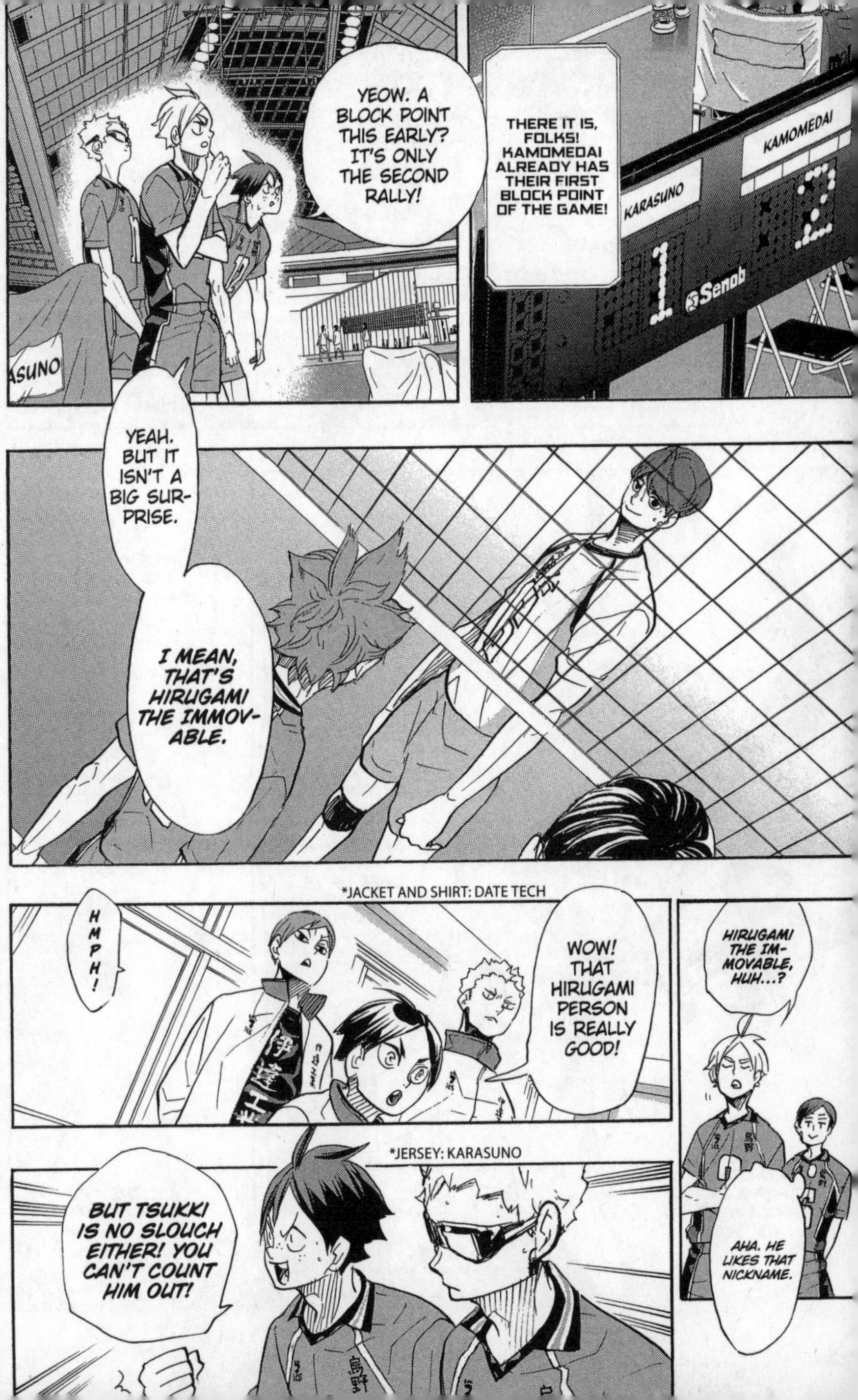
KAMOMEDAI
KARASUNO
THERE IT IS, FOLKS! KAMOMEDAI ALREADY HAS THEIR FIRST BLOCK POINT OF THE GAME!
YEOW. A BLOCK POINT THIS EARLY? IT'S ONLY THE SECOND RALLY!
YEAH. BUT IT ISN'T A BIG SURPRISE.
I MEAN, THAT'S HIRUGAMI THE IMMOVABLE.
*JACKET AND SHIRT: DATE TECH
HIRUGAMI THE IMMOVABLE, HUH...?
AHA. HE LIKES THAT NICKNAME.
WOW! THAT HIRUGAMI PERSON IS REALLY GOOD!
HMPH!
*JERSEY: KARASUNO
BUT TSUKKI IS NO SLOUCH EITHER! YOU CAN'T COUNT HIM OUT!

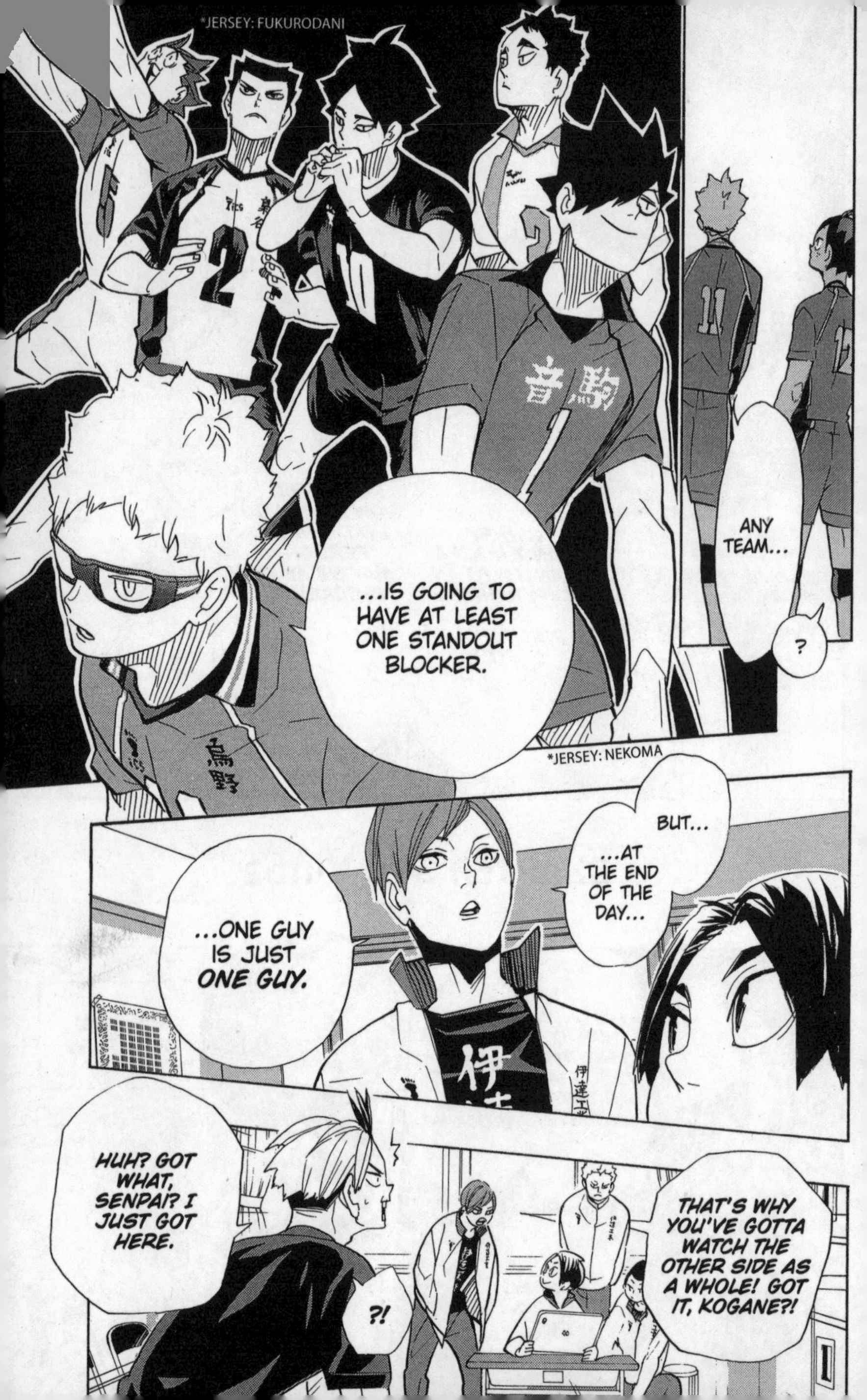
ANY TEAM...
?
*JERSEY: FUKURODANI
...IS GOING TO HAVE AT LEAST ONE STANDOUT BLOCKER.
*JERSEY: NEKOMA
BUT...
...AT THE END OF THE DAY...
...ONE GUY IS JUST ONE GUY.
THAT'S WHY YOU'VE GOTTA WATCH THE OTHER SIDE AS A WHOLE! GOT IT, KOGANE?!
?!
HUH? GOT WHAT, SENPAI? I JUST GOT HERE.

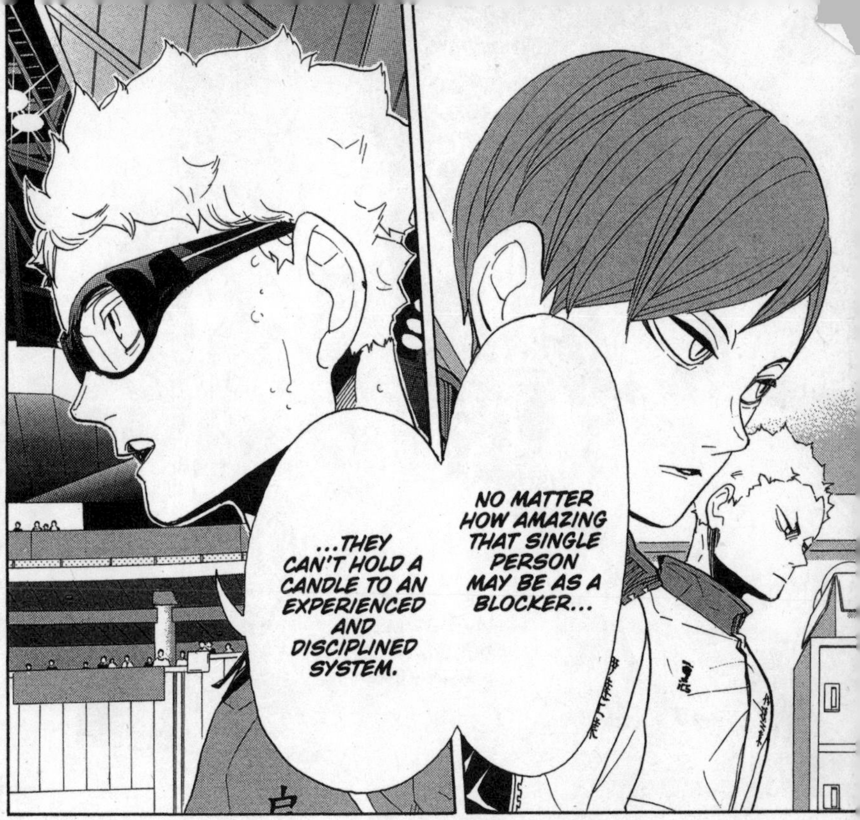
NO MATTER HOW AMAZING THAT SINGLE PERSON MAY BE AS A BLOCKER...
...THEY CAN'T HOLD A CANDLE TO AN EXPERIENCED AND DISCIPLINED SYSTEM.

CHAPTER 341: Vines

*JERSEY: KAMOMEDAI

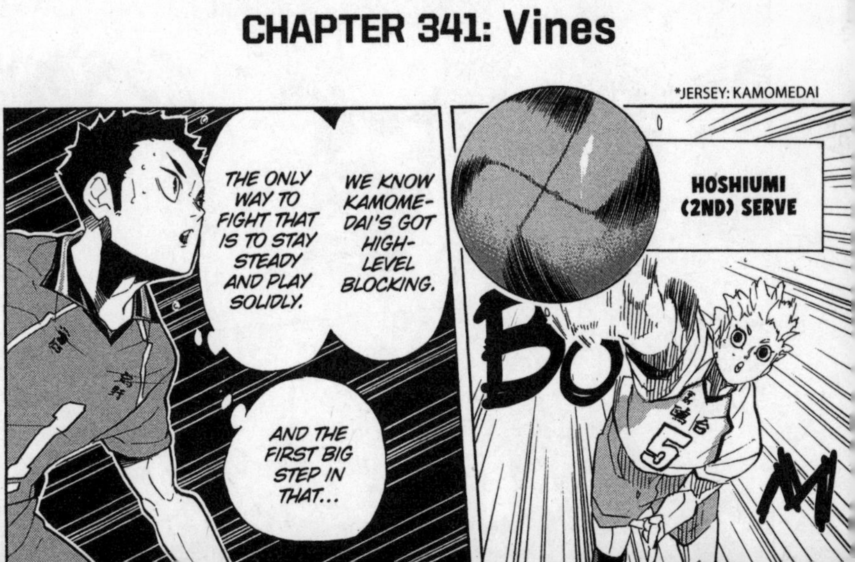
HOSHIUMI (2ND) SERVE
BO
M
WE KNOW KAMOME-DAI'S GOT HIGH-LEVEL BLOCKING.
THE ONLY WAY TO FIGHT THAT IS TO STAY STEADY AND PLAY SOLIDLY.
AND THE FIRST BIG STEP IN THAT...

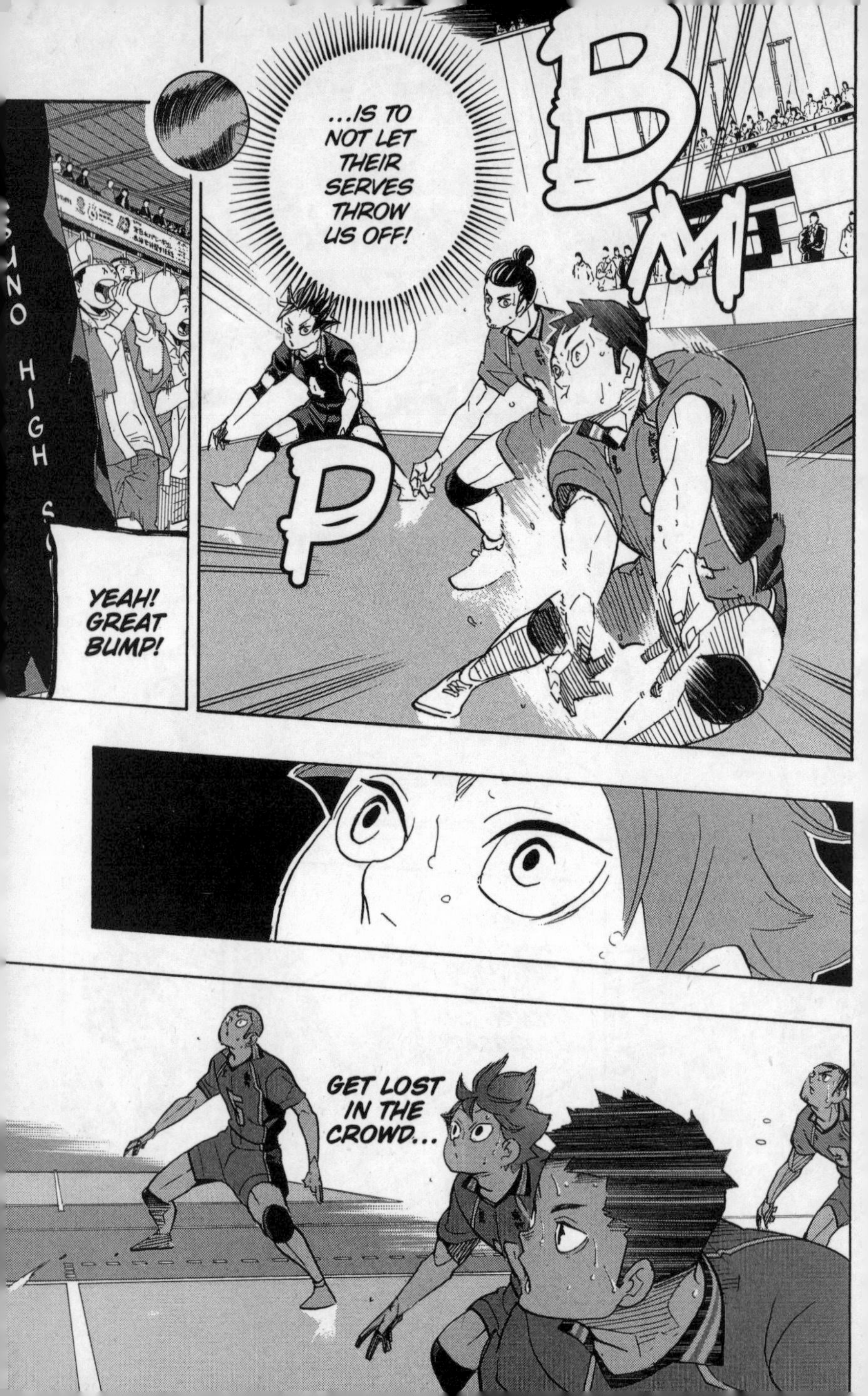
...IS TO NOT LET THEIR SERVES THROW US OFF!
BMP
YEAH! GREAT BUMP!
GET LOST IN THE CROWD...

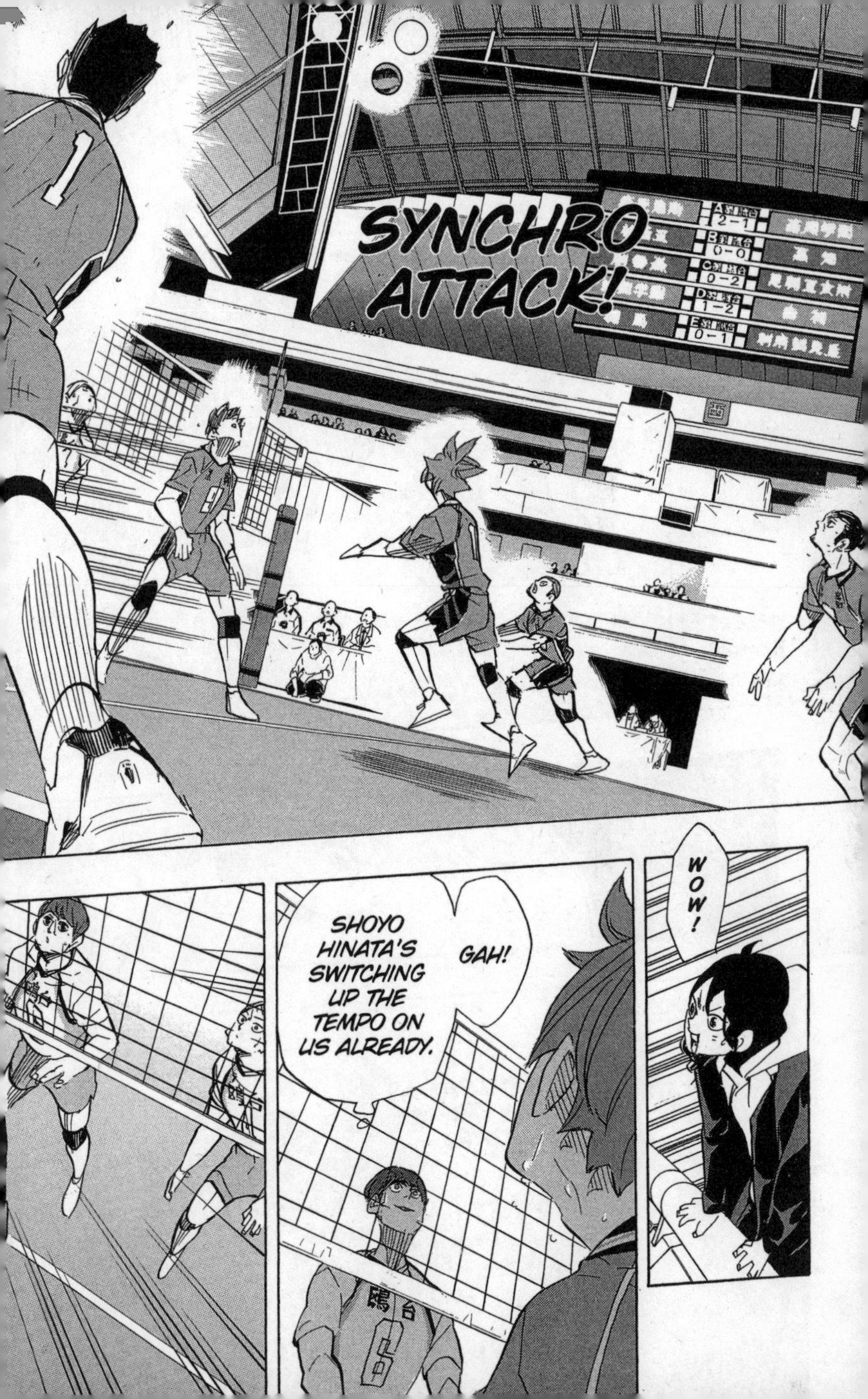

SYNCHRO ATTACK!
WOW!
SHOYO HINATA'S SWITCHING UP THE TEMPO ON US ALREADY.
GAH!

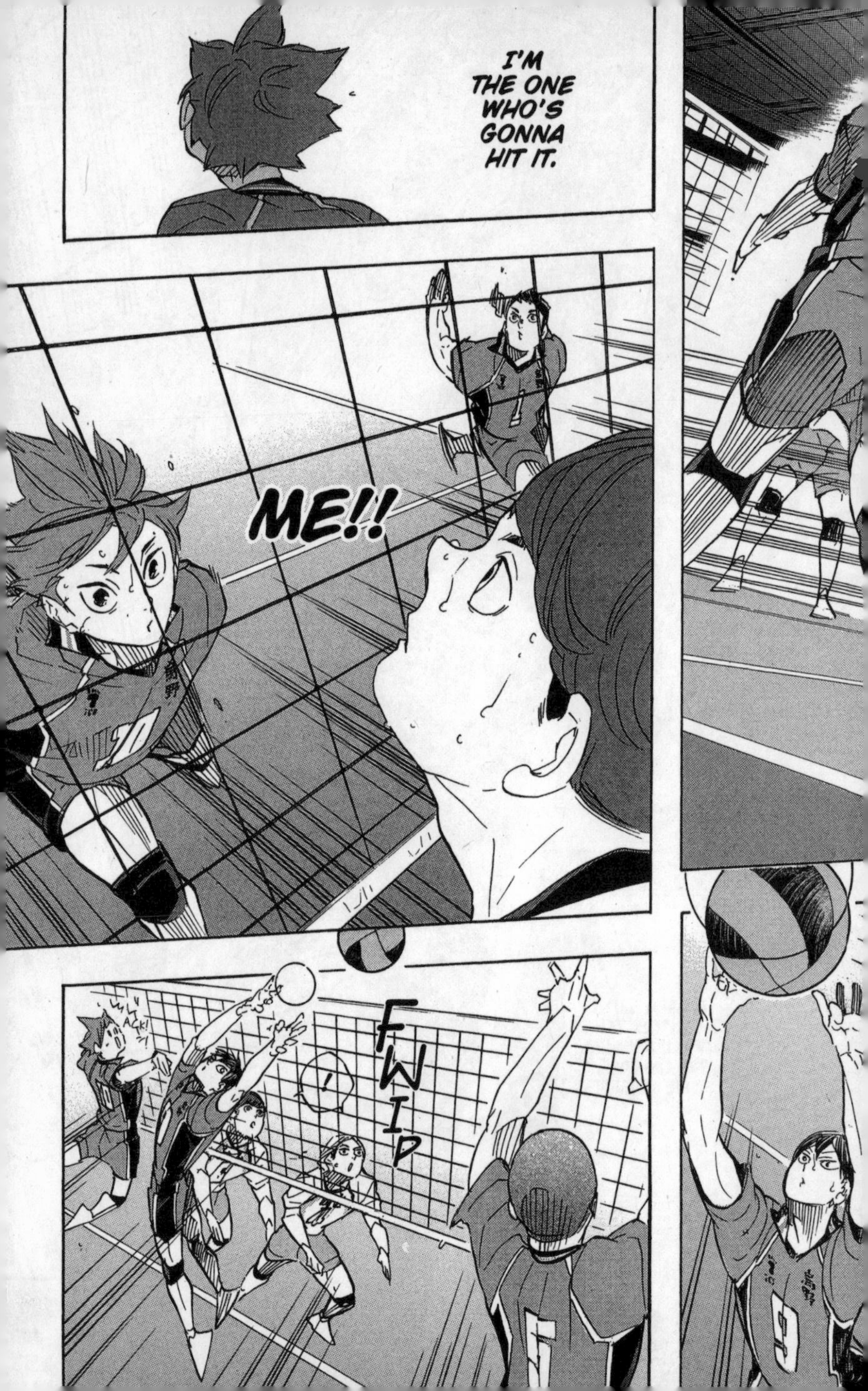
I'M THE ONE WHO'S GONNA HIT IT.
ME!!
FWIP
!
ACK!

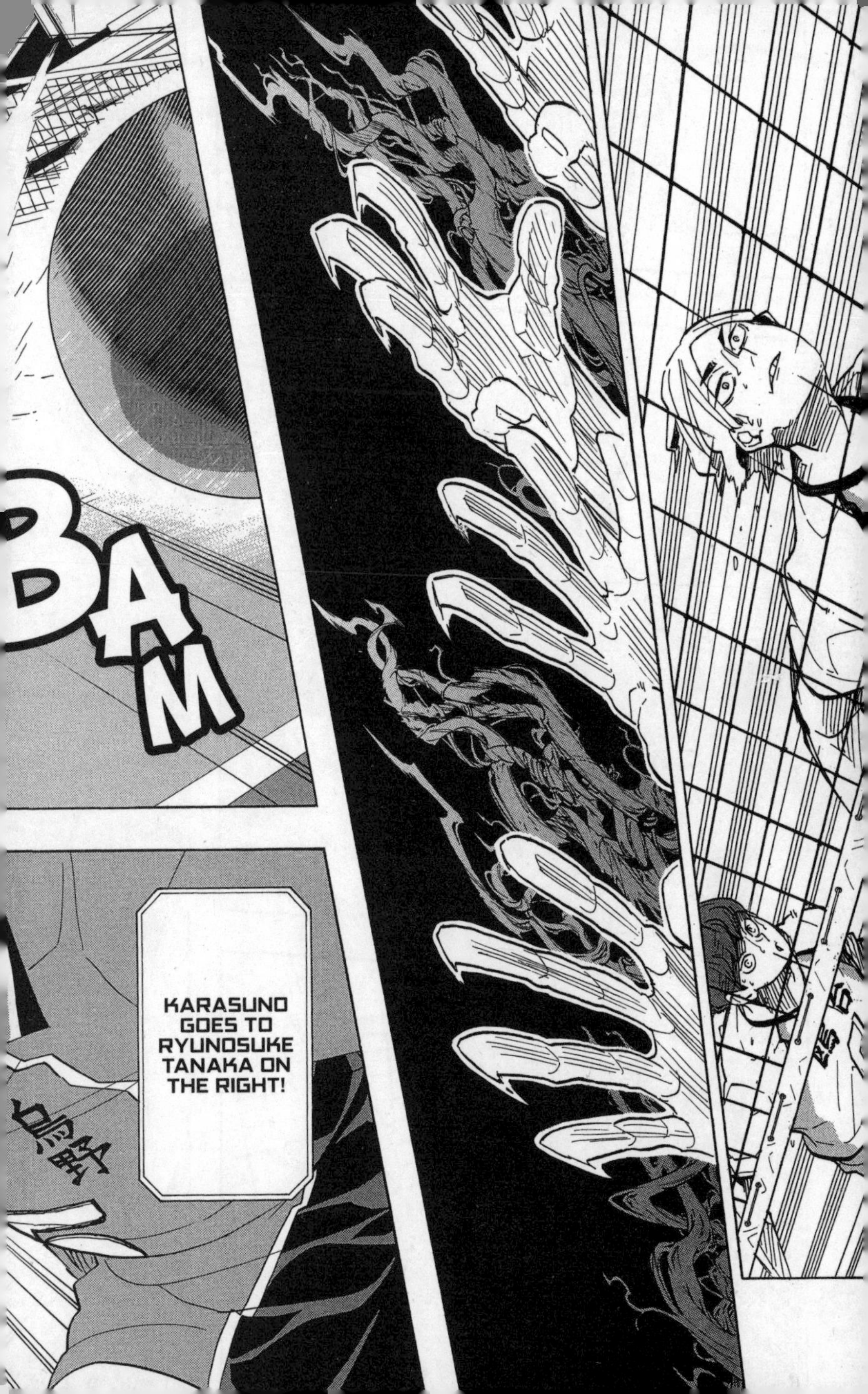
BAM
KARASUNO GOES TO RYUNOSUKE TANAKA ON THE RIGHT!

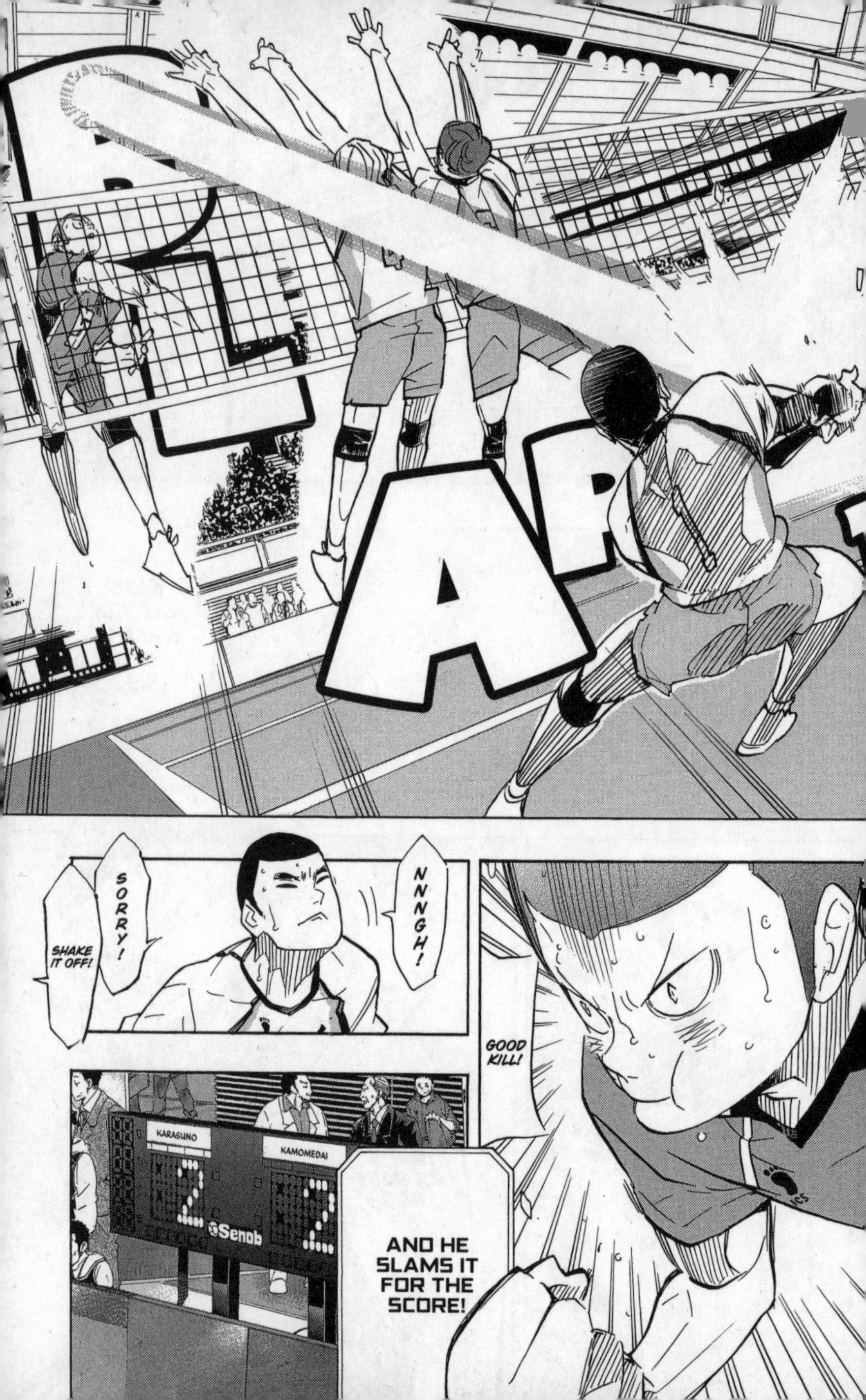
GOOD KILL!
AND HE SLAMS IT FOR THE SCORE!
NNNGH!
SORRY!
SHAKE IT OFF!
KARASUNO
KAMOMEDAI
Senob

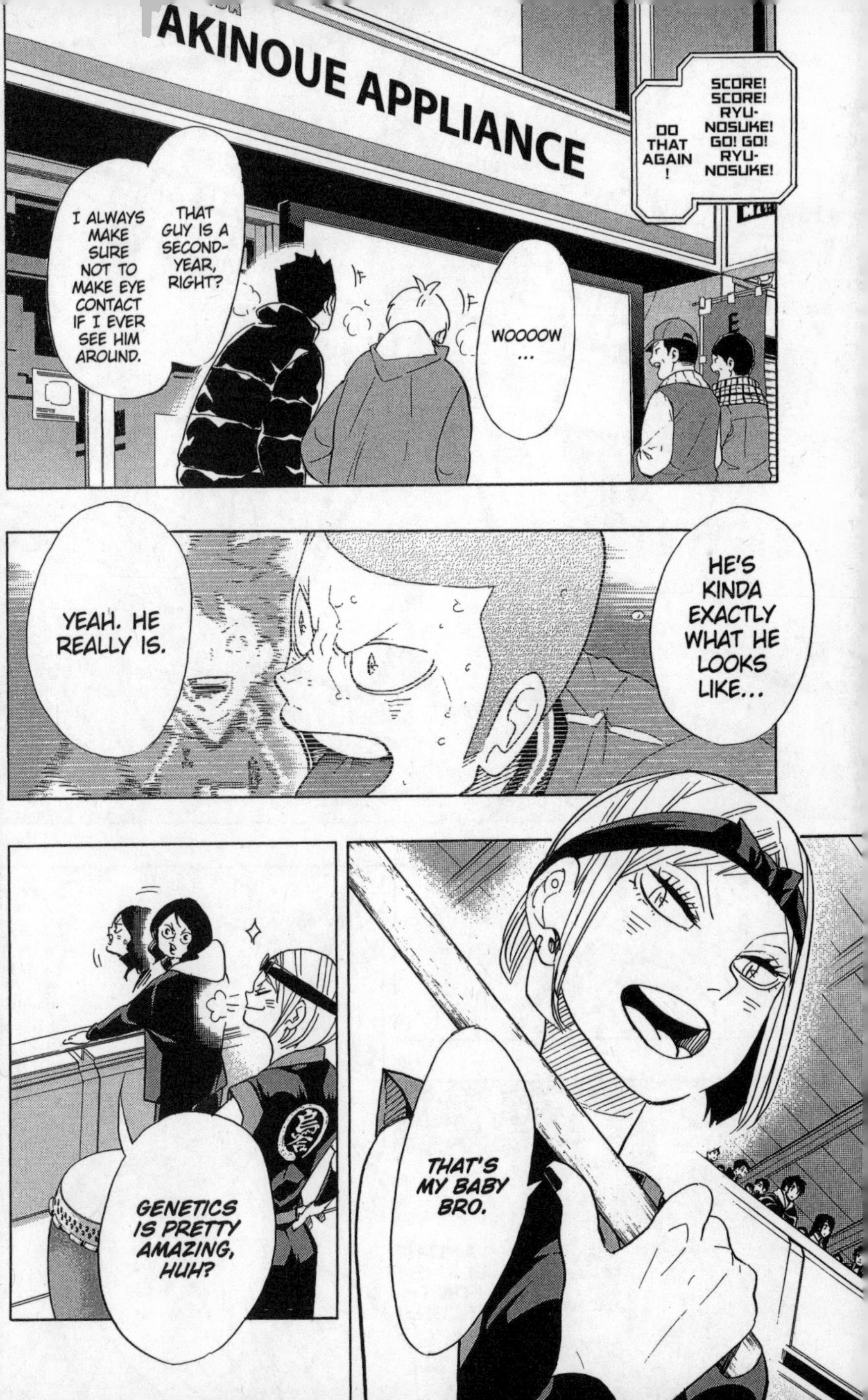
AKINOUE APPLIANCE
SCORE! SCORE! RYU-NOSUKE! GO! GO! RYU-NOSUKE!
DO THAT AGAIN!
WOOOOW...
THAT GUY IS A SECOND-YEAR, RIGHT?
I ALWAYS MAKE SURE NOT TO MAKE EYE CONTACT IF I EVER SEE HIM AROUND.
HE'S KINDA EXACTLY WHAT HE LOOKS LIKE...
YEAH. HE REALLY IS.
THAT'S MY BABY BRO.
GENETICS IS PRETTY AMAZING, HUH?

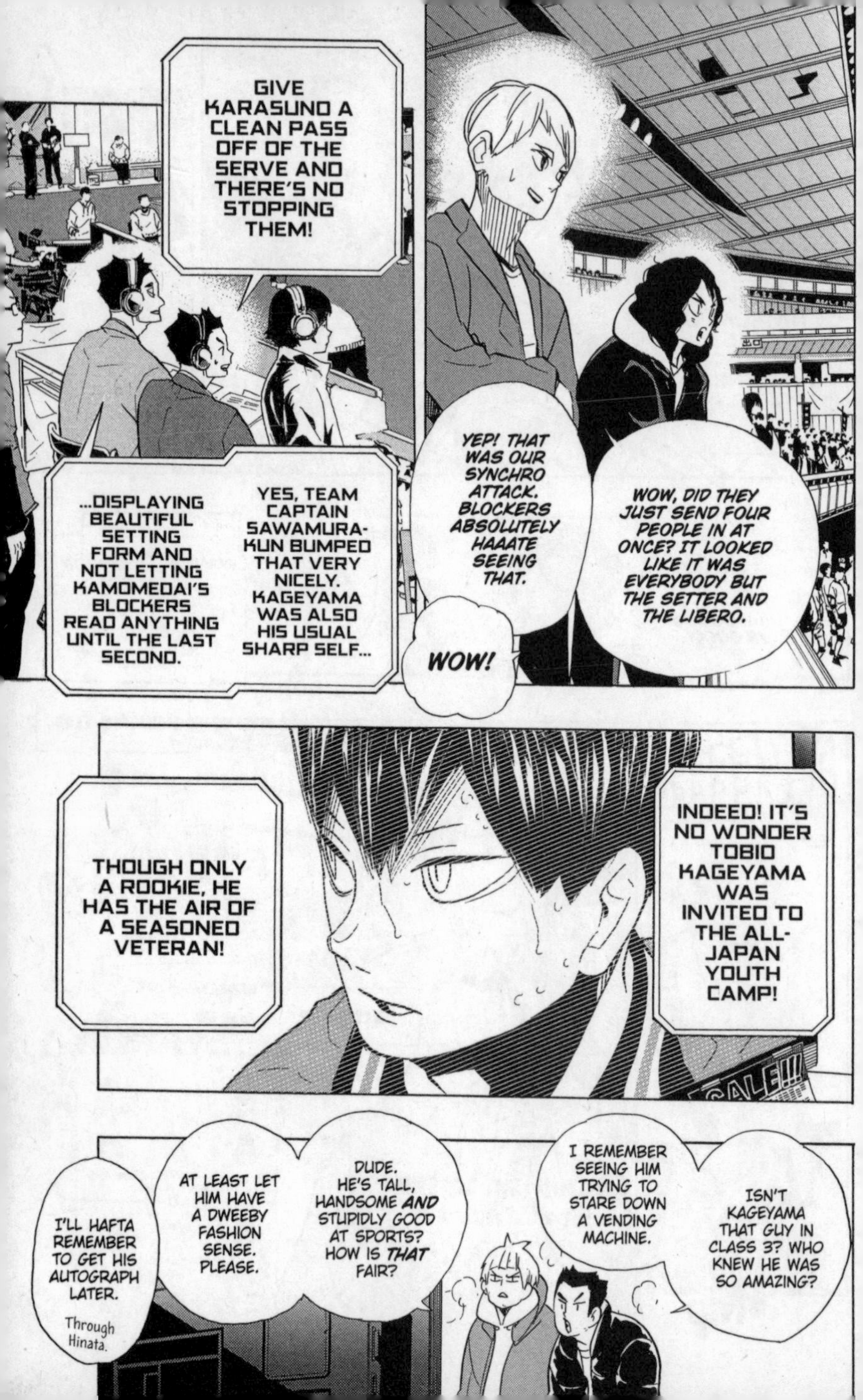
WOW, DID THEY JUST SEND FOUR PEOPLE IN AT ONCE? IT LOOKED LIKE IT WAS EVERYBODY BUT THE SETTER AND THE LIBERO.
YEP! THAT WAS OUR SYNCHRO ATTACK. BLOCKERS ABSOLUTELY HAAATE SEEING THAT.
WOW!
GIVE KARASUNO A CLEAN PASS OFF OF THE SERVE AND THERE'S NO STOPPING THEM!
YES, TEAM CAPTAIN SAWAMURA-KUN BUMPED THAT VERY NICELY. KAGEYAMA WAS ALSO HIS USUAL SHARP SELF...
...DISPLAYING BEAUTIFUL SETTING FORM AND NOT LETTING KAMOMEDAI'S BLOCKERS READ ANYTHING UNTIL THE LAST SECOND.
INDEED! IT'S NO WONDER TOBIO KAGEYAMA WAS INVITED TO THE ALL-JAPAN YOUTH CAMP!
THOUGH ONLY A ROOKIE, HE HAS THE AIR OF A SEASONED VETERAN!
SALE!!!
ISN'T KAGEYAMA THAT GUY IN CLASS 3? WHO KNEW HE WAS SO AMAZING?
I REMEMBER SEEING HIM TRYING TO STARE DOWN A VENDING MACHINE.
DUDE. HE'S TALL, HANDSOME AND STUPIDLY GOOD AT SPORTS? HOW IS THAT FAIR?
AT LEAST LET HIM HAVE A DWEEBY FASHION SENSE. PLEASE.
I'LL HAFTA REMEMBER TO GET HIS AUTOGRAPH LATER.
Through Hinata.

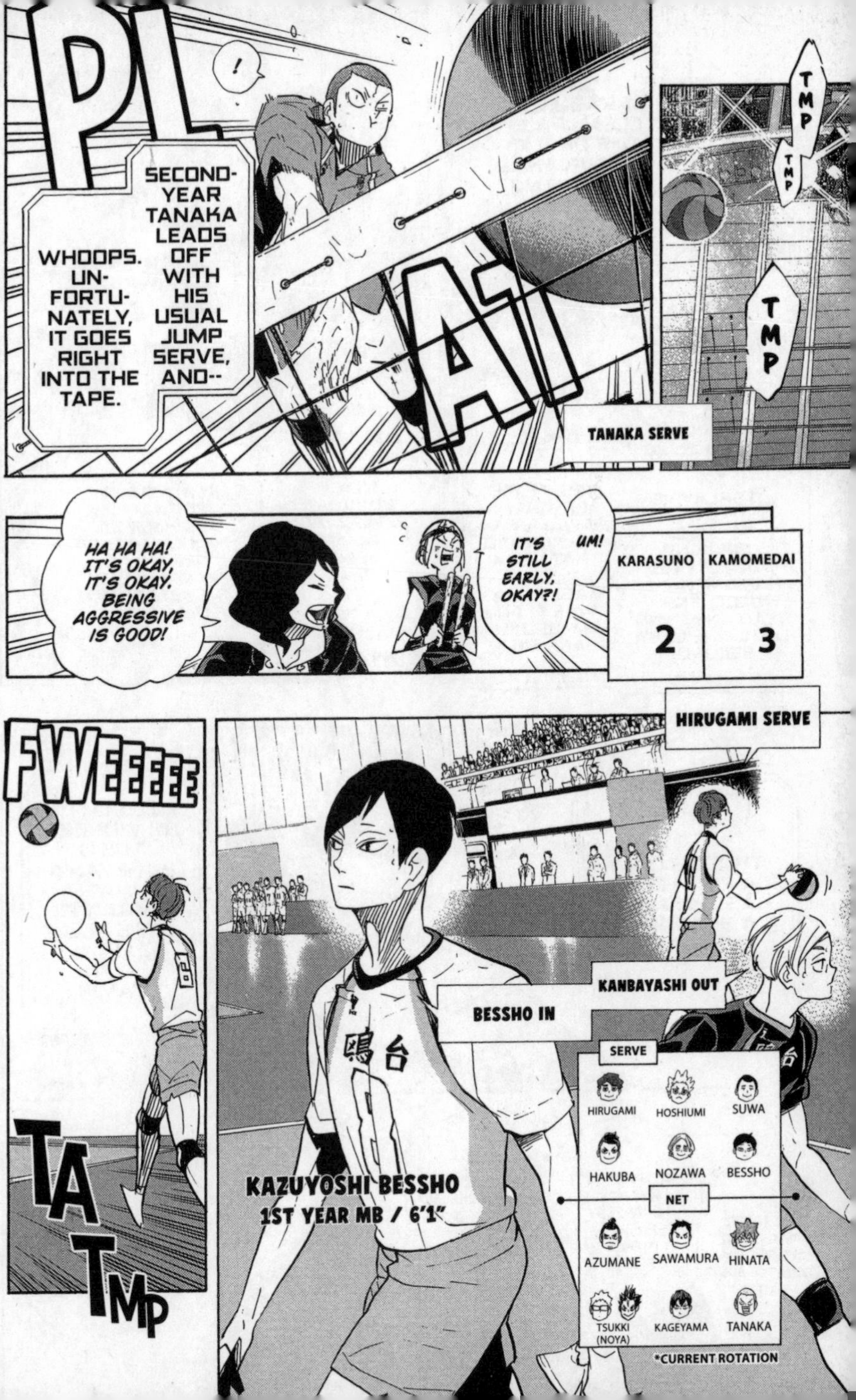
TMP
TMP
TMP
TANAKA SERVE
!
SECOND-YEAR TANAKA LEADS OFF WITH HIS USUAL JUMP SERVE, AND--
PLAI
WHOOPS. UNFORTUNATELY, IT GOES RIGHT INTO THE TAPE.
KARASUNO 2
KAMOMEDAI 3
UM!
IT'S STILL EARLY, OKAY?!
HA HA HA! IT'S OKAY, IT'S OKAY. BEING AGGRESSIVE IS GOOD!
HIRUGAMI SERVE
KANBAYASHI OUT
BESSHO IN
KAZUYOSHI BESSHO
1ST YEAR MB / 6'1"
SERVE
HIRUGAMI
HOSHIUMI
SUWA
HAKUBA
NOZAWA
BESSHO
NET
AZUMANE
SAWAMURA
HINATA
TSUKKI (NOYA)
KAGEYAMA
TANAKA
*CURRENT ROTATION
FWEEEEE
TA
TMP

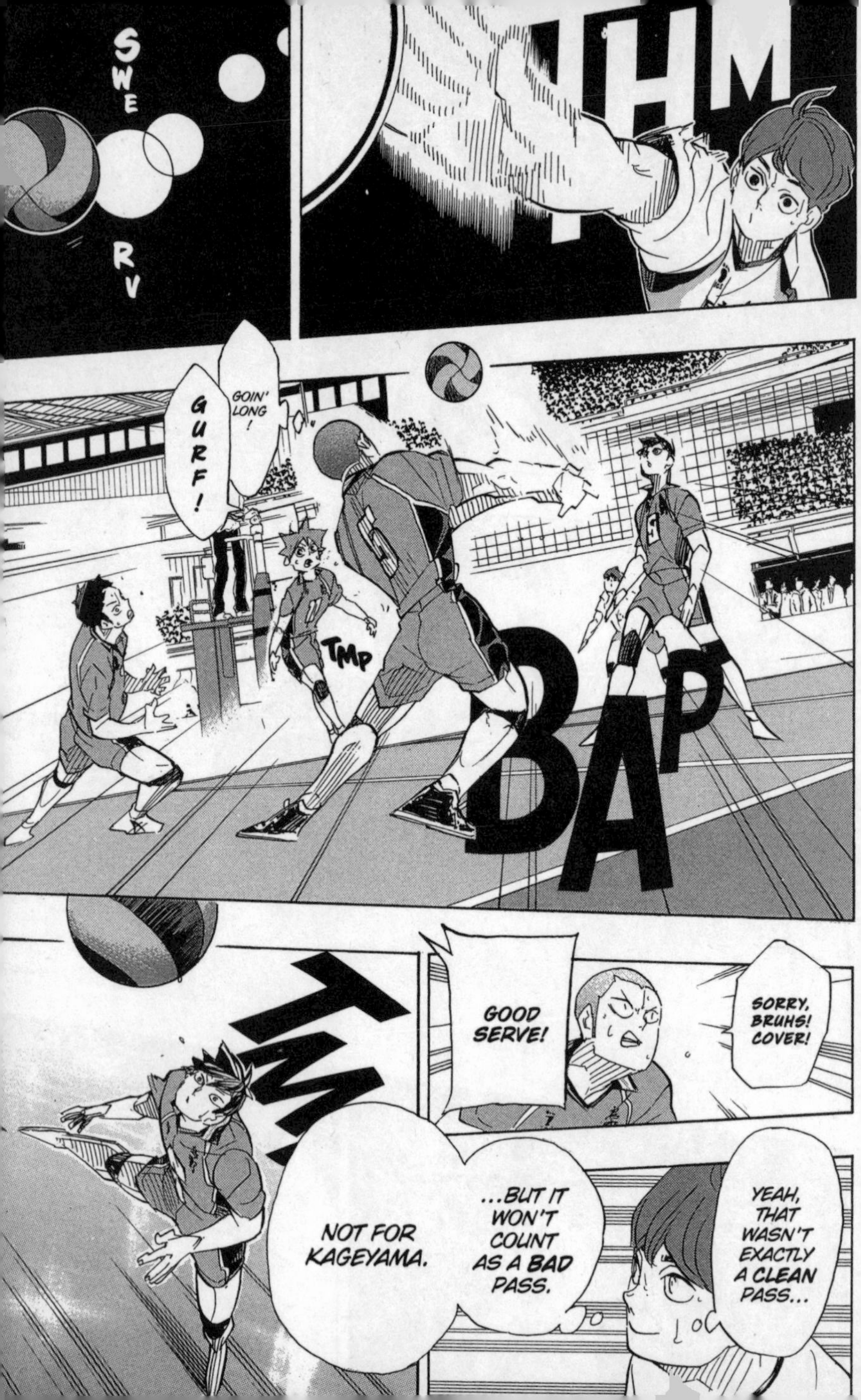
THM
SWE
RV
GOIN' LONG!
GURF!
TMP
BAP
SORRY, BRUHS! COVER!
GOOD SERVE!
YEAH, THAT WASN'T EXACTLY A CLEAN PASS...
...BUT IT WON'T COUNT AS A BAD PASS.
NOT FOR KAGEYAMA.
TM

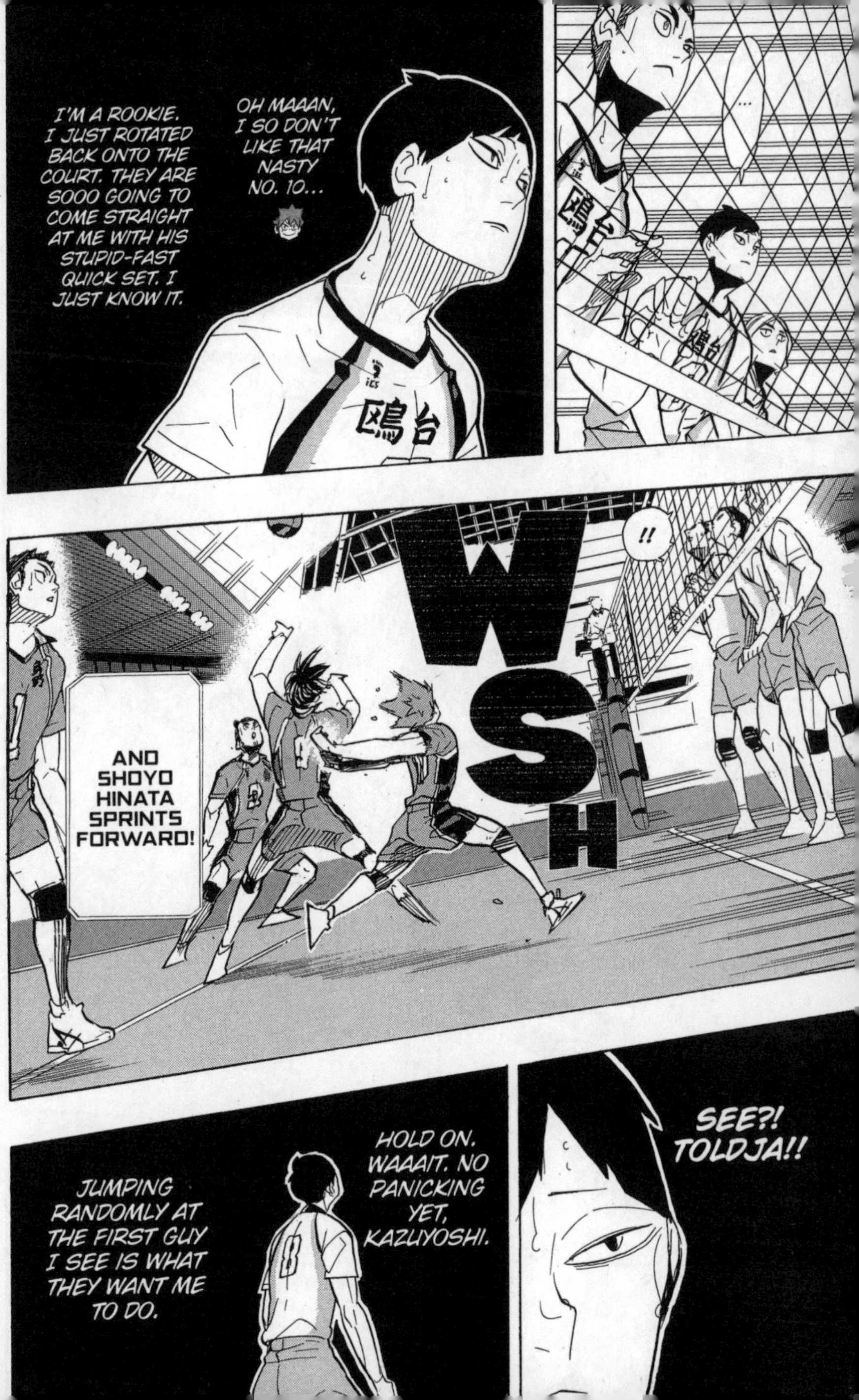
...
OH MAAAN, I SO DON'T LIKE THAT NASTY NO. 10...
I'M A ROOKIE. I JUST ROTATED BACK ONTO THE COURT. THEY ARE SOOO GOING TO COME STRAIGHT AT ME WITH HIS STUPID-FAST QUICK SET. I JUST KNOW IT.
!!
WSH
AND SHOYO HINATA SPRINTS FORWARD!
SEE?! TOLDJA!!
HOLD ON. WAAAIT. NO PANICKING YET, KAZUYOSHI.
JUMPING RANDOMLY AT THE FIRST GUY I SEE IS WHAT THEY WANT ME TO DO.

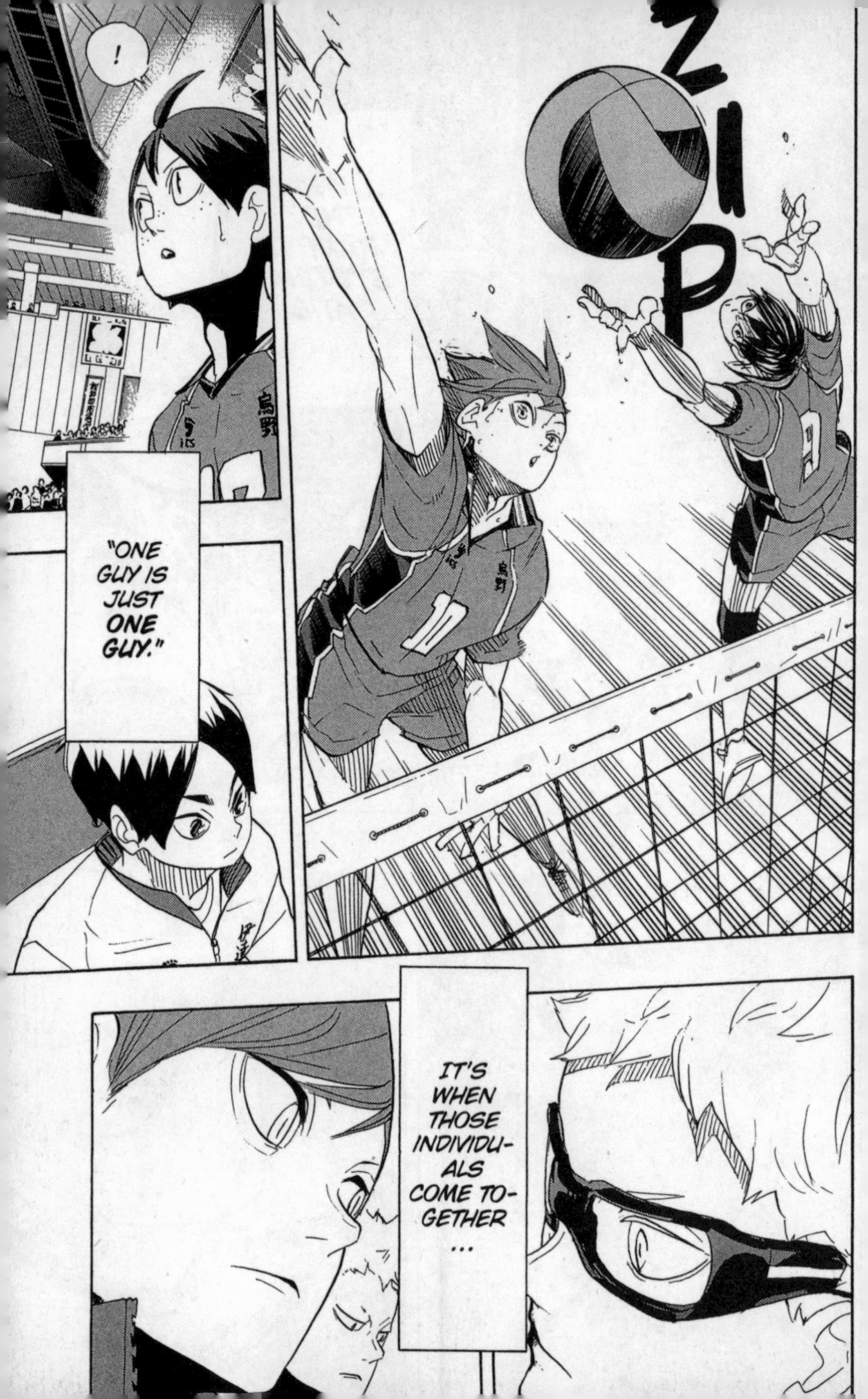
ZIP
!
"ONE GUY IS JUST ONE GUY."
IT'S WHEN THOSE INDIVIDU-ALS COME TO-GETHER ...

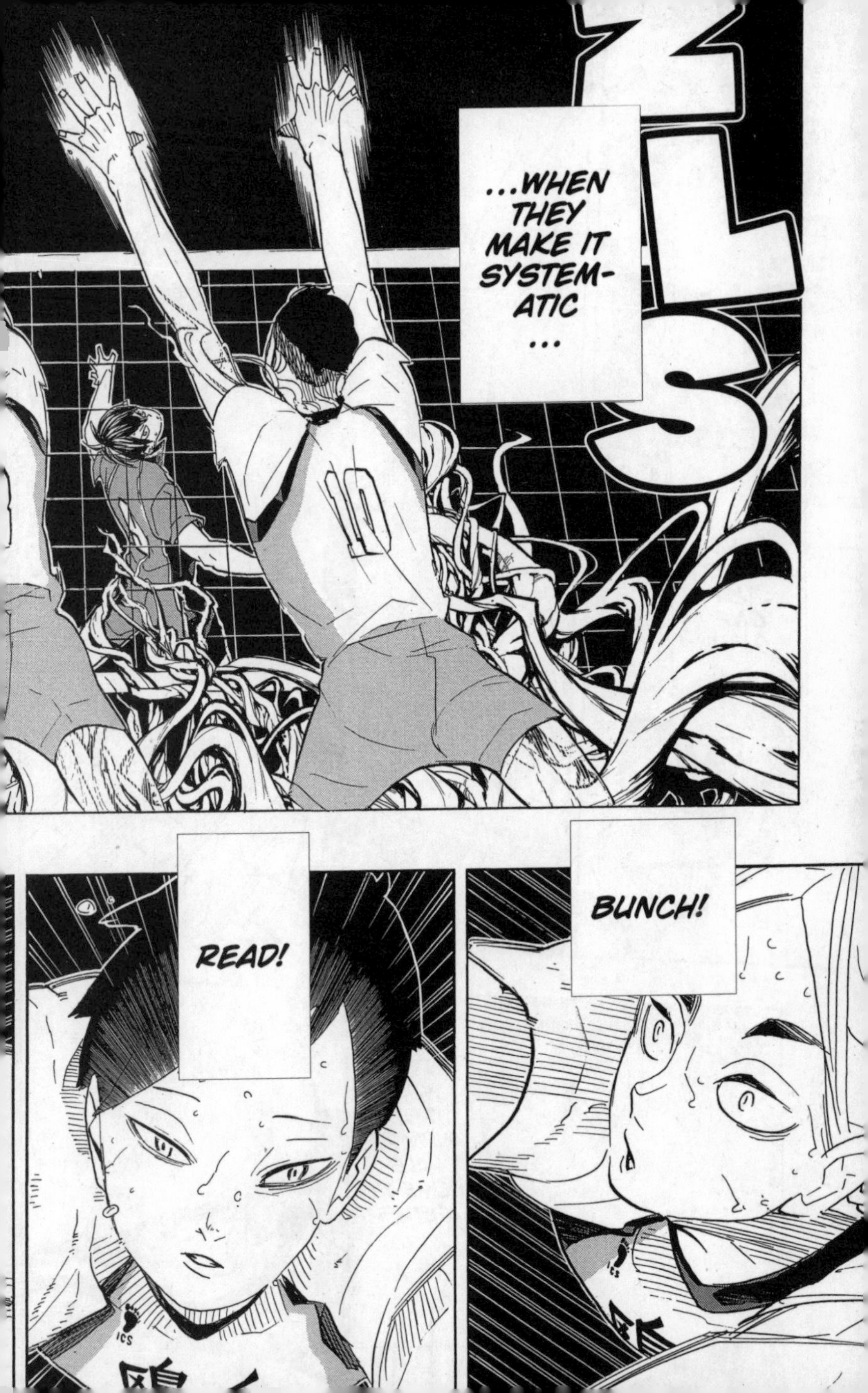
...WHEN THEY MAKE IT SYSTEM-ATIC ...
BUNCH!
READ!

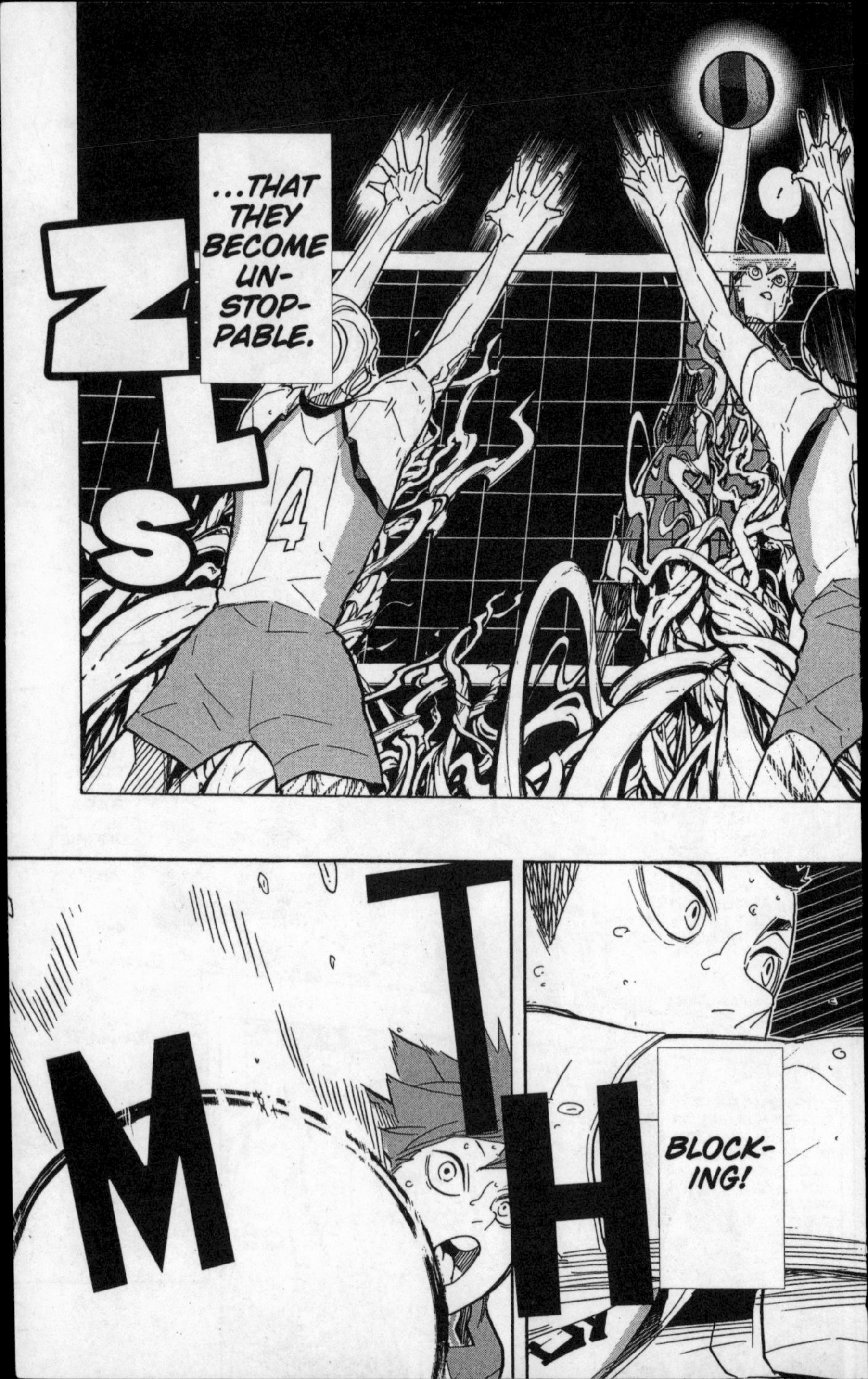
...THAT THEY BECOME UN-STOPPABLE.
ZLS
BLOCKING!
THM

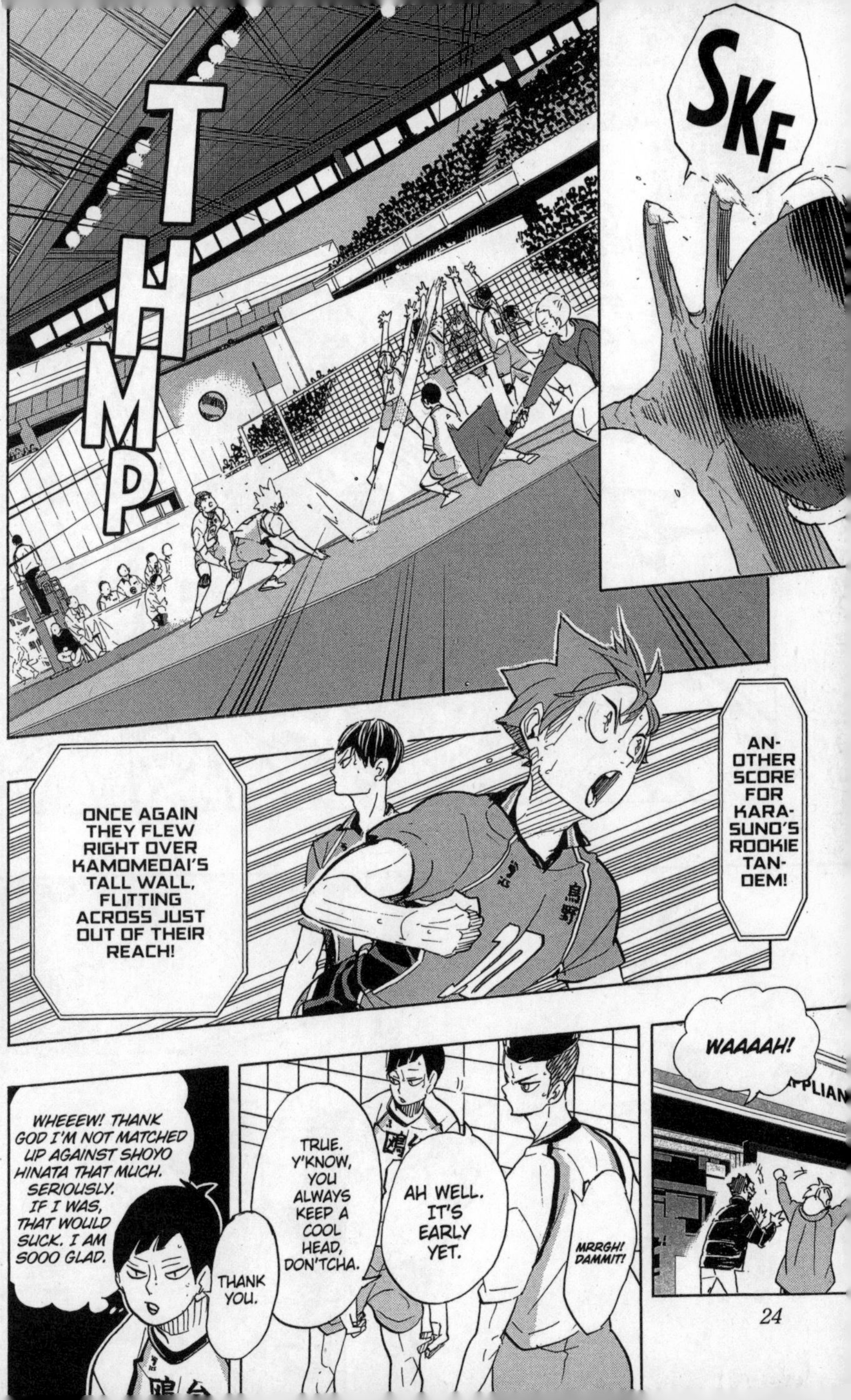
SKF
THMP
AN-OTHER SCORE FOR KARA-SUNO'S ROOKIE TAN-DEM!
ONCE AGAIN THEY FLEW RIGHT OVER KAMOMEDAI'S TALL WALL, FLITTING ACROSS JUST OUT OF THEIR REACH!
WAAAAH!
MRRGH! DAMMIT!
AH WELL. IT'S EARLY YET.
TRUE. Y'KNOW, YOU ALWAYS KEEP A COOL HEAD, DON'TCHA.
WHEEEW! THANK GOD I'M NOT MATCHED UP AGAINST SHOYO HINATA THAT MUCH. SERIOUSLY. IF I WAS, THAT WOULD SUCK. I AM SOOO GLAD.
THANK YOU.

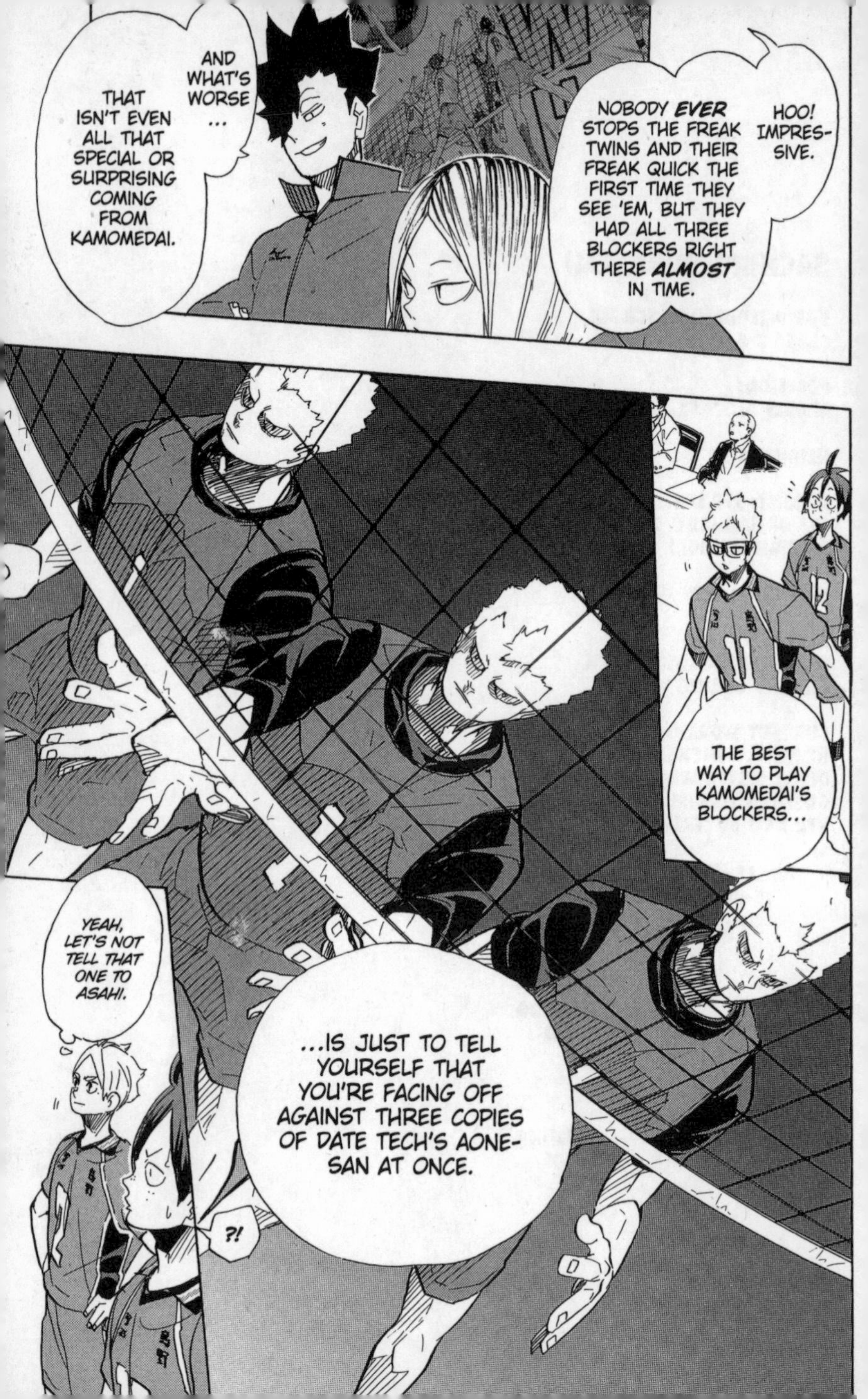
HOO! IMPRES-SIVE.
NOBODY EVER STOPS THE FREAK TWINS AND THEIR FREAK QUICK THE FIRST TIME THEY SEE 'EM, BUT THEY HAD ALL THREE BLOCKERS RIGHT THERE ALMOST IN TIME.
AND WHAT'S WORSE...
THAT ISN'T EVEN ALL THAT SPECIAL OR SURPRISING COMING FROM KAMOMEDAI.
THE BEST WAY TO PLAY KAMOMEDAI'S BLOCKERS...
...IS JUST TO TELL YOURSELF THAT YOU'RE FACING OFF AGAINST THREE COPIES OF DATE TECH'S AONE-SAN AT ONCE.
?!
YEAH, LET'S NOT TELL THAT ONE TO ASAHI.

SACHIRO HIRUGAMI

KAMOMEDAI HIGH SCHOOL, CLASS 2-6

POSITION:
MIDDLE BLOCKER

HEIGHT: 6'3"

WEIGHT: 178 LBS.
(AS OF JANUARY, 2ND YEAR OF HIGH SCHOOL)

BIRTHDAY: FEBRUARY 3

FAVORITE FOOD:
SHUMAI DUMPLINGS WITH CHUNKY FILLING

CURRENT WORRY:
HE REALLY WISHES HIS OLDER SISTER WOULD STOP GUSHING TO HIM ABOUT HER NEW BOYFRIEND.

ABILITY PARAMETERS
(5-POINT SCALE)

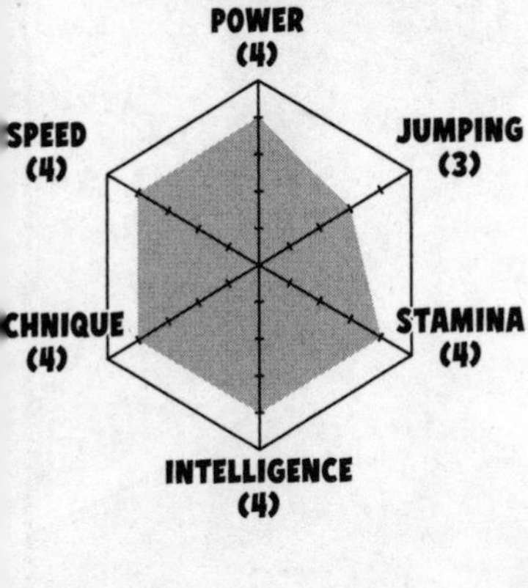
POWER
(4)
JUMPING
(3)
STAMINA
(4)
INTELLIGENCE
(4)
CHNIQUE
(4)
SPEED
(4)

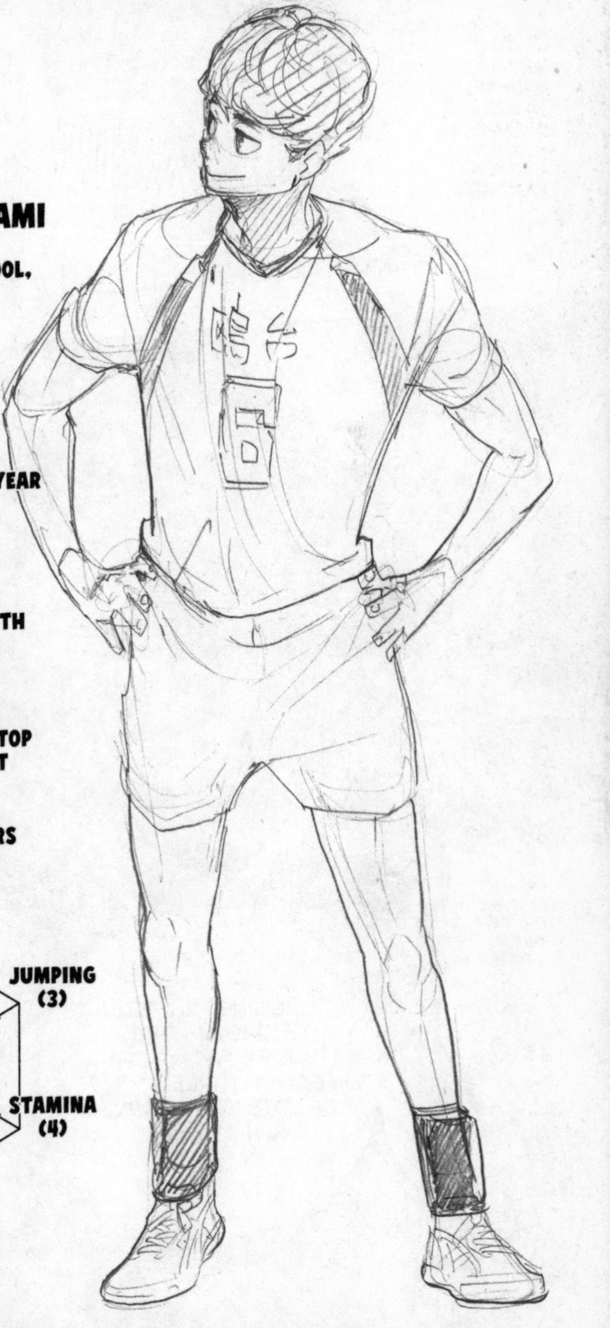

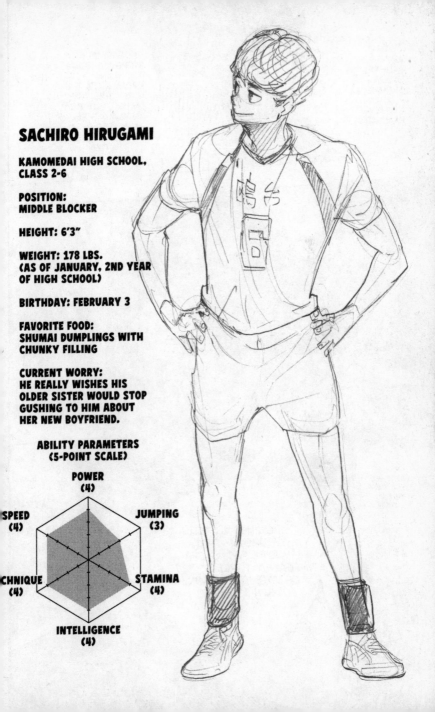

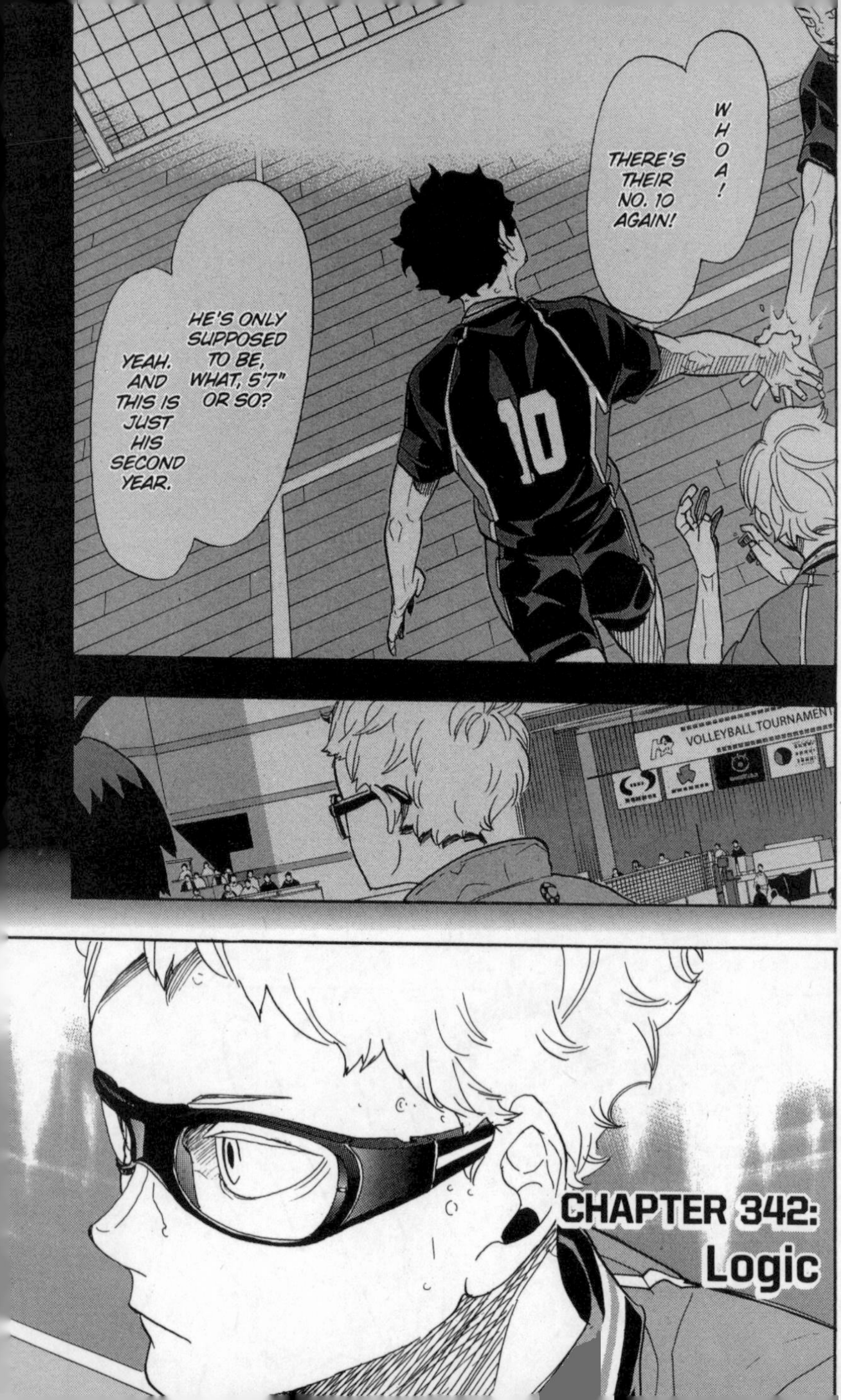
WHOA!
THERE'S THEIR NO. 10 AGAIN!
HE'S ONLY SUPPOSED TO BE, WHAT, 5'7" OR SO?
YEAH. AND THIS IS JUST HIS SECOND YEAR.
VOLLEYBALL TOURNAMENT
CHAPTER 342:
Logic

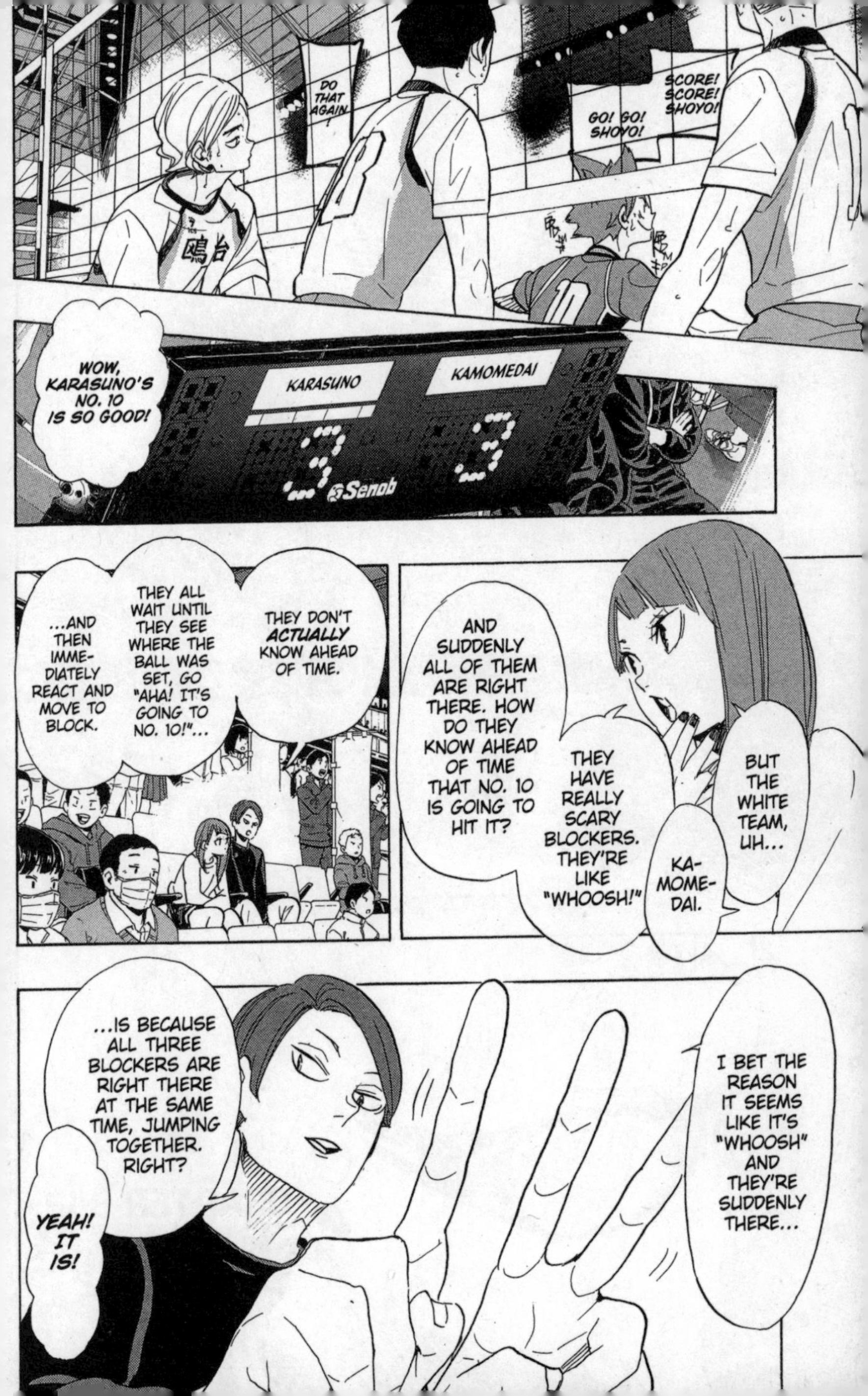
SCORE! SCORE! SHOYO!
GO! GO! SHOYO!
DO THAT AGAIN!
WOW, KARASUNO'S NO. 10 IS SO GOOD!
KAMOMEDAI
KARASUNO
Senob
BUT THE WHITE TEAM, UH...
KA-MOME-DAI.
THEY HAVE REALLY SCARY BLOCKERS. THEY'RE LIKE "WHOOSH!"
AND SUDDENLY ALL OF THEM ARE RIGHT THERE. HOW DO THEY KNOW AHEAD OF TIME THAT NO. 10 IS GOING TO HIT IT?
THEY DON'T ACTUALLY KNOW AHEAD OF TIME.
THEY ALL WAIT UNTIL THEY SEE WHERE THE BALL WAS SET, GO "AHA! IT'S GOING TO NO. 10!"...
...AND THEN IMME-DIATELY REACT AND MOVE TO BLOCK.
I BET THE REASON IT SEEMS LIKE IT'S "WHOOSH" AND THEY'RE SUDDENLY THERE...
...IS BECAUSE ALL THREE BLOCKERS ARE RIGHT THERE AT THE SAME TIME, JUMPING TOGETHER. RIGHT?
YEAH! IT IS!

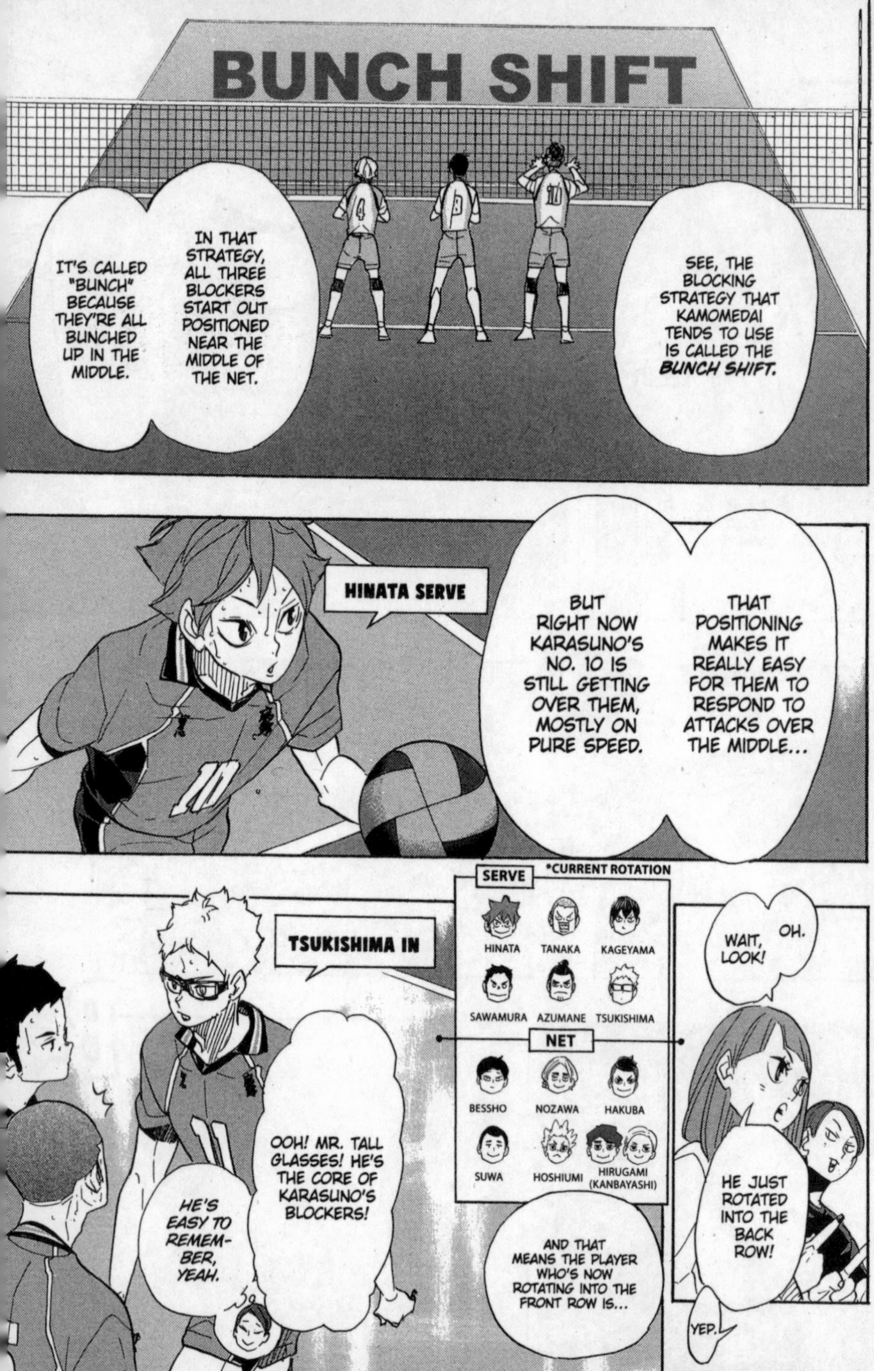
BUNCH SHIFT
SEE, THE BLOCKING STRATEGY THAT KAMOMEDAI TENDS TO USE IS CALLED THE *BUNCH SHIFT.*
IN THAT STRATEGY, ALL THREE BLOCKERS START OUT POSITIONED NEAR THE MIDDLE OF THE NET.
IT'S CALLED "BUNCH" BECAUSE THEY'RE ALL BUNCHED UP IN THE MIDDLE.
THAT POSITIONING MAKES IT REALLY EASY FOR THEM TO RESPOND TO ATTACKS OVER THE MIDDLE...
BUT RIGHT NOW KARASUNO'S NO. 10 IS STILL GETTING OVER THEM, MOSTLY ON PURE SPEED.
HINATA SERVE
OH.
WAIT, LOOK!
HE JUST ROTATED INTO THE BACK ROW!
YEP.
SERVE
*CURRENT ROTATION
HINATA
TANAKA
KAGEYAMA
SAWAMURA
AZUMANE
TSUKISHIMA
NET
BESSHO
NOZAWA
HAKUBA
SUWA
HOSHIUMI
HIRUGAMI (KANBAYASHI)
TSUKISHIMA IN
AND THAT MEANS THE PLAYER WHO'S NOW ROTATING INTO THE FRONT ROW IS...
OOH! MR. TALL GLASSES! HE'S THE CORE OF KARASUNO'S BLOCKERS!
HE'S EASY TO REMEMBER, YEAH.

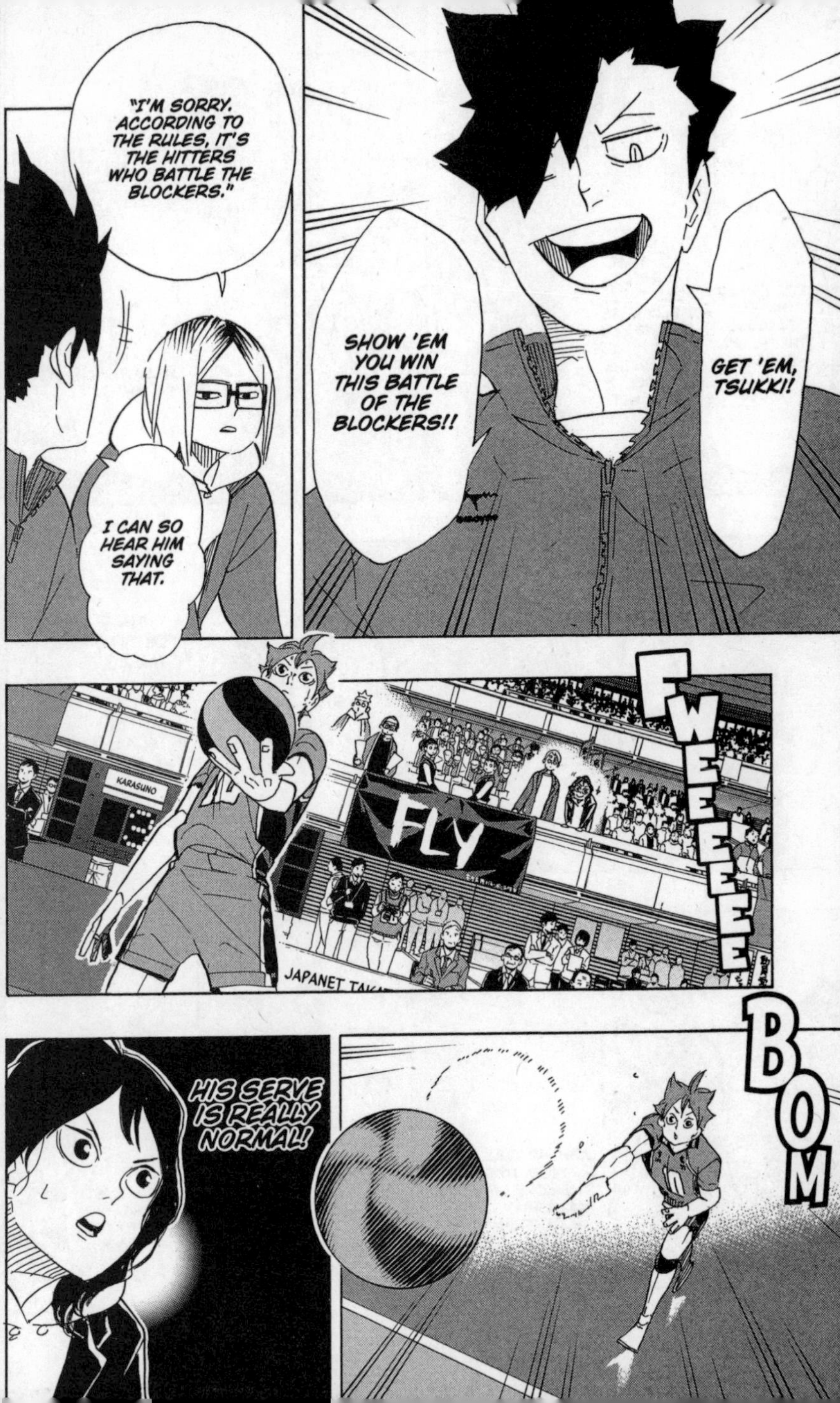
GET 'EM, TSUKKI!
SHOW 'EM YOU WIN THIS BATTLE OF THE BLOCKERS!!
"I'M SORRY. ACCORDING TO THE RULES, IT'S THE HITTERS WHO BATTLE THE BLOCKERS."
I CAN SO HEAR HIM SAYING THAT.
FWEEEEEE
FLY
KARASUNO
BOM
HIS SERVE IS REALLY NORMAL!

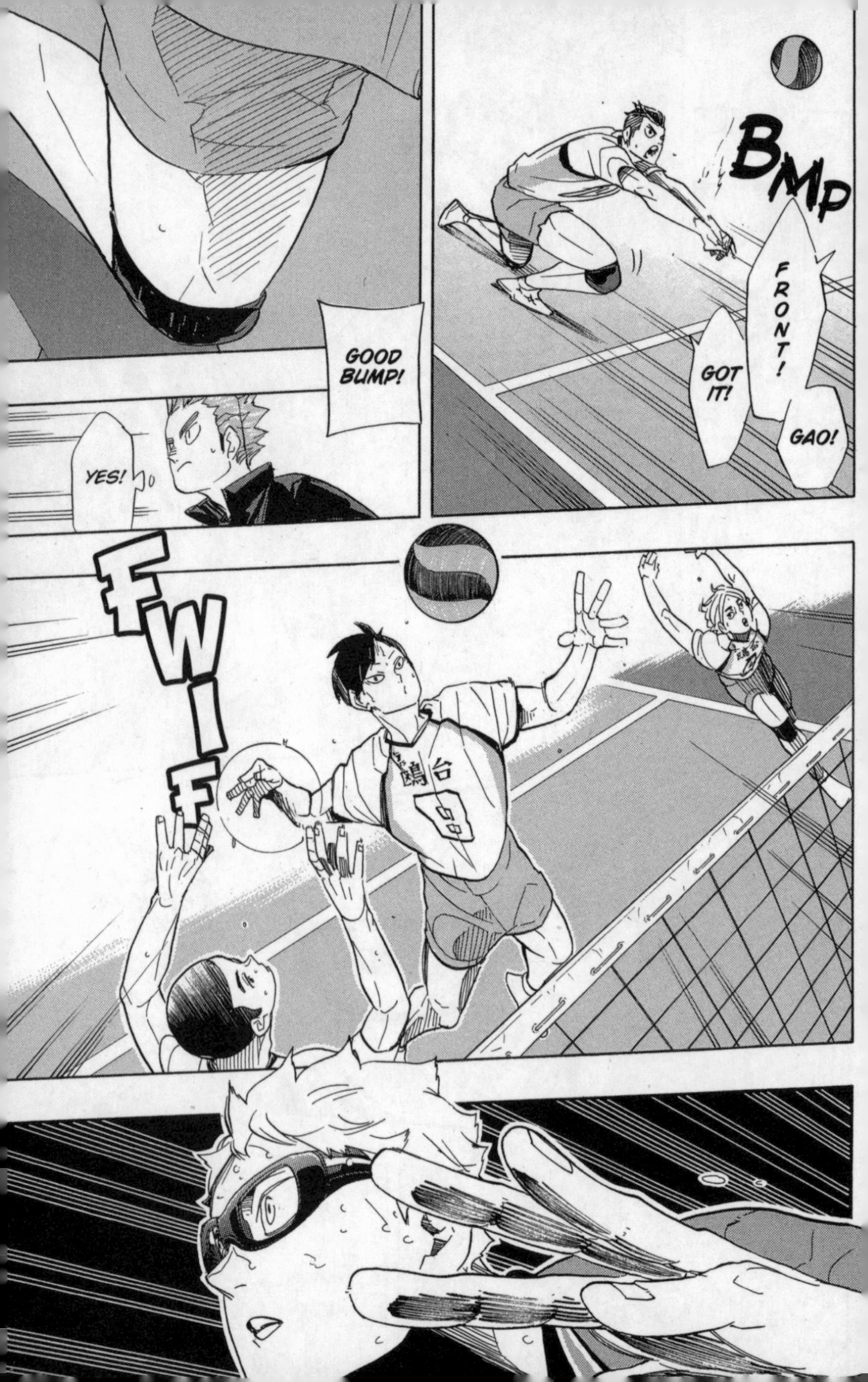
BMP
FRONT!
GOT IT!
GAO!
GOOD BUMP!
YES!
FWIF

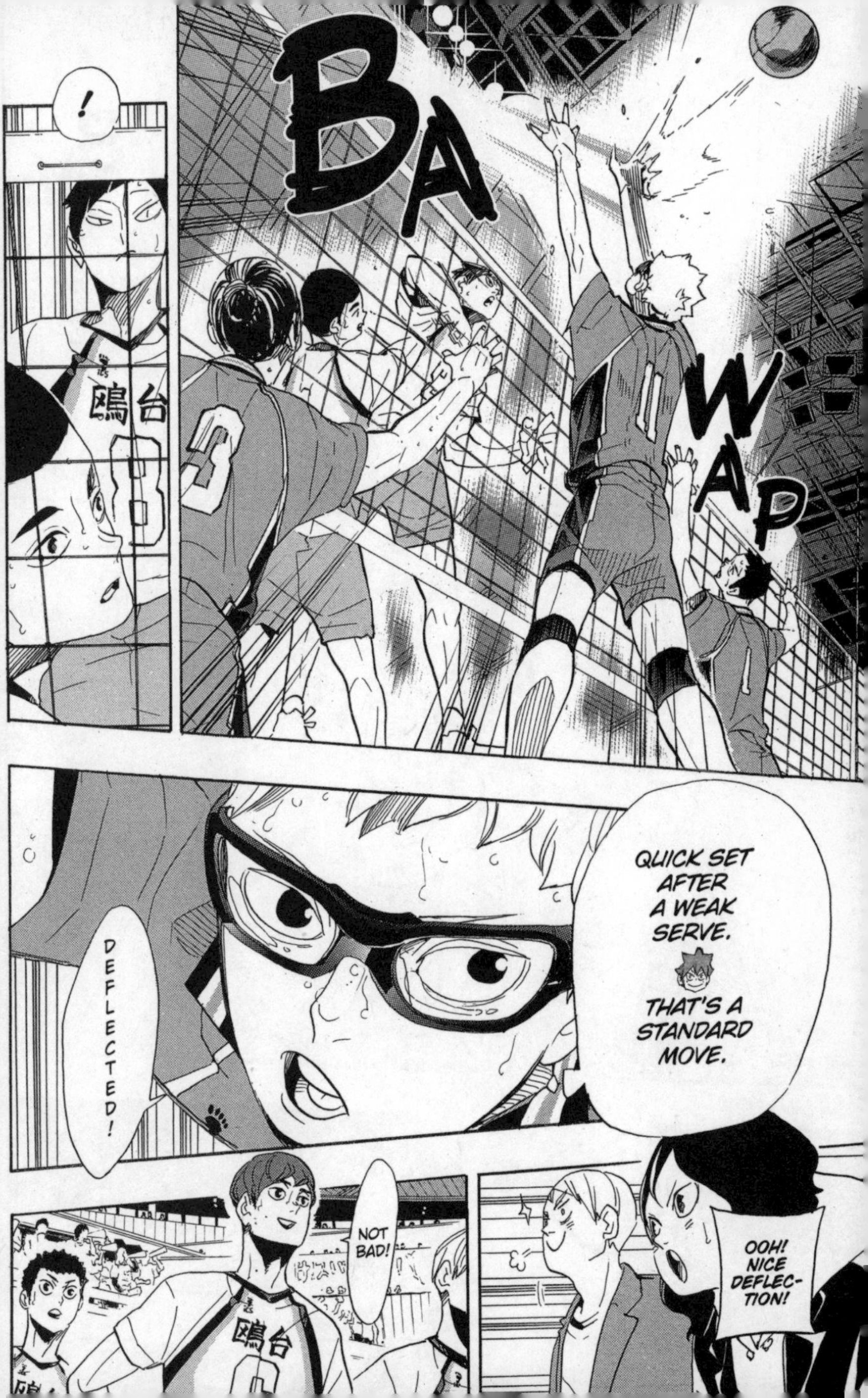
BA
WAP
!
鴎台
QUICK SET AFTER A WEAK SERVE. THAT'S A STANDARD MOVE.
DEFLECTED!
OOH! NICE DEFLECTION!
NOT BAD!
鴎台

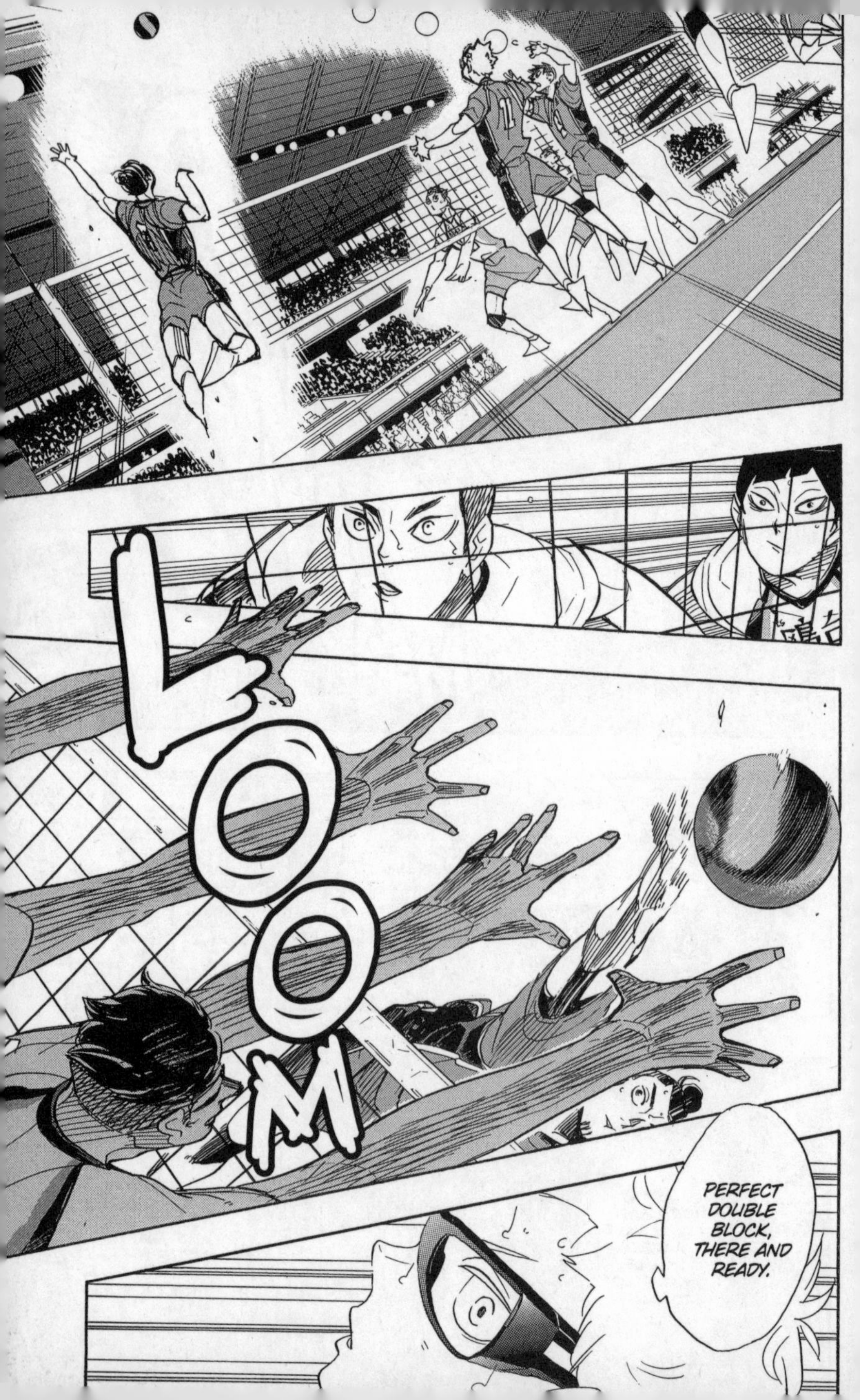
LOOOM
PERFECT DOUBLE BLOCK, THERE AND READY.

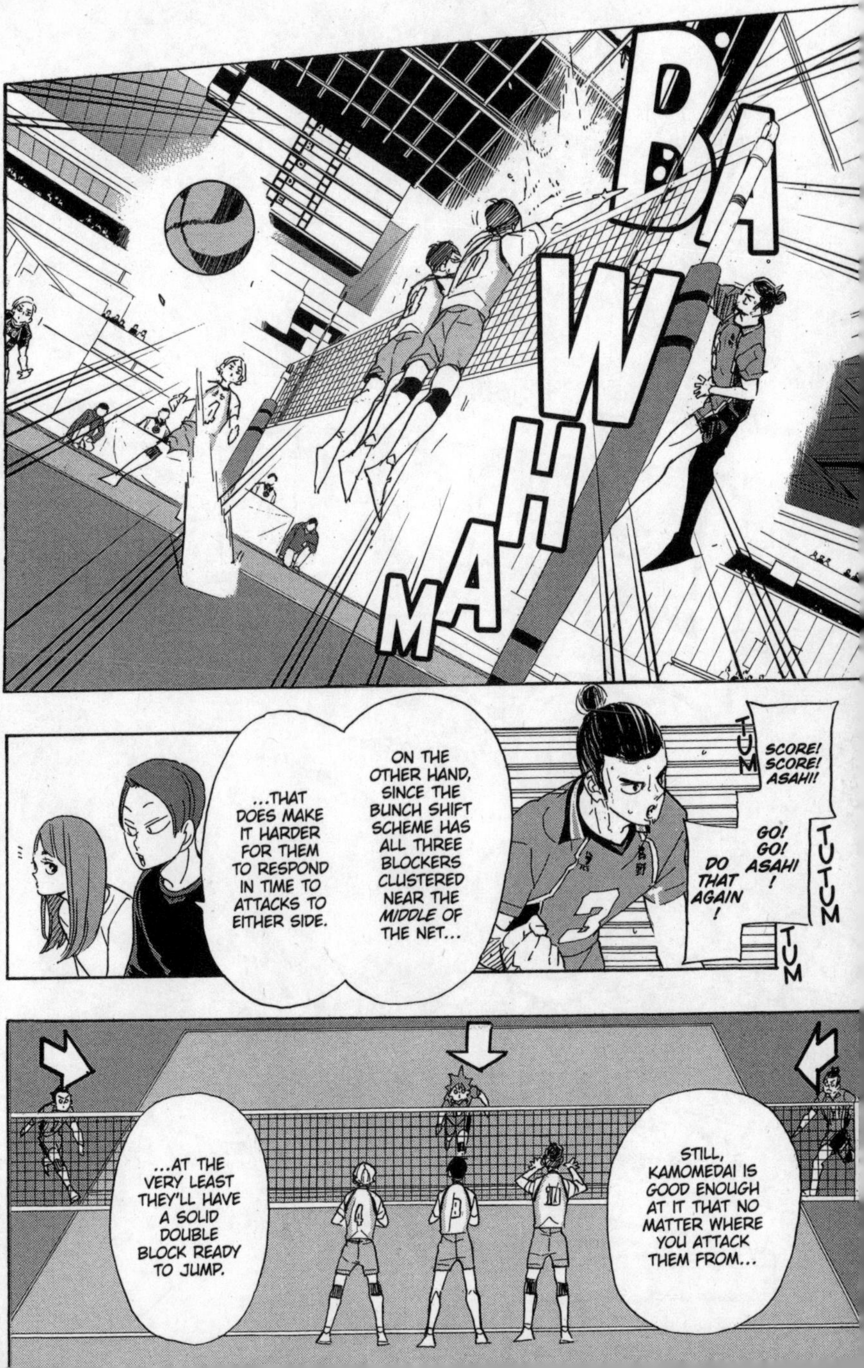
BAWHAM
TUM TUM
SCORE! SCORE! ASAHI!
GO! GO! ASAHI!
DO THAT AGAIN!
TUTUM
TUM
ON THE OTHER HAND, SINCE THE BUNCH SHIFT SCHEME HAS ALL THREE BLOCKERS CLUSTERED NEAR THE *MIDDLE* OF THE NET...
...THAT DOES MAKE IT HARDER FOR THEM TO RESPOND IN TIME TO ATTACKS TO EITHER SIDE.
STILL, KAMOMEDAI IS GOOD ENOUGH AT IT THAT NO MATTER WHERE YOU ATTACK THEM FROM...
...AT THE VERY LEAST THEY'LL HAVE A SOLID DOUBLE BLOCK READY TO JUMP.

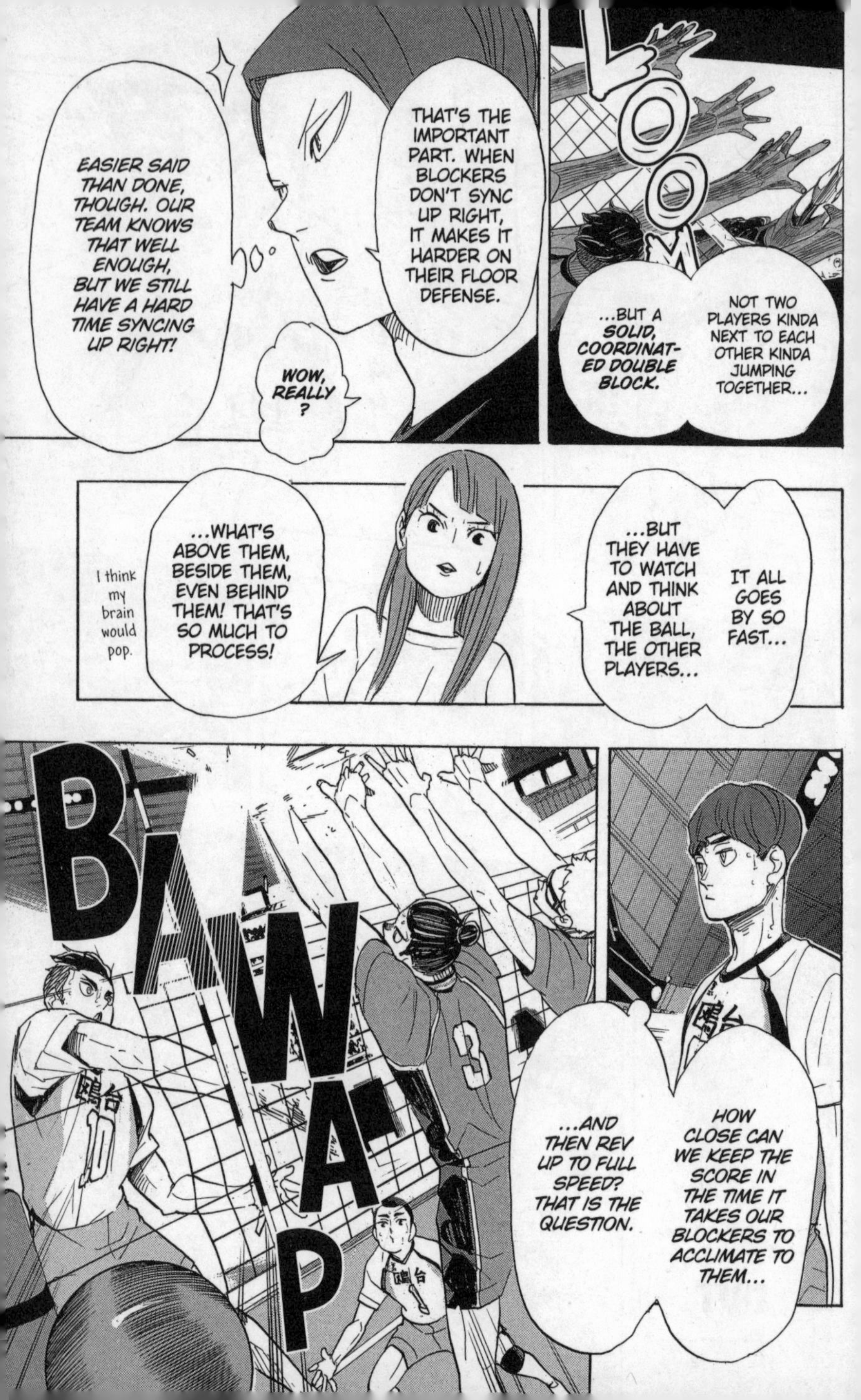
LOOOM
NOT TWO PLAYERS KINDA NEXT TO EACH OTHER KINDA JUMPING TOGETHER...
...BUT A SOLID, COORDINATED DOUBLE BLOCK.
THAT'S THE IMPORTANT PART. WHEN BLOCKERS DON'T SYNC UP RIGHT, IT MAKES IT HARDER ON THEIR FLOOR DEFENSE.
EASIER SAID THAN DONE, THOUGH. OUR TEAM KNOWS THAT WELL ENOUGH, BUT WE STILL HAVE A HARD TIME SYNCING UP RIGHT!
WOW, REALLY?
IT ALL GOES BY SO FAST...
...BUT THEY HAVE TO WATCH AND THINK ABOUT THE BALL, THE OTHER PLAYERS...
...WHAT'S ABOVE THEM, BESIDE THEM, EVEN BEHIND THEM! THAT'S SO MUCH TO PROCESS!
I think my brain would pop.
HOW CLOSE CAN WE KEEP THE SCORE IN THE TIME IT TAKES OUR BLOCKERS TO ACCLIMATE TO THEM...
...AND THEN REV UP TO FULL SPEED? THAT IS THE QUESTION.
BAWAP

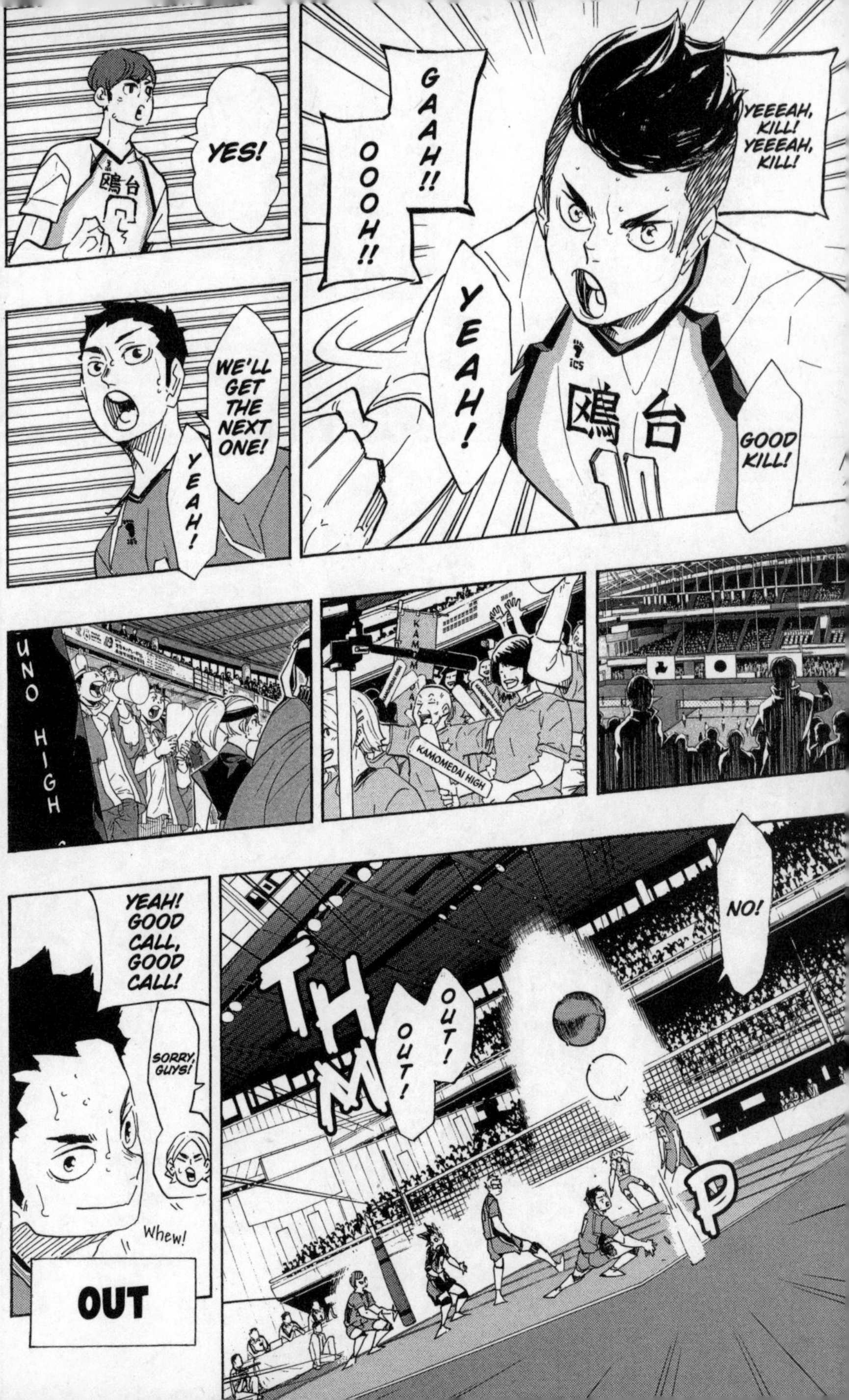
YEEEAH, KILL! YEEEAH, KILL!
GAAH!!
OOOOH!!
GOOD KILL!
YEAH!
YES!
WE'LL GET THE NEXT ONE!
YEAH!
KAMOMEDAI HIGH
UNO HIGH
NO!
OUT!
OUT!
THM
P
YEAH! GOOD CALL, GOOD CALL!
SORRY, GUYS!
Whew!
OUT

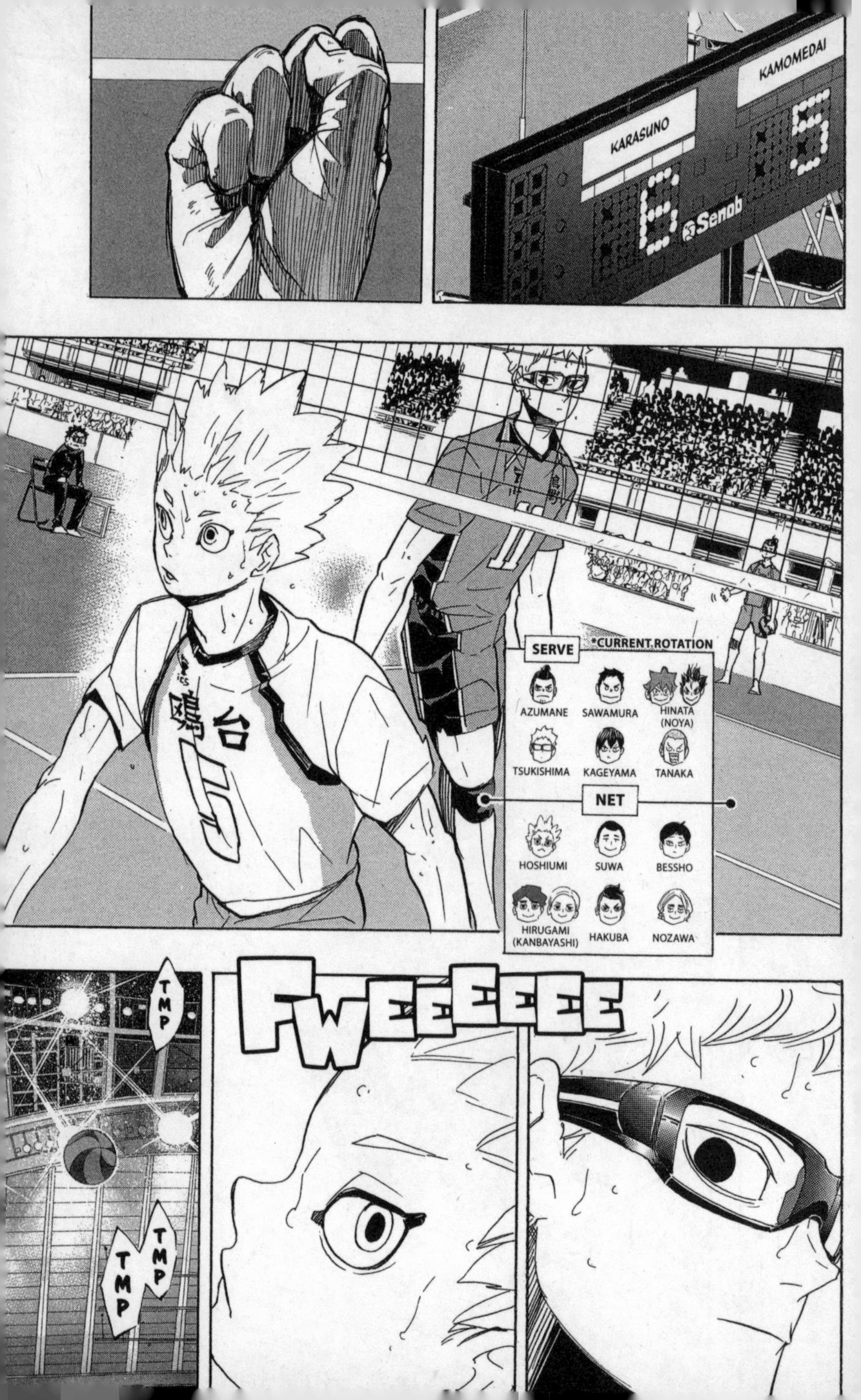

KAMOMEDAI
KARASUNO
Senob
SERVE
*CURRENT ROTATION
AZUMANE
SAWAMURA
HINATA (NOYA)
TSUKISHIMA
KAGEYAMA
TANAKA
NET
HOSHIUMI
SUWA
BESSHO
HIRUGAMI (KANBAYASHI)
HAKUBA
NOZAWA
FWEEEEEE
TMP
TMP
TMP

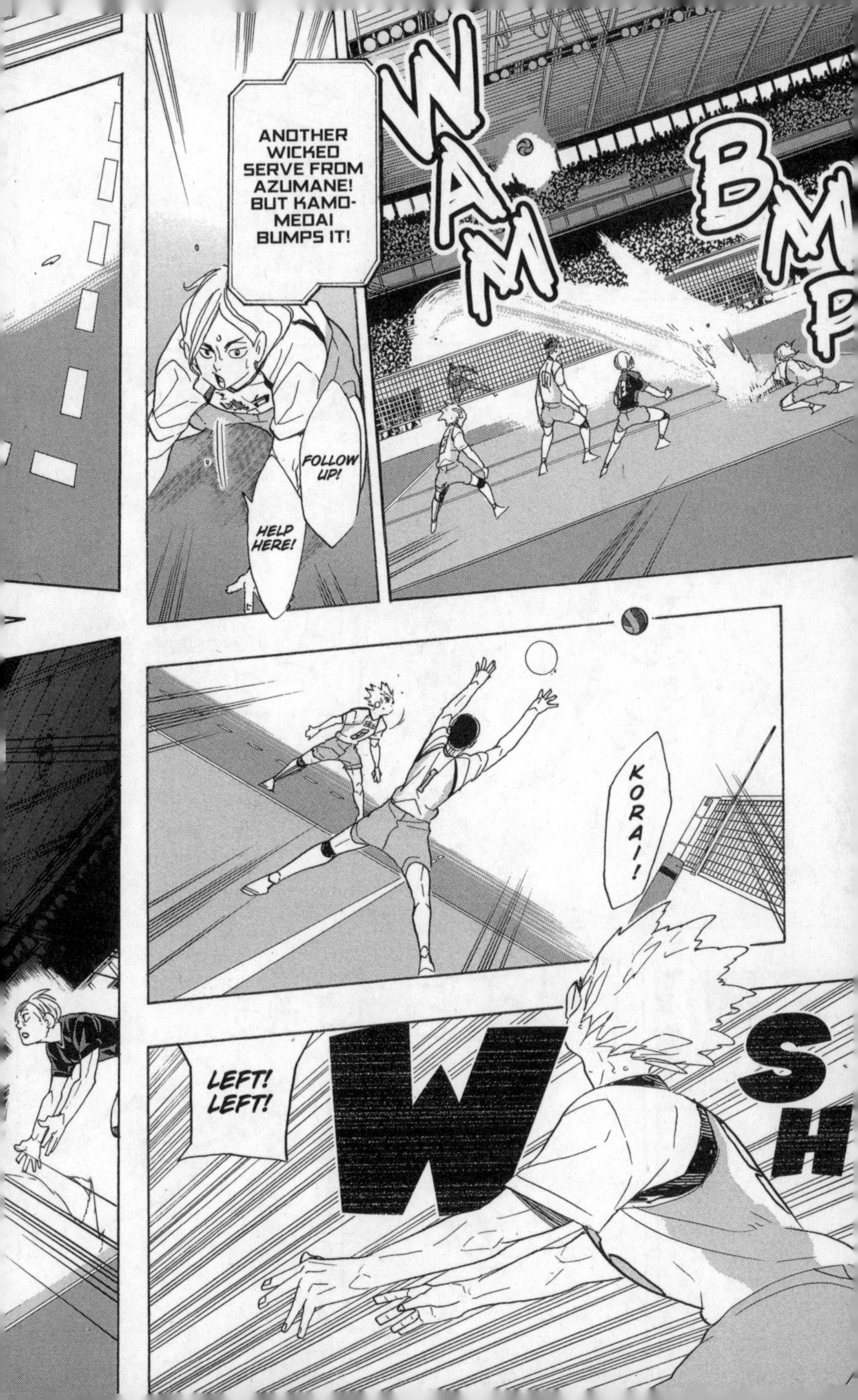
ANOTHER WICKED SERVE FROM AZUMANE! BUT KAMO-MEDAI BUMPS IT!
WAM
BMP
FOLLOW UP!
HELP HERE!
KORAI!
SH
W
LEFT! LEFT!

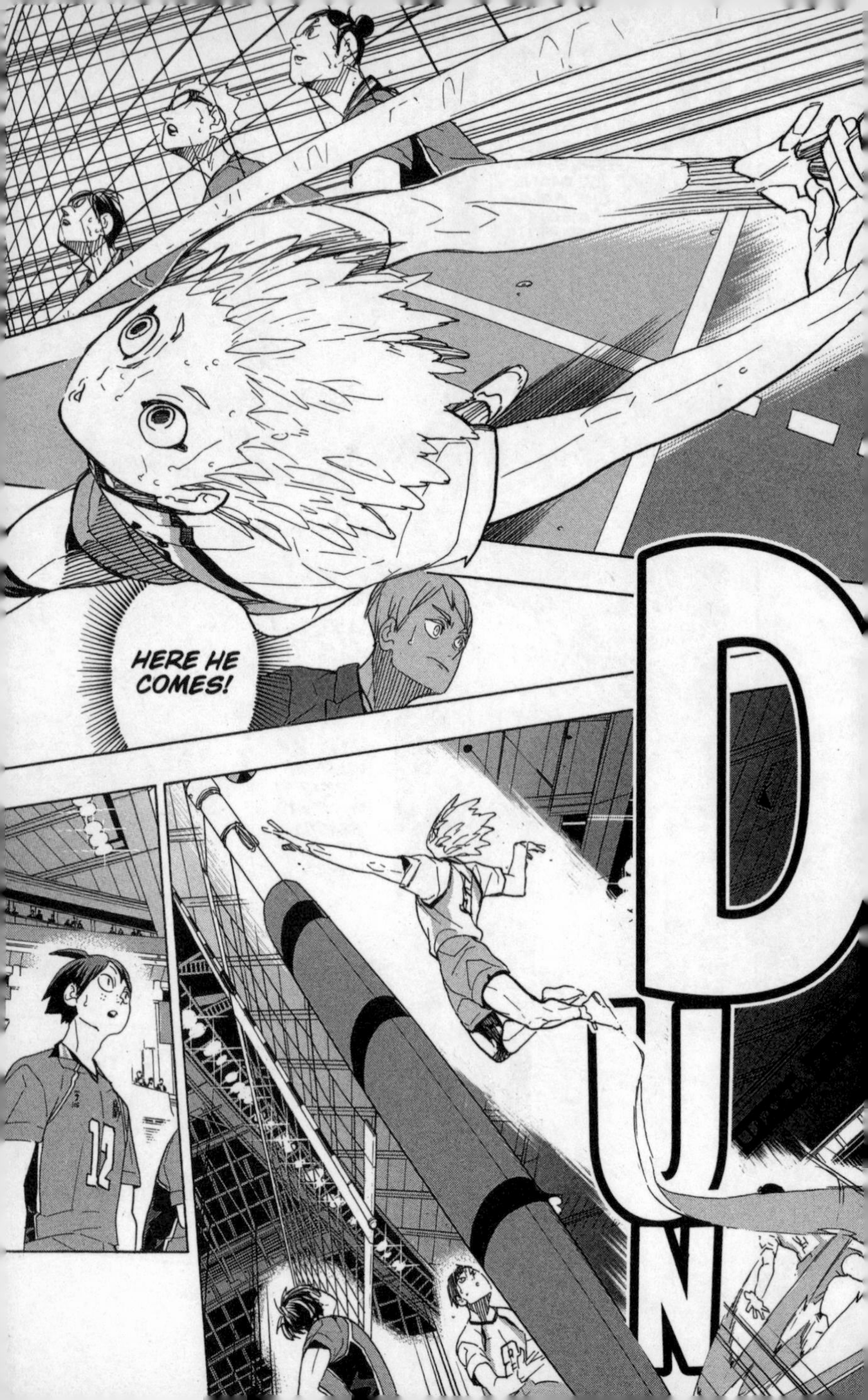
HERE HE COMES!
DUN

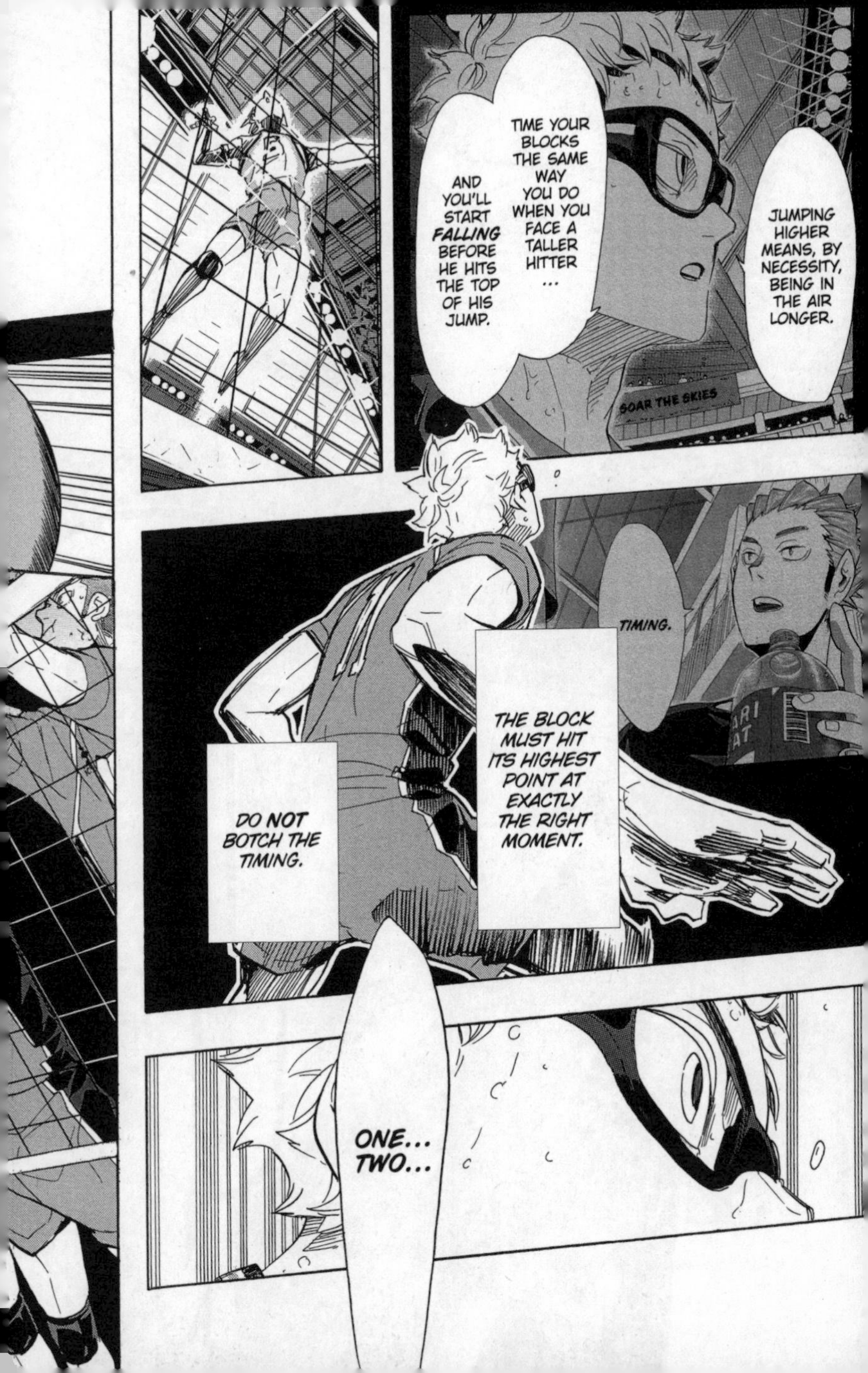

JUMPING HIGHER MEANS, BY NECESSITY, BEING IN THE AIR LONGER.
SOAR THE SKIES
TIME YOUR BLOCKS THE SAME WAY YOU DO WHEN YOU FACE A TALLER HITTER ...
AND YOU'LL START FALLING BEFORE HE HITS THE TOP OF HIS JUMP.
TIMING.
THE BLOCK MUST HIT ITS HIGHEST POINT AT EXACTLY THE RIGHT MOMENT.
DO NOT BOTCH THE TIMING.
ONE... TWO...

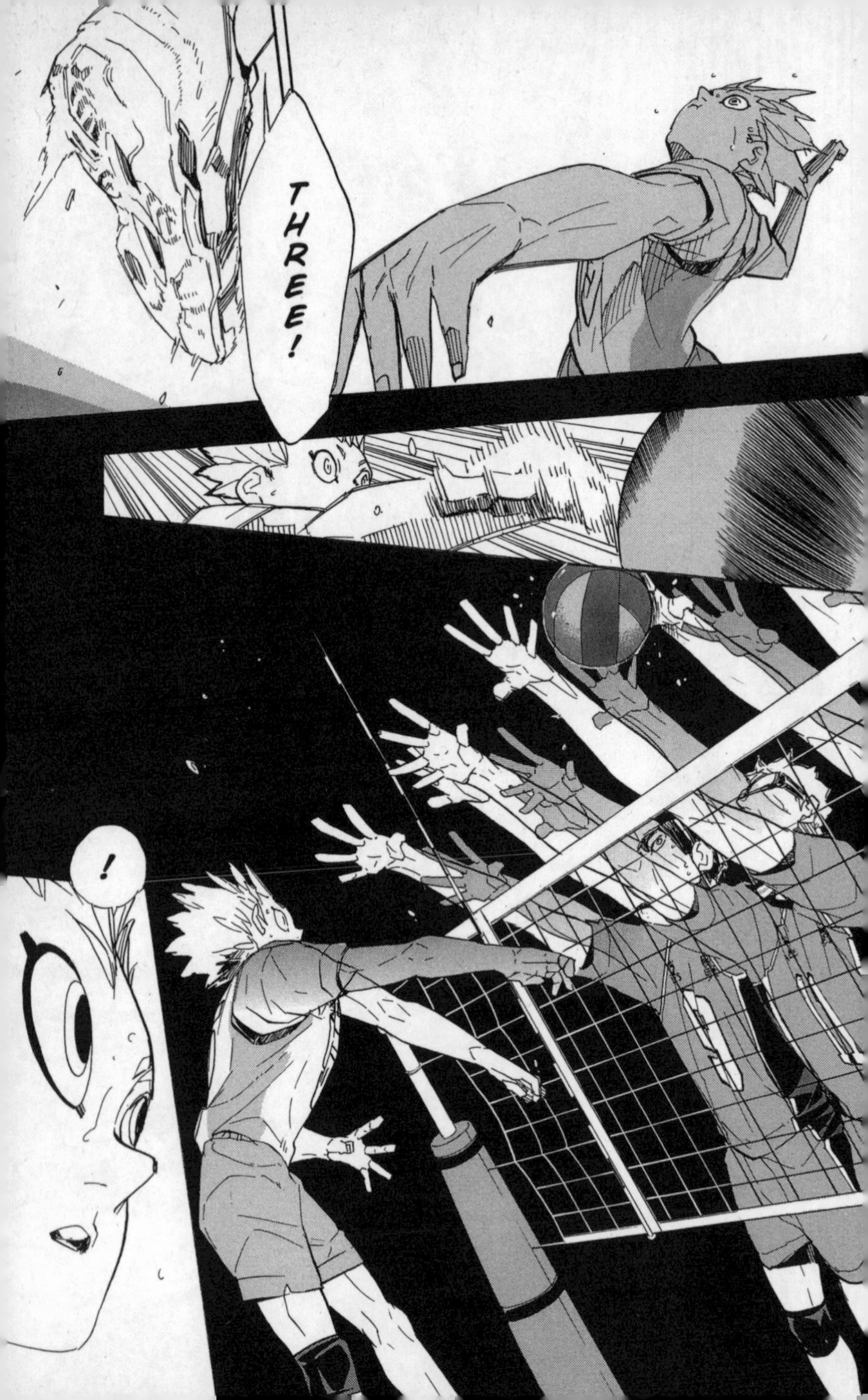
THREE!
!

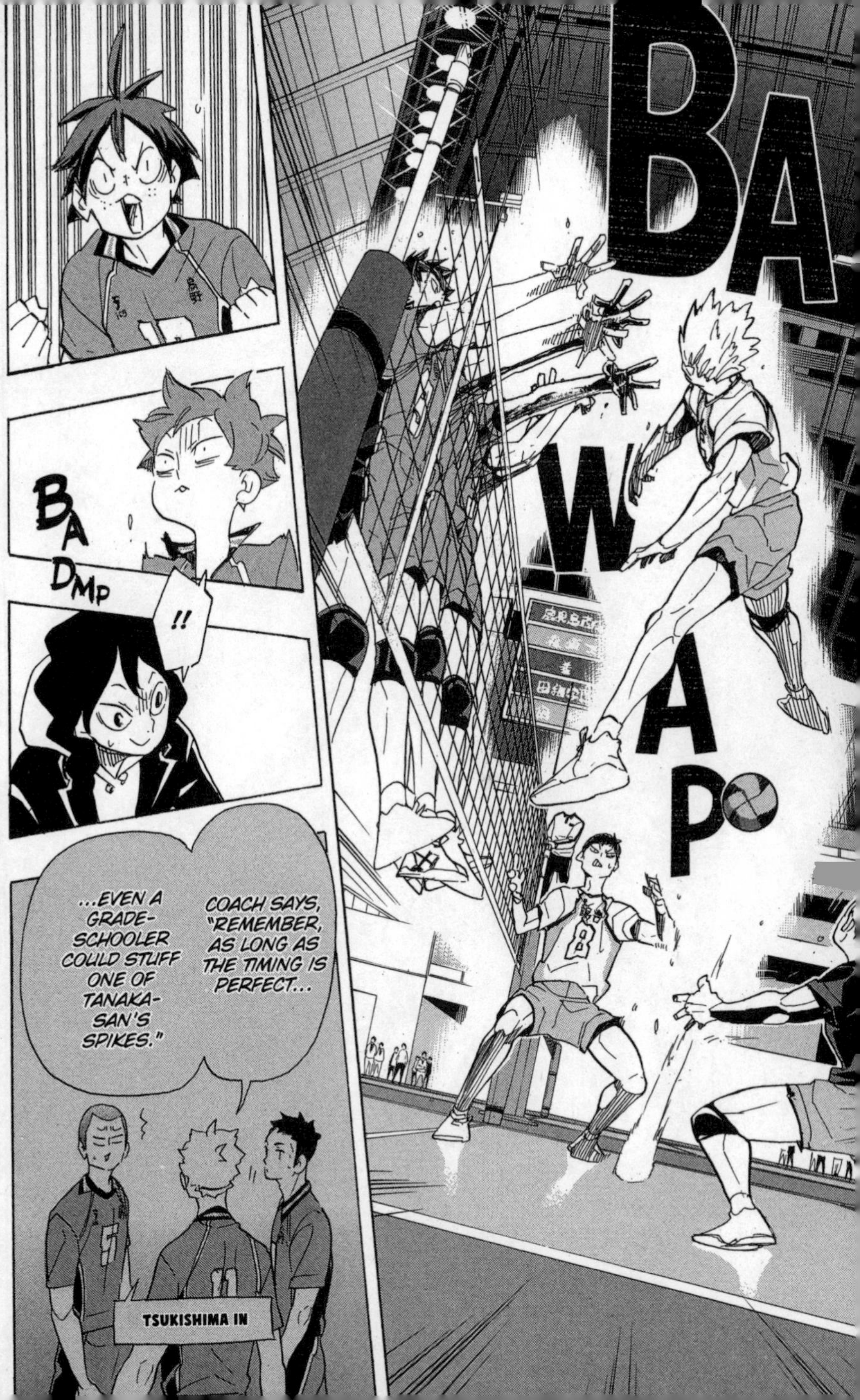
BAWAP
BADMP
!!
COACH SAYS, "REMEMBER, AS LONG AS THE TIMING IS PERFECT...
...EVEN A GRADE-SCHOOLER COULD STUFF ONE OF TANAKA-SAN'S SPIKES."
TSUKISHIMA IN

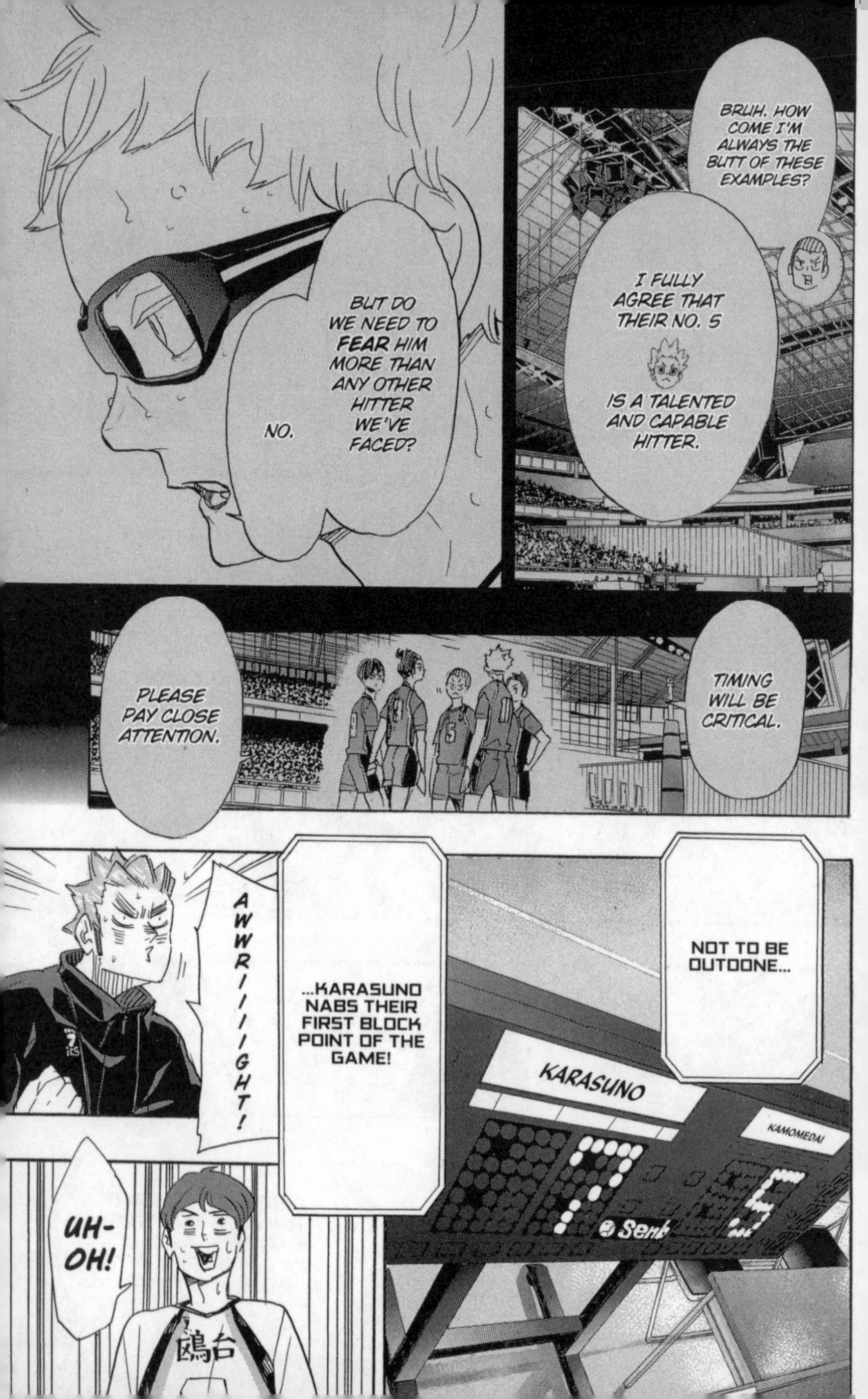
BRUH. HOW COME I'M ALWAYS THE BUTT OF THESE EXAMPLES?
I FULLY AGREE THAT THEIR NO. 5 IS A TALENTED AND CAPABLE HITTER.
BUT DO WE NEED TO **FEAR** HIM MORE THAN ANY OTHER HITTER WE'VE FACED?
NO.
TIMING WILL BE CRITICAL.
PLEASE PAY CLOSE ATTENTION.
NOT TO BE OUTDONE...
...KARASUNO NABS THEIR FIRST BLOCK POINT OF THE GAME!
KARASUNO
KAMOMEDAI
7
5
AWWRIIIIIGHT!
UH-OH!

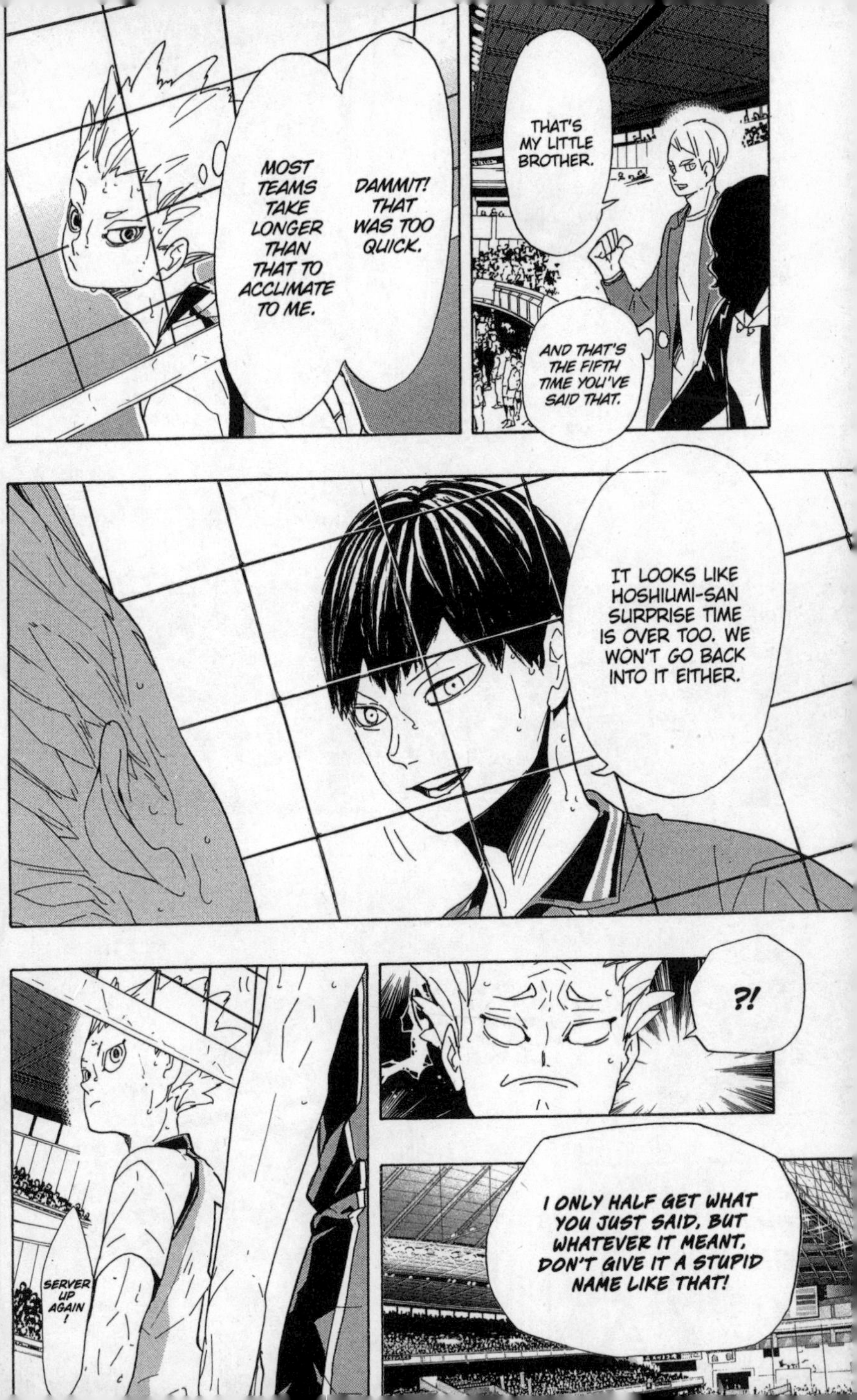
THAT'S MY LITTLE BROTHER.
AND THAT'S THE FIFTH TIME YOU'VE SAID THAT.
DAMMIT! THAT WAS TOO QUICK.
MOST TEAMS TAKE LONGER THAN THAT TO ACCLIMATE TO ME.
IT LOOKS LIKE HOSHIUMI-SAN SURPRISE TIME IS OVER TOO. WE WON'T GO BACK INTO IT EITHER.
?!
I ONLY HALF GET WHAT YOU JUST SAID, BUT WHATEVER IT MEANT, DON'T GIVE IT A STUPID NAME LIKE THAT!
SERVER UP AGAIN!

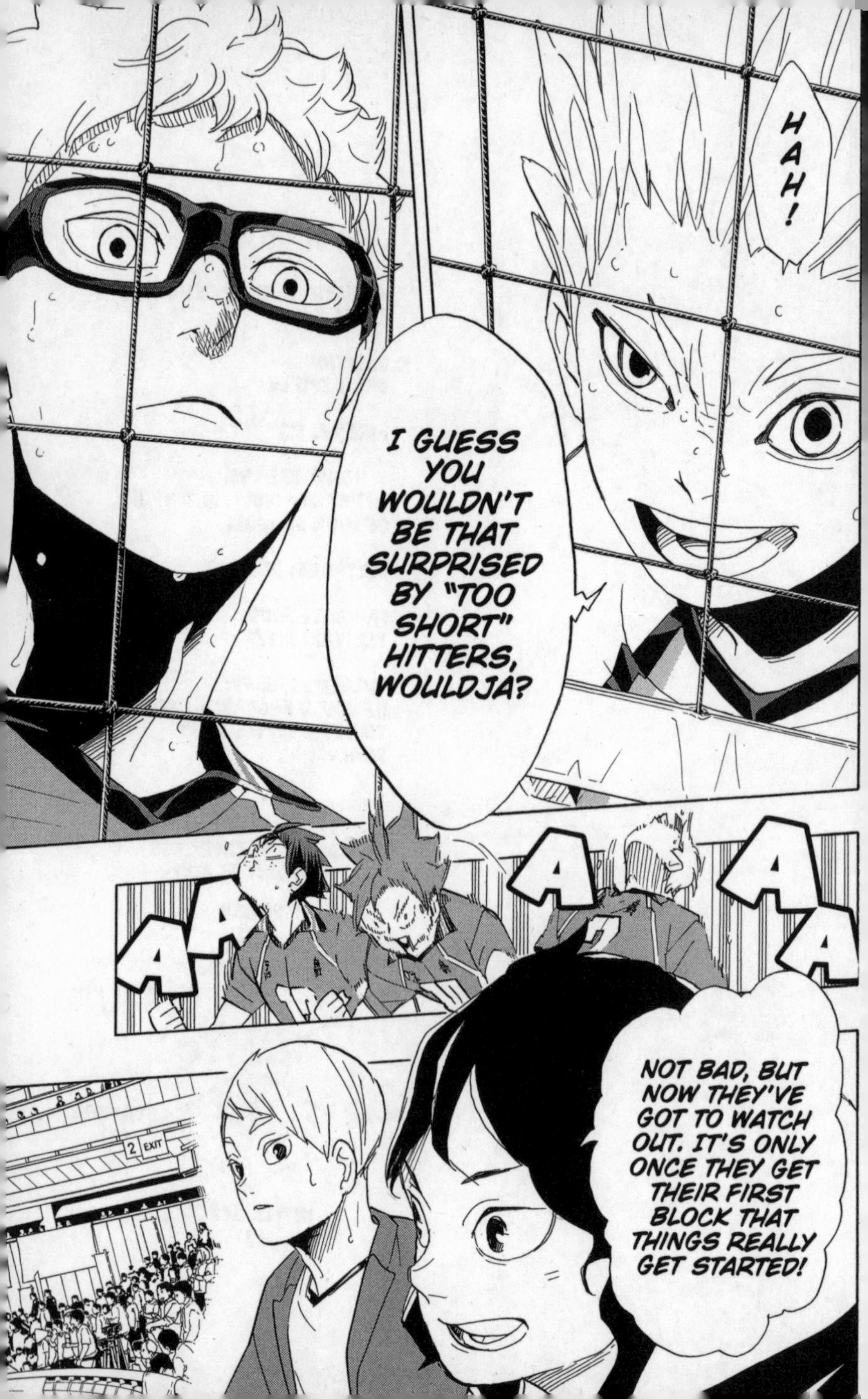
HAH!
I GUESS YOU WOULDN'T BE THAT SURPRISED BY "TOO SHORT" HITTERS, WOULDJA?
A A
A A
A A
NOT BAD, BUT NOW THEY'VE GOT TO WATCH OUT. IT'S ONLY ONCE THEY GET THEIR FIRST BLOCK THAT THINGS REALLY GET STARTED!
2 EXIT

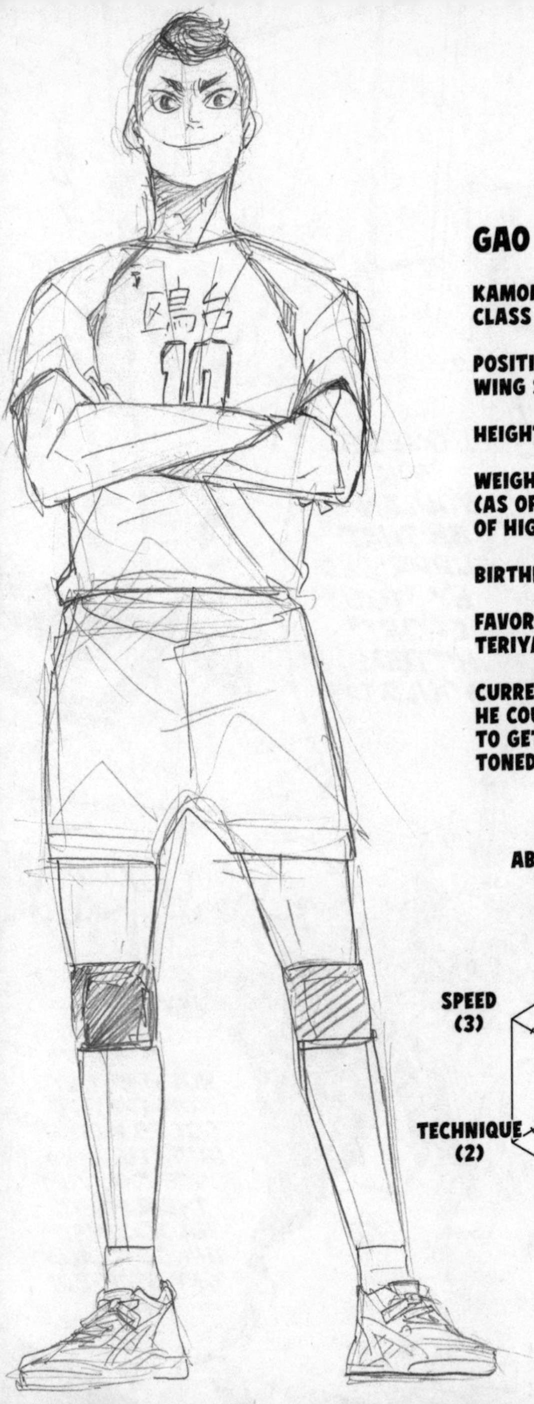

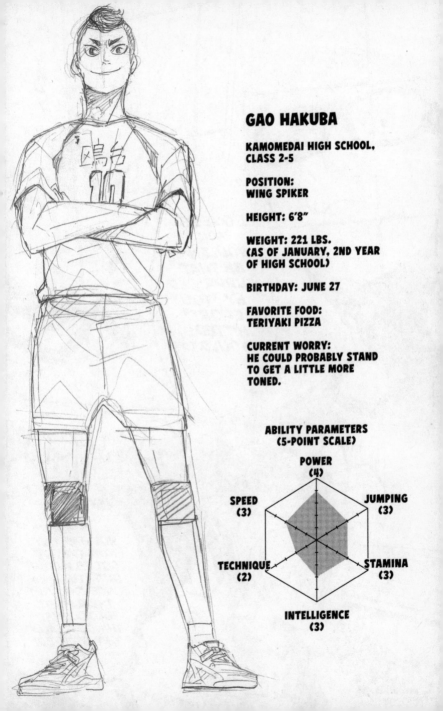

GAO HAKUBA

KAMOMEDAI HIGH SCHOOL, CLASS 2-5

POSITION:
WING SPIKER

HEIGHT: 6'8"

WEIGHT: 221 LBS.
(AS OF JANUARY, 2ND YEAR OF HIGH SCHOOL)

BIRTHDAY: JUNE 27

FAVORITE FOOD:
TERIYAKI PIZZA

CURRENT WORRY:
HE COULD PROBABLY STAND TO GET A LITTLE MORE TONED.

ABILITY PARAMETERS
(5-POINT SCALE)

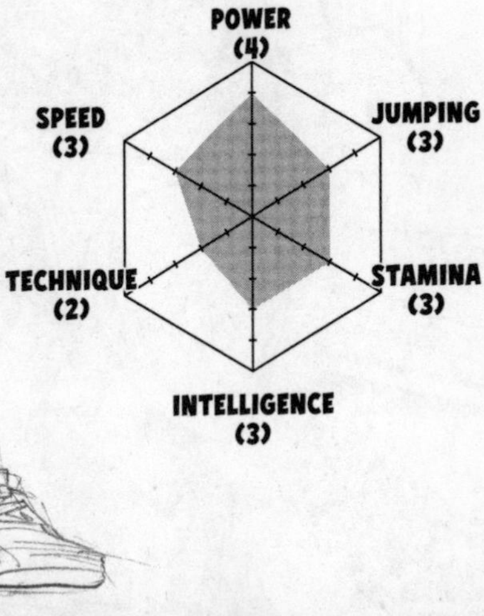
POWER (4)
JUMPING (3)
STAMINA (3)
INTELLIGENCE (3)
TECHNIQUE (2)
SPEED (3)

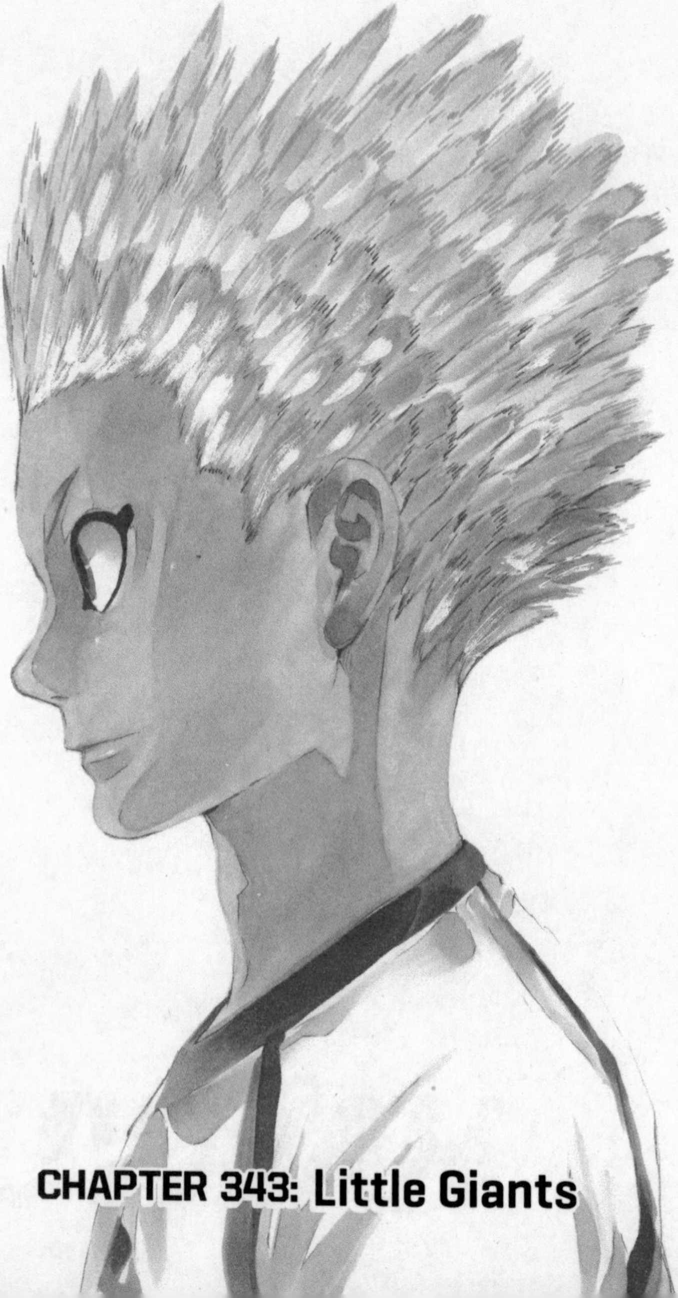

CHAPTER 343: Little Giants

HAIKYU!!

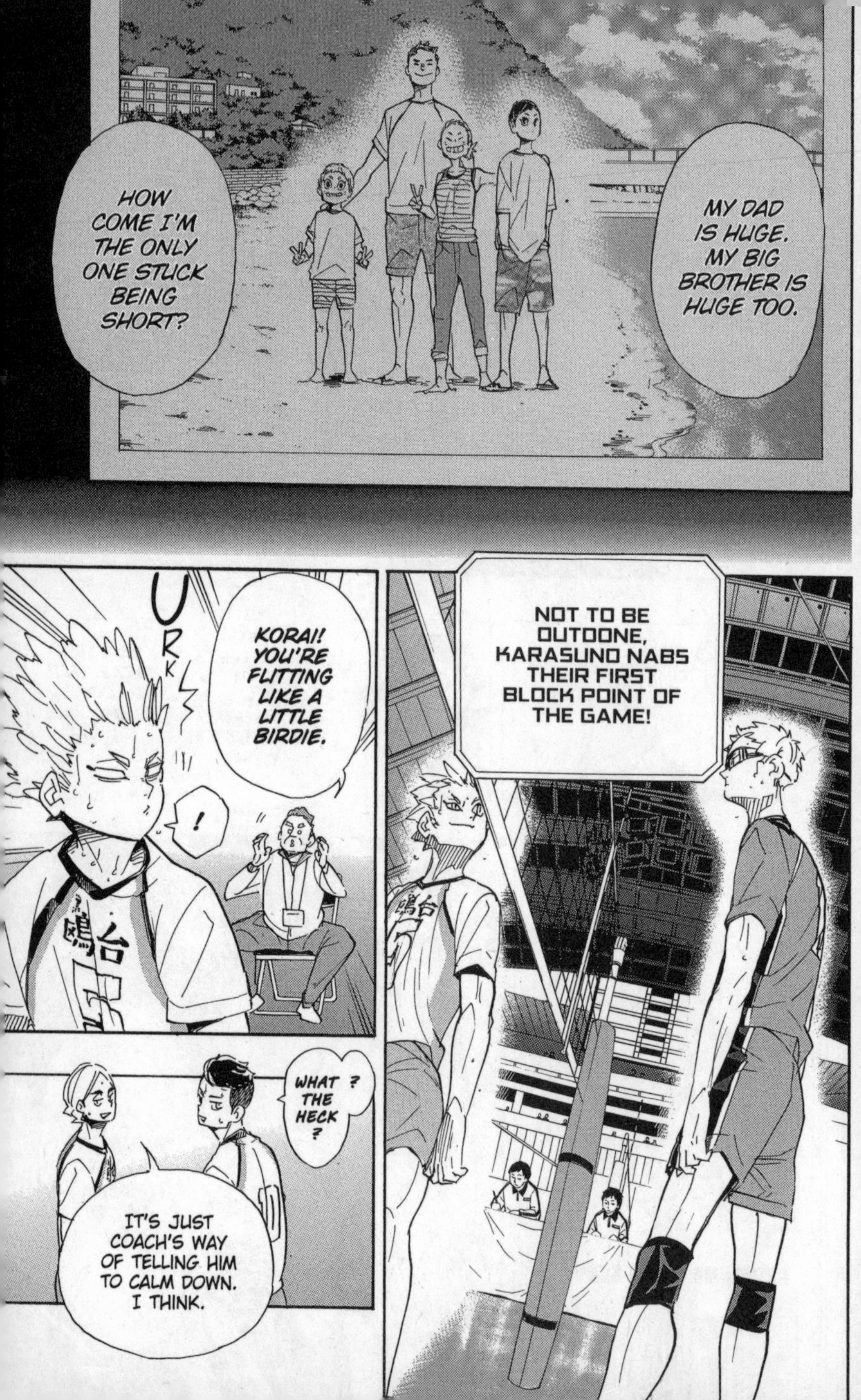
MY DAD IS HUGE. MY BIG BROTHER IS HUGE TOO.
HOW COME I'M THE ONLY ONE STUCK BEING SHORT?
NOT TO BE OUTDONE, KARASUNO NABS THEIR FIRST BLOCK POINT OF THE GAME!
KORAI! YOU'RE FLITTING LIKE A LITTLE BIRDIE.
URK
!
WHAT THE HECK ??
IT'S JUST COACH'S WAY OF TELLING HIM TO CALM DOWN. I THINK.

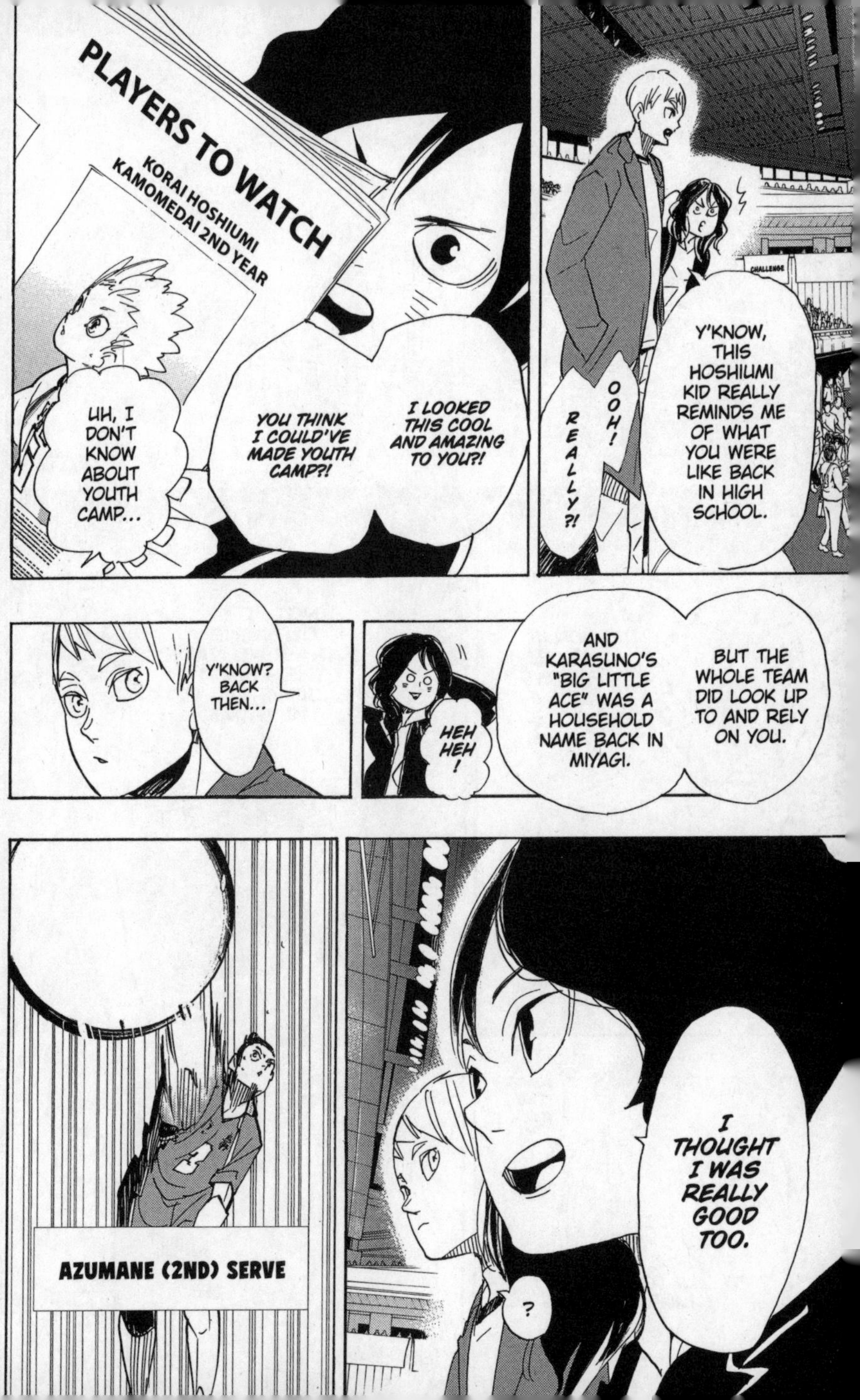
Y'KNOW, THIS HOSHIUMI KID REALLY REMINDS ME OF WHAT YOU WERE LIKE BACK IN HIGH SCHOOL.
OOH!
REALLY?!
CHALLENGE
PLAYERS TO WATCH
KORAI HOSHIUMI KAMOMEDAI 2ND YEAR
I LOOKED THIS COOL AND AMAZING TO YOU?!
YOU THINK I COULD'VE MADE YOUTH CAMP?!
UH, I DON'T KNOW ABOUT YOUTH CAMP...
BUT THE WHOLE TEAM DID LOOK UP TO AND RELY ON YOU.
AND KARASUNO'S "BIG LITTLE ACE" WAS A HOUSEHOLD NAME BACK IN MIYAGI.
HEH HEH!
Y'KNOW? BACK THEN...
I THOUGHT I WAS REALLY GOOD TOO.
?
AZUMANE (2ND) SERVE

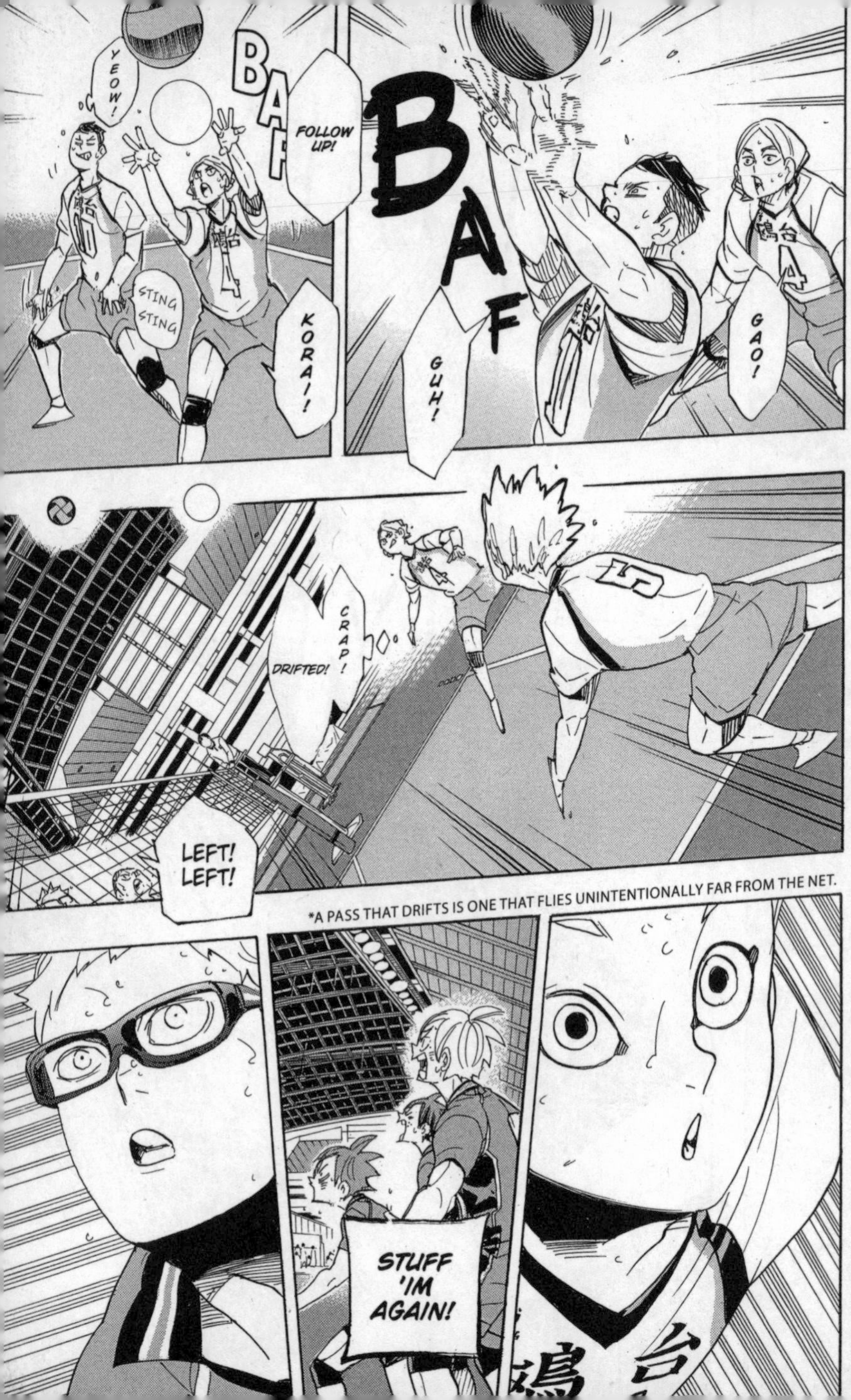
BAF
GAO!
GUH!
FOLLOW UP!
BAF
YEOW!
KORA!!
STING STING
CRAP!
DRIFTED!
LEFT! LEFT!
STUFF 'IM AGAIN!

*A PASS THAT DRIFTS IS ONE THAT FLIES UNINTENTIONALLY FAR FROM THE NET.

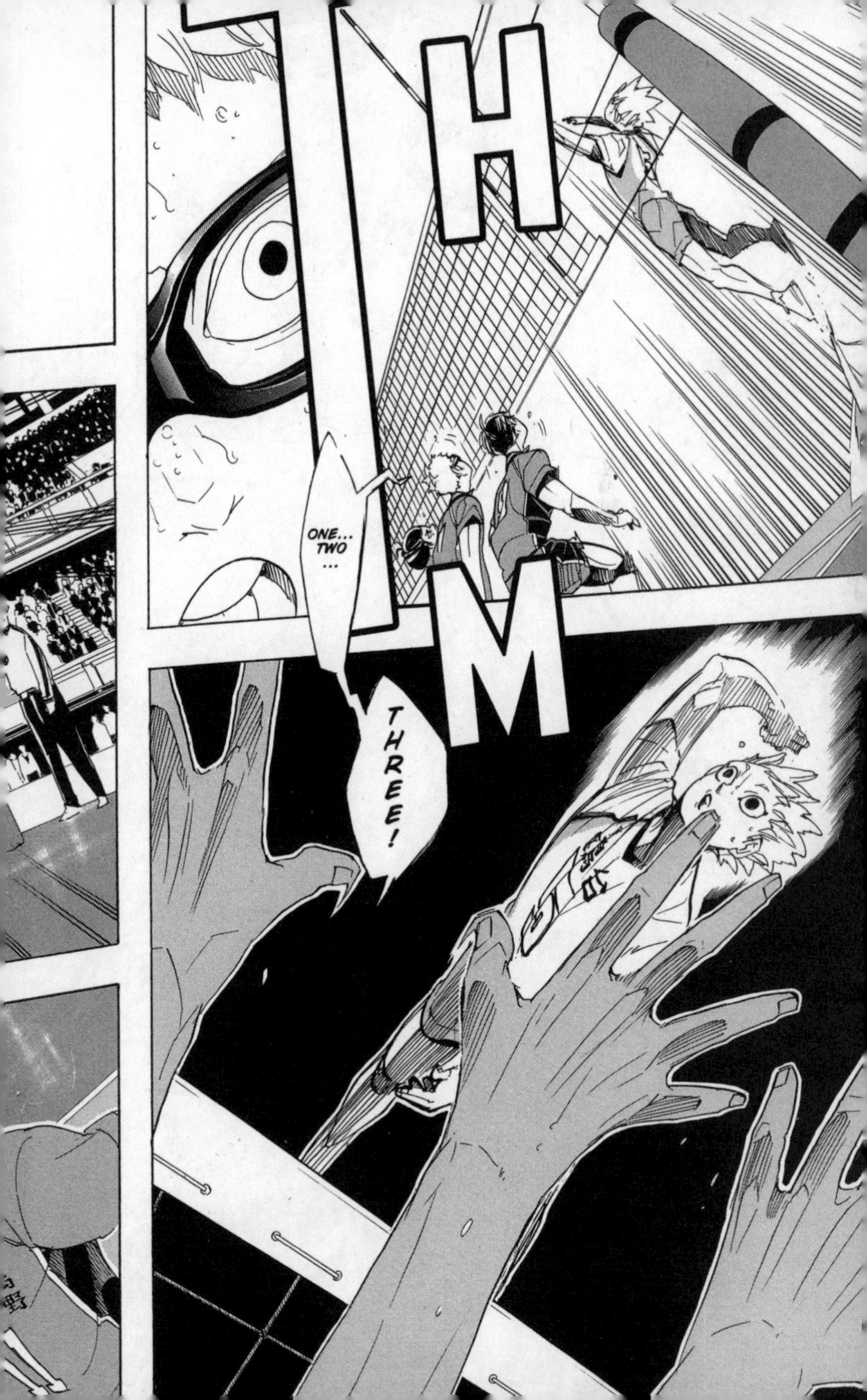
H
M
ONE... TWO ...
THREE!

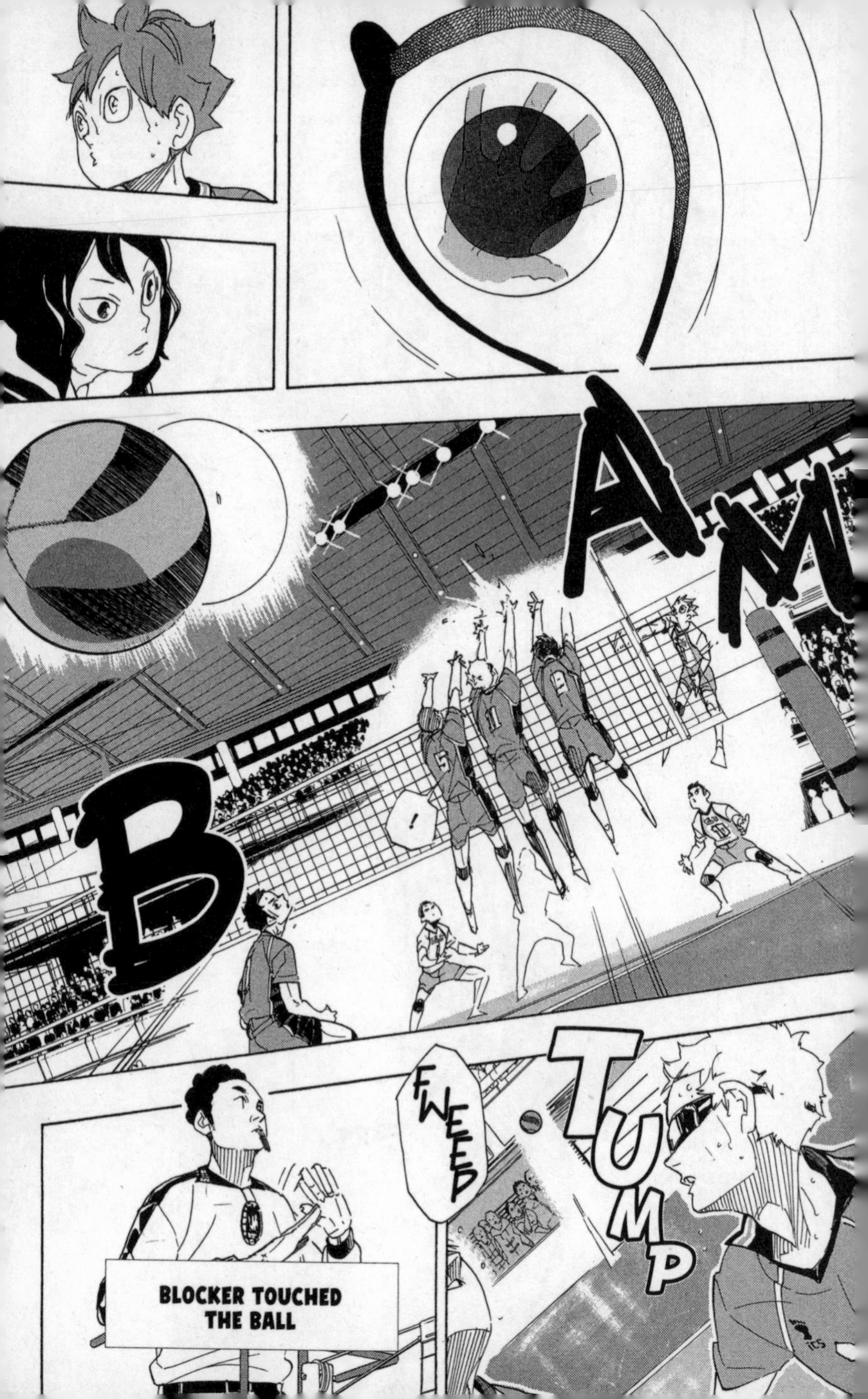
BAM
!
TUMP
FWEEP
BLOCKER TOUCHED THE BALL

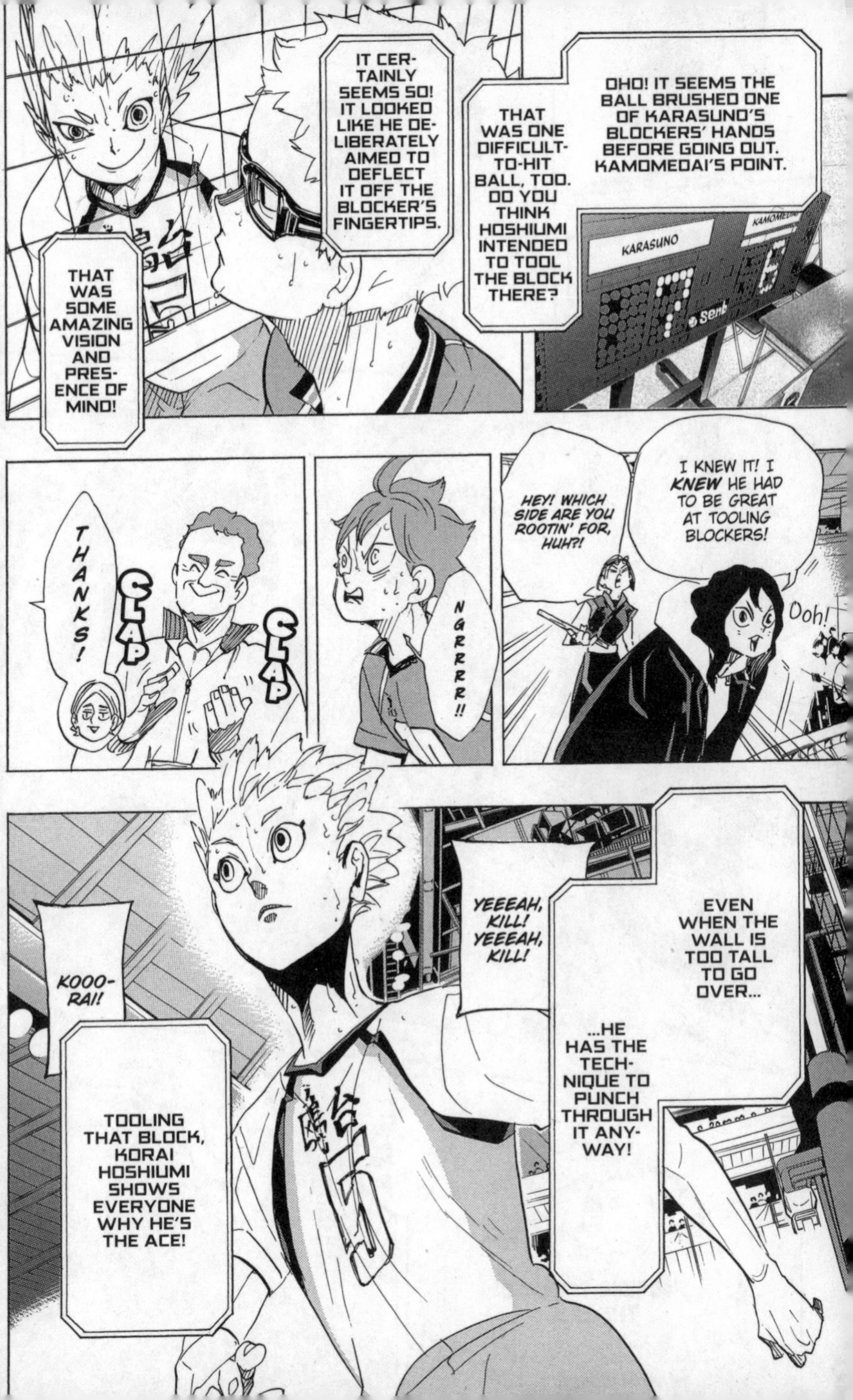
OHO! IT SEEMS THE BALL BRUSHED ONE OF KARASUNO'S BLOCKERS' HANDS BEFORE GOING OUT. KAMOMEDAI'S POINT.
KARASUNO
THAT WAS ONE DIFFICULT-TO-HIT BALL, TOO. DO YOU THINK HOSHIUMI INTENDED TO TOOL THE BLOCK THERE?
IT CER-TAINLY SEEMS SO! IT LOOKED LIKE HE DE-LIBERATELY AIMED TO DEFLECT IT OFF THE BLOCKER'S FINGERTIPS.
THAT WAS SOME AMAZING VISION AND PRES-ENCE OF MIND!
I KNEW IT! I KNEW HE HAD TO BE GREAT AT TOOLING BLOCKERS!
HEY! WHICH SIDE ARE YOU ROOTIN' FOR, HUH?!
Ooh!
NGRRRR!!
THANKS!
CLAP
CLAP
EVEN WHEN THE WALL IS TOO TALL TO GO OVER...
...HE HAS THE TECH-NIQUE TO PUNCH THROUGH IT ANY-WAY!
YEEEAH, KILL! YEEEAH, KILL!
KOOO-RAI!
TOOLING THAT BLOCK, KORAI HOSHIUMI SHOWS EVERYONE WHY HE'S THE ACE!

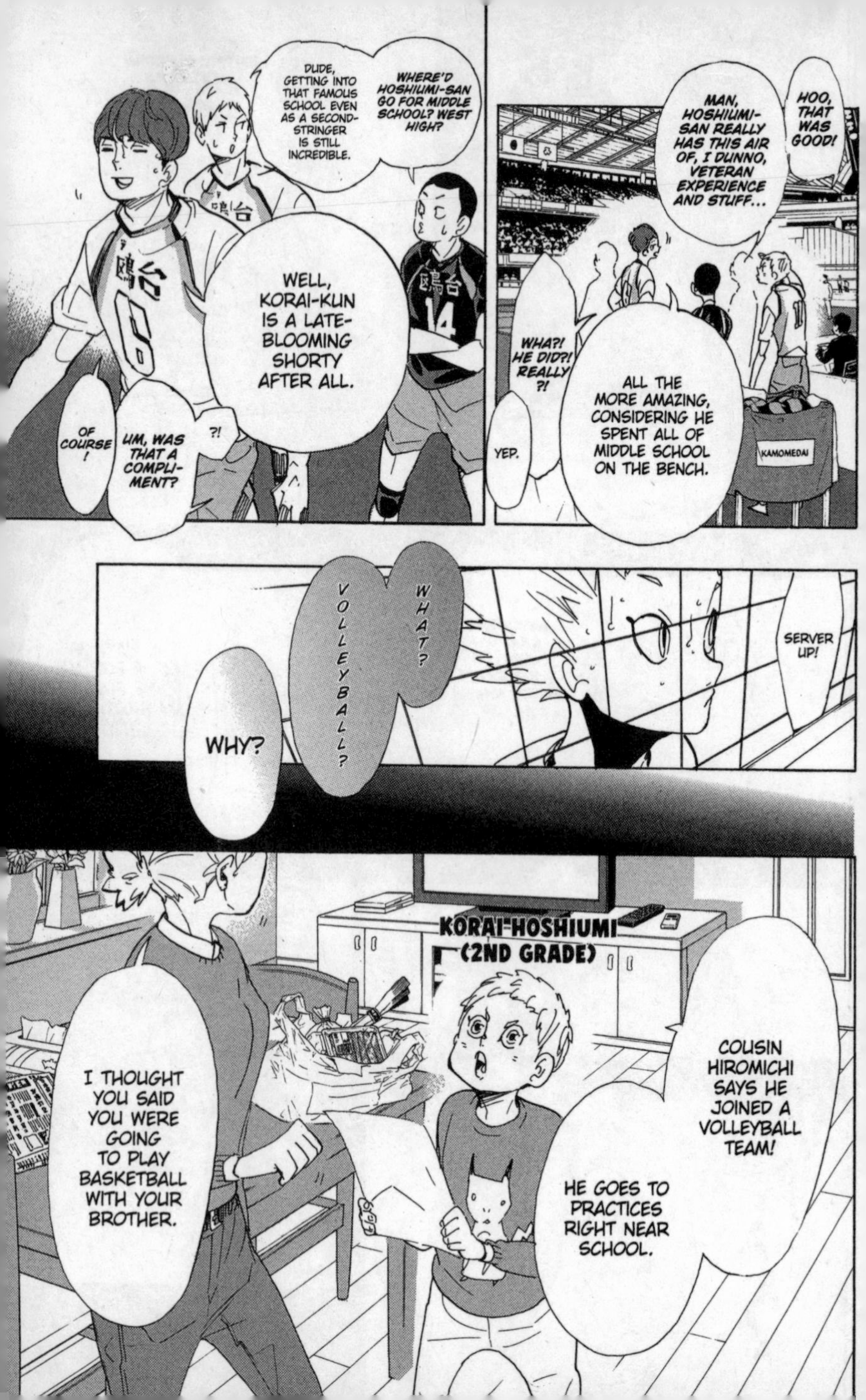
HOO, THAT WAS GOOD!
MAN, HOSHIUMI-SAN REALLY HAS THIS AIR OF, I DUNNO, VETERAN EXPERIENCE AND STUFF...
KAMOMEDAI
ALL THE MORE AMAZING, CONSIDERING HE SPENT ALL OF MIDDLE SCHOOL ON THE BENCH.
WHA?! HE DID?! REALLY ?!
YEP.
WHERE'D HOSHIUMI-SAN GO FOR MIDDLE SCHOOL? WEST HIGH?
DUDE, GETTING INTO THAT FAMOUS SCHOOL EVEN AS A SECOND-STRINGER IS STILL INCREDIBLE.
WELL, KORAI-KUN IS A LATE-BLOOMING SHORTY AFTER ALL.
?!
UM, WAS THAT A COMPLIMENT?
OF COURSE!
SERVER UP!
WHAT?
VOLLEYBALL?
WHY?
KORAI HOSHIUMI (2ND GRADE)
COUSIN HIROMICHI SAYS HE JOINED A VOLLEYBALL TEAM!
HE GOES TO PRACTICES RIGHT NEAR SCHOOL.
I THOUGHT YOU SAID YOU WERE GOING TO PLAY BASKETBALL WITH YOUR BROTHER.

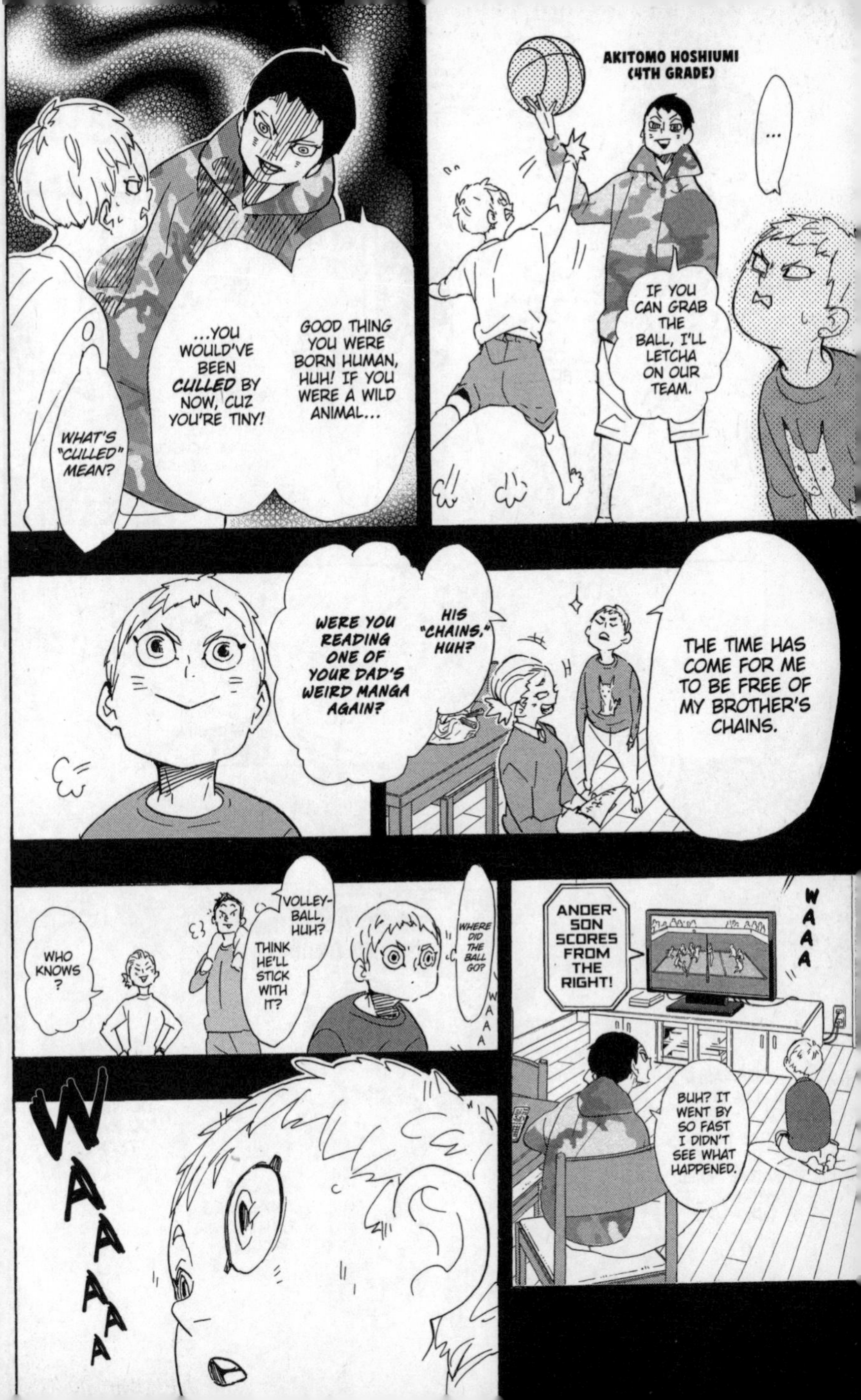
AKITOMO HOSHIUMI (4TH GRADE)
...
IF YOU CAN GRAB THE BALL, I'LL LETCHA ON OUR TEAM.
GOOD THING YOU WERE BORN HUMAN, HUH! IF YOU WERE A WILD ANIMAL...
...YOU WOULD'VE BEEN CULLED BY NOW, CUZ YOU'RE TINY!
WHAT'S "CULLED" MEAN?
THE TIME HAS COME FOR ME TO BE FREE OF MY BROTHER'S CHAINS.
HIS "CHAINS," HUH?
WERE YOU READING ONE OF YOUR DAD'S WEIRD MANGA AGAIN?
ANDER-SON SCORES FROM THE RIGHT!
WAAA
BUH? IT WENT BY SO FAST I DIDN'T SEE WHAT HAPPENED.
WHERE DID THE BALL GO?
WAAA
VOLLEY-BALL, HUH? THINK HE'LL STICK WITH IT?
WHO KNOWS?
WAAAAAA

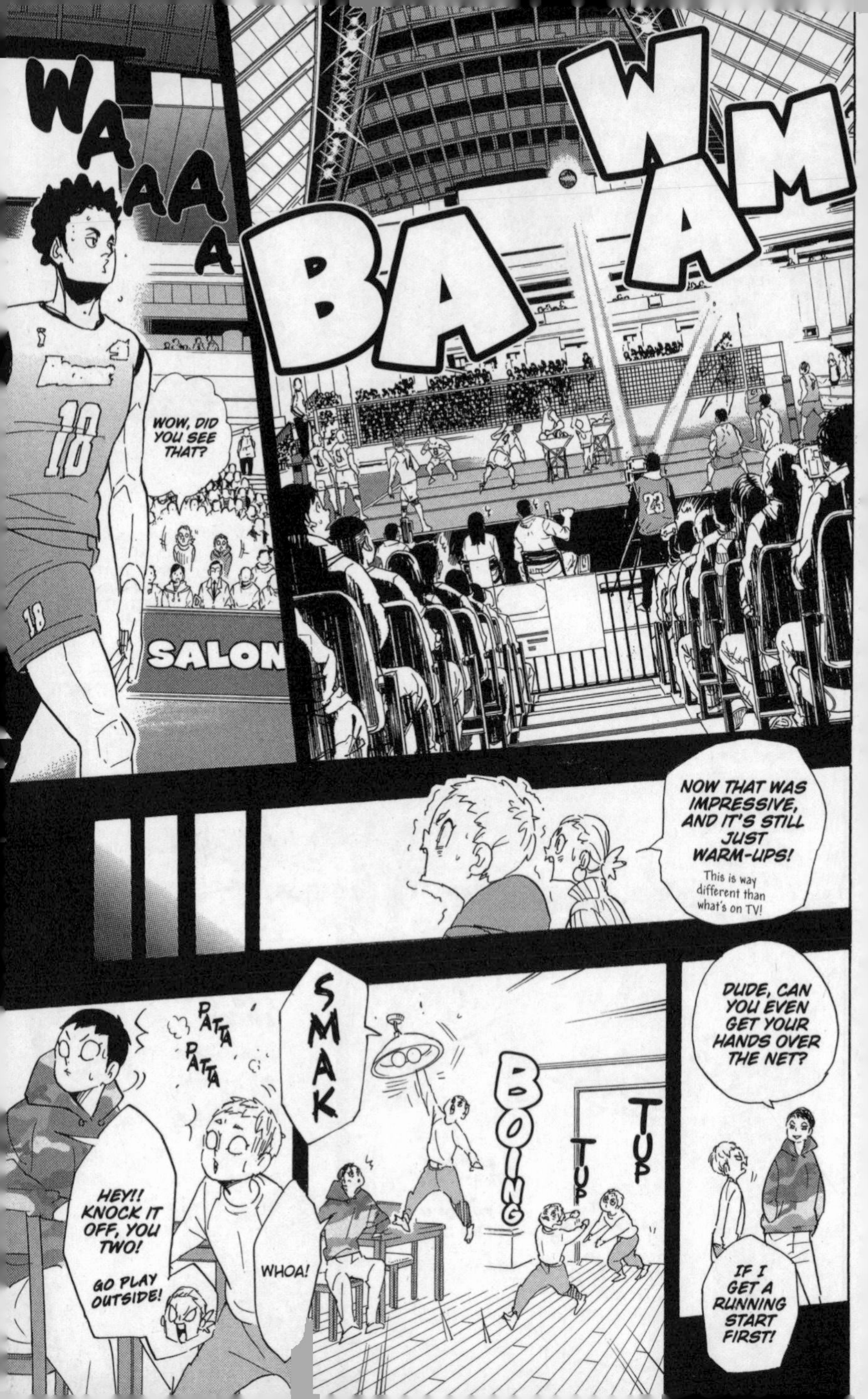
BA WAM
WAAAAA
WOW, DID YOU SEE THAT?
SALON
NOW THAT WAS IMPRESSIVE, AND IT'S STILL JUST WARM-UPS!
This is way different than what's on TV!
DUDE, CAN YOU EVEN GET YOUR HANDS OVER THE NET?
IF I GET A RUNNING START FIRST!
TUP TUP
BOING
SMAK
PATTA PATTA
HEY!! KNOCK IT OFF, YOU TWO!
GO PLAY OUTSIDE!
WHOA!

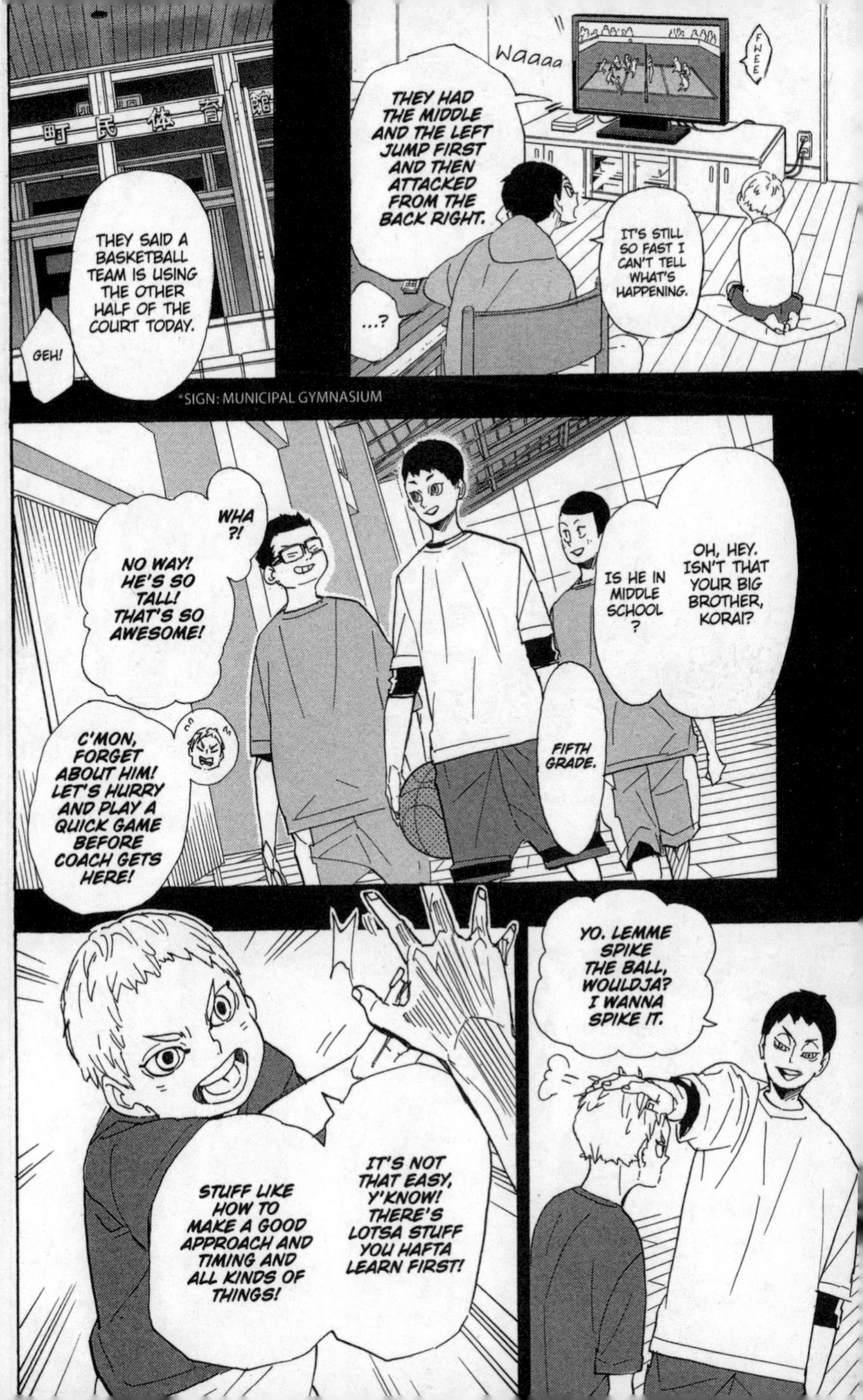
FWEE
Waaaa
THEY HAD THE MIDDLE AND THE LEFT JUMP FIRST AND THEN ATTACKED FROM THE BACK RIGHT.
IT'S STILL SO FAST I CAN'T TELL WHAT'S HAPPENING.
...?
町民体育館
THEY SAID A BASKETBALL TEAM IS USING THE OTHER HALF OF THE COURT TODAY.
GEH!
*SIGN: MUNICIPAL GYMNASIUM
OH, HEY. ISN'T THAT YOUR BIG BROTHER, KORAI?
IS HE IN MIDDLE SCHOOL?
WHA?!
NO WAY! HE'S SO TALL! THAT'S SO AWESOME!
FIFTH GRADE.
C'MON, FORGET ABOUT HIM! LET'S HURRY AND PLAY A QUICK GAME BEFORE COACH GETS HERE!
YO. LEMME SPIKE THE BALL, WOULDJA? I WANNA SPIKE IT.
IT'S NOT THAT EASY, Y'KNOW! THERE'S LOTSA STUFF YOU HAFTA LEARN FIRST!
STUFF LIKE HOW TO MAKE A GOOD APPROACH AND TIMING AND ALL KINDS OF THINGS!

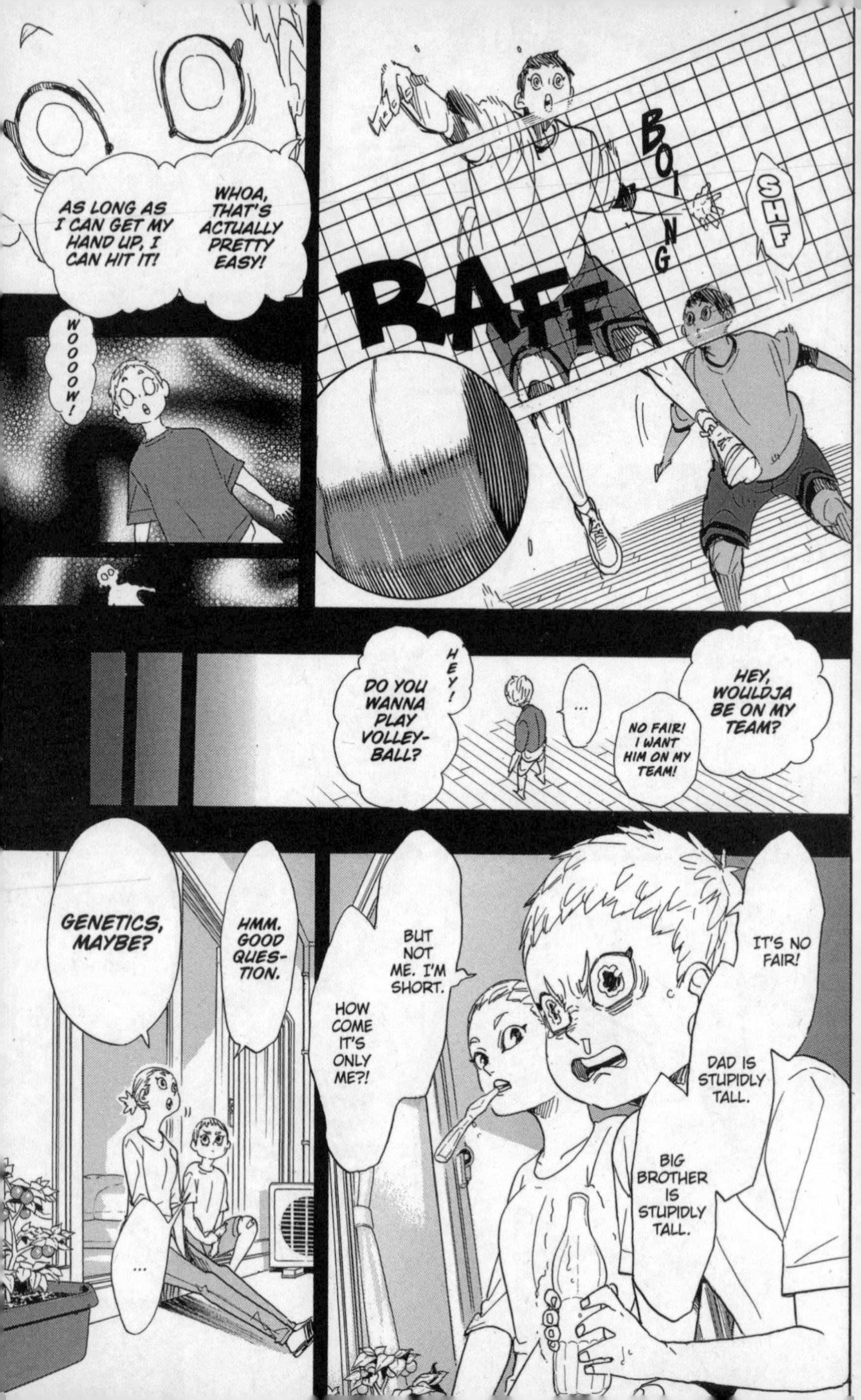
SHF
BOING
RAFF
WHOA, THAT'S ACTUALLY PRETTY EASY!
AS LONG AS I CAN GET MY HAND UP, I CAN HIT IT!
WOOOOOW!
HEY, WOULDJA BE ON MY TEAM?
NO FAIR! I WANT HIM ON MY TEAM!
...
HEY!
DO YOU WANNA PLAY VOLLEY-BALL?
IT'S NO FAIR!
DAD IS STUPIDLY TALL.
BIG BROTHER IS STUPIDLY TALL.
BUT NOT ME. I'M SHORT.
HOW COME IT'S ONLY ME?!
HMM. GOOD QUES-TION.
GENETICS, MAYBE?
...

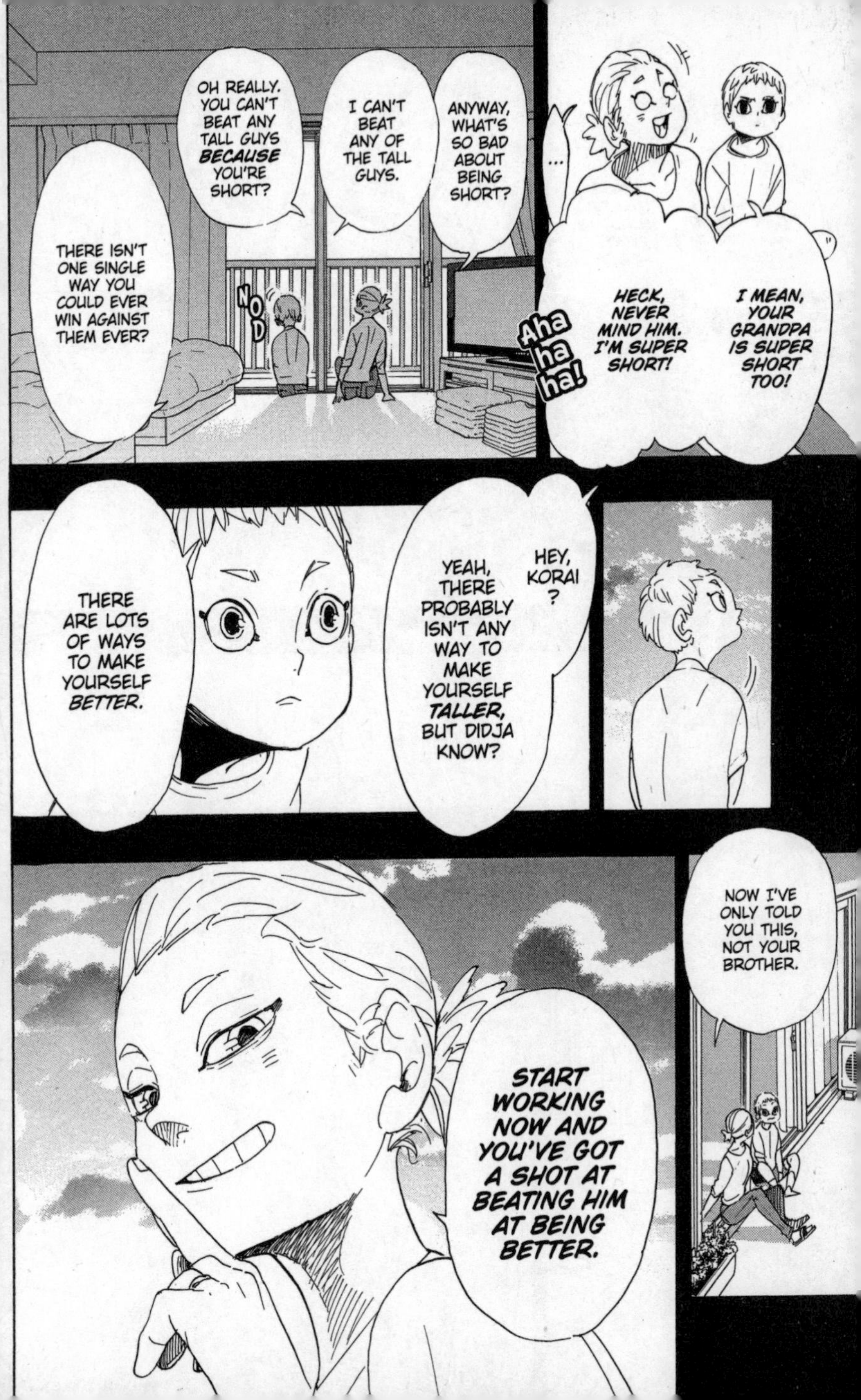

I MEAN, YOUR GRANDPA IS SUPER SHORT TOO!
HECK, NEVER MIND HIM. I'M SUPER SHORT!
Aha ha ha!
...
ANYWAY, WHAT'S SO BAD ABOUT BEING SHORT?
I CAN'T BEAT ANY OF THE TALL GUYS.
NOD
OH REALLY. YOU CAN'T BEAT ANY TALL GUYS *BECAUSE* YOU'RE SHORT?
THERE ISN'T ONE SINGLE WAY YOU COULD EVER WIN AGAINST THEM EVER?
HEY, KORAI?
YEAH, THERE PROBABLY ISN'T ANY WAY TO MAKE YOURSELF *TALLER,* BUT DIDJA KNOW?
THERE ARE LOTS OF WAYS TO MAKE YOURSELF *BETTER.*
NOW I'VE ONLY TOLD YOU THIS, NOT YOUR BROTHER.
START WORKING NOW AND YOU'VE GOT A SHOT AT BEATING HIM AT BEING BETTER.

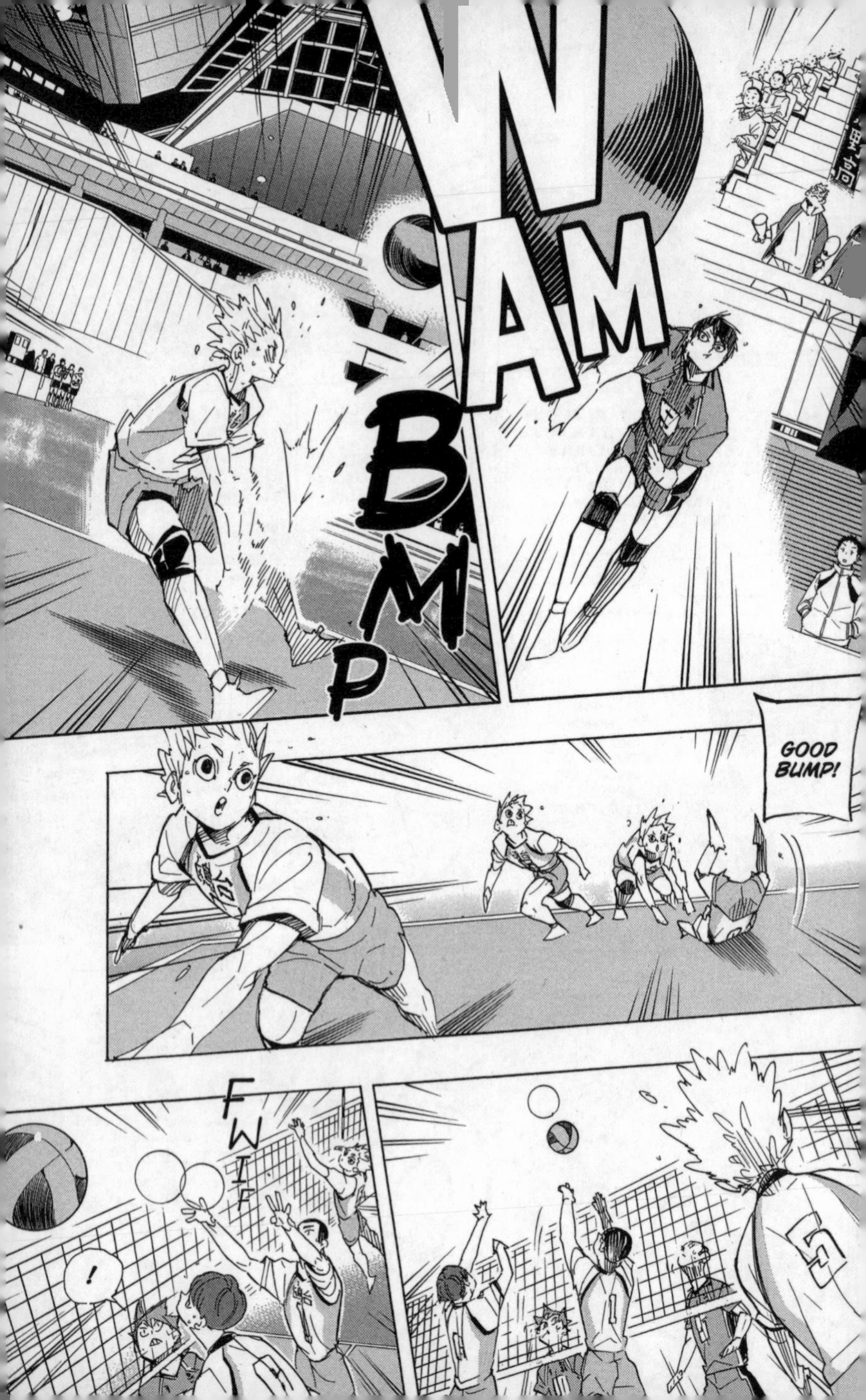
WAM
BMP
GOOD BUMP!
FWIF
!

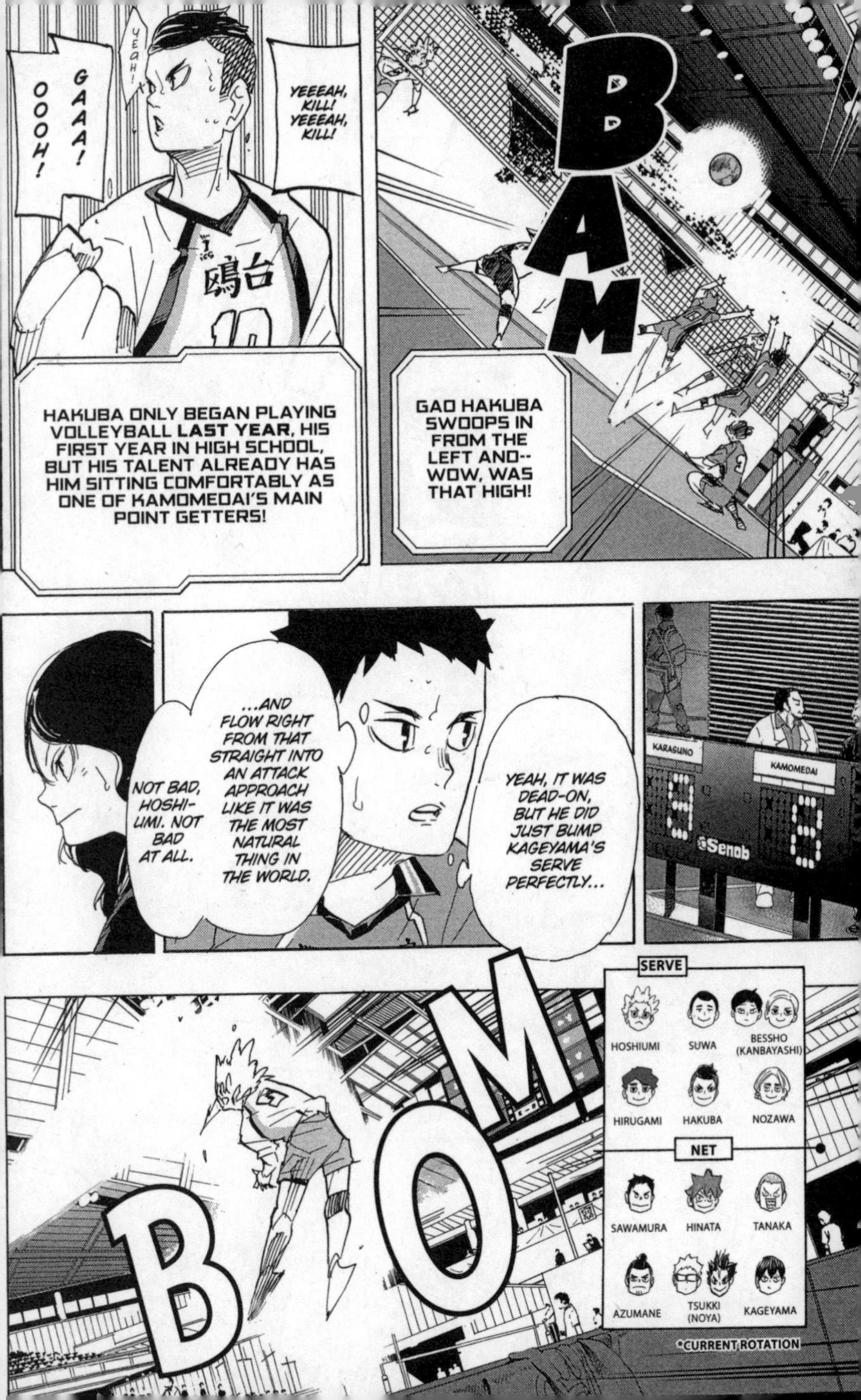
BAM
GAO HAKUBA SWOOPS IN FROM THE LEFT AND-- WOW, WAS THAT HIGH!
YEEEAH, KILL! YEEEAH, KILL!
YEAH!
GAAA!
OOOH!
HAKUBA ONLY BEGAN PLAYING VOLLEYBALL **LAST YEAR**, HIS FIRST YEAR IN HIGH SCHOOL, BUT HIS TALENT ALREADY HAS HIM SITTING COMFORTABLY AS ONE OF KAMOMEDAI'S MAIN POINT GETTERS!
KARASUNO
KAMOMEDAI
Senob
YEAH, IT WAS DEAD-ON, BUT HE DID JUST BUMP KAGEYAMA'S SERVE PERFECTLY...
...AND FLOW RIGHT FROM THAT STRAIGHT INTO AN ATTACK APPROACH LIKE IT WAS THE MOST NATURAL THING IN THE WORLD.
NOT BAD, HOSHI-UMI. NOT BAD AT ALL.
SERVE
HOSHIUMI
SUWA
BESSHO (KANBAYASHI)
HIRUGAMI
HAKUBA
NOZAWA
NET
SAWAMURA
HINATA
TANAKA
AZUMANE
TSUKKI (NOYA)
KAGEYAMA
*CURRENT ROTATION
BOOM

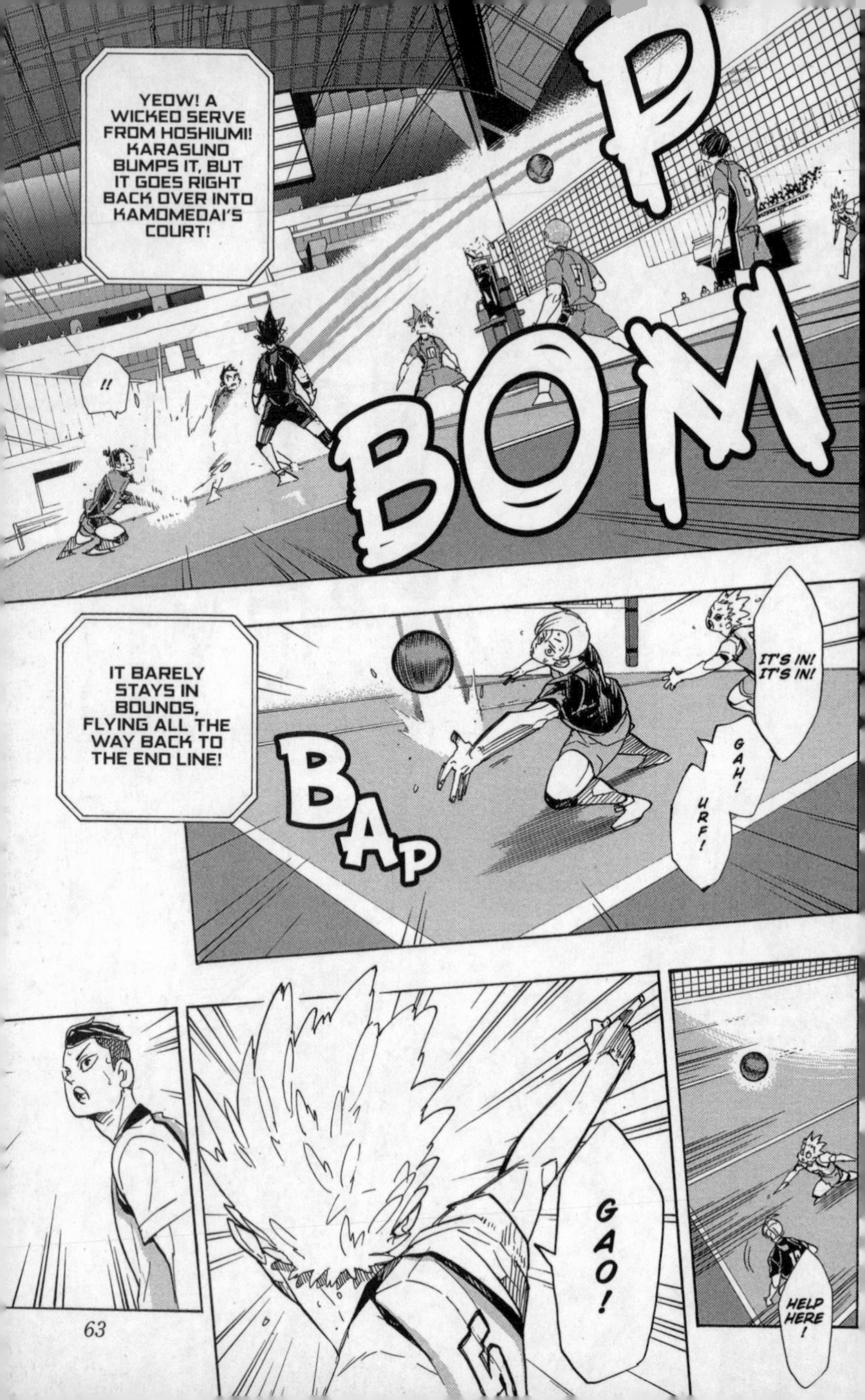
YEOW! A WICKED SERVE FROM HOSHIUMI! KARASUNO BUMPS IT, BUT IT GOES RIGHT BACK OVER INTO KAMOMEDAI'S COURT!
P
BOM
!!
IT'S IN! IT'S IN!
GAH!
URF!
IT BARELY STAYS IN BOUNDS, FLYING ALL THE WAY BACK TO THE END LINE!
BAP
HELP HERE!
GAO!

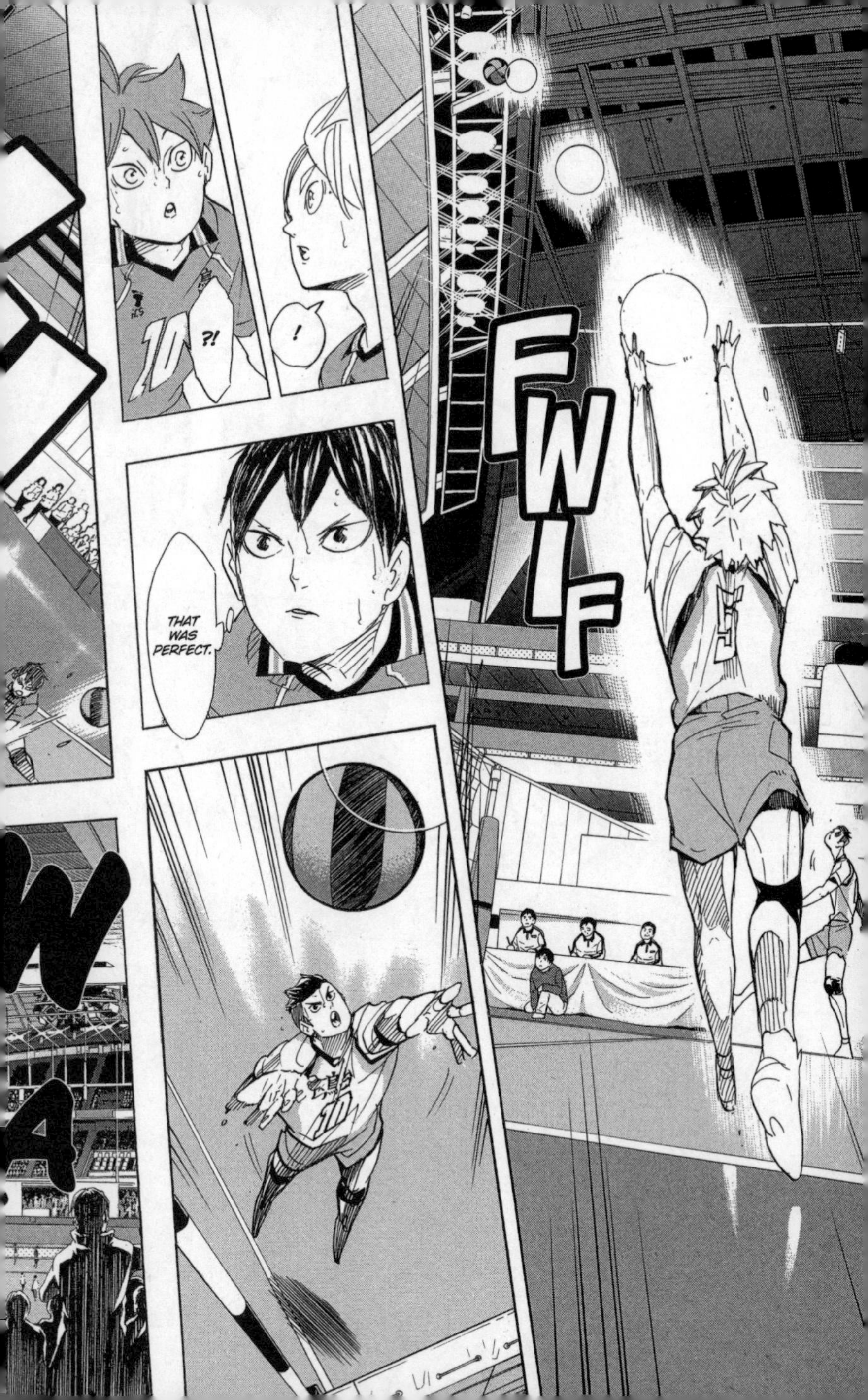
FWIF
!
?!
THAT WAS PERFECT.

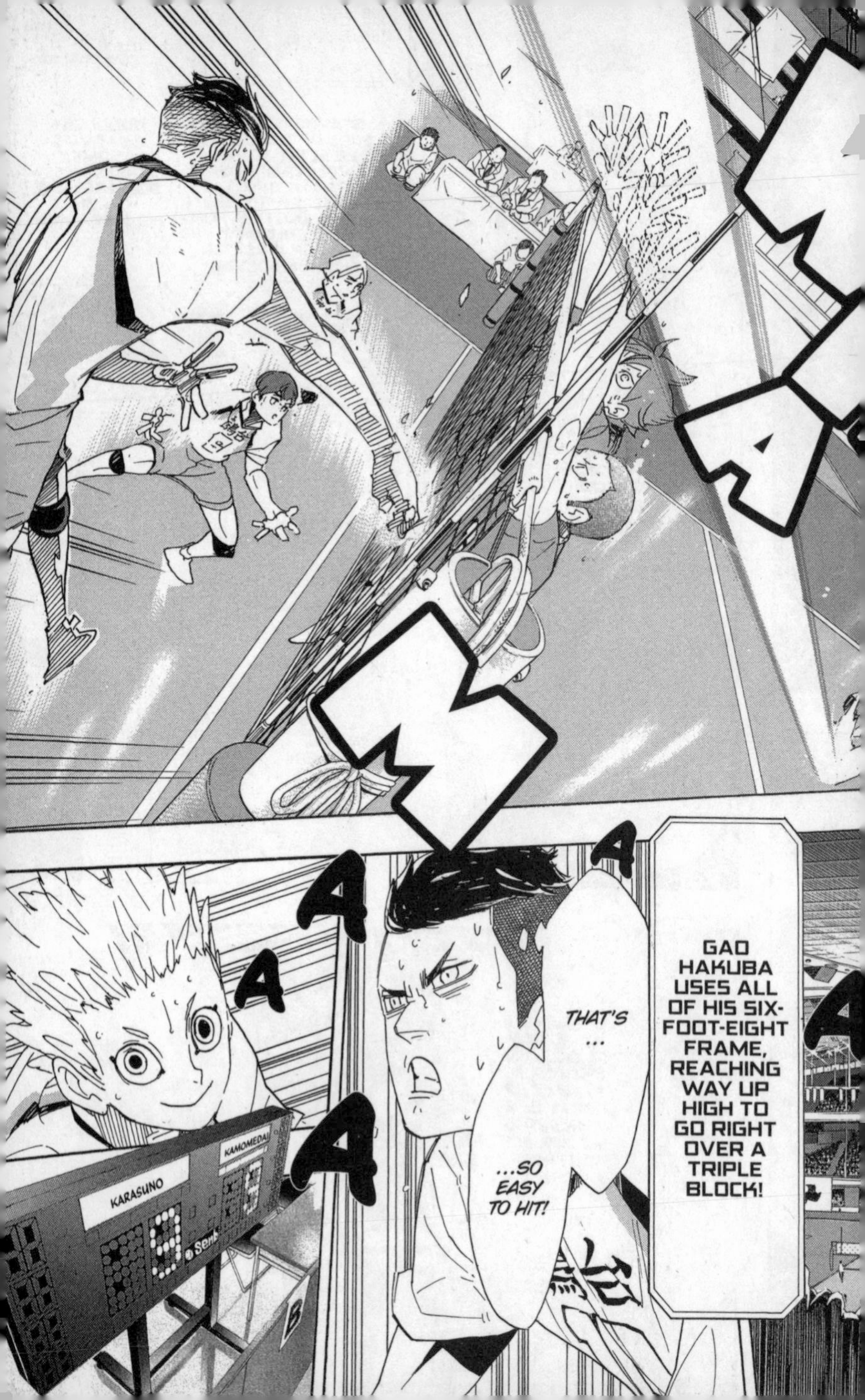
GAO HAKUBA USES ALL OF HIS SIX-FOOT-EIGHT FRAME, REACHING WAY UP HIGH TO GO RIGHT OVER A TRIPLE BLOCK!
THAT'S ...
...SO EASY TO HIT!
KAMOMEDAI
KARASUNO

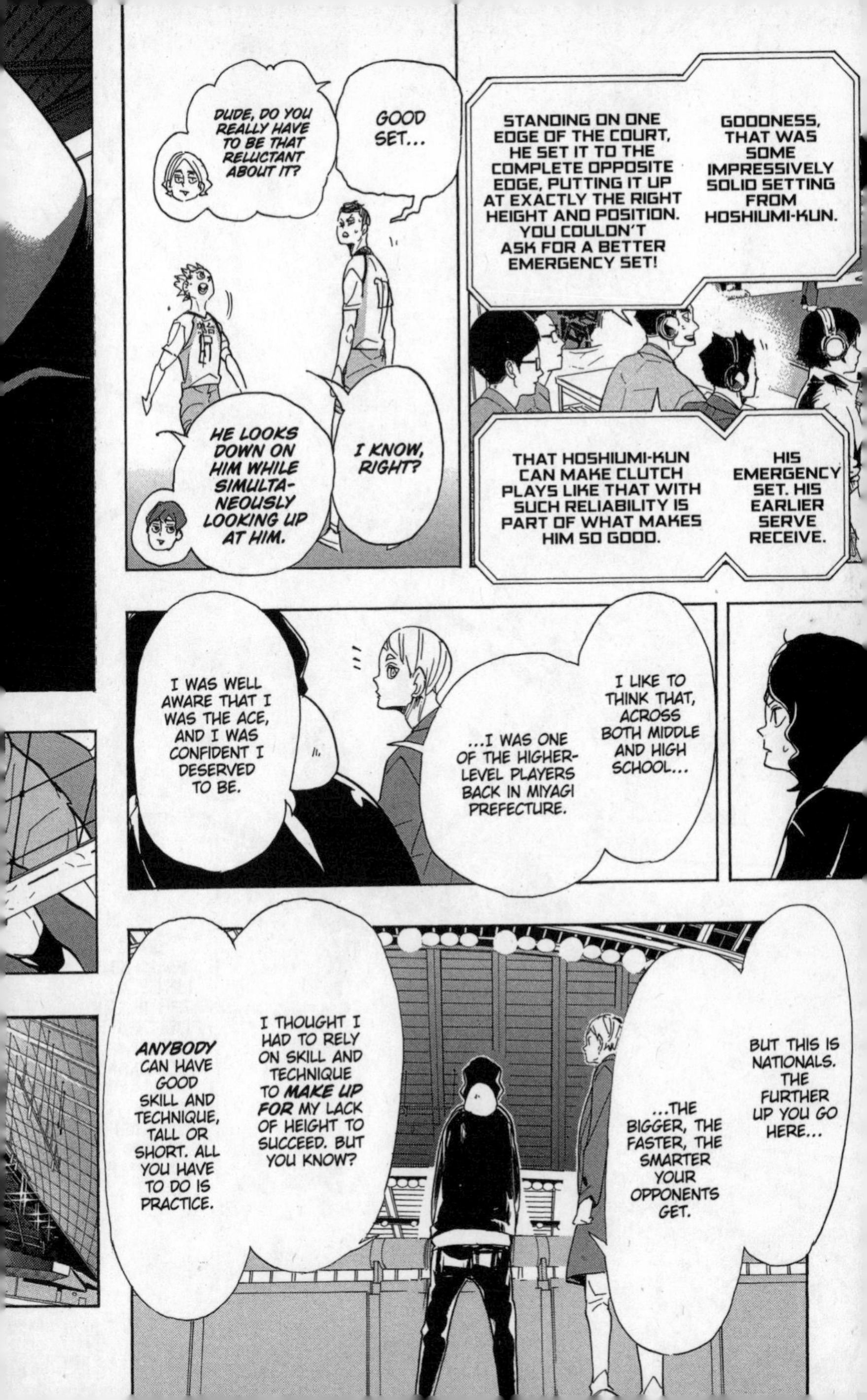
GOODNESS, THAT WAS SOME IMPRESSIVELY SOLID SETTING FROM HOSHIUMI-KUN.
STANDING ON ONE EDGE OF THE COURT, HE SET IT TO THE COMPLETE OPPOSITE EDGE, PUTTING IT UP AT EXACTLY THE RIGHT HEIGHT AND POSITION. YOU COULDN'T ASK FOR A BETTER EMERGENCY SET!
HIS EMERGENCY SET. HIS EARLIER SERVE RECEIVE.
THAT HOSHIUMI-KUN CAN MAKE CLUTCH PLAYS LIKE THAT WITH SUCH RELIABILITY IS PART OF WHAT MAKES HIM SO GOOD.
GOOD SET...
DUDE, DO YOU REALLY HAVE TO BE THAT RELUCTANT ABOUT IT?
I KNOW, RIGHT?
HE LOOKS DOWN ON HIM WHILE SIMULTA-NEOUSLY LOOKING UP AT HIM.
I LIKE TO THINK THAT, ACROSS BOTH MIDDLE AND HIGH SCHOOL...
...I WAS ONE OF THE HIGHER-LEVEL PLAYERS BACK IN MIYAGI PREFECTURE.
I WAS WELL AWARE THAT I WAS THE ACE, AND I WAS CONFIDENT I DESERVED TO BE.
BUT THIS IS NATIONALS. THE FURTHER UP YOU GO HERE...
...THE BIGGER, THE FASTER, THE SMARTER YOUR OPPONENTS GET.
I THOUGHT I HAD TO RELY ON SKILL AND TECHNIQUE TO MAKE UP FOR MY LACK OF HEIGHT TO SUCCEED. BUT YOU KNOW?
ANYBODY CAN HAVE GOOD SKILL AND TECHNIQUE, TALL OR SHORT. ALL YOU HAVE TO DO IS PRACTICE.

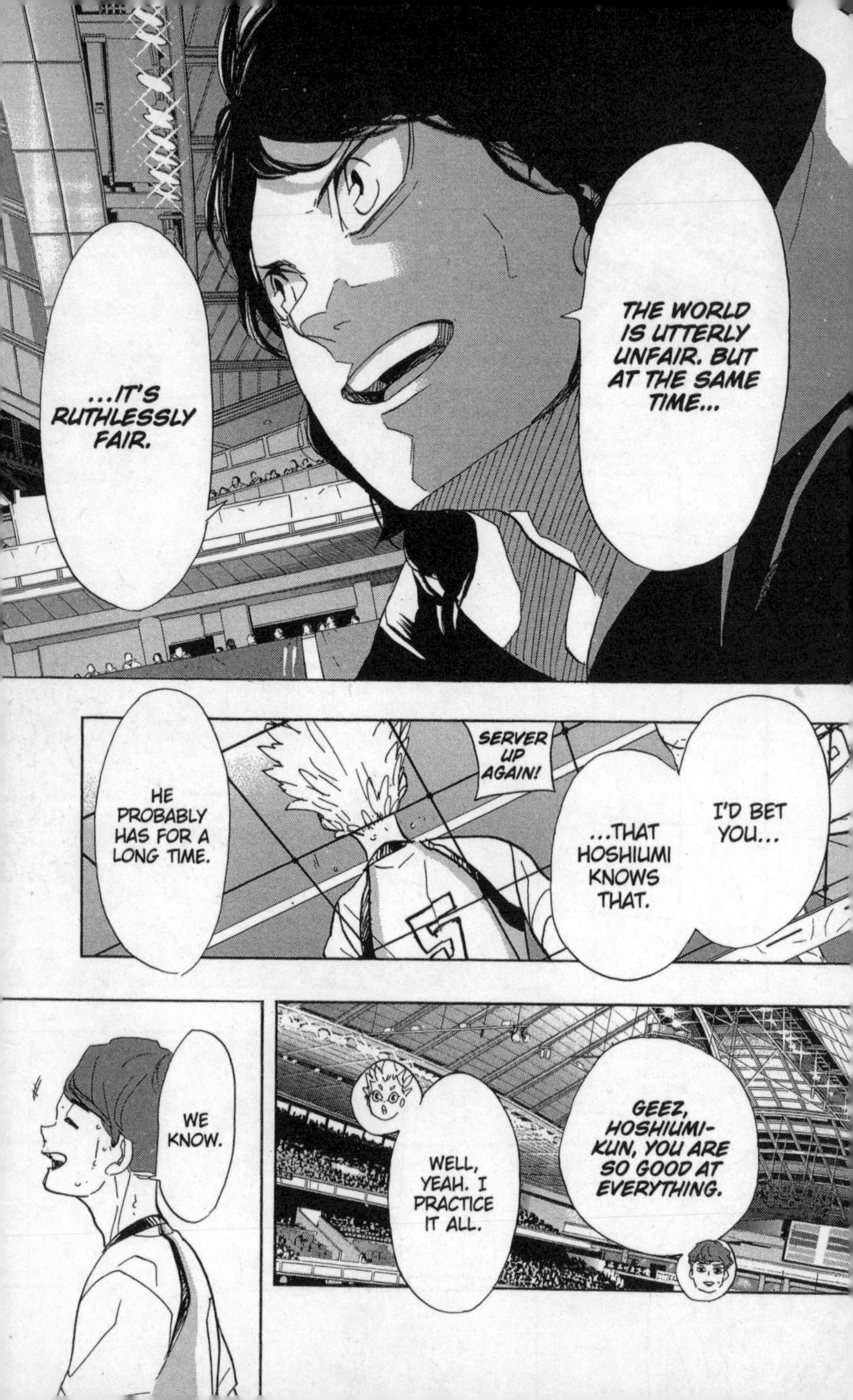
THE WORLD IS UTTERLY UNFAIR. BUT AT THE SAME TIME...
...IT'S RUTHLESSLY FAIR.
I'D BET YOU...
...THAT HOSHIUMI KNOWS THAT.
SERVER UP AGAIN!
HE PROBABLY HAS FOR A LONG TIME.
GEEZ, HOSHIUMI-KUN, YOU ARE SO GOOD AT EVERYTHING.
WELL, YEAH. I PRACTICE IT ALL.
WE KNOW.

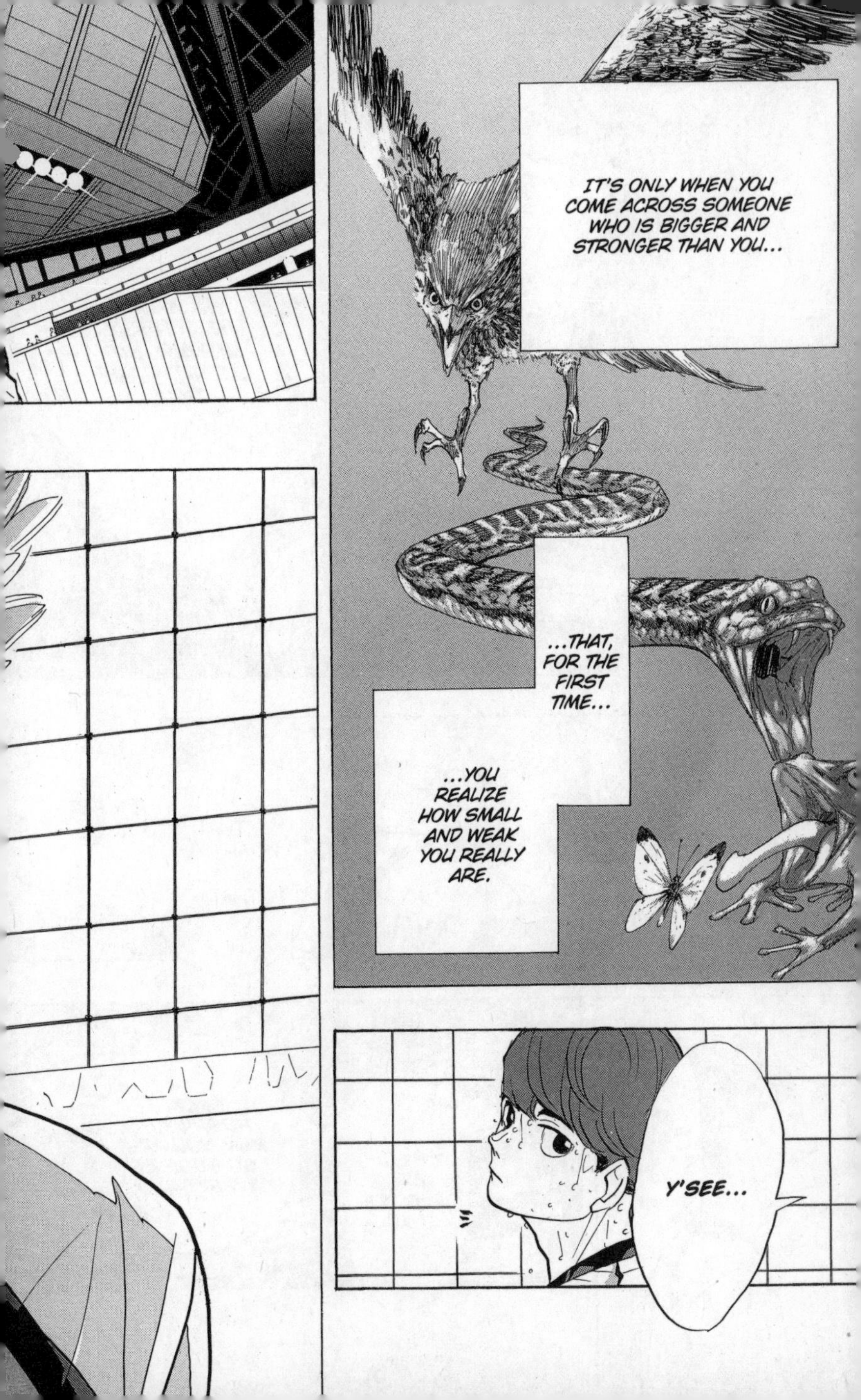
IT'S ONLY WHEN YOU COME ACROSS SOMEONE WHO IS BIGGER AND STRONGER THAN YOU...
...THAT, FOR THE FIRST TIME...
...YOU REALIZE HOW SMALL AND WEAK YOU REALLY ARE.
Y'SEE...

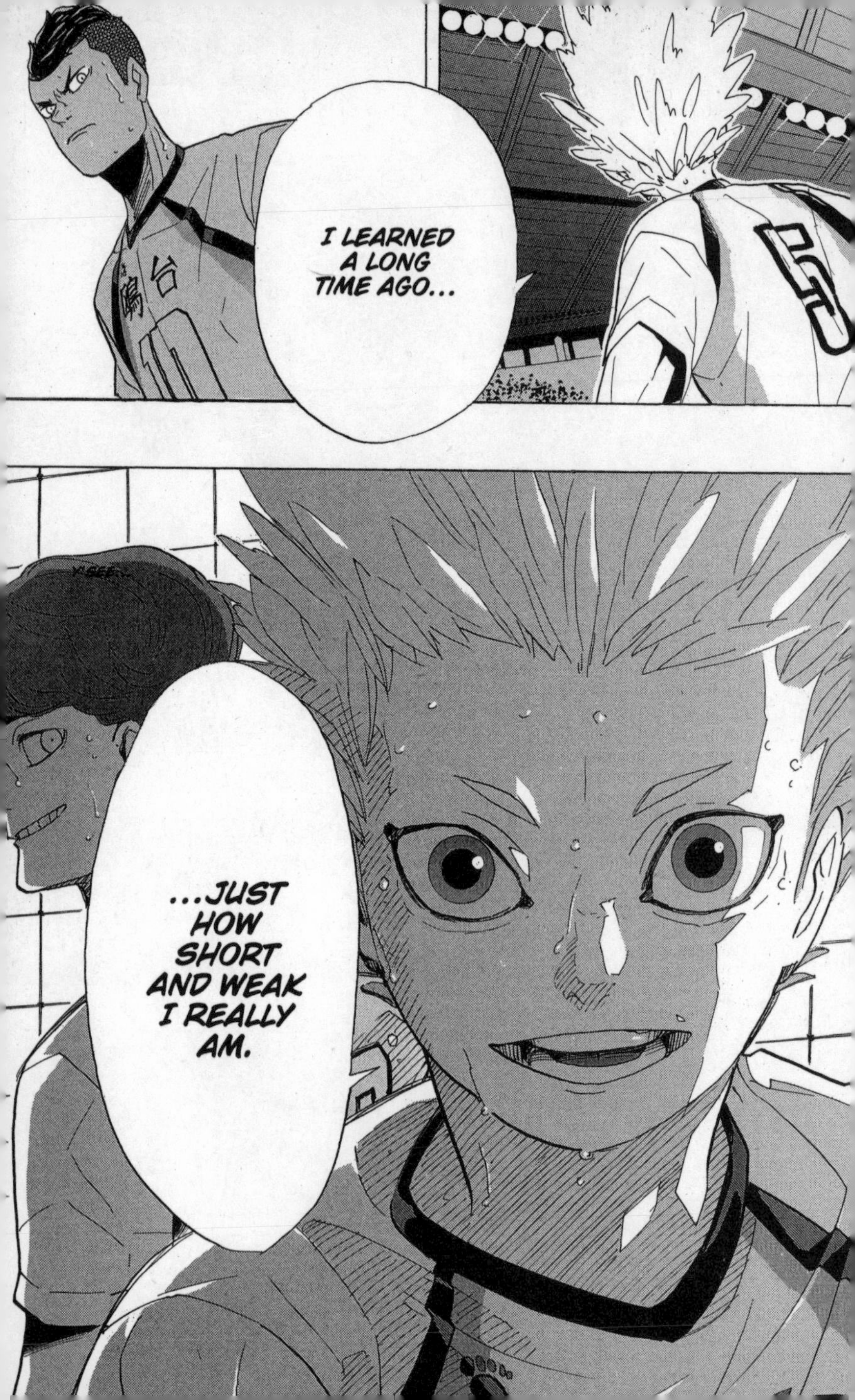
I LEARNED A LONG TIME AGO...
...JUST HOW SHORT AND WEAK I REALLY AM.

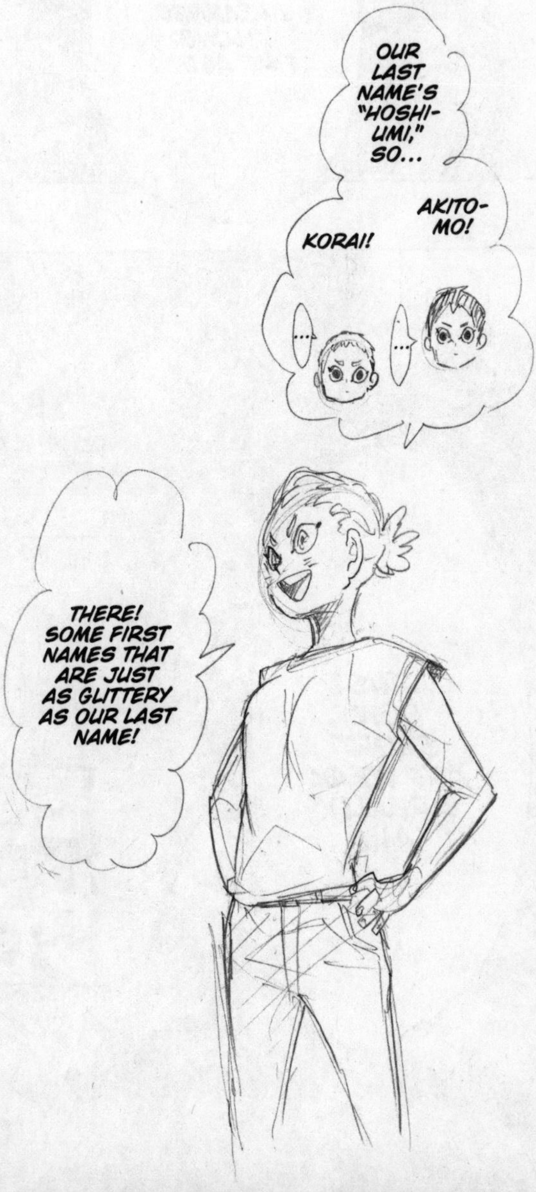
OUR LAST NAME'S "HOSHI-UMI," SO...
AKITO-MO!
KORAI!
...
...
THERE! SOME FIRST NAMES THAT ARE JUST AS GLITTERY AS OUR LAST NAME!

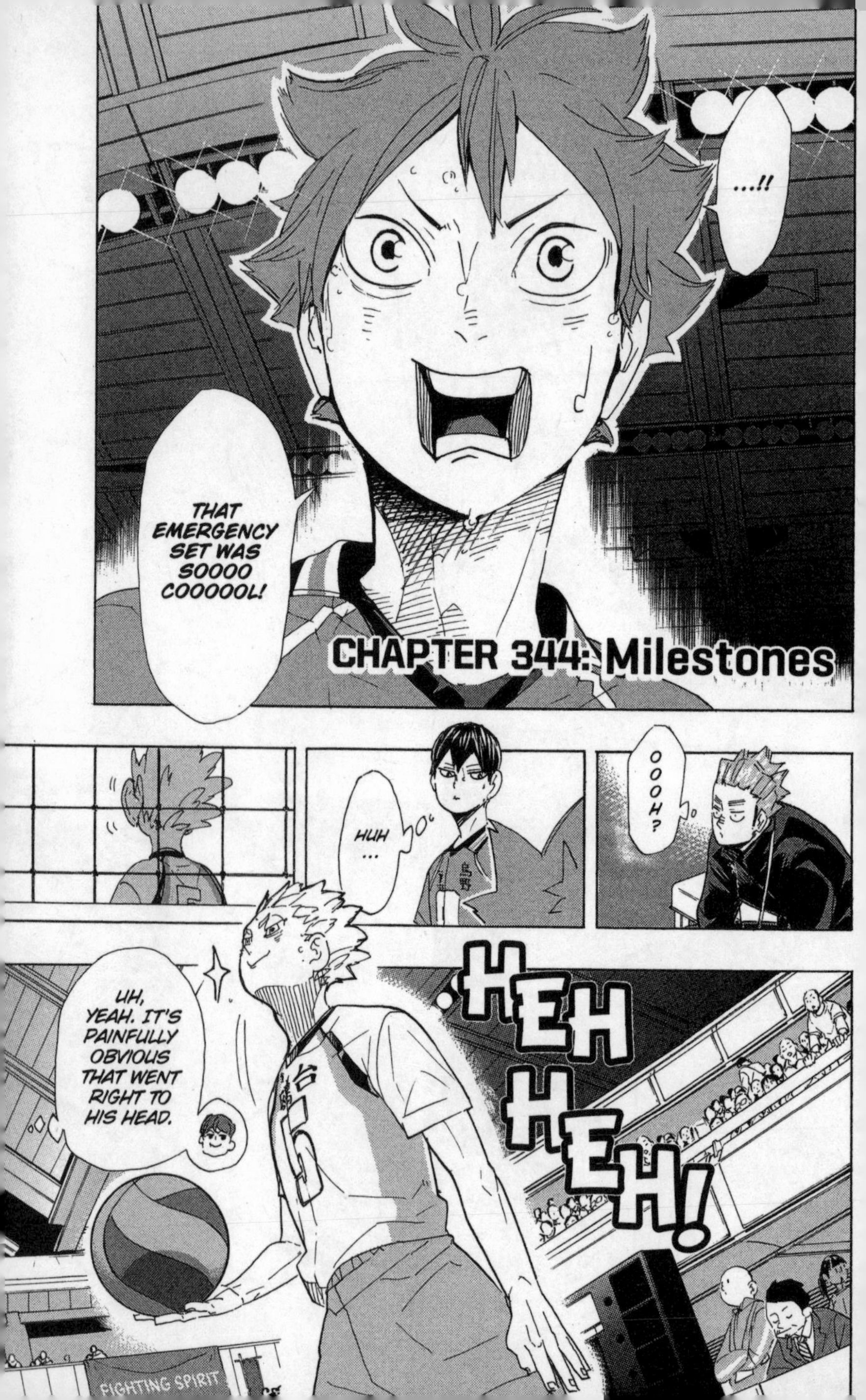
...!!
THAT EMERGENCY SET WAS SOOOO COOOOOL!
CHAPTER 344: Milestones
OOOH?
HUH...
HEH HEH HEH!
UH, YEAH. IT'S PAINFULLY OBVIOUS THAT WENT RIGHT TO HIS HEAD.
FIGHTING SPIRIT

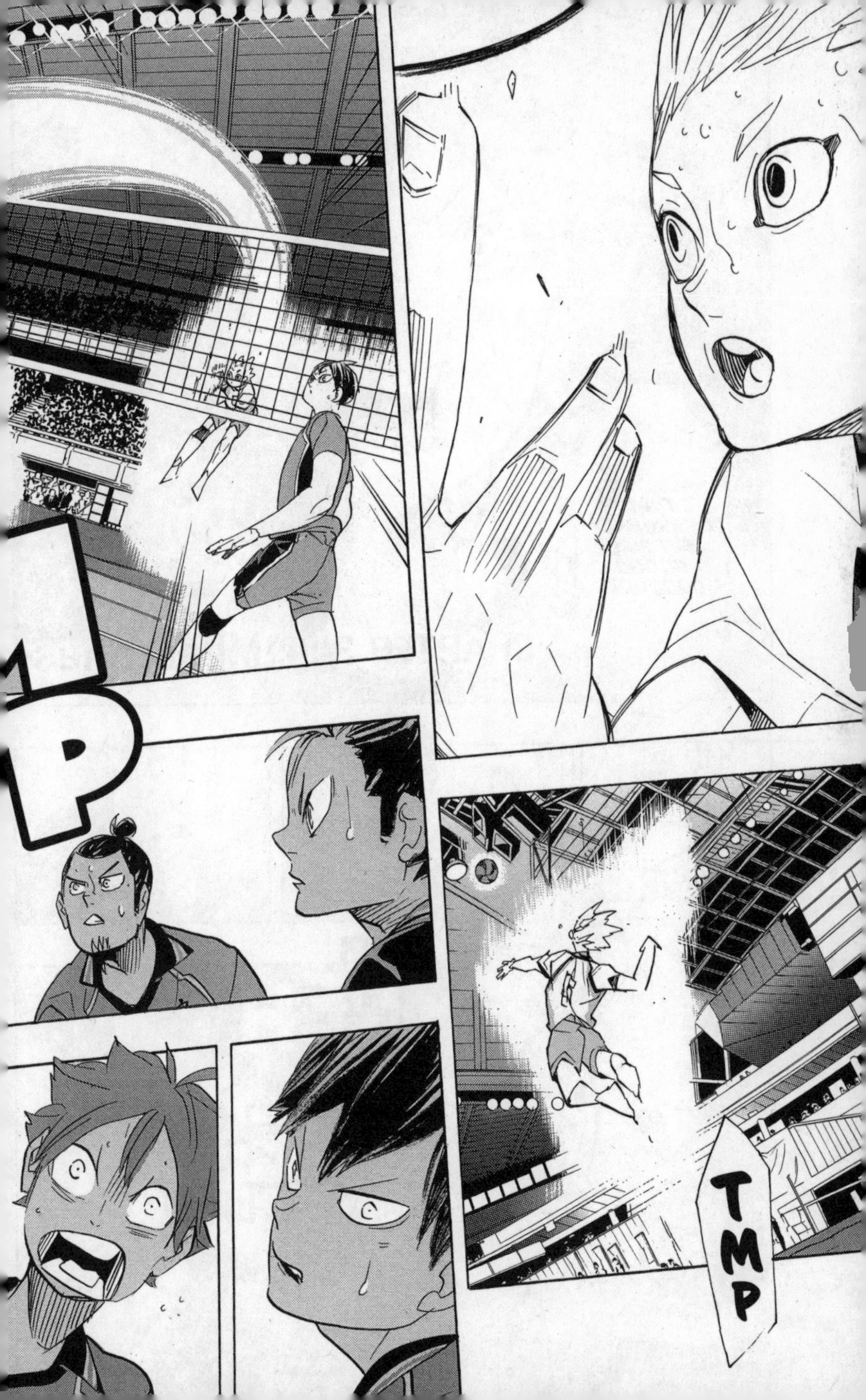
TMP
P

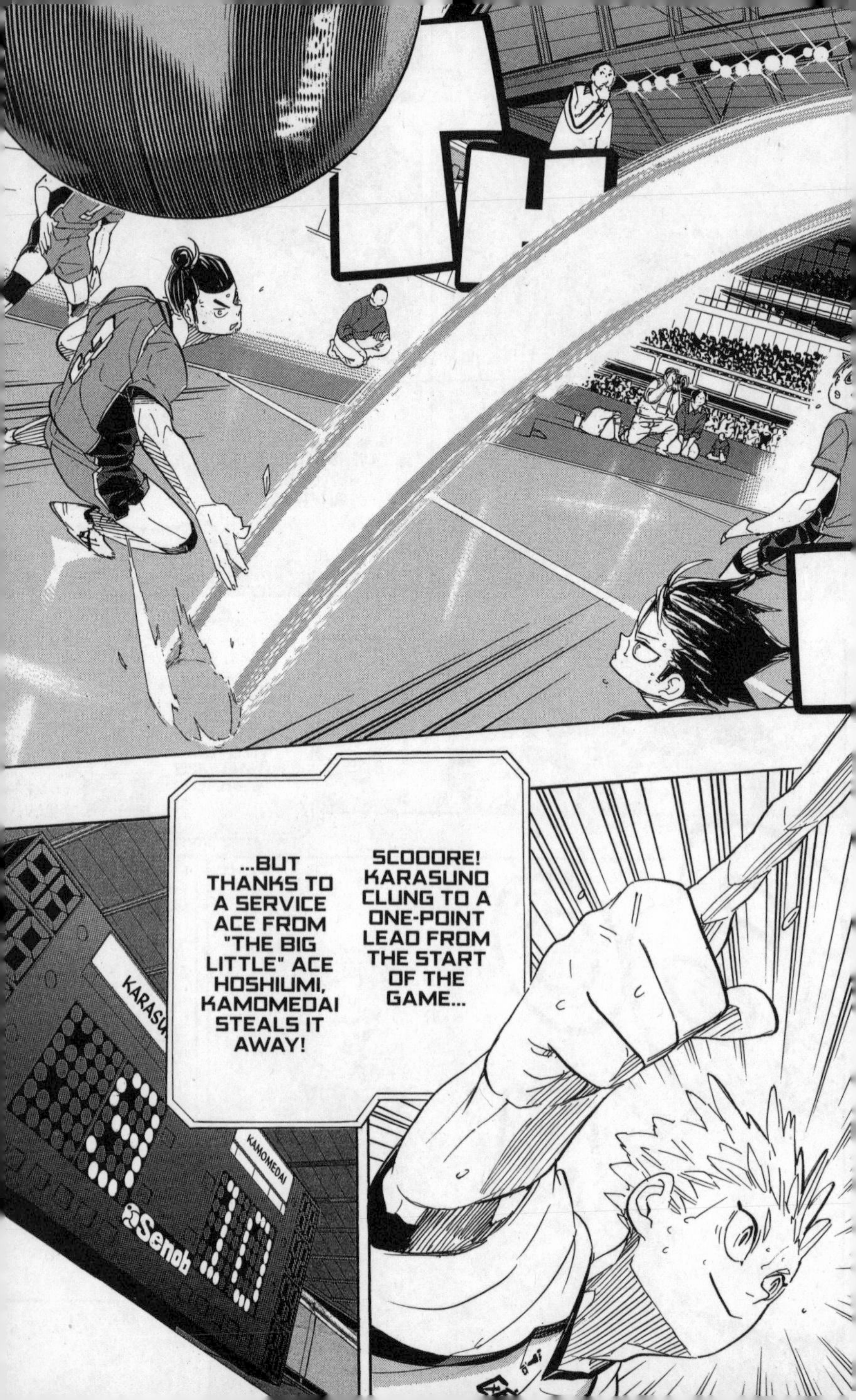
SCOOORE! KARASUNO CLUNG TO A ONE-POINT LEAD FROM THE START OF THE GAME...
...BUT THANKS TO A SERVICE ACE FROM "THE BIG LITTLE" ACE HOSHIUMI, KAMOMEDAI STEALS IT AWAY!
KAMOMEDAI

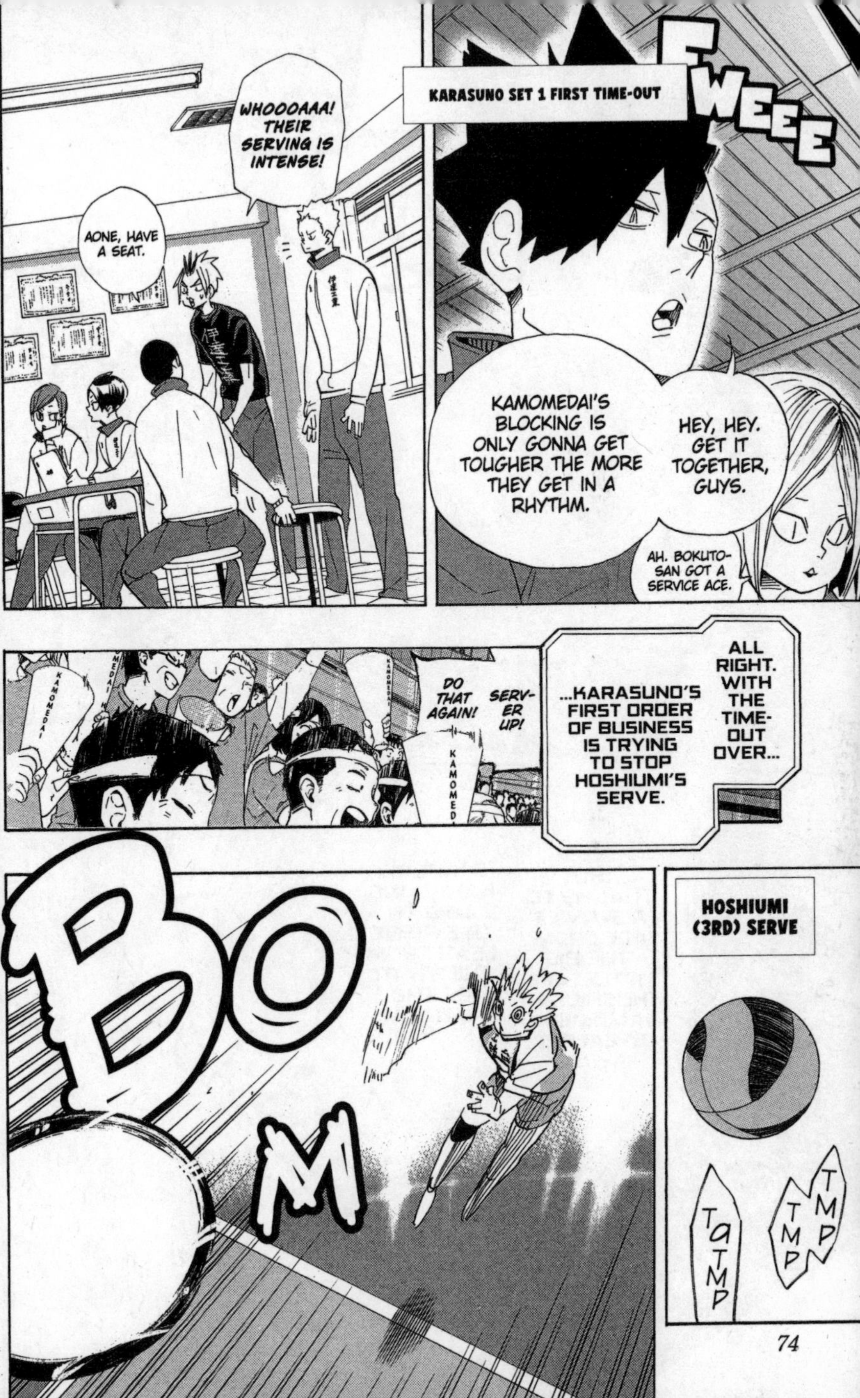
KARASUNO SET 1 FIRST TIME-OUT
FWEEE
HEY, HEY. GET IT TOGETHER, GUYS.
KAMOMEDAI'S BLOCKING IS ONLY GONNA GET TOUGHER THE MORE THEY GET IN A RHYTHM.
AH. BOKUTO-SAN GOT A SERVICE ACE.
WHOOOAAA! THEIR SERVING IS INTENSE!
AONE, HAVE A SEAT.
ALL RIGHT. WITH THE TIME-OUT OVER...
...KARASUNO'S FIRST ORDER OF BUSINESS IS TRYING TO STOP HOSHIUMI'S SERVE.
KAMOMEDAI
SERV-ER UP!
DO THAT AGAIN!
HOSHIUMI (3RD) SERVE
TMP TMP
TATMP
BOOM

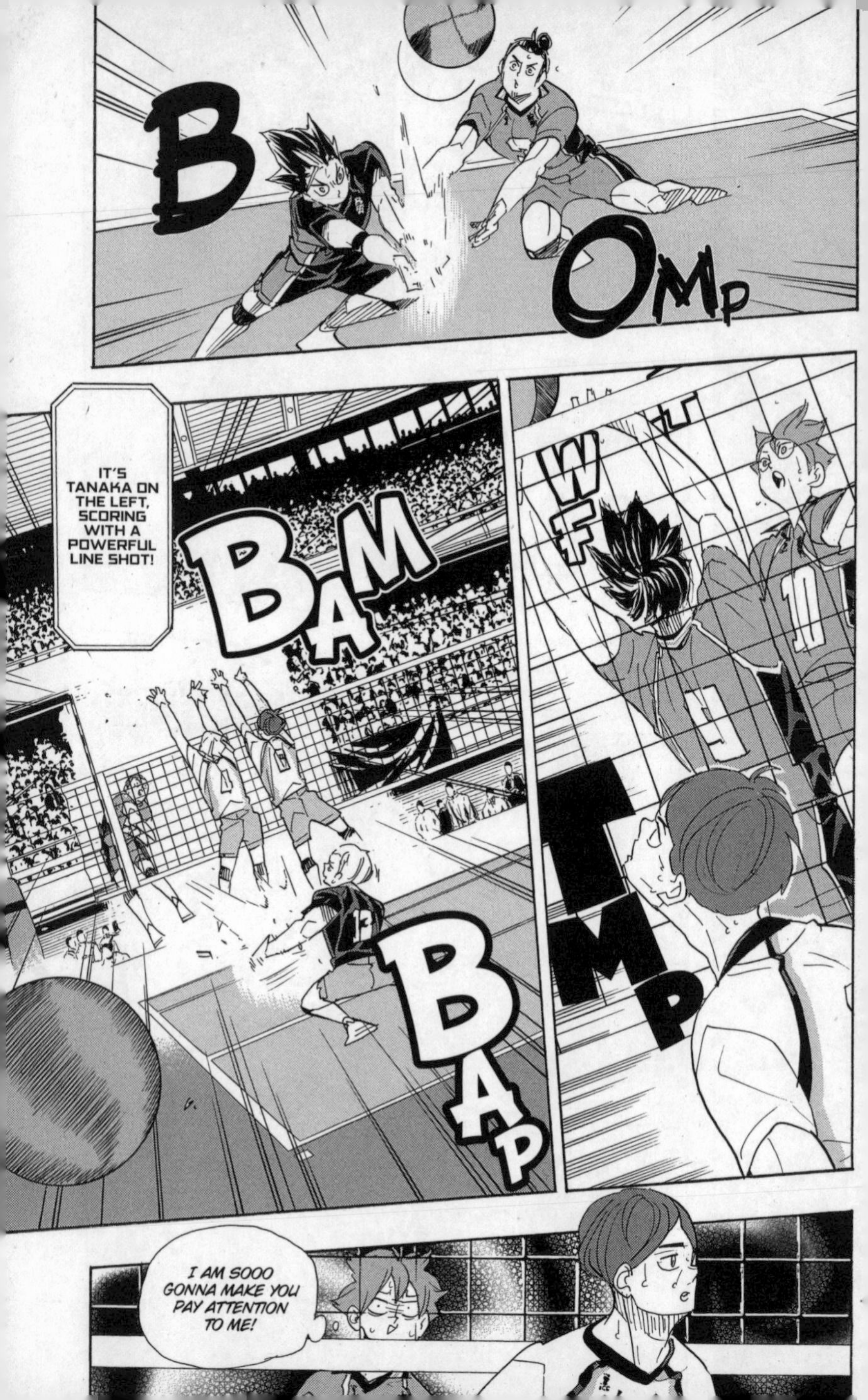
BOMP
WF
TMP
IT'S TANAKA ON THE LEFT, SCORING WITH A POWERFUL LINE SHOT!
BAM
BAP
I AM SOOO GONNA MAKE YOU PAY ATTENTION TO ME!

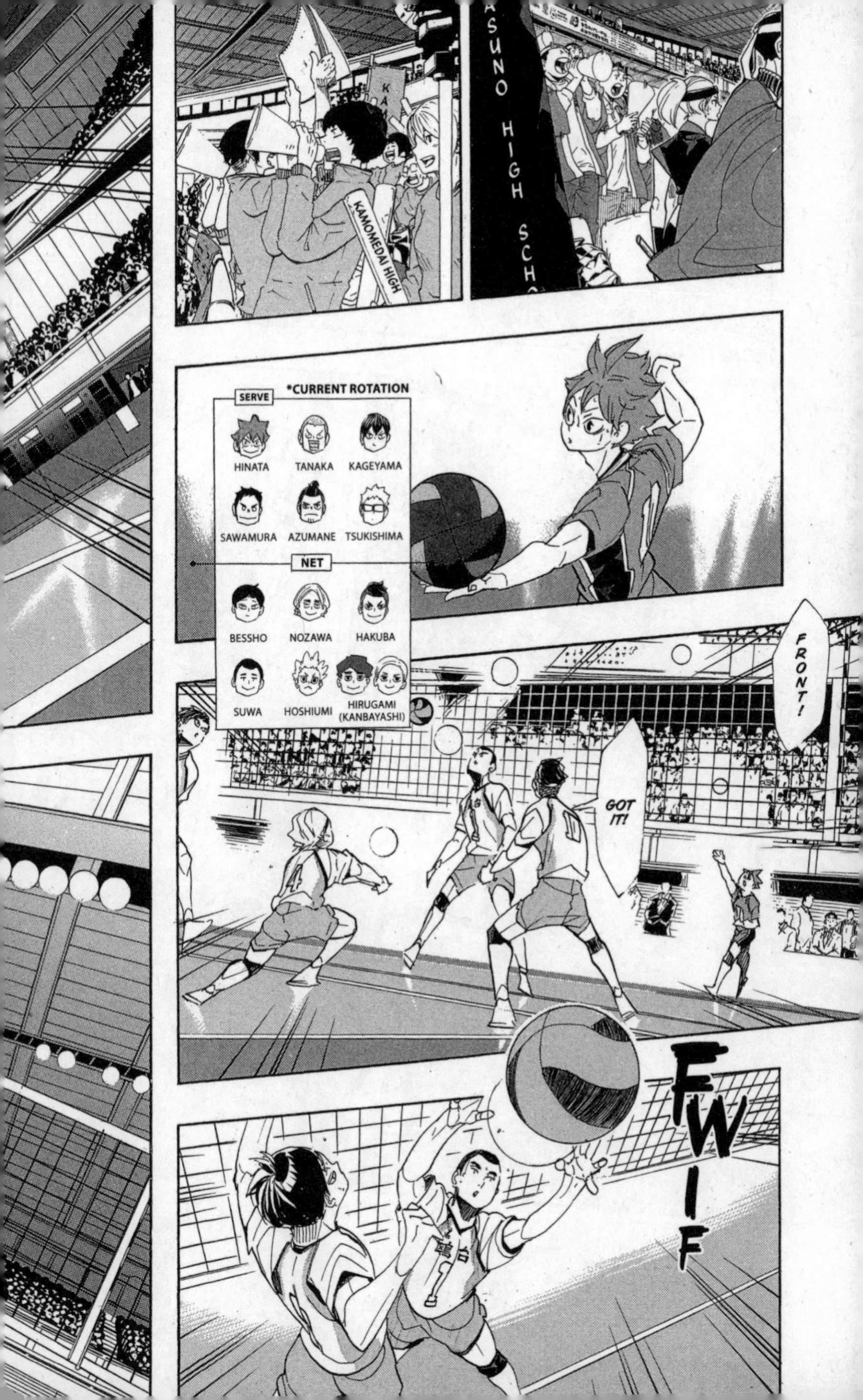
ASUNO HIGH SCHO
KAMOMEDAI HIGH
*CURRENT ROTATION
SERVE
HINATA
TANAKA
KAGEYAMA
SAWAMURA
AZUMANE
TSUKISHIMA
NET
BESSHO
NOZAWA
HAKUBA
SUWA
HOSHIUMI
HIRUGAMI (KANBAYASHI)
FRONT!
GOT IT!
FWIF

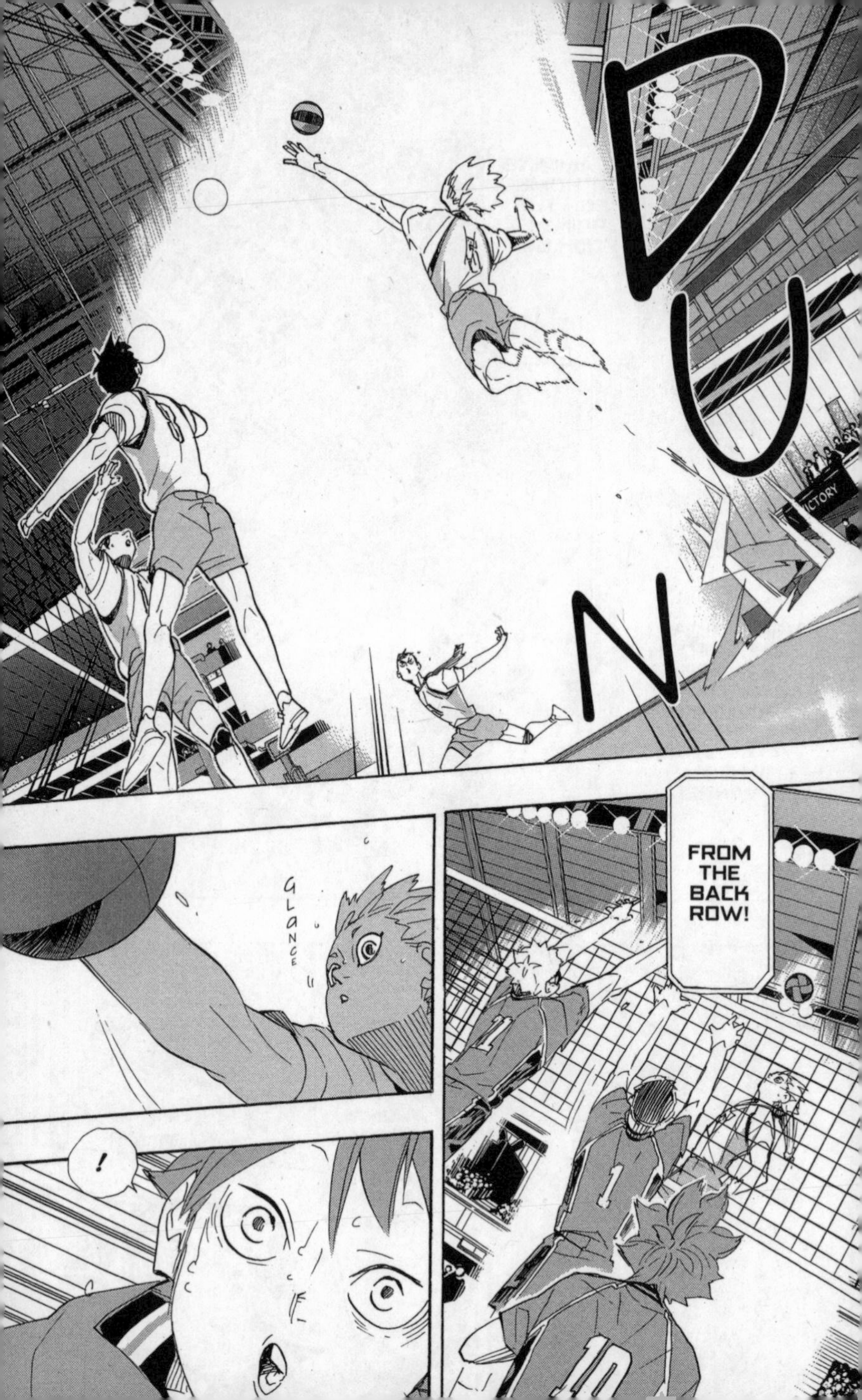
DUN
FROM THE BACK ROW!
GLANCE
!

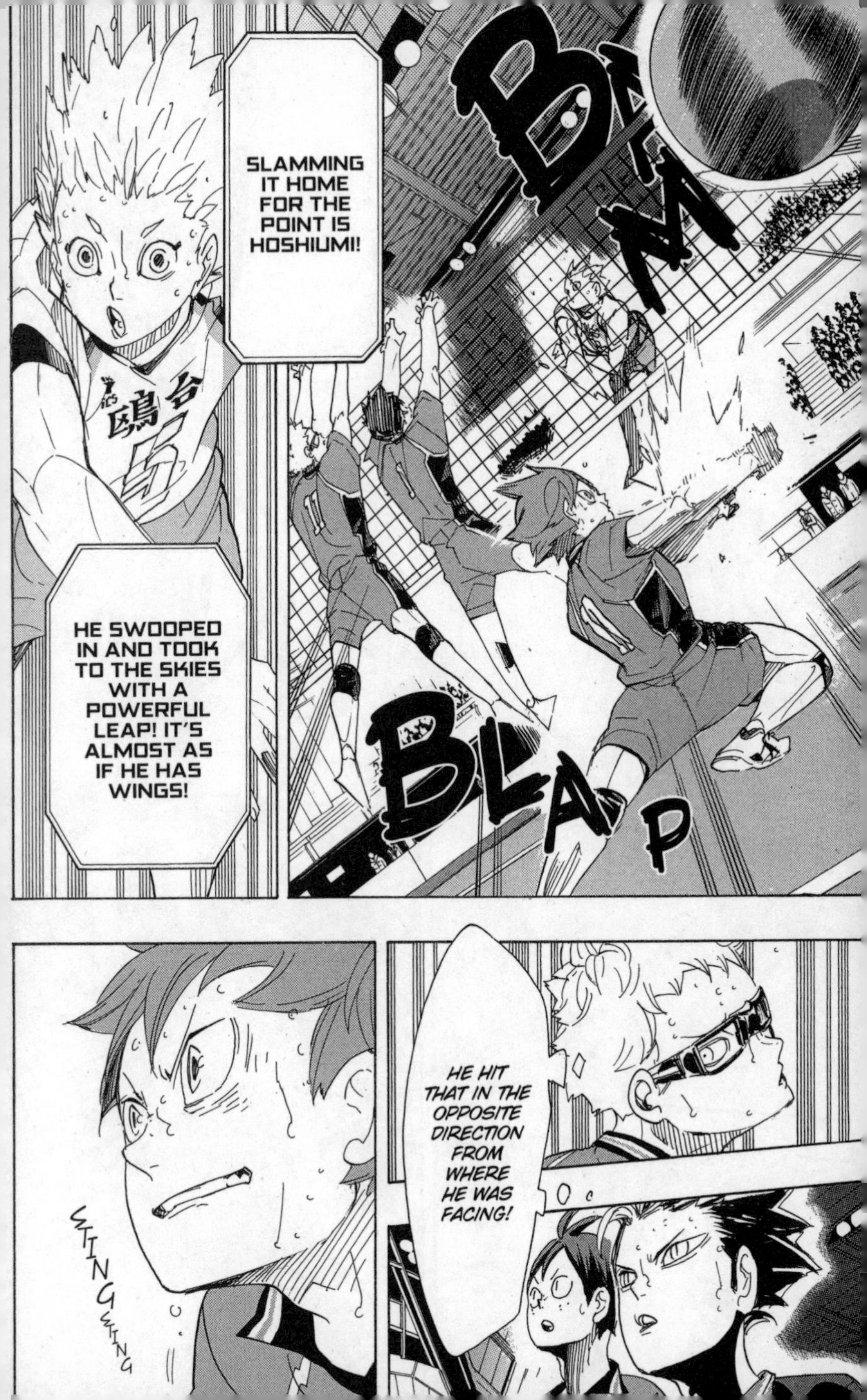
BAM
BLAP
SLAMMING IT HOME FOR THE POINT IS HOSHIUMI!
HE SWOOPED IN AND TOOK TO THE SKIES WITH A POWERFUL LEAP! IT'S ALMOST AS IF HE HAS WINGS!
HE HIT THAT IN THE OPPOSITE DIRECTION FROM WHERE HE WAS FACING!
STING
STING

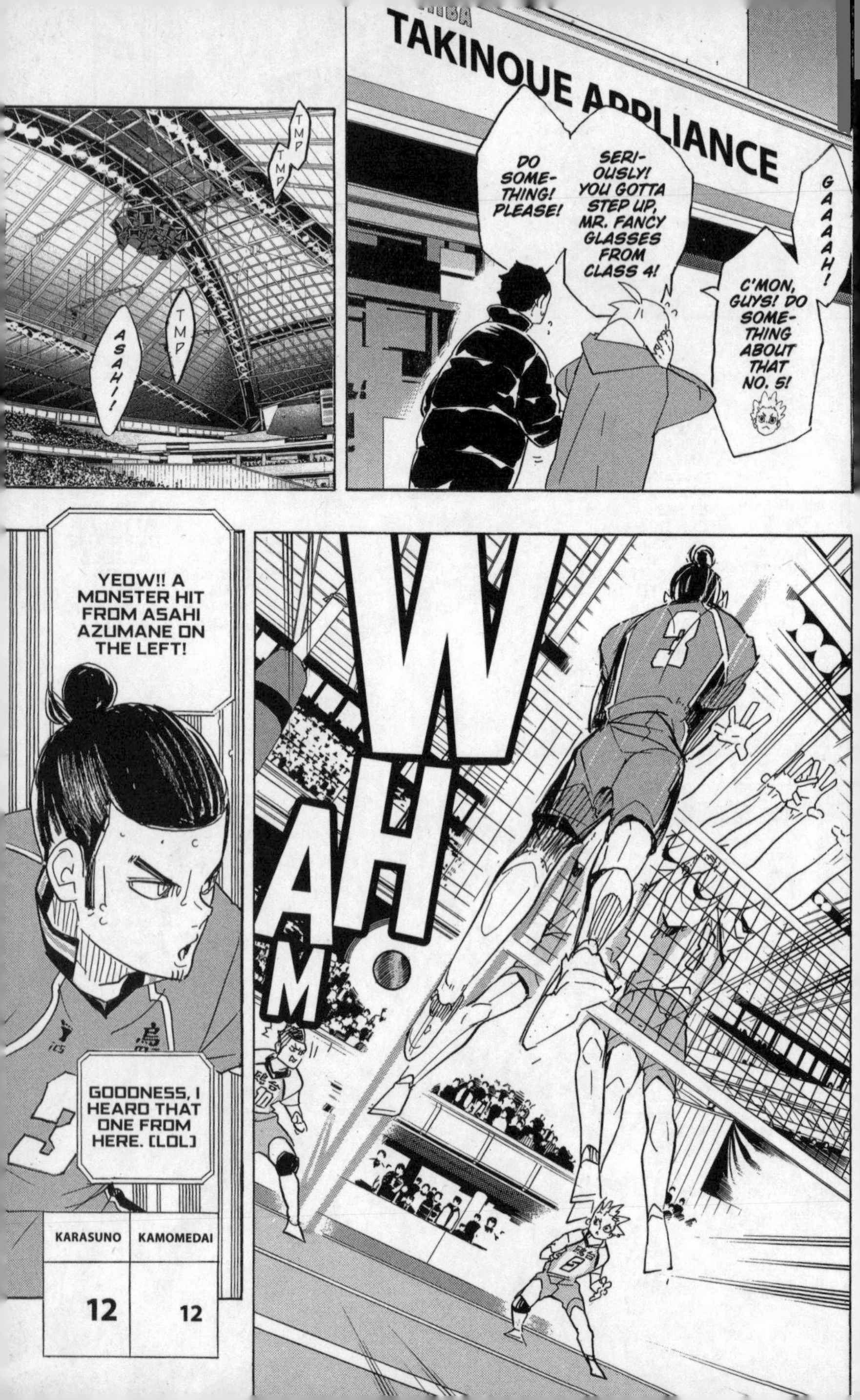
TAKINOUE APPLIANCE
GAAAAAH!
C'MON, GUYS! DO SOMETHING ABOUT THAT NO. 5!
SERIOUSLY! YOU GOTTA STEP UP, MR. FANCY GLASSES FROM CLASS 4!
DO SOMETHING! PLEASE!
TMP TMP TMP
TMP
ASAHI!!
WHAM
YEOW!! A MONSTER HIT FROM ASAHI AZUMANE ON THE LEFT!
GOODNESS, I HEARD THAT ONE FROM HERE. [LOL]
KARASUNO 12
KAMOMEDAI 12

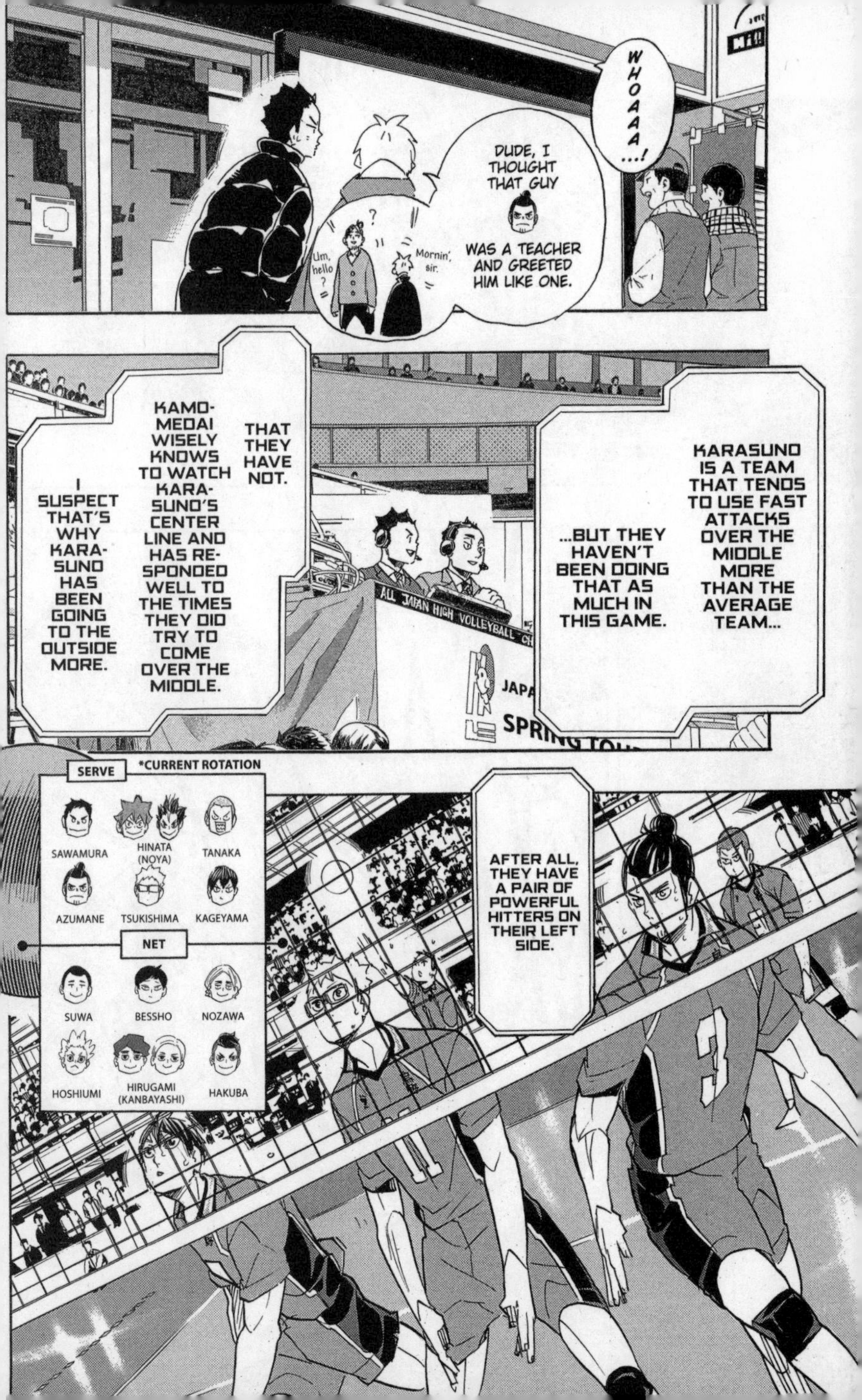
WHOAAA...!
DUDE, I THOUGHT THAT GUY
WAS A TEACHER AND GREETED HIM LIKE ONE.
Mornin', sir.
Um, hello ?
KARASUNO IS A TEAM THAT TENDS TO USE FAST ATTACKS OVER THE MIDDLE MORE THAN THE AVERAGE TEAM...
...BUT THEY HAVEN'T BEEN DOING THAT AS MUCH IN THIS GAME.
THAT THEY HAVE NOT.
KAMO-MEDAI WISELY KNOWS TO WATCH KARA-SUNO'S CENTER LINE AND HAS RE-SPONDED WELL TO THE TIMES THEY DID TRY TO COME OVER THE MIDDLE.
I SUSPECT THAT'S WHY KARA-SUNO HAS BEEN GOING TO THE OUTSIDE MORE.
AFTER ALL, THEY HAVE A PAIR OF POWERFUL HITTERS ON THEIR LEFT SIDE.
SERVE
*CURRENT ROTATION
SAWAMURA
HINATA (NOYA)
TANAKA
AZUMANE
TSUKISHIMA
KAGEYAMA
NET
SUWA
BESSHO
NOZAWA
HOSHIUMI
HIRUGAMI (KANBAYASHI)
HAKUBA

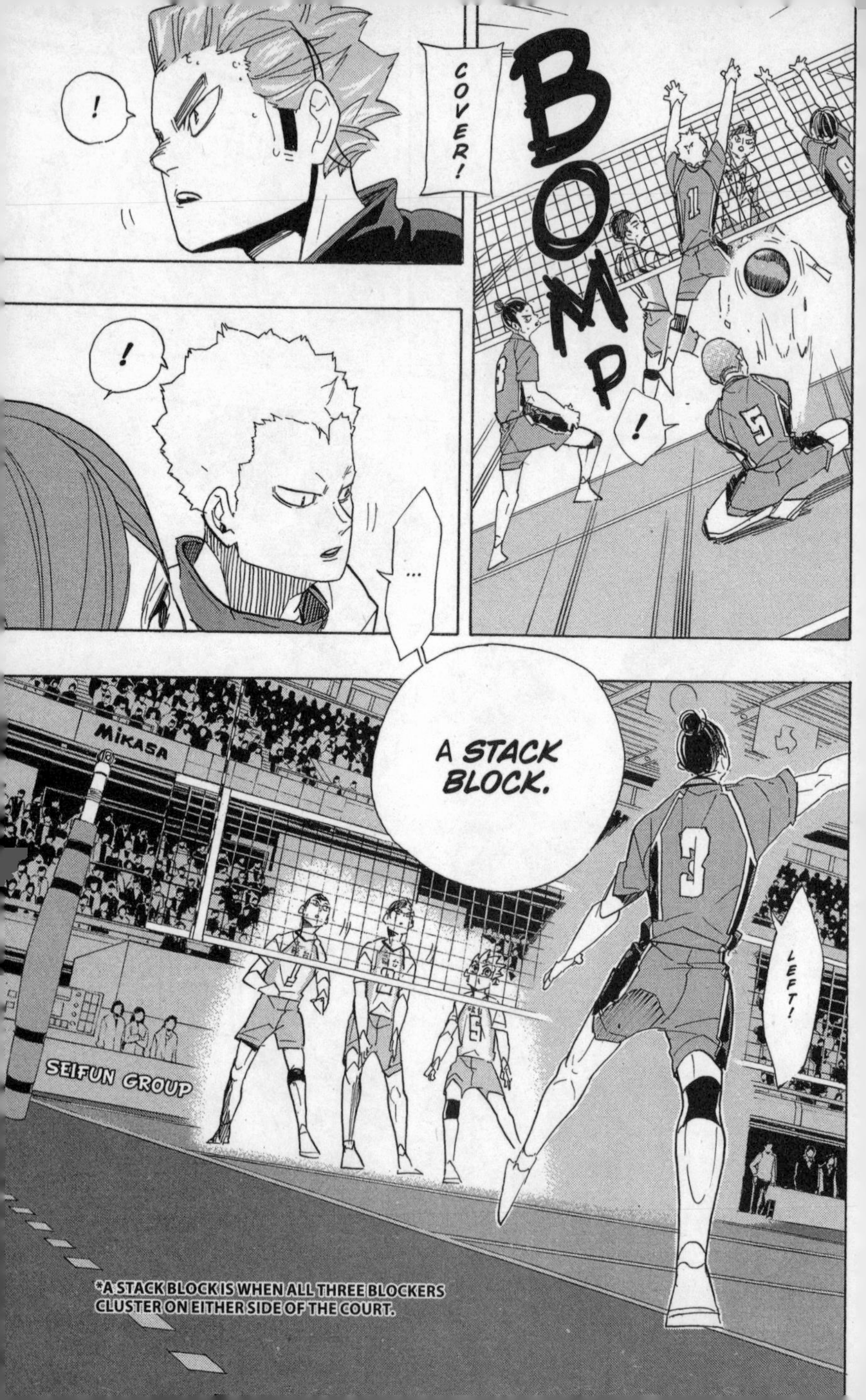
COVER!
BOMP
!
!
!
...
A STACK BLOCK.
LEFT!
MIKASA
SEIFUN GROUP

*A STACK BLOCK IS WHEN ALL THREE BLOCKERS CLUSTER ON EITHER SIDE OF THE COURT.

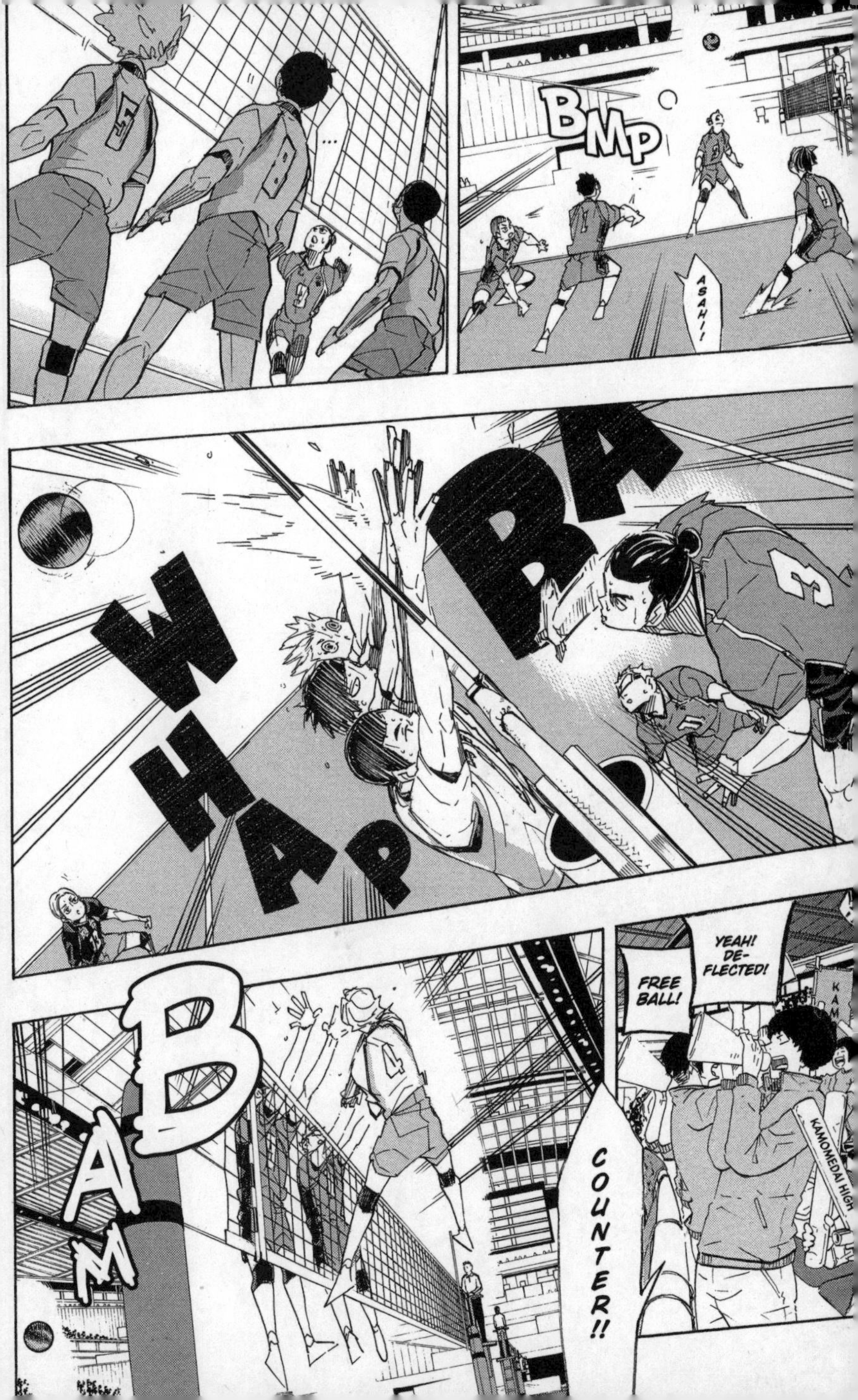
BMP
ASAHI!
...
BA
WHAP
YEAH! DE-FLECTED!
FREE BALL!
KAMOMEDAI HIGH
BAM
COUNTER!!

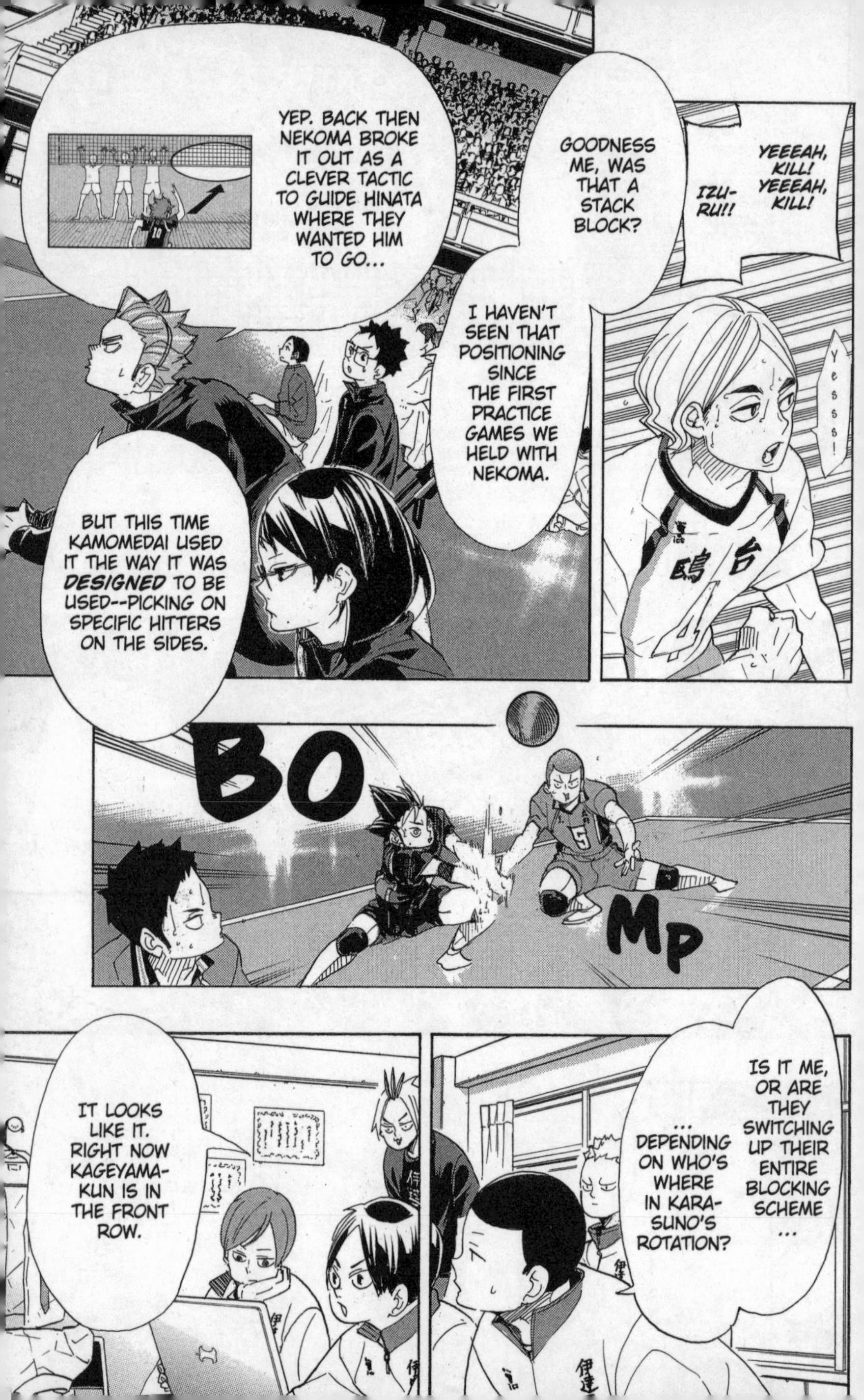

YEEEAH, KILL! YEEEAH, KILL!
IZU-RU!!
Yesss!
GOODNESS ME, WAS THAT A STACK BLOCK?
I HAVEN'T SEEN THAT POSITIONING SINCE THE FIRST PRACTICE GAMES WE HELD WITH NEKOMA.
YEP. BACK THEN NEKOMA BROKE IT OUT AS A CLEVER TACTIC TO GUIDE HINATA WHERE THEY WANTED HIM TO GO...
BUT THIS TIME KAMOMEDAI USED IT THE WAY IT WAS ***DESIGNED*** TO BE USED--PICKING ON SPECIFIC HITTERS ON THE SIDES.
BO
MP
IS IT ME, OR ARE THEY SWITCHING UP THEIR ENTIRE BLOCKING SCHEME...
...DEPENDING ON WHO'S WHERE IN KARA-SUNO'S ROTATION?
IT LOOKS LIKE IT. RIGHT NOW KAGEYAMA-KUN IS IN THE FRONT ROW.

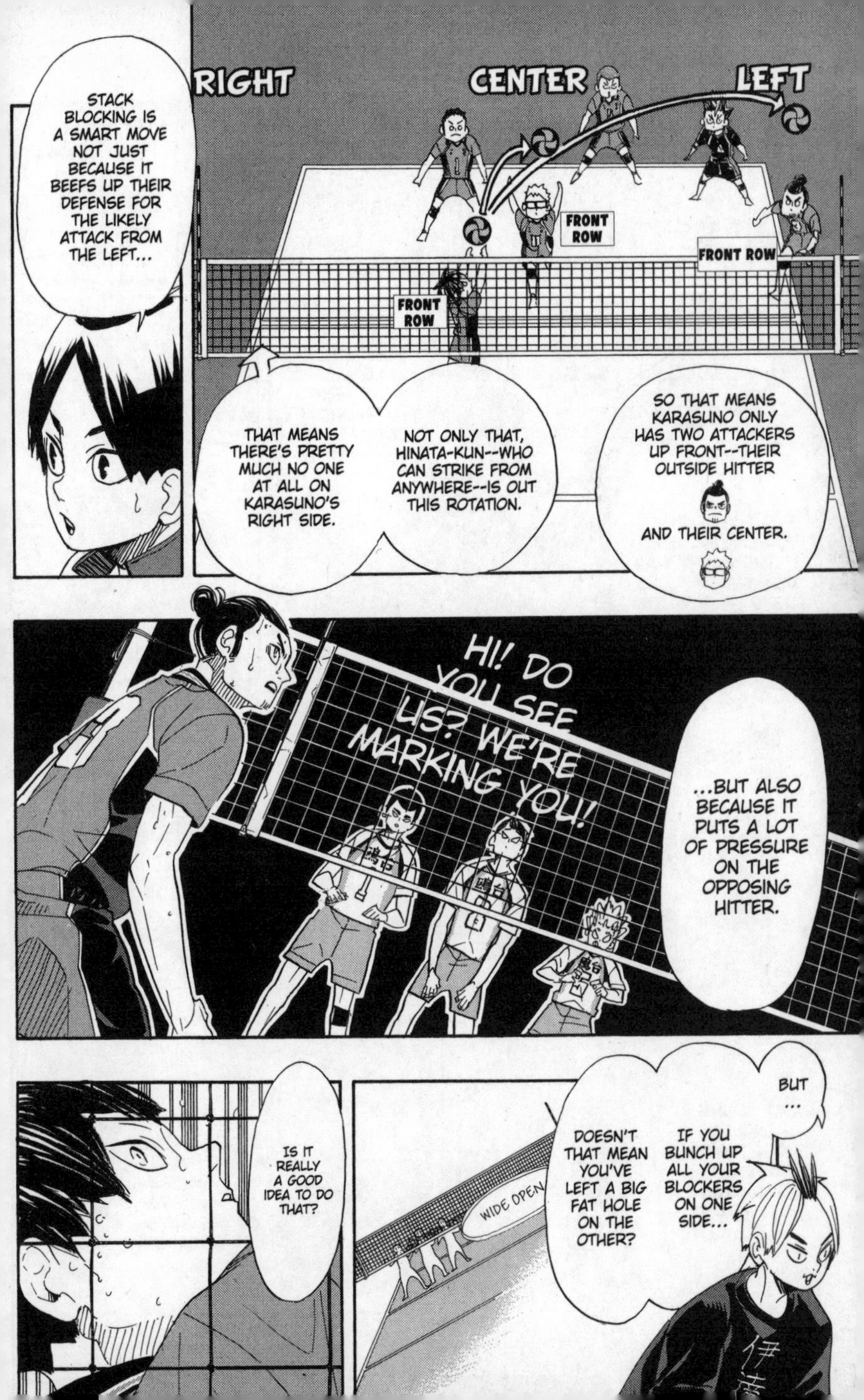
RIGHT
CENTER
LEFT
FRONT ROW
FRONT ROW
FRONT ROW
SO THAT MEANS KARASUNO ONLY HAS TWO ATTACKERS UP FRONT--THEIR OUTSIDE HITTER
AND THEIR CENTER.
NOT ONLY THAT, HINATA-KUN--WHO CAN STRIKE FROM ANYWHERE--IS OUT THIS ROTATION.
THAT MEANS THERE'S PRETTY MUCH NO ONE AT ALL ON KARASUNO'S RIGHT SIDE.
STACK BLOCKING IS A SMART MOVE NOT JUST BECAUSE IT BEEFS UP THEIR DEFENSE FOR THE LIKELY ATTACK FROM THE LEFT...
...BUT ALSO BECAUSE IT PUTS A LOT OF PRESSURE ON THE OPPOSING HITTER.
HI! DO YOU SEE US? WE'RE MARKING YOU!
BUT ...
IF YOU BUNCH UP ALL YOUR BLOCKERS ON ONE SIDE...
DOESN'T THAT MEAN YOU'VE LEFT A BIG FAT HOLE ON THE OTHER?
WIDE OPEN
IS IT REALLY A GOOD IDEA TO DO THAT?

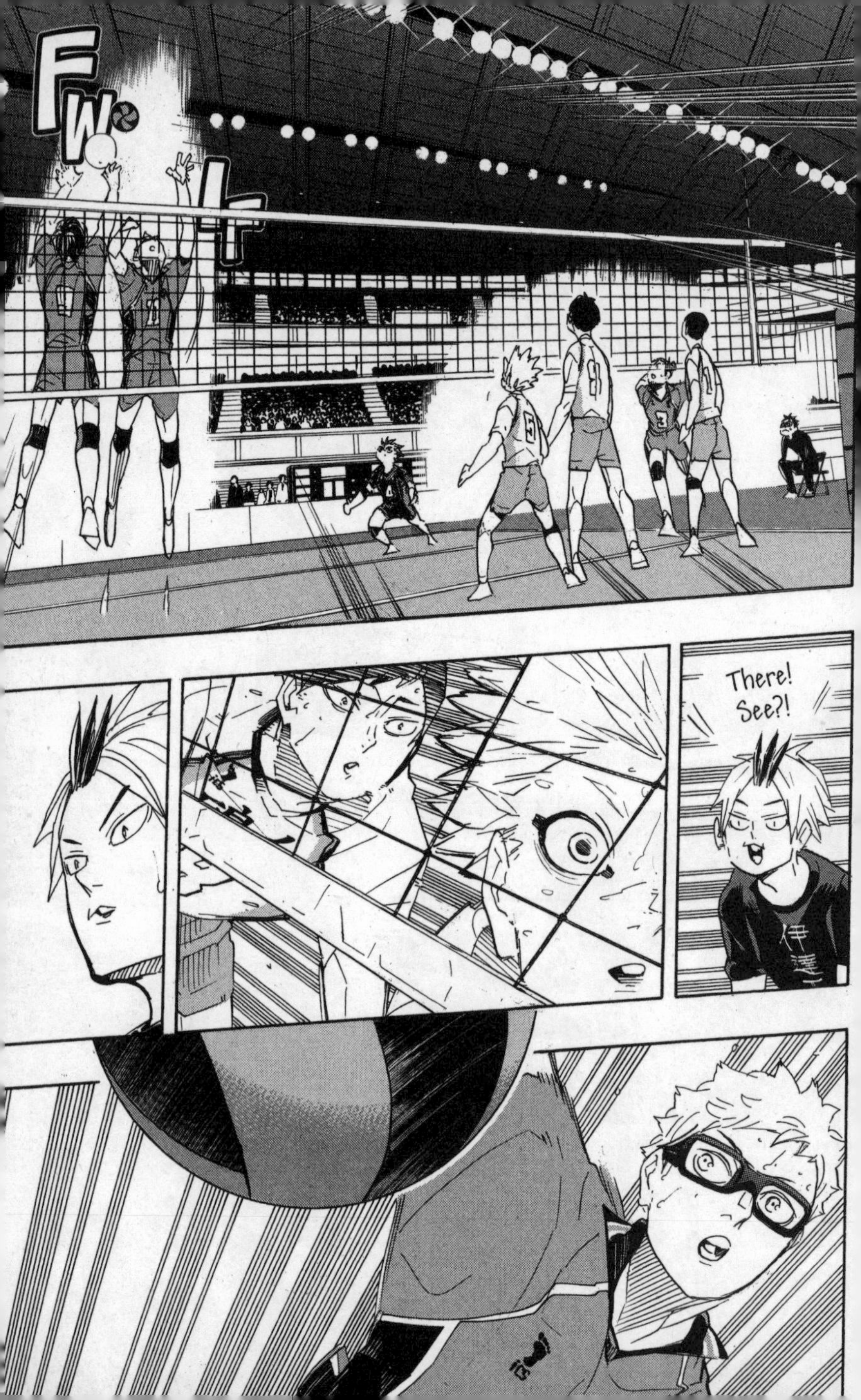
FWIP
There!
See?!

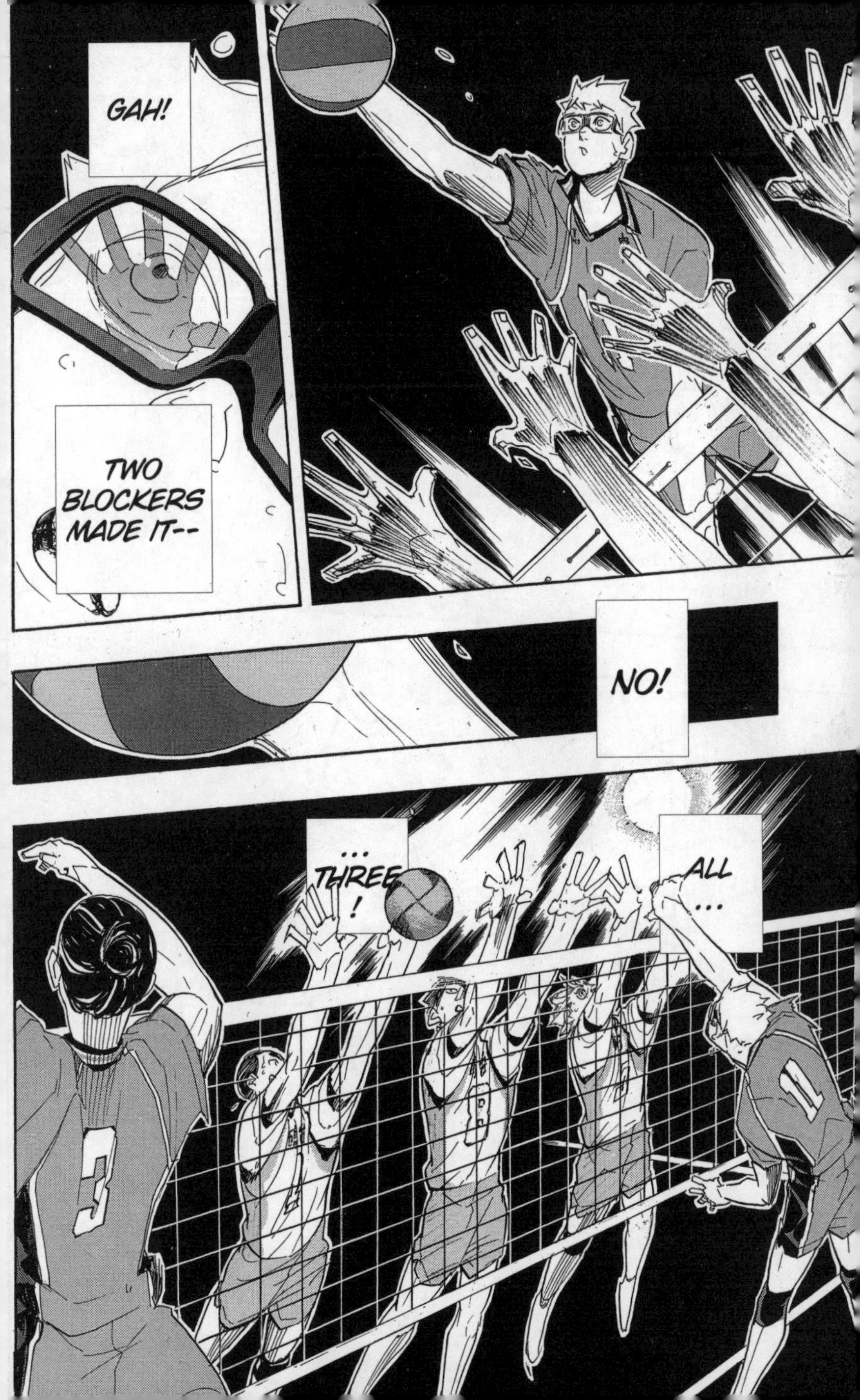
GAH!
TWO BLOCKERS MADE IT--
NO!
ALL ...
... THREE!

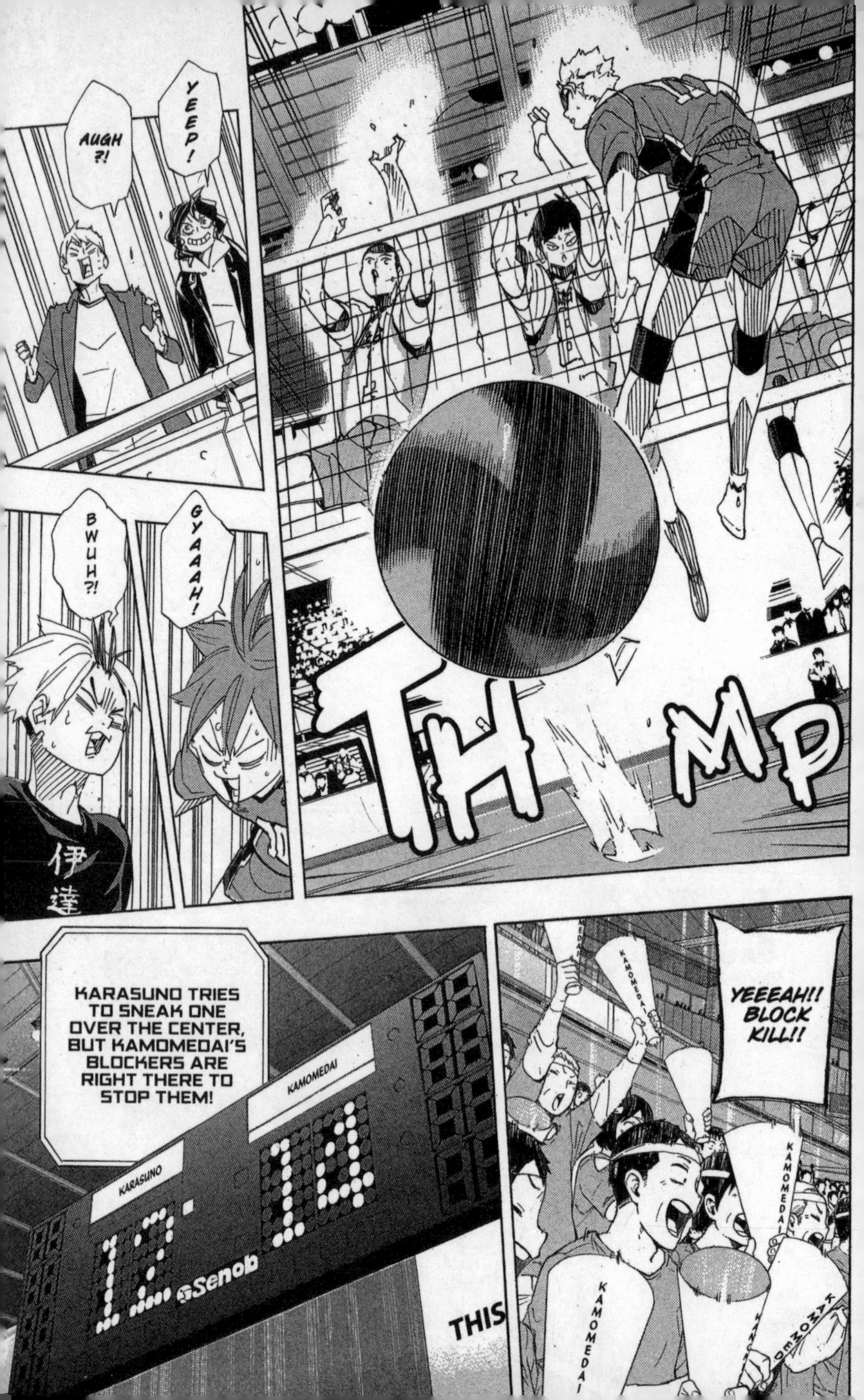

TH MP
YEEP!
AUGH?!
GYAAAH!
BWUH?!
YEEEAH!! BLOCK KILL!!
KAMOMEDAI
KAMOMEDAI
KAMOMEDAI
KAMOMEDAI
KAMOMEDAI
KARASUNO TRIES TO SNEAK ONE OVER THE CENTER, BUT KAMOMEDAI'S BLOCKERS ARE RIGHT THERE TO STOP THEM!
KARASUNO
KAMOMEDAI
12
14
Senob
THIS

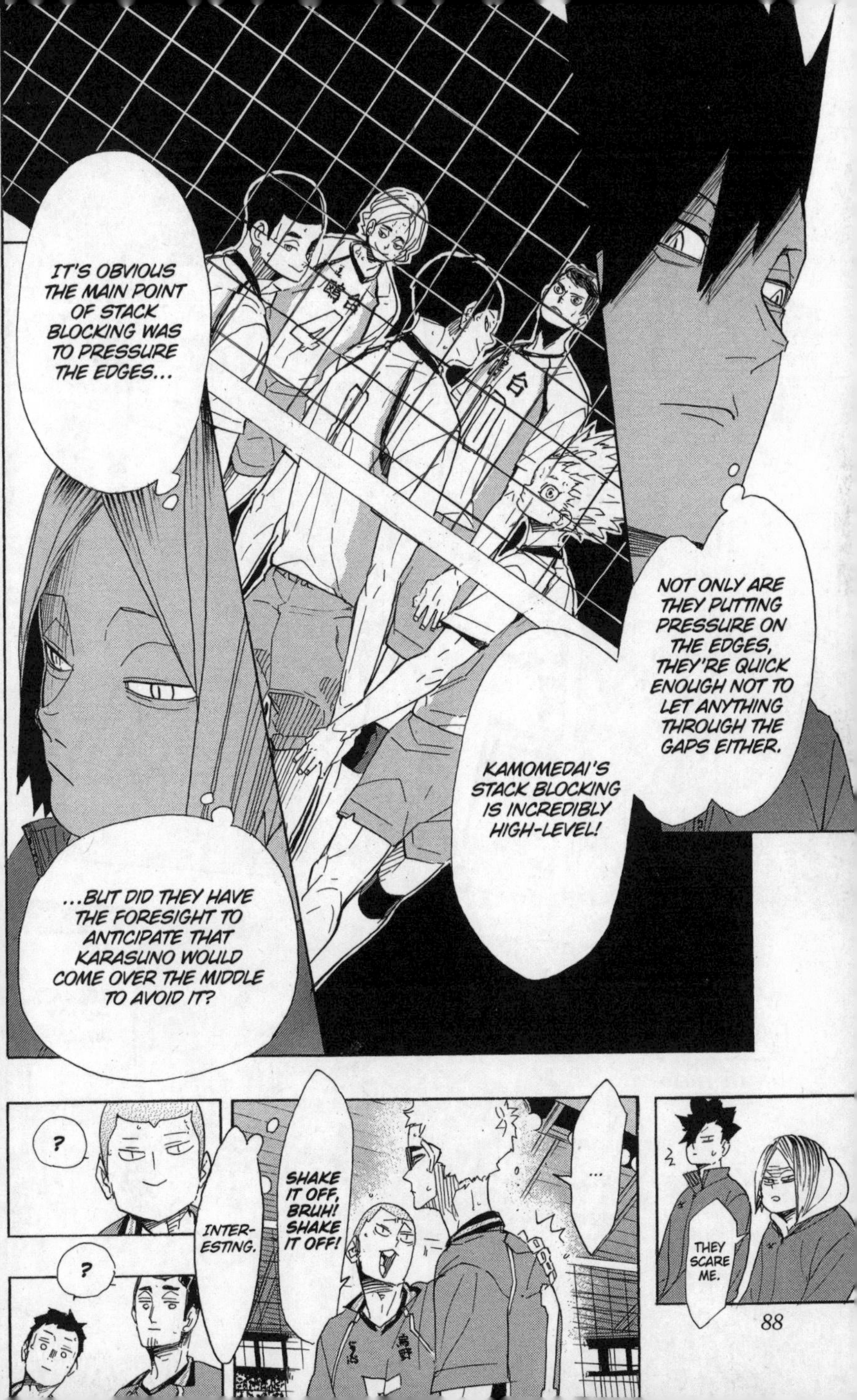
NOT ONLY ARE THEY PUTTING PRESSURE ON THE EDGES, THEY'RE QUICK ENOUGH NOT TO LET ANYTHING THROUGH THE GAPS EITHER.
KAMOMEDAI'S STACK BLOCKING IS INCREDIBLY HIGH-LEVEL!
IT'S OBVIOUS THE MAIN POINT OF STACK BLOCKING WAS TO PRESSURE THE EDGES...
...BUT DID THEY HAVE THE FORESIGHT TO ANTICIPATE THAT KARASUNO WOULD COME OVER THE MIDDLE TO AVOID IT?
THEY SCARE ME.
...
SHAKE IT OFF, BRUH! SHAKE IT OFF!
?
INTER-ESTING.
?

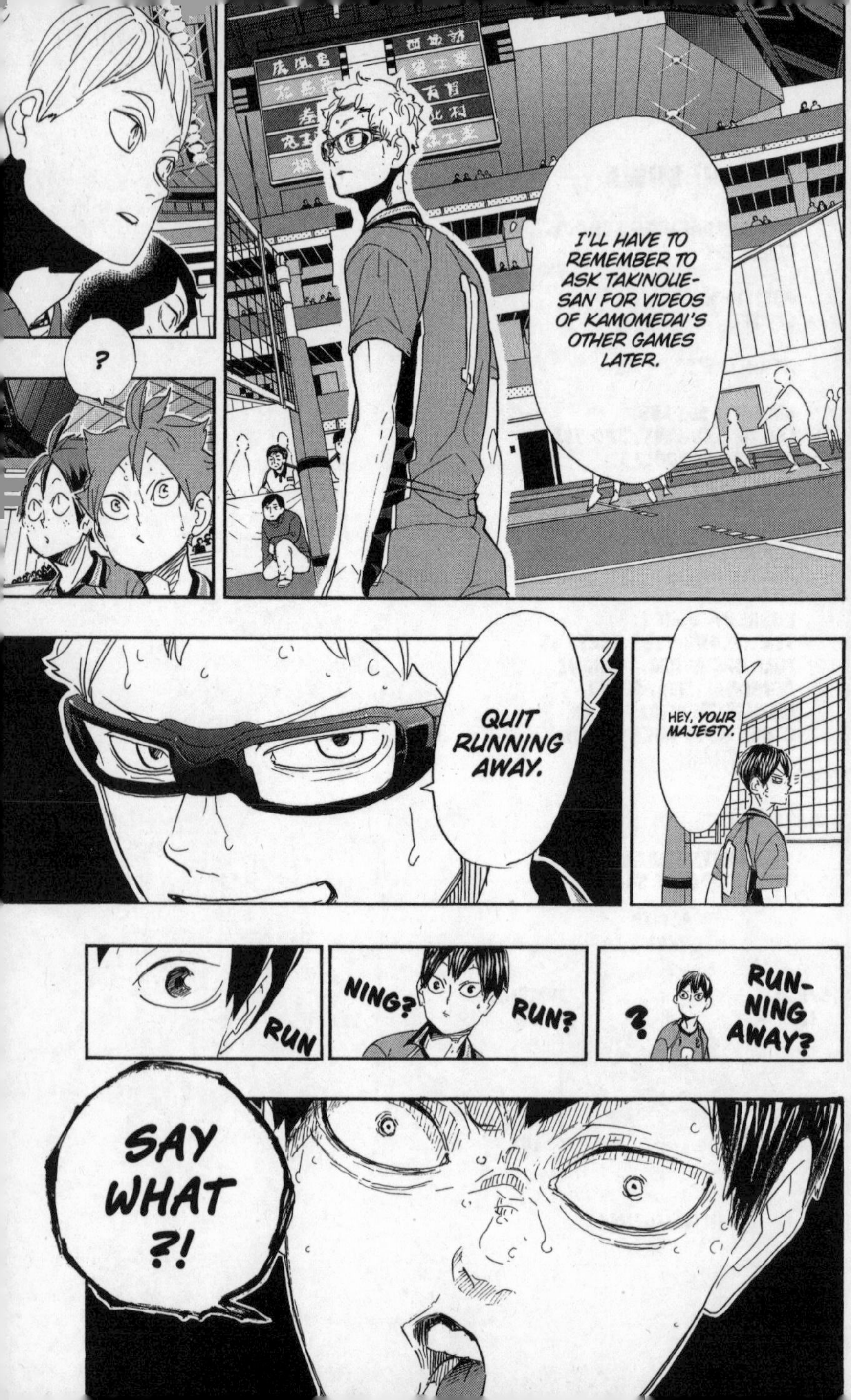
I'LL HAVE TO REMEMBER TO ASK TAKINOUE-SAN FOR VIDEOS OF KAMOMEDAI'S OTHER GAMES LATER.
?
HEY, YOUR MAJESTY.
QUIT RUNNING AWAY.
RUN-NING AWAY?
?
RUN?
NING?
RUN
SAY WHAT ?!

AIKICHI SUWA

KAMOMEDAI HIGH SCHOOL, CLASS 3-1

POSITION:
SETTER

HEIGHT: 5'9"

WEIGHT: 155 LBS.
(AS OF JANUARY, 3RD YEAR OF HIGH SCHOOL)

BIRTHDAY: JUNE 8

FAVORITE FOOD:
BONITO TATAKI

CURRENT WORRY:
THE SECOND-YEAR CLASS IS FULL OF RATHER...UNIQUE PERSONALITIES, SO HE WISHES THE FIRST-YEAR CLASS GOOD LUCK DEALING WITH THEM.

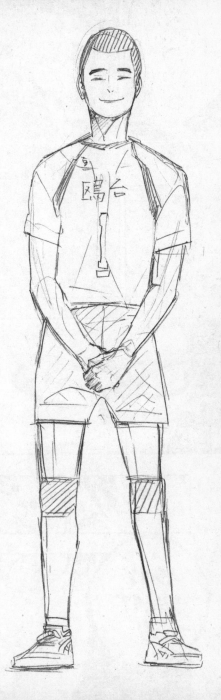

ABILITY PARAMETERS
(5-POINT SCALE)

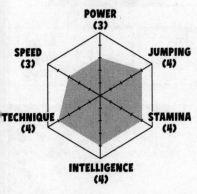

POWER (3)

JUMPING (4)

SPEED (3)

STAMINA (4)

TECHNIQUE (4)

INTELLIGENCE (4)

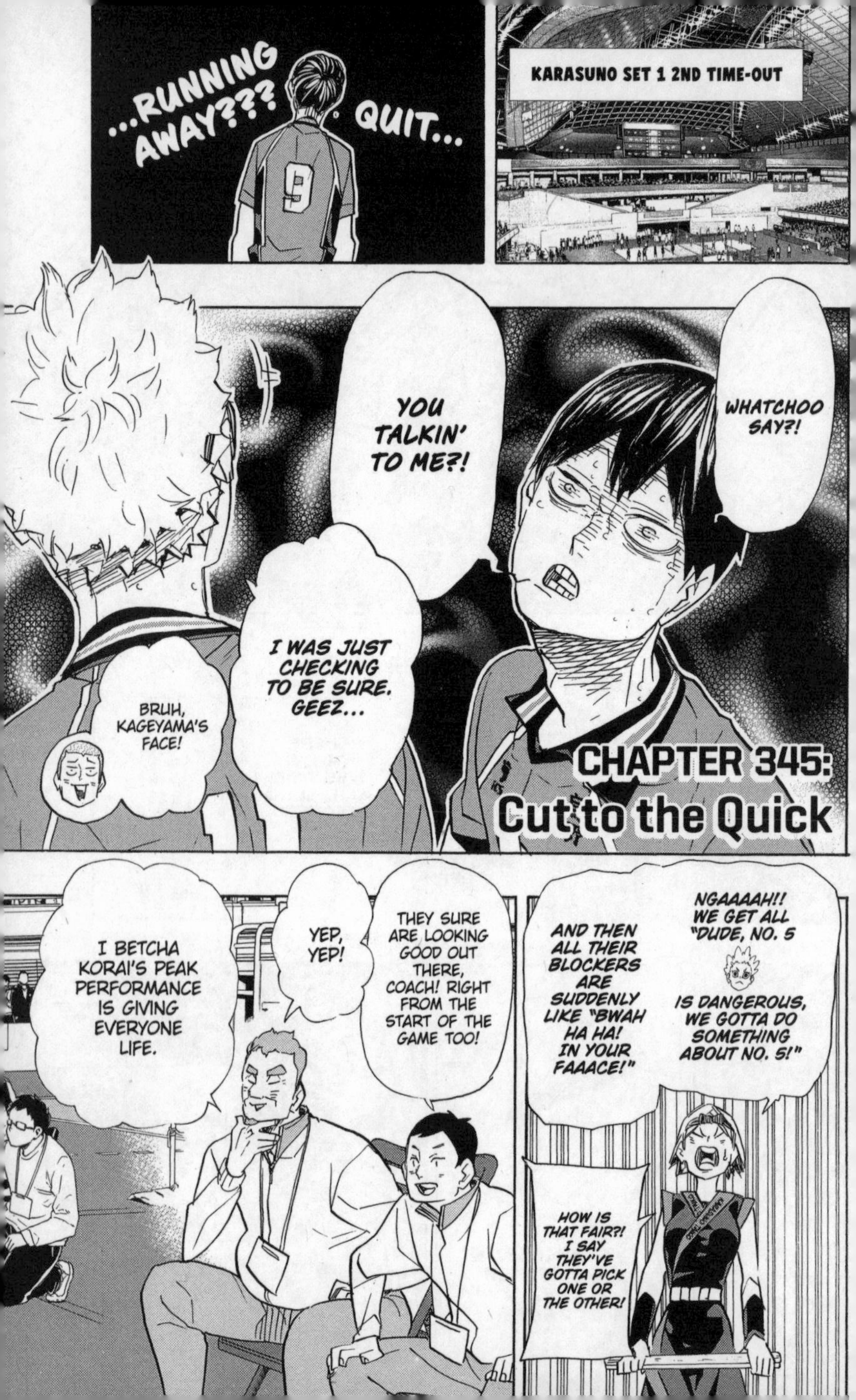
KARASUNO SET 1 2ND TIME-OUT
QUIT...
...RUNNING AWAY???
WHATCHOO SAY?!
YOU TALKIN' TO ME?!
I WAS JUST CHECKING TO BE SURE. GEEZ...
CHAPTER 345:
Cut to the Quick
BRUH, KAGEYAMA'S FACE!
NGAAAAH!! WE GET ALL "DUDE, NO. 5
IS DANGEROUS, WE GOTTA DO SOMETHING ABOUT NO. 5!"
AND THEN ALL THEIR BLOCKERS ARE SUDDENLY LIKE "BWAH HA HA! IN YOUR FAAACE!"
HOW IS THAT FAIR?! I SAY THEY'VE GOTTA PICK ONE OR THE OTHER!
THEY SURE ARE LOOKING GOOD OUT THERE, COACH! RIGHT FROM THE START OF THE GAME TOO!
YEP, YEP!
I BETCHA KORAI'S PEAK PERFORMANCE IS GIVING EVERYONE LIFE.

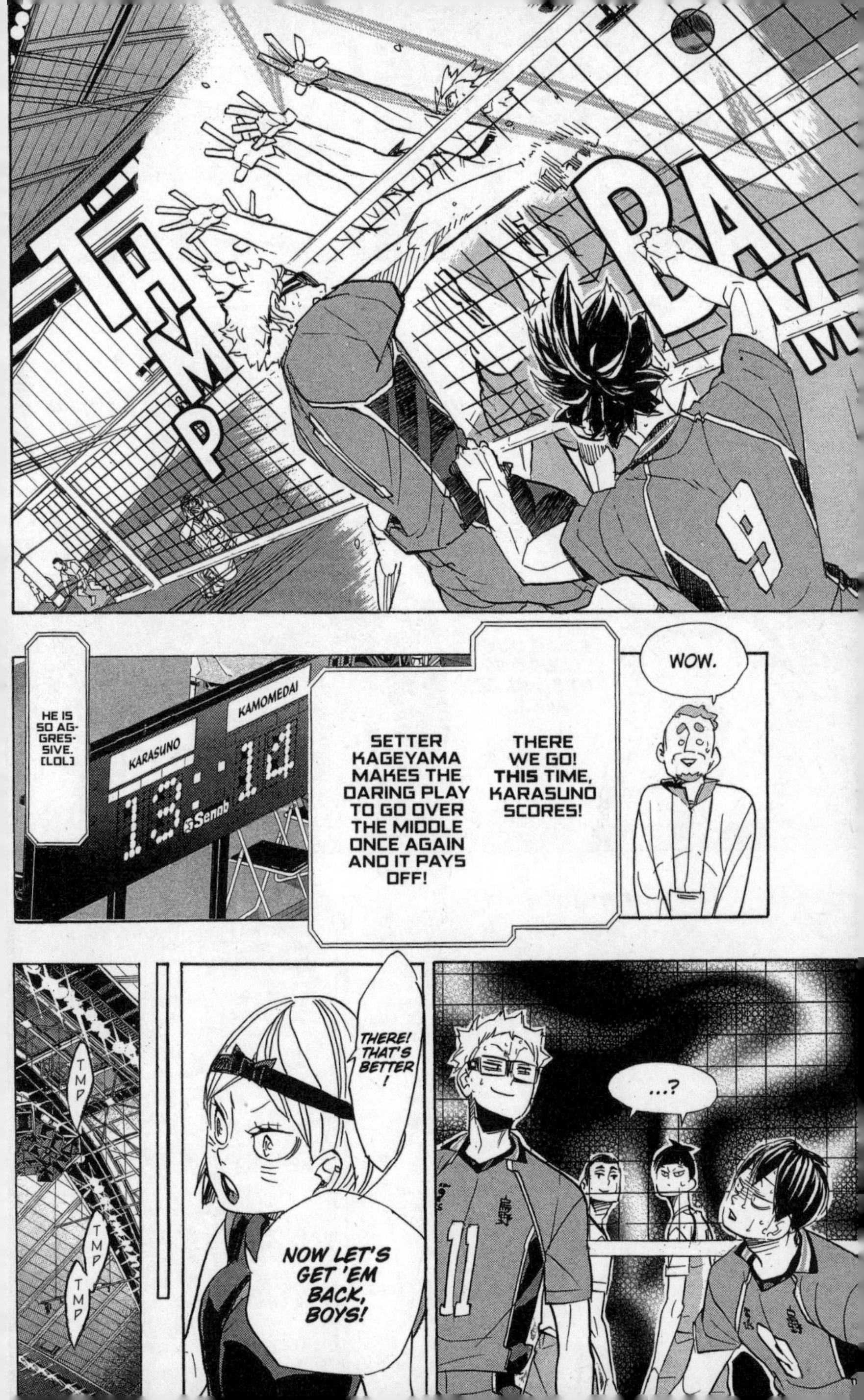
DAMM
THUMP
WOW.
THERE WE GO! THIS TIME, KARASUNO SCORES!
SETTER KAGEYAMA MAKES THE DARING PLAY TO GO OVER THE MIDDLE ONCE AGAIN AND IT PAYS OFF!
KAMOMEDAI
KARASUNO
Senoh
HE IS SO AGGRESSIVE. [LOL]
...?
THERE! THAT'S BETTER!
NOW LET'S GET 'EM BACK, BOYS!
TMP
TMP
TMP

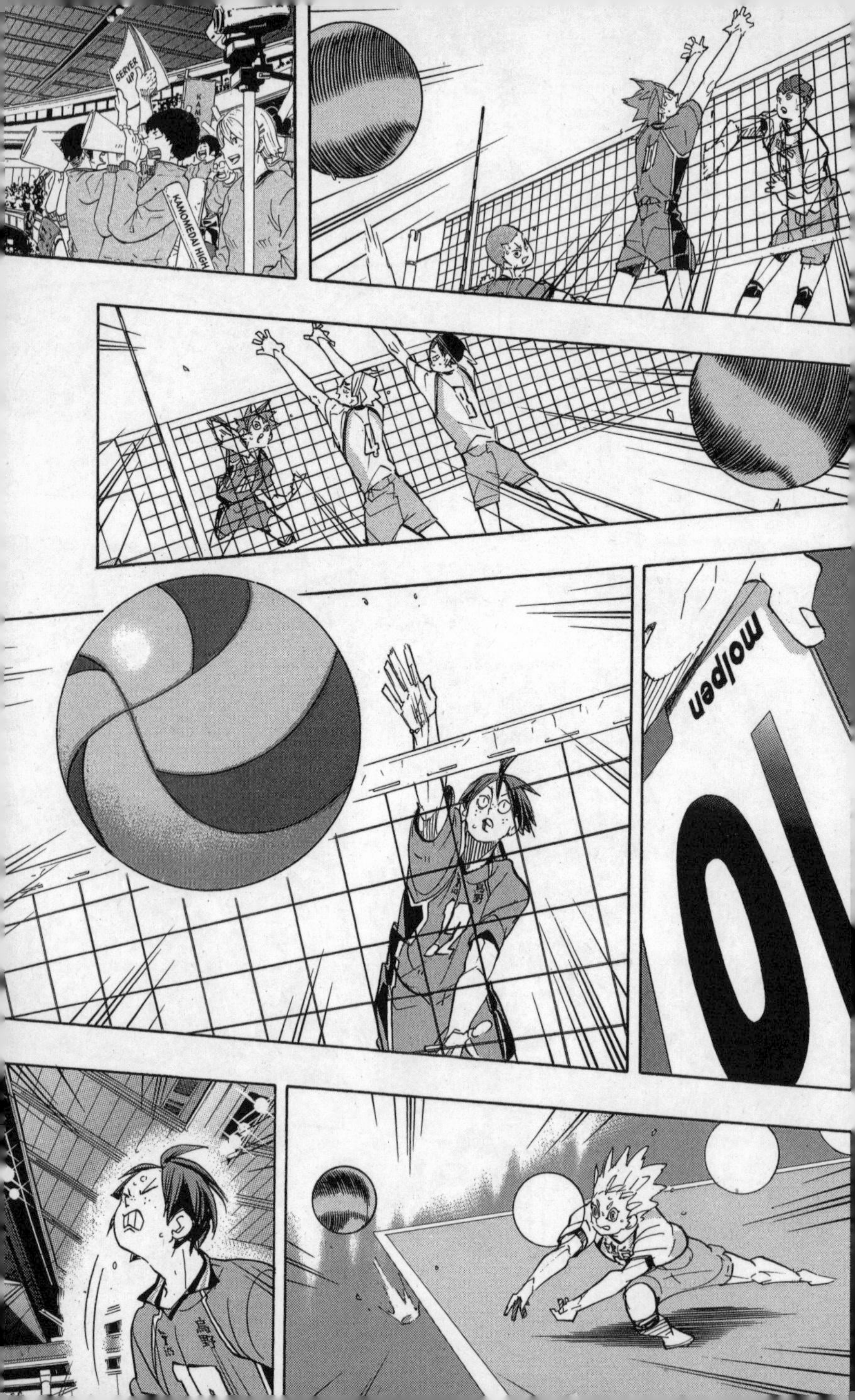
SERVER UP
KAMOMEDAI HIGH

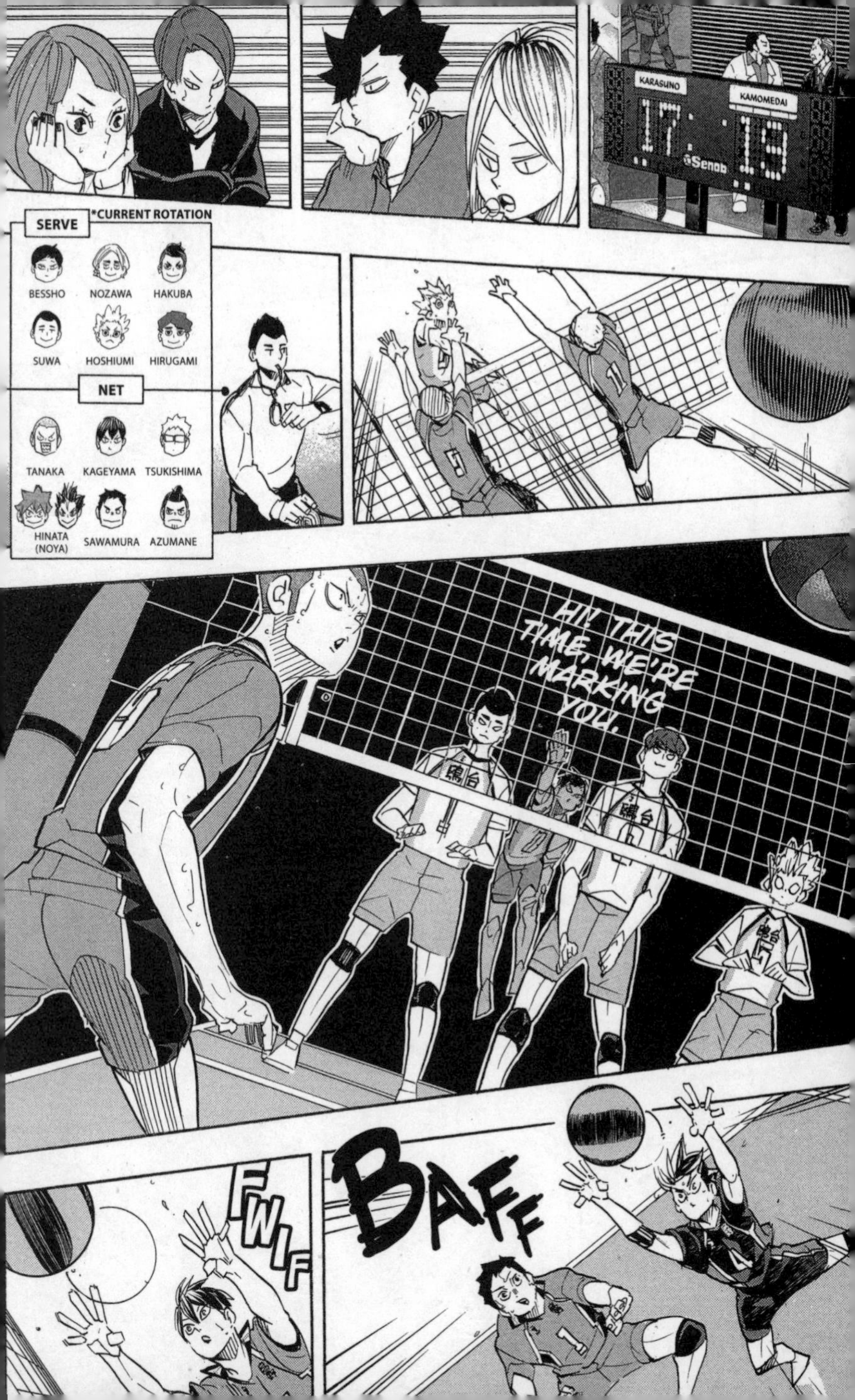

KARASUNO
KAMOMEDAI
17
19
Senob
SERVE
*CURRENT ROTATION
BESSHO
NOZAWA
HAKUBA
SUWA
HOSHIUMI
HIRUGAMI
NET
TANAKA
KAGEYAMA
TSUKISHIMA
HINATA (NOYA)
SAWAMURA
AZUMANE
HI! THIS TIME, WE'RE MARKING YOU.
BAFF
FWIF

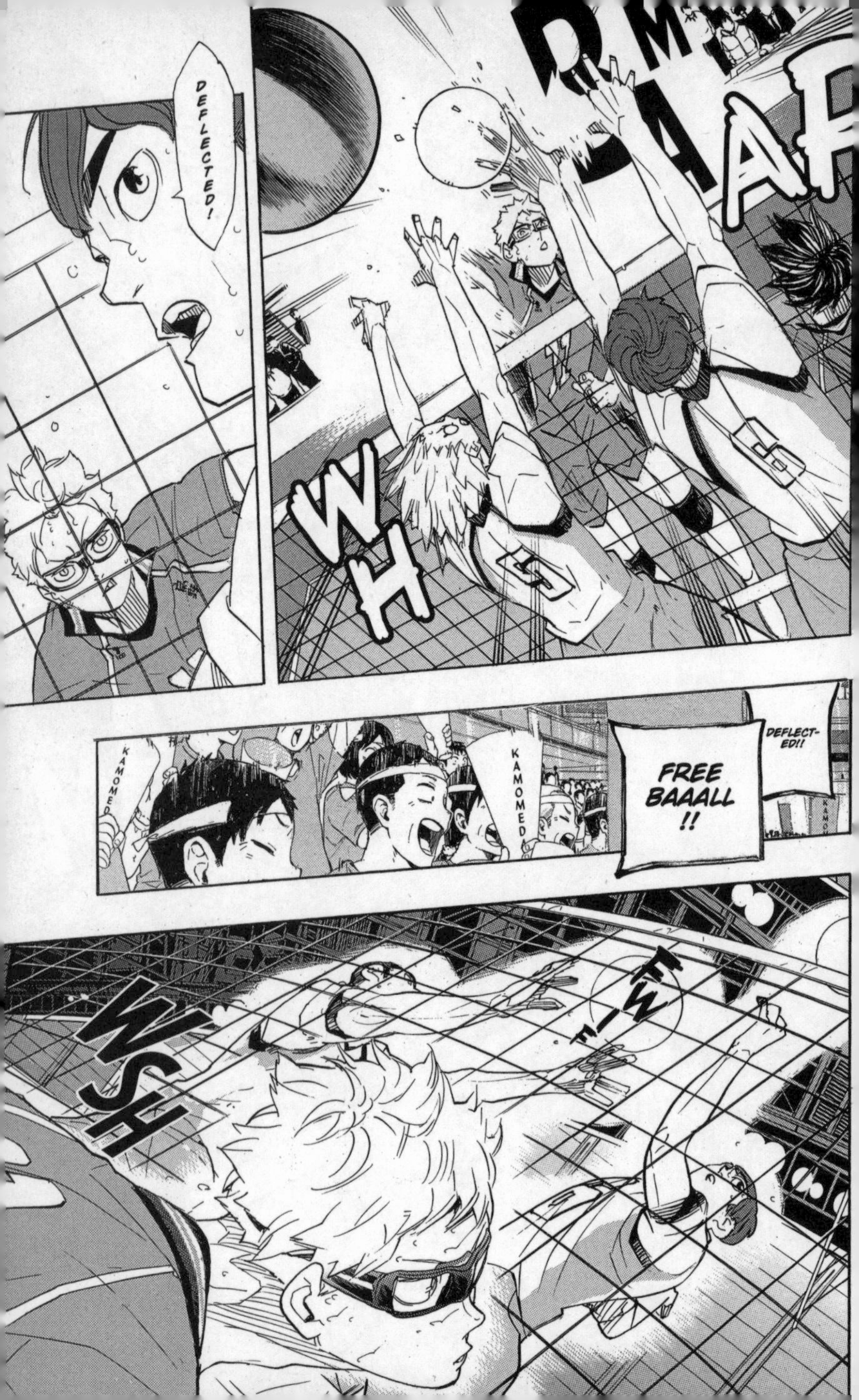
RMMM
DEFLECTED!
WH
DEFLECTED!!
FREE BAAALL!!
KAMOMEDA
KAMOMEDA
FWM
WSH

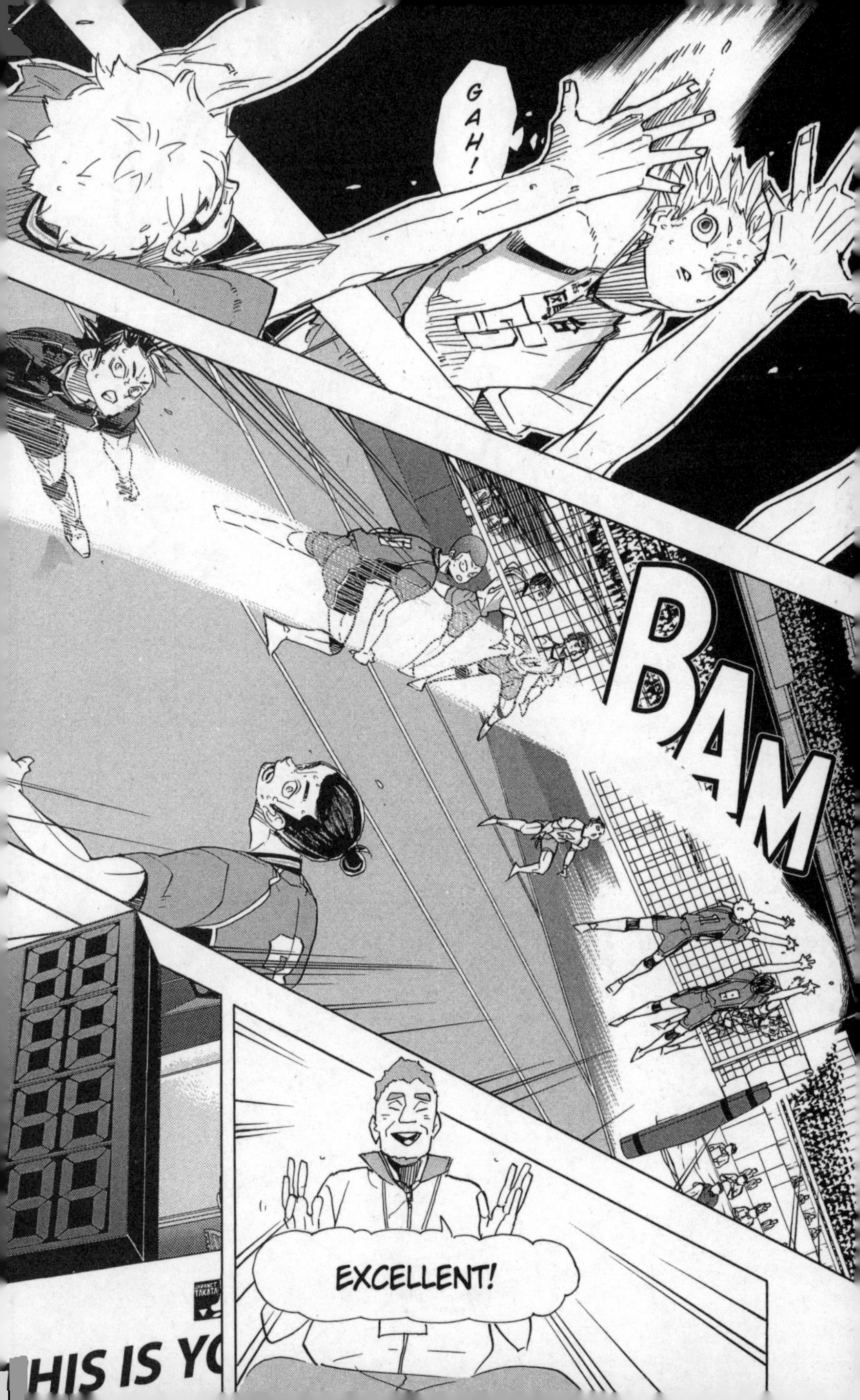
GAH!
BAM
EXCELLENT!
HIS IS YO

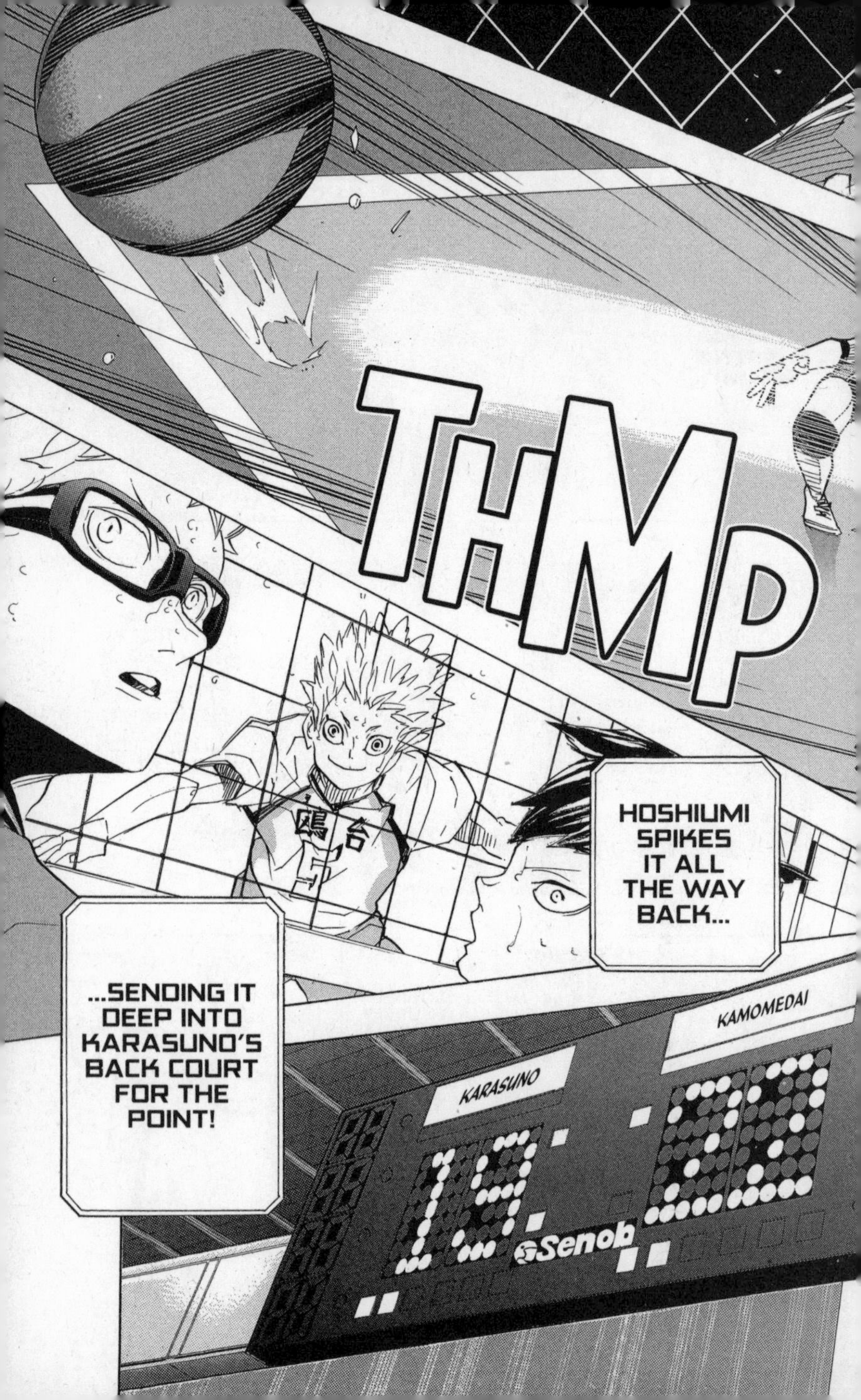
THMP
HOSHIUMI SPIKES IT ALL THE WAY BACK...
...SENDING IT DEEP INTO KARASUNO'S BACK COURT FOR THE POINT!
KAMOMEDAI
KARASUNO
Senob

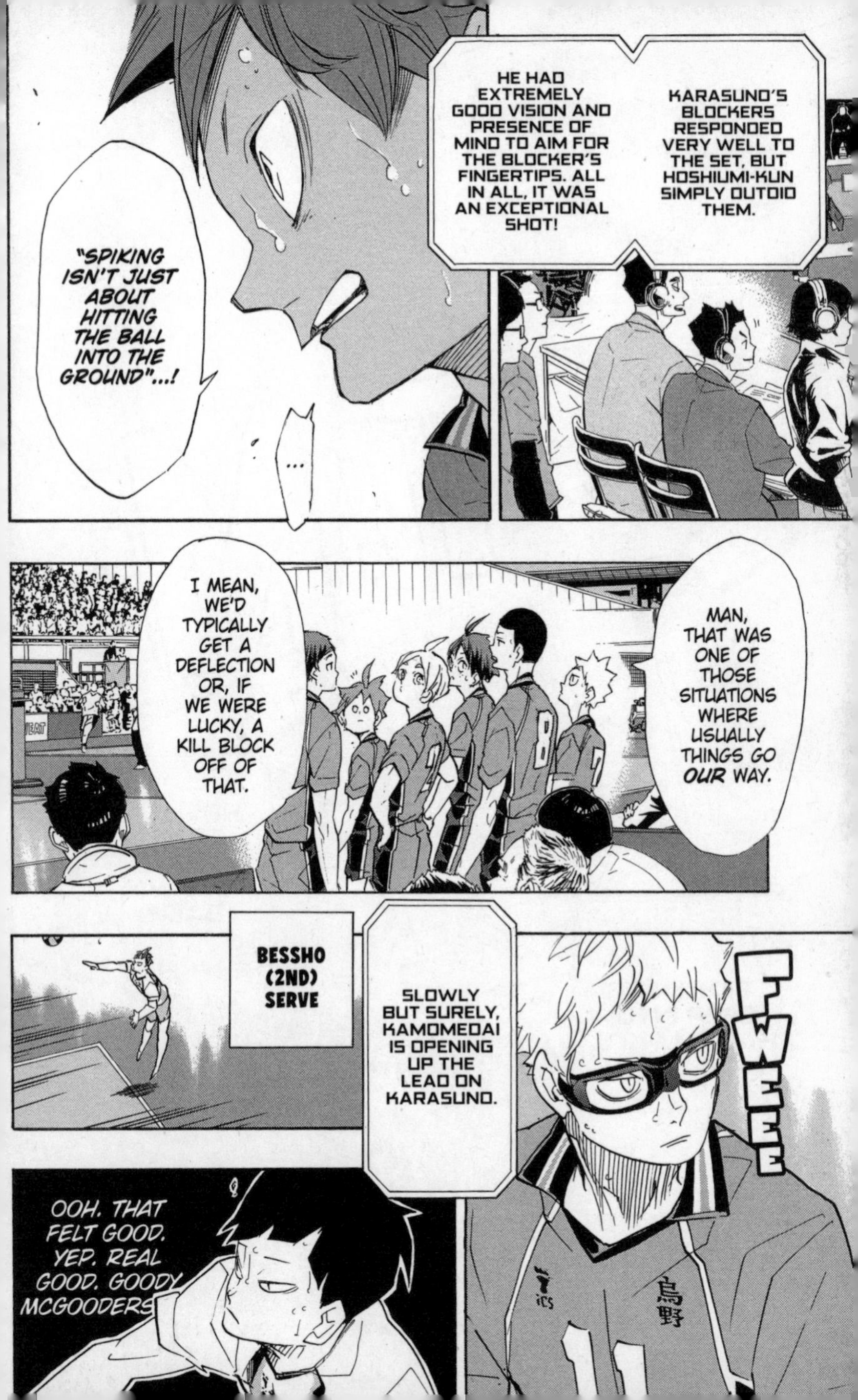
KARASUNO'S BLOCKERS RESPONDED VERY WELL TO THE SET, BUT HOSHIUMI-KUN SIMPLY OUTDID THEM.
HE HAD EXTREMELY GOOD VISION AND PRESENCE OF MIND TO AIM FOR THE BLOCKER'S FINGERTIPS. ALL IN ALL, IT WAS AN EXCEPTIONAL SHOT!
"SPIKING ISN'T JUST ABOUT HITTING THE BALL INTO THE GROUND"...!
...
MAN, THAT WAS ONE OF THOSE SITUATIONS WHERE USUALLY THINGS GO *OUR* WAY.
I MEAN, WE'D TYPICALLY GET A DEFLECTION OR, IF WE WERE LUCKY, A KILL BLOCK OFF OF THAT.
FWEEE
SLOWLY BUT SURELY, KAMOMEDAI IS OPENING UP THE LEAD ON KARASUNO.
BESSHO (2ND) SERVE
OOH. THAT FELT GOOD. YEP. REAL GOOD. GOODY MCGOODERS

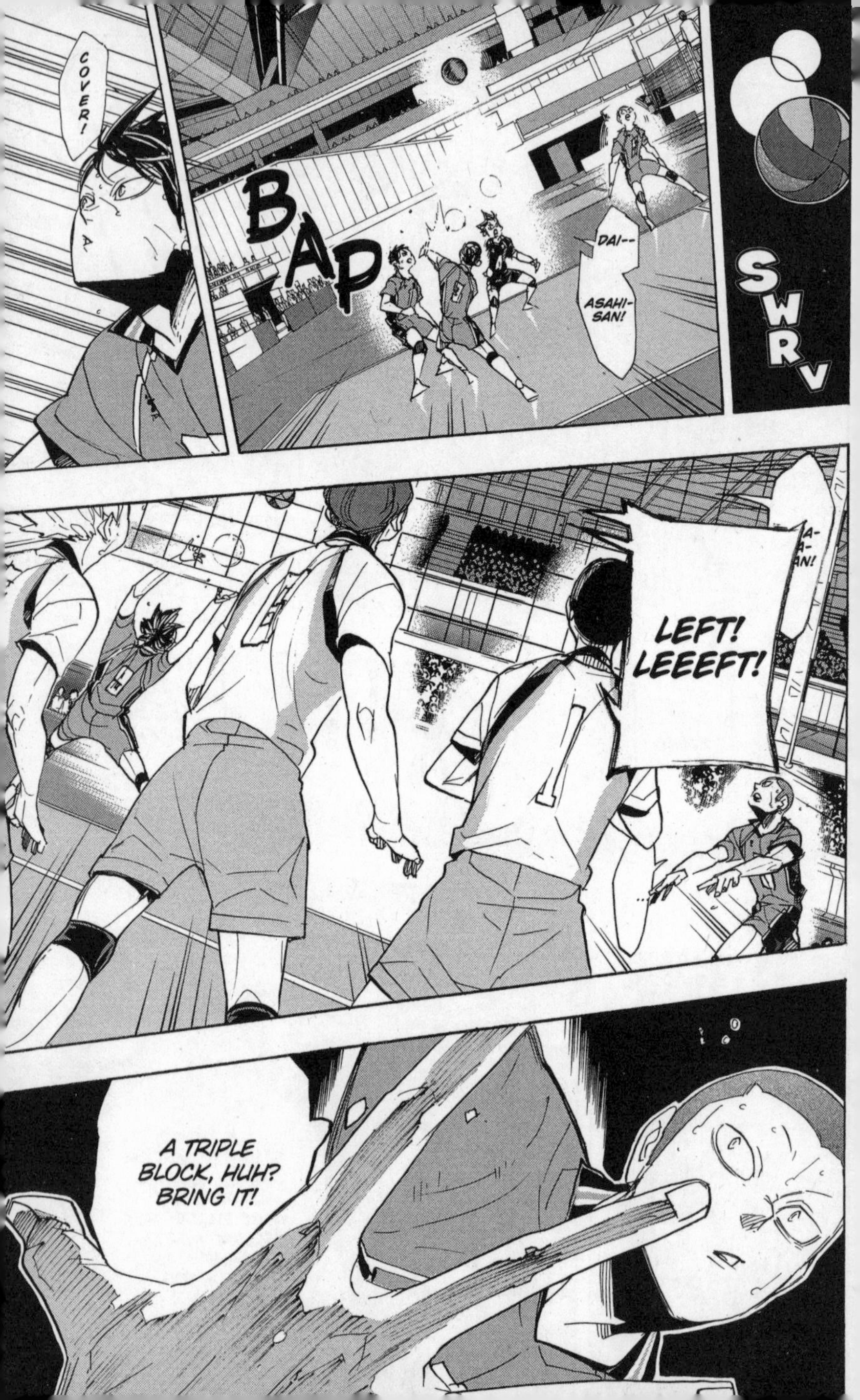
SWRV
DAI--
ASAHI-SAN!
BAP
COVER!
A-
A-
AN!
LEFT! LEEEFT!
A TRIPLE BLOCK, HUH? BRING IT!

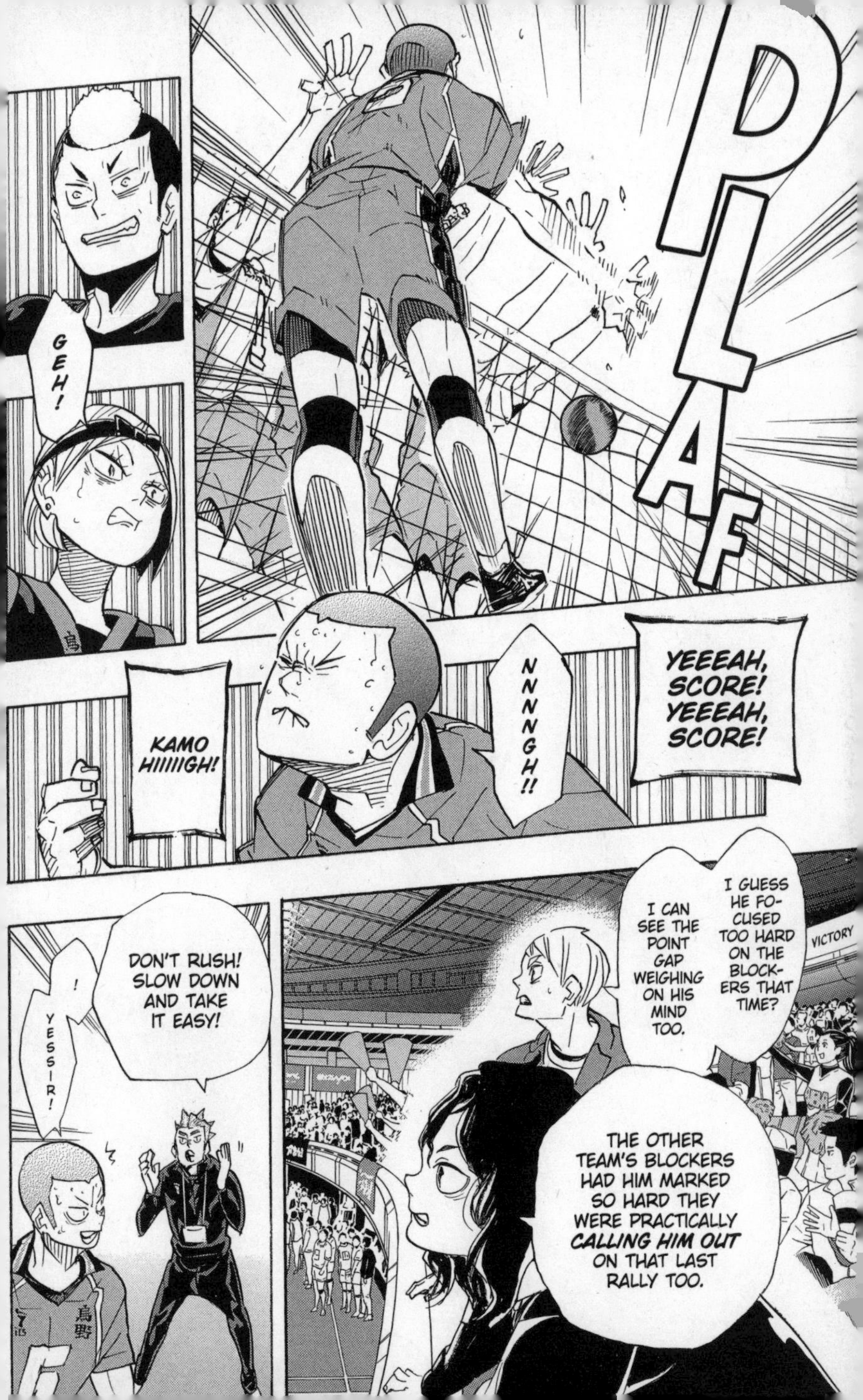
PLAF
GEH!
YEEEAH, SCORE! YEEEAH, SCORE!
NNNNGH!!
KAMO HIIIIIGH!
I GUESS HE FO-CUSED TOO HARD ON THE BLOCK-ERS THAT TIME?
I CAN SEE THE POINT GAP WEIGHING ON HIS MIND TOO.
VICTORY
THE OTHER TEAM'S BLOCKERS HAD HIM MARKED SO HARD THEY WERE PRACTICALLY *CALLING HIM OUT* ON THAT LAST RALLY TOO.
DON'T RUSH! SLOW DOWN AND TAKE IT EASY!
!
YESSIR!

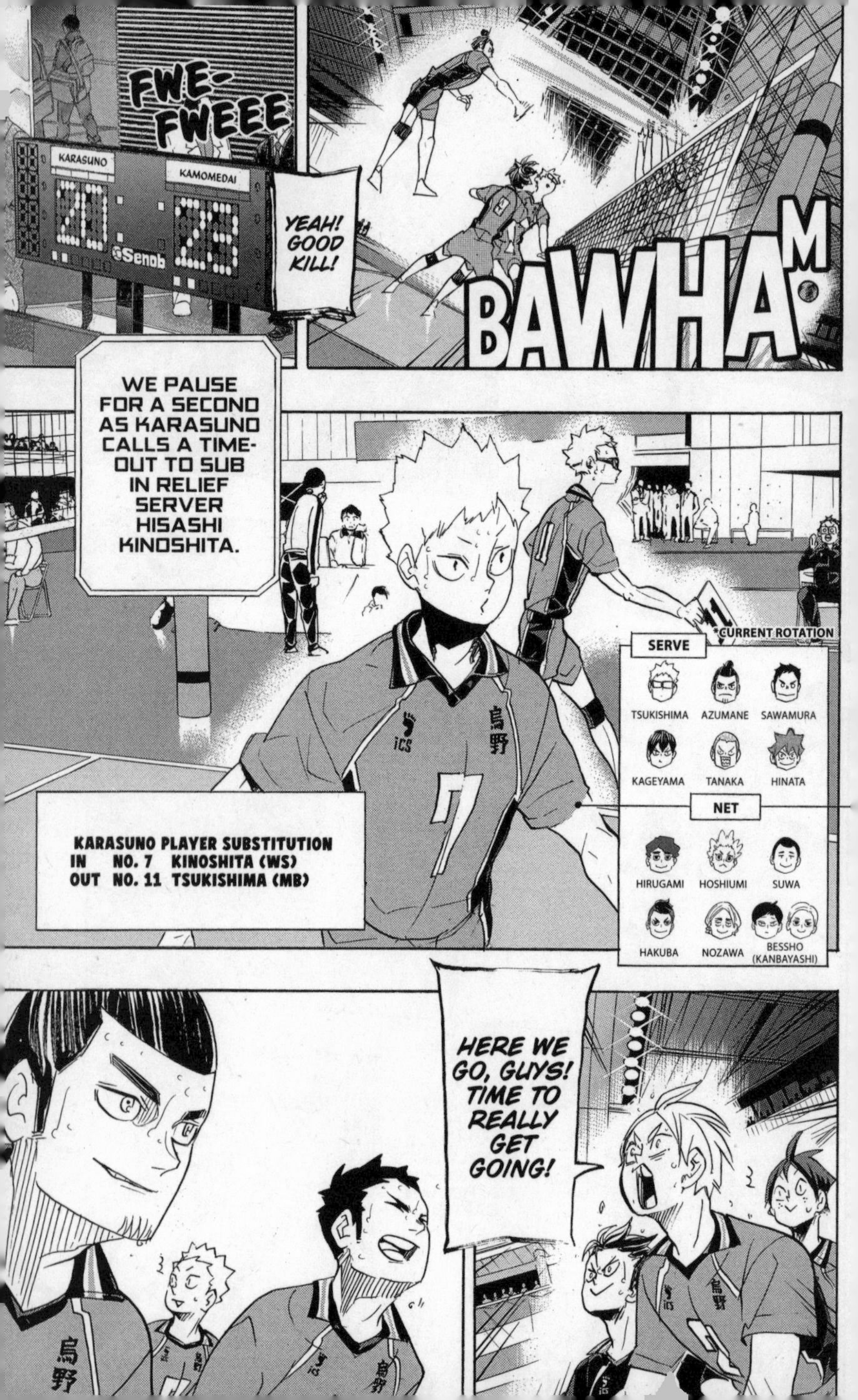
BAWHAM
YEAH! GOOD KILL!
FWE-FWEEE
KARASUNO
KAMOMEDAI
Senob
WE PAUSE FOR A SECOND AS KARASUNO CALLS A TIME-OUT TO SUB IN RELIEF SERVER HISASHI KINOSHITA.
*CURRENT ROTATION
SERVE
TSUKISHIMA
AZUMANE
SAWAMURA
KAGEYAMA
TANAKA
HINATA
NET
HIRUGAMI
HOSHIUMI
SUWA
HAKUBA
NOZAWA
BESSHO (KANBAYASHI)
KARASUNO PLAYER SUBSTITUTION
IN NO. 7 KINOSHITA (WS)
OUT NO. 11 TSUKISHIMA (MB)
HERE WE GO, GUYS! TIME TO REALLY GET GOING!

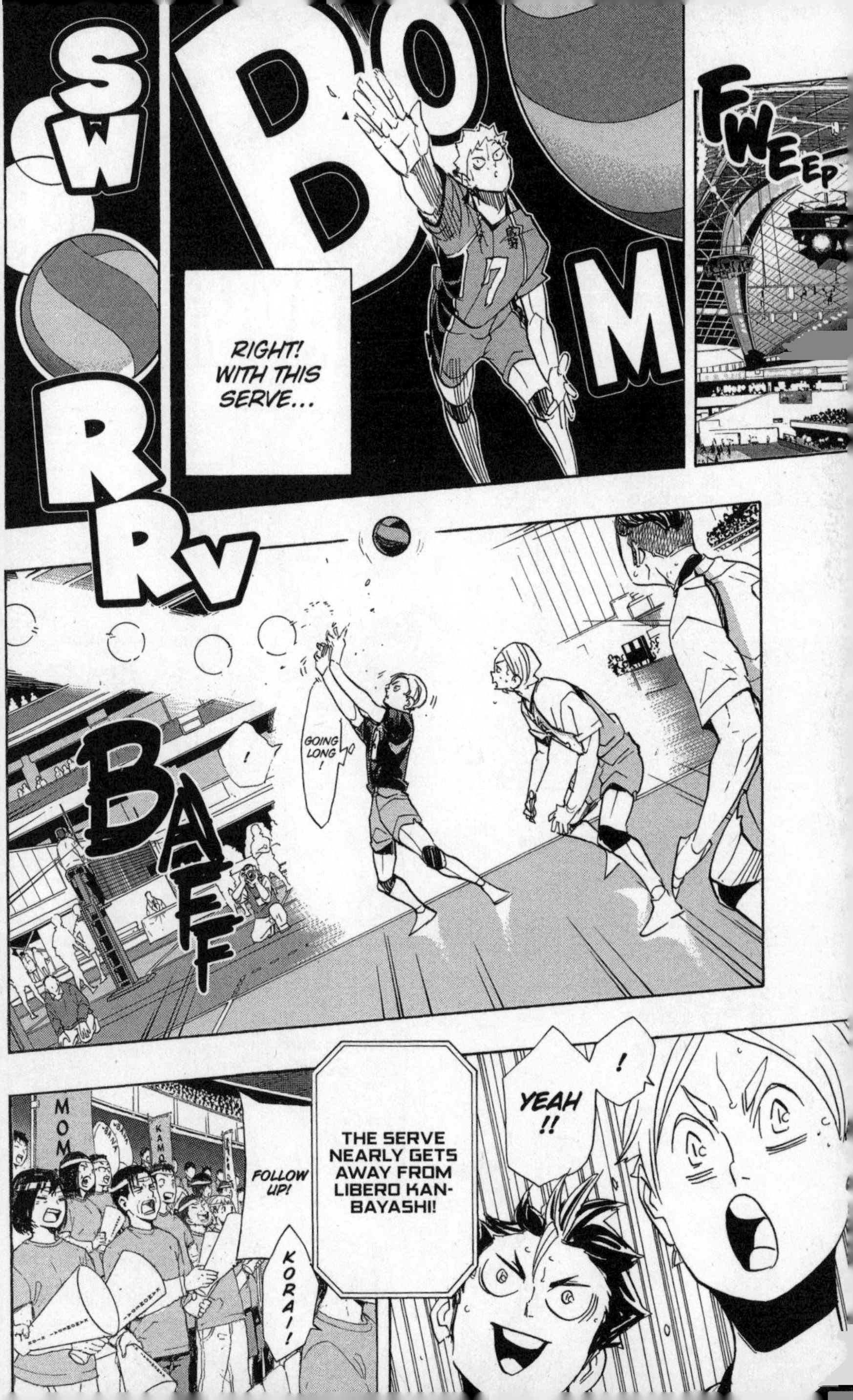
SWOOSH
RIGHT! WITH THIS SERVE...
DOOM
FWEEP
RRV
BAFF
GOING LONG!
!
YEAH!!
!
THE SERVE NEARLY GETS AWAY FROM LIBERO KANBAYASHI!
FOLLOW UP!
KORA!!

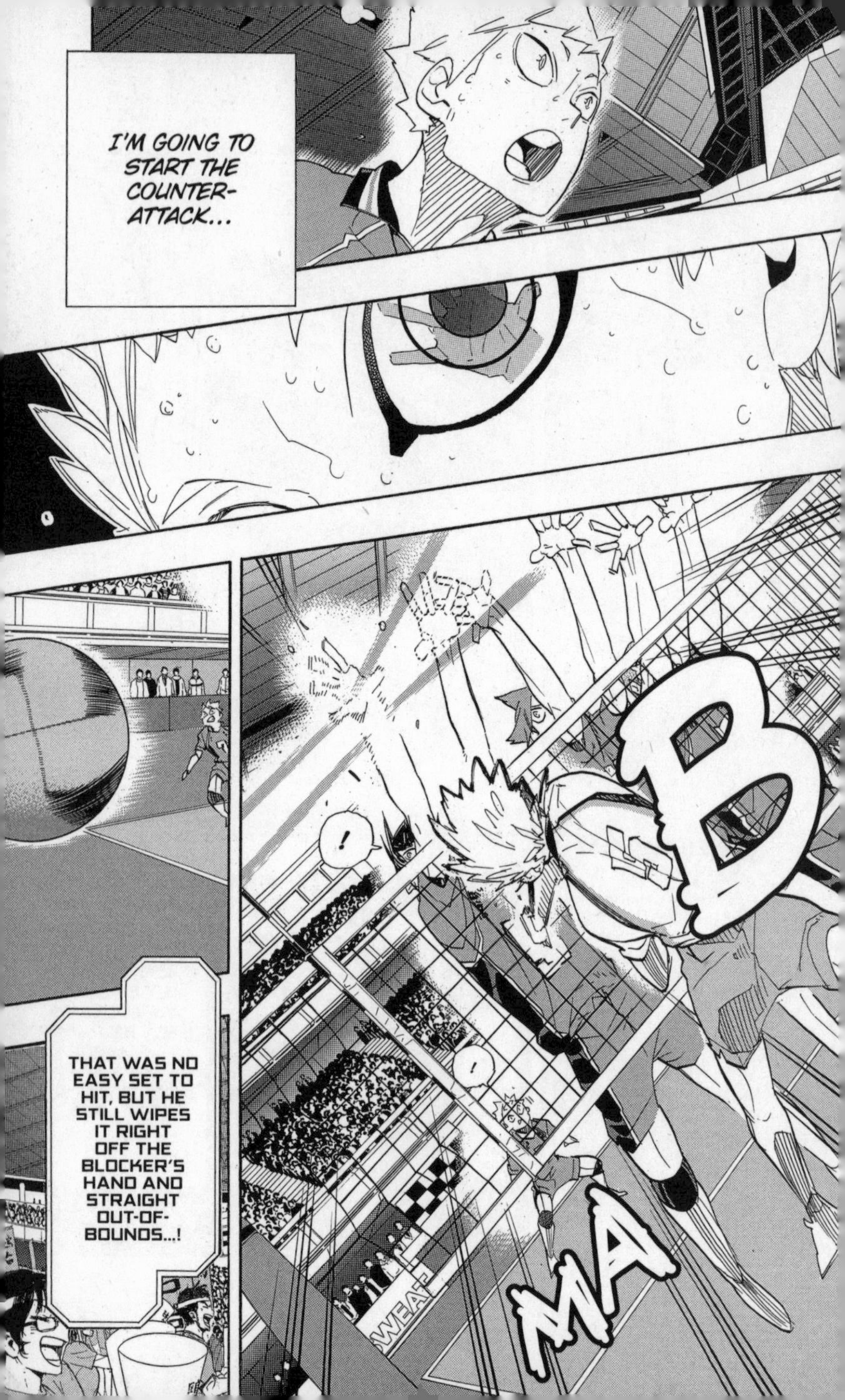
I'M GOING TO START THE COUNTER-ATTACK...
!
!
BAM
THAT WAS NO EASY SET TO HIT, BUT HE STILL WIPES IT RIGHT OFF THE BLOCKER'S HAND AND STRAIGHT OUT-OF-BOUNDS...!

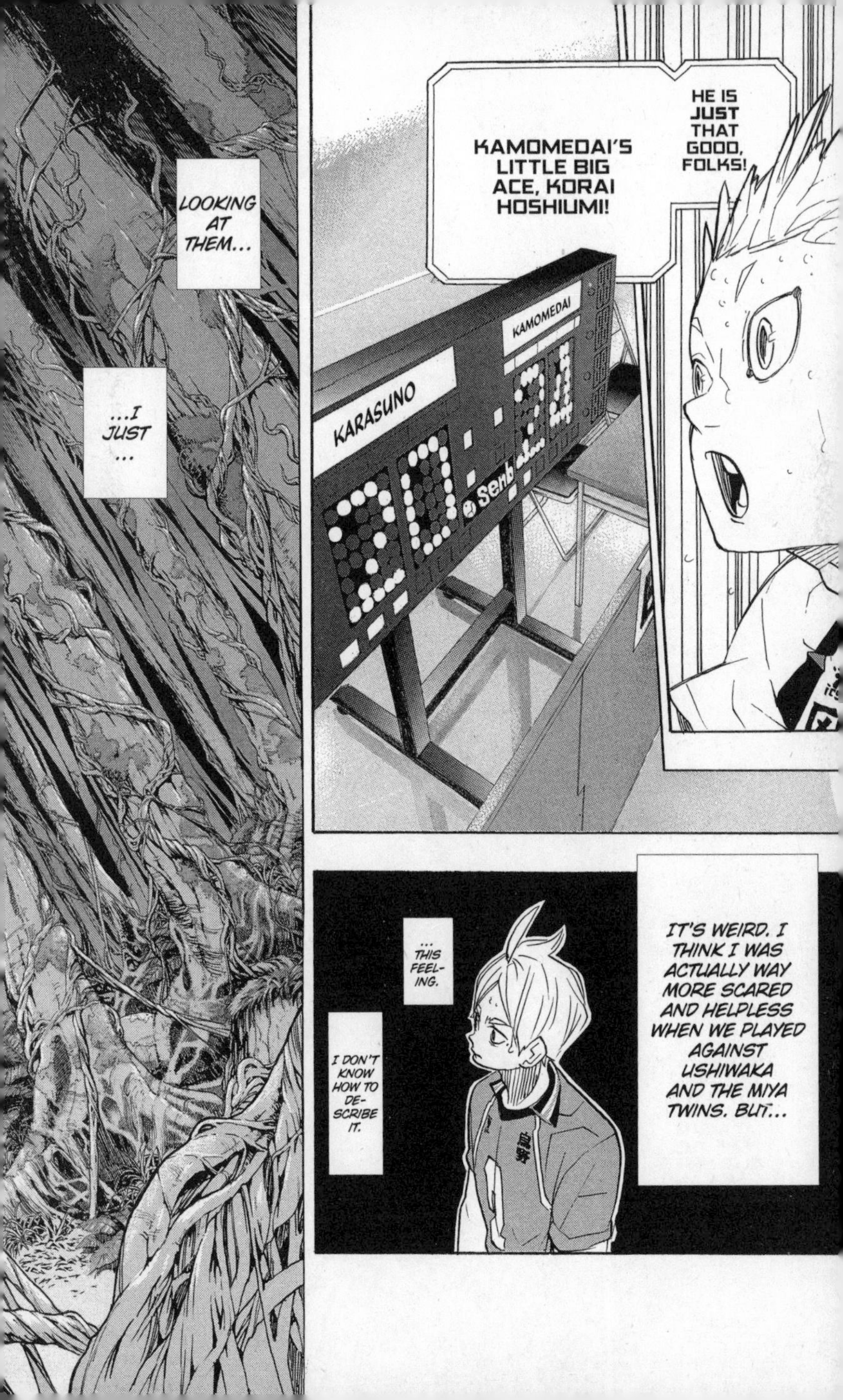

HE IS JUST THAT GOOD, FOLKS!
KAMOMEDAI'S LITTLE BIG ACE, KORAI HOSHIUMI!
KAMOMEDAI
KARASUNO
IT'S WEIRD. I THINK I WAS ACTUALLY WAY MORE SCARED AND HELPLESS WHEN WE PLAYED AGAINST USHIWAKA AND THE MIYA TWINS. BUT...
...THIS FEEL-ING.
I DON'T KNOW HOW TO DE-SCRIBE IT.
LOOKING AT THEM...
...I JUST ...

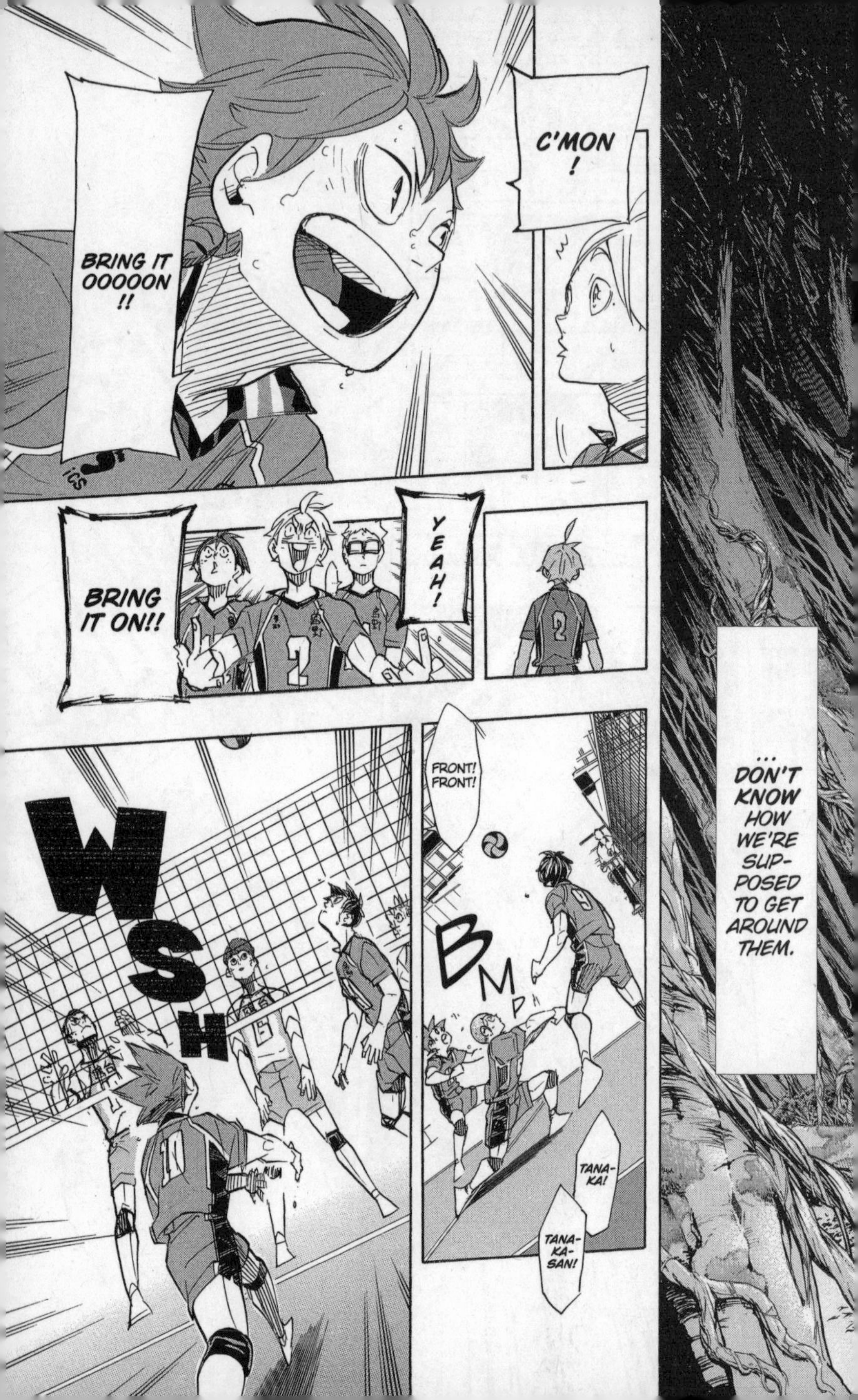
... DON'T KNOW HOW WE'RE SUP-POSED TO GET AROUND THEM.
C'MON!
BRING IT OOOOON!!
YEAH!
BRING IT ON!!
FRONT! FRONT!
BMP
TANA-KA!
TANA-KA-SAN!
WSH

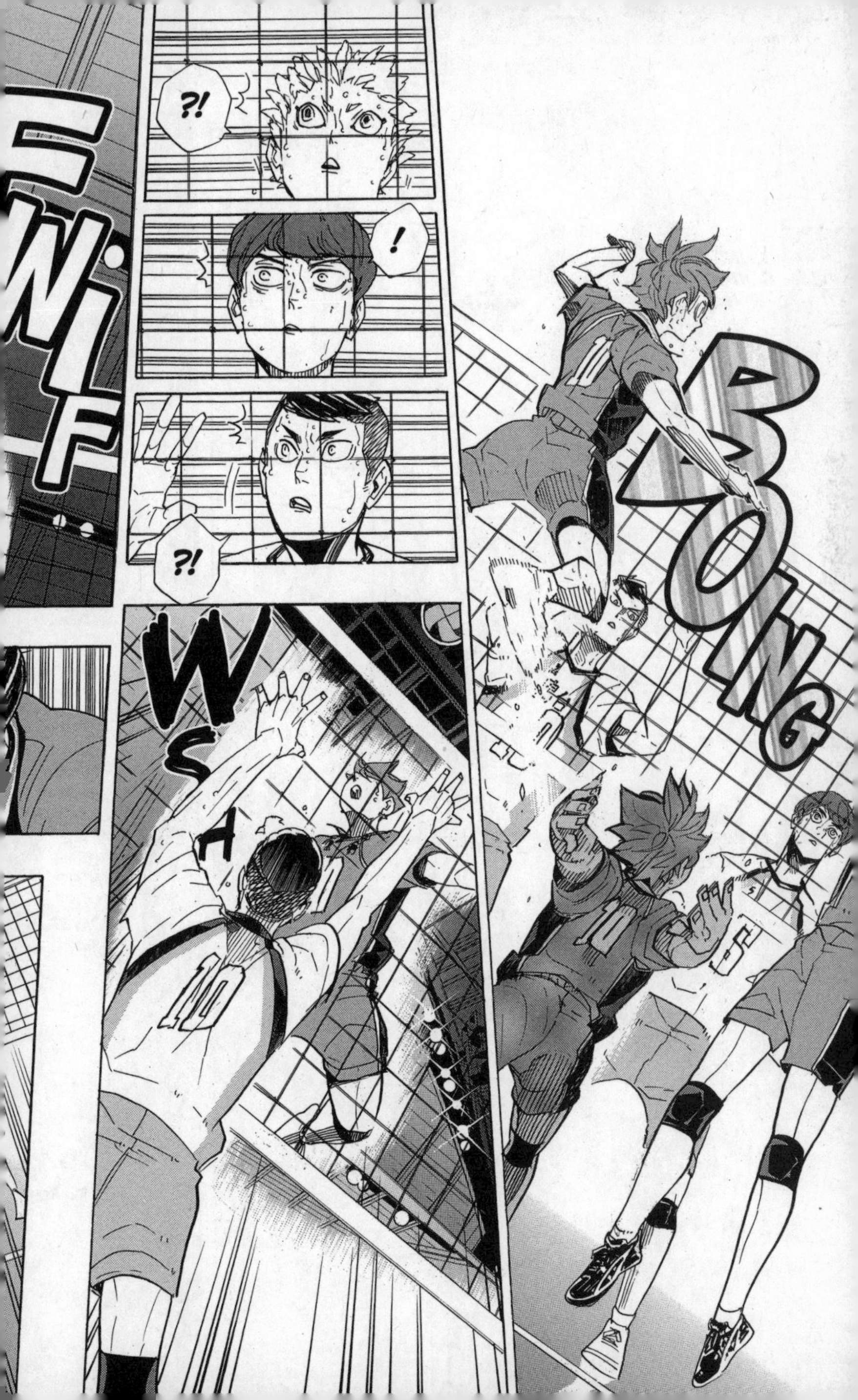
BOING
?!
!
?!
WSH

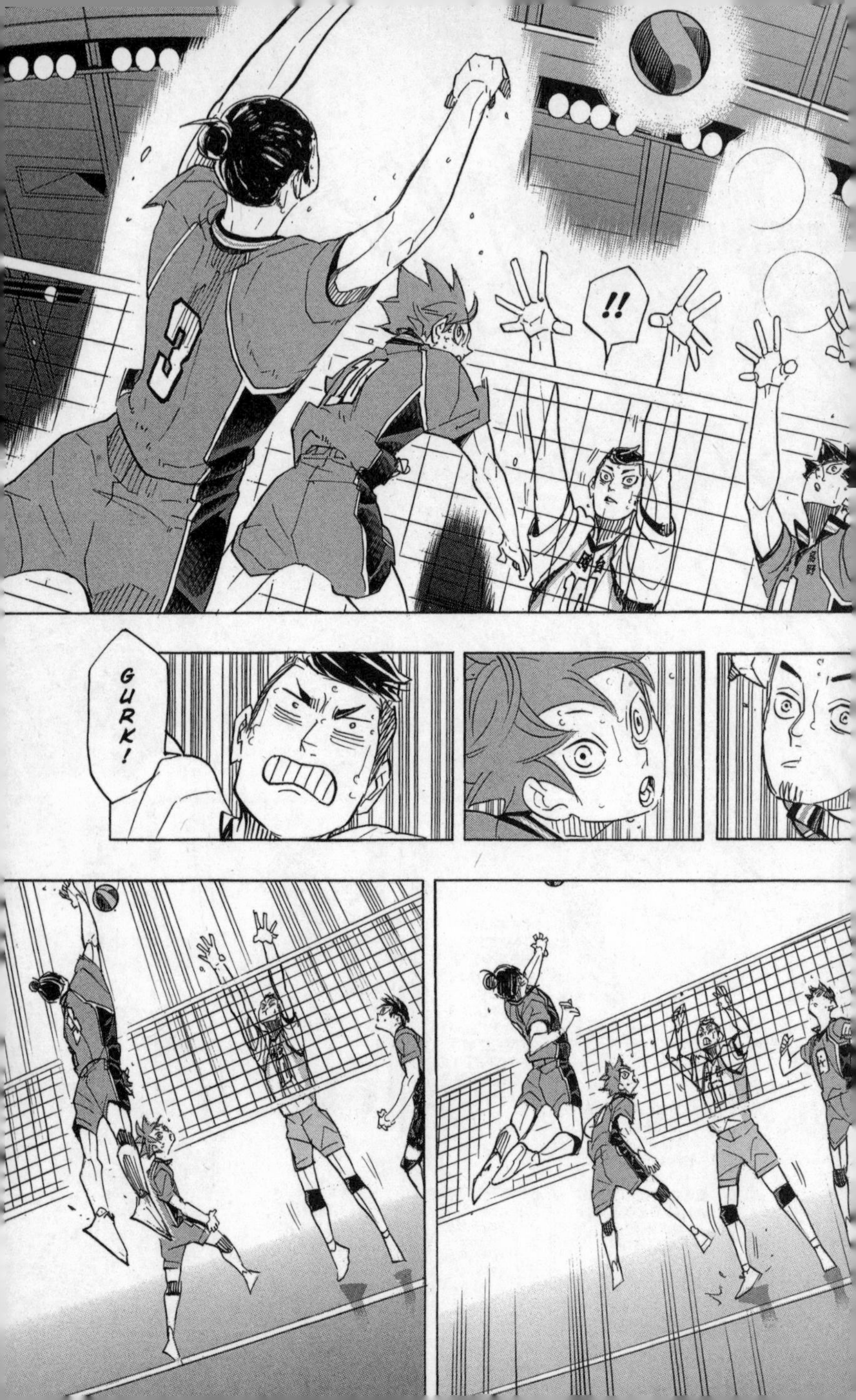
!!
GURK!

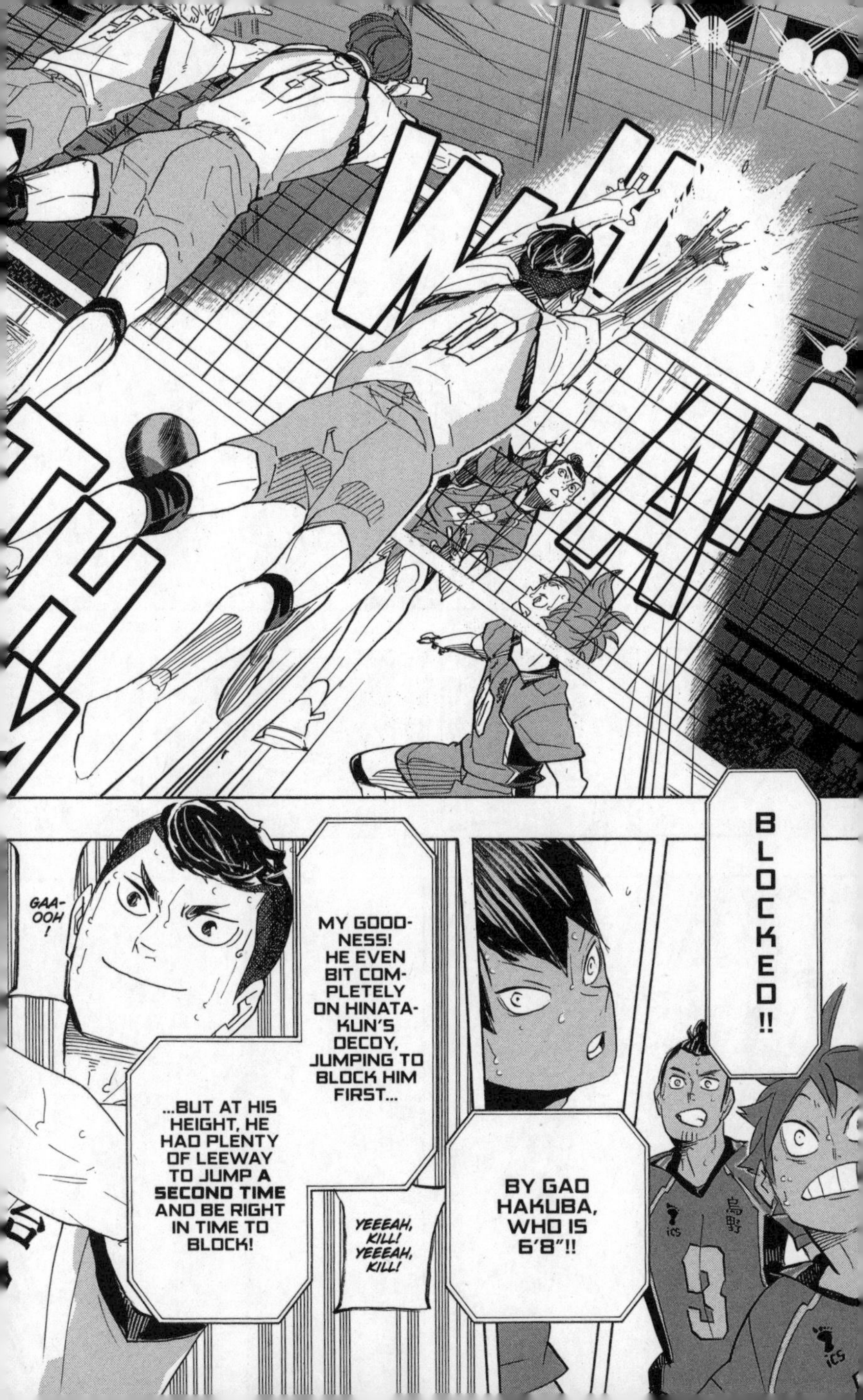
WHAP
BLOCKED!!
BY GAO HAKUBA, WHO IS 6'8"!!
MY GOOD-NESS! HE EVEN BIT COM-PLETELY ON HINATA-KUN'S DECOY, JUMPING TO BLOCK HIM FIRST...
...BUT AT HIS HEIGHT, HE HAD PLENTY OF LEEWAY TO JUMP A SECOND TIME AND BE RIGHT IN TIME TO BLOCK!
YEEEAH, KILL! YEEEAH, KILL!
GAA-OOH!

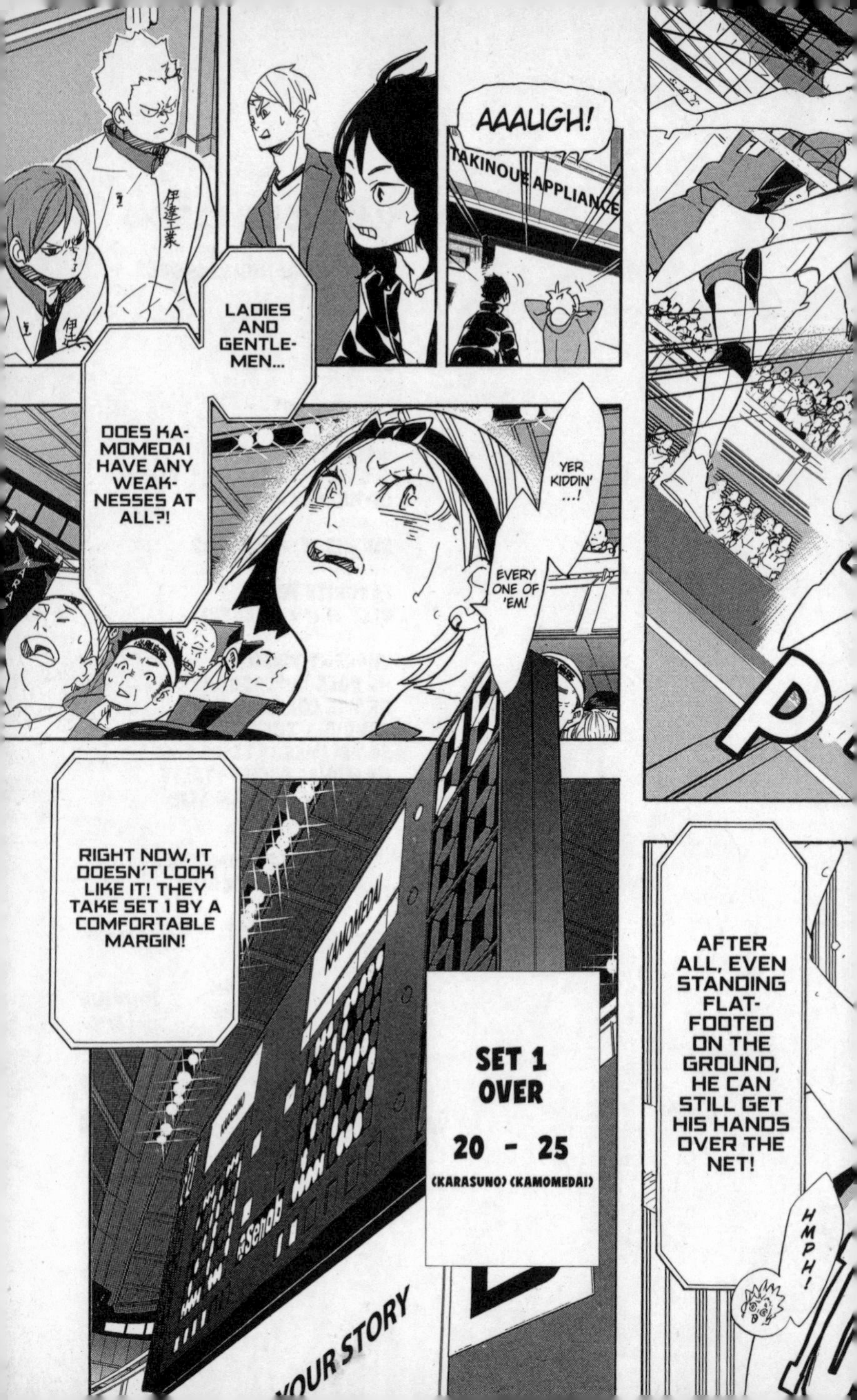
AFTER ALL, EVEN STANDING FLAT-FOOTED ON THE GROUND, HE CAN STILL GET HIS HANDS OVER THE NET!
HMPH!
AAAUGH!
TAKINOUE APPLIANCE
LADIES AND GENTLE-MEN...
DOES KA-MOMEDAI HAVE ANY WEAK-NESSES AT ALL?!
YER KIDDIN' ...!
EVERY ONE OF 'EM!
RIGHT NOW, IT DOESN'T LOOK LIKE IT! THEY TAKE SET 1 BY A COMFORTABLE MARGIN!
KAMOMEDAI
SET 1 OVER
20 - 25
(KARASUNO) (KAMOMEDAI)
YOUR STORY

KAZUYOSHI BESSHO

KAMOMEDAI HIGH SCHOOL, CLASS 1-4

POSITION: MIDDLE BLOCKER

HEIGHT: 6'1"

WEIGHT: 162 LBS. (AS OF JANUARY, 1ST YEAR OF HIGH SCHOOL)

BIRTHDAY: MARCH 22

FAVORITE FOOD: DEEP-FRIED MACKEREL

CURRENT WORRY: HE DOES IMPERSONATIONS OF THE COACH IN HIS MIND ALL THE TIME, AND SOMETIMES IT FEELS LIKE HE MIGHT ACCIDENTALLY LET SOME OF THEM SLIP.

ABILITY PARAMETERS (5-POINT SCALE)

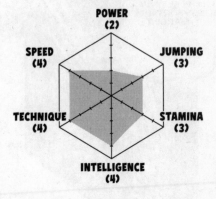

POWER (2)

JUMPING (3)

STAMINA (3)

INTELLIGENCE (4)

TECHNIQUE (4)

SPEED (4)

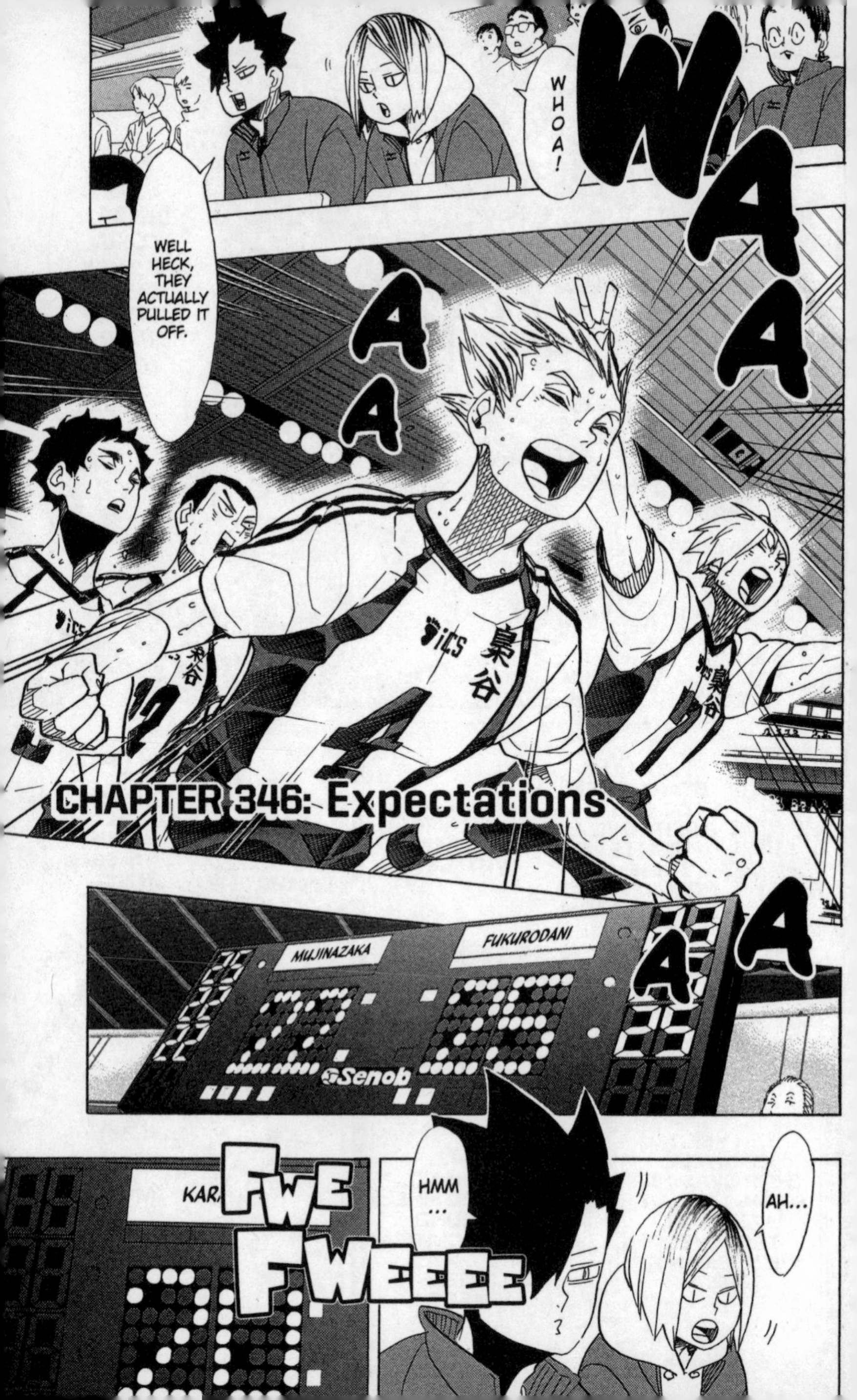
WAAAA
WHOA!
WELL HECK, THEY ACTUALLY PULLED IT OFF.
AAA
CHAPTER 346: Expectations
MUJINAZAKA
FUKURODANI
Senob
A
KAR
FWE FWEEEE
AH...
HMM ...

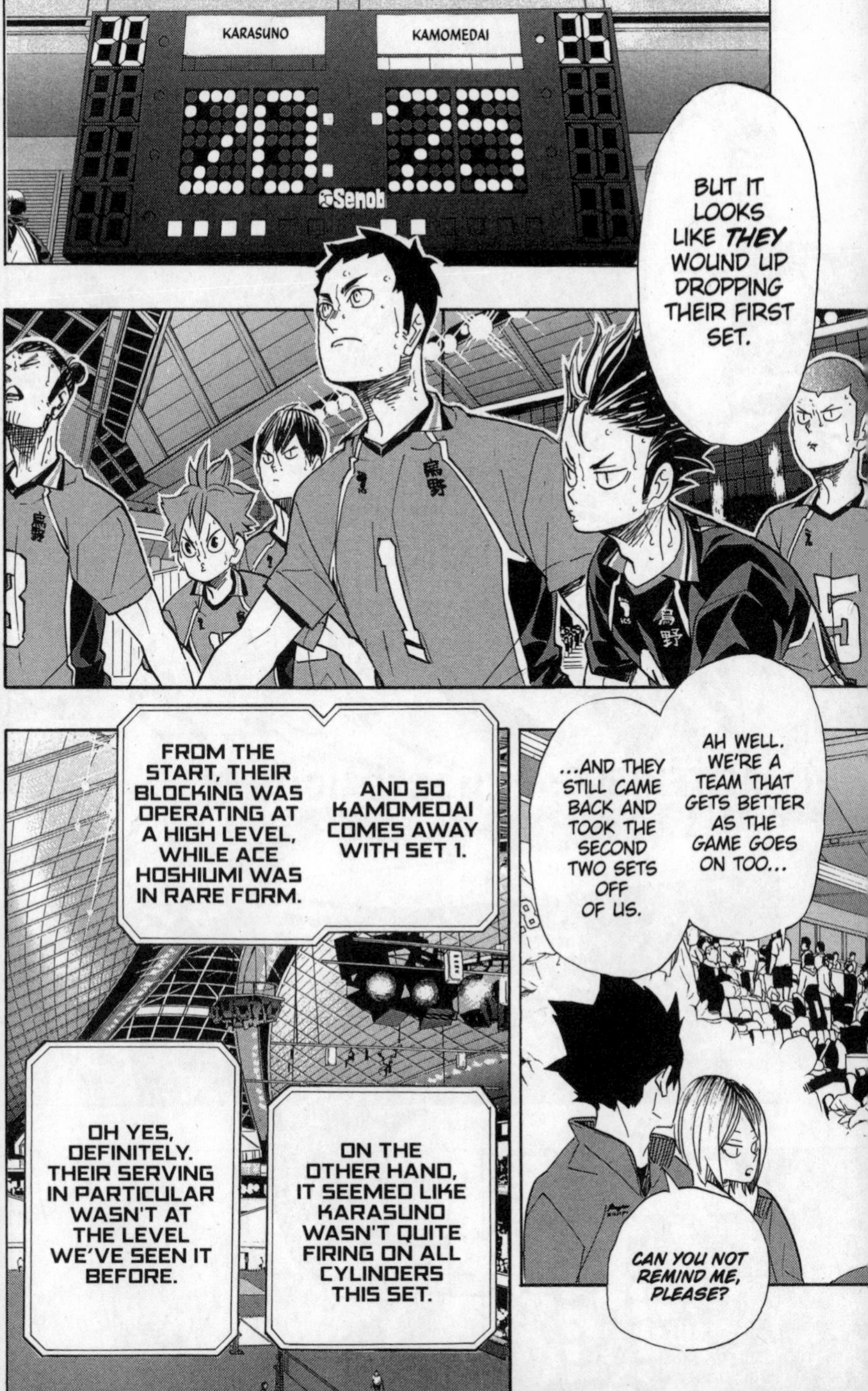
KARASUNO
KAMOMEDAI
20:25
BUT IT LOOKS LIKE THEY WOUND UP DROPPING THEIR FIRST SET.
AH WELL. WE'RE A TEAM THAT GETS BETTER AS THE GAME GOES ON TOO...
...AND THEY STILL CAME BACK AND TOOK THE SECOND TWO SETS OFF OF US.
CAN YOU NOT REMIND ME, PLEASE?
AND SO KAMOMEDAI COMES AWAY WITH SET 1.
FROM THE START, THEIR BLOCKING WAS OPERATING AT A HIGH LEVEL, WHILE ACE HOSHIUMI WAS IN RARE FORM.
ON THE OTHER HAND, IT SEEMED LIKE KARASUNO WASN'T QUITE FIRING ON ALL CYLINDERS THIS SET.
OH YES, DEFINITELY. THEIR SERVING IN PARTICULAR WASN'T AT THE LEVEL WE'VE SEEN IT BEFORE.

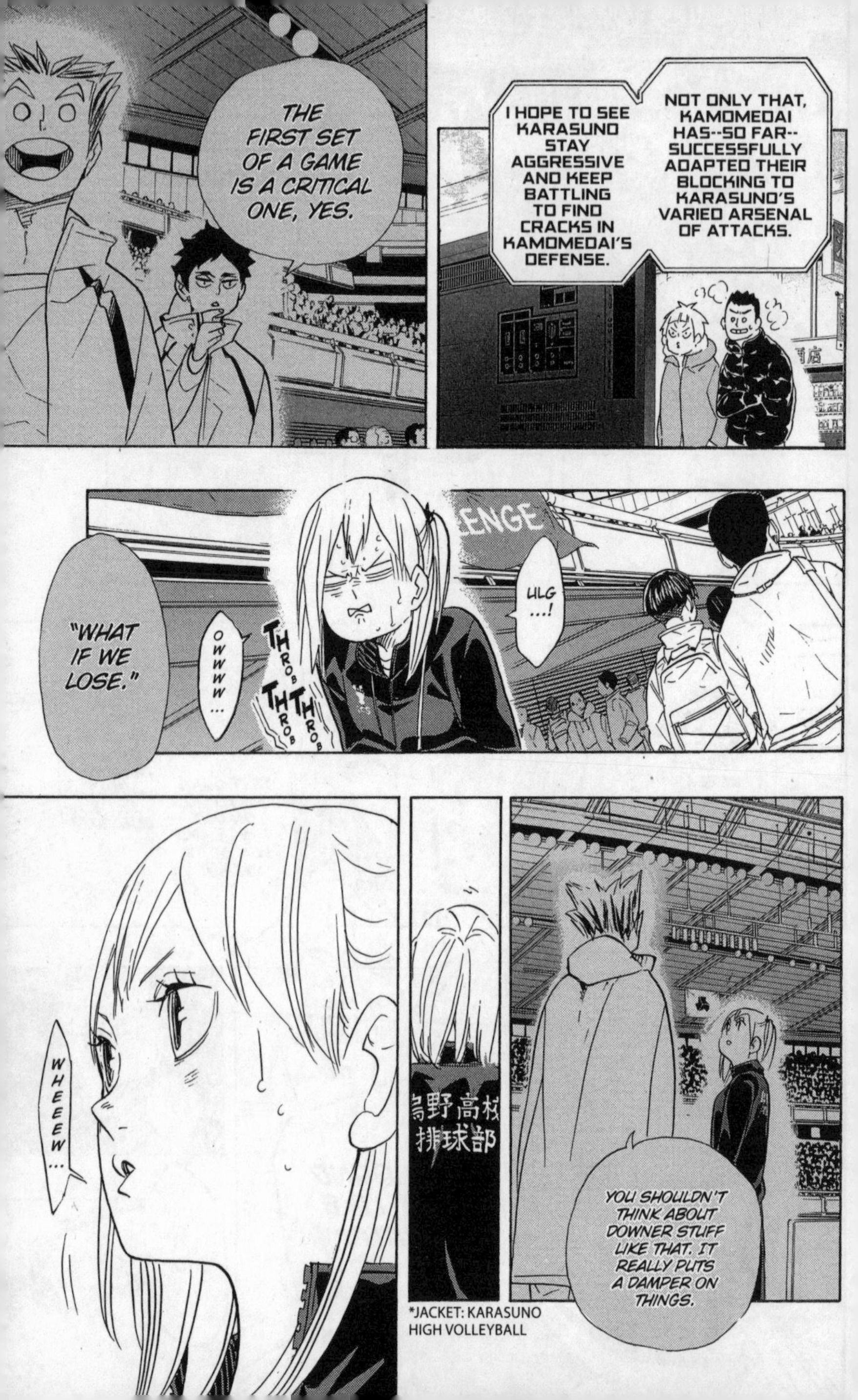
NOT ONLY THAT, KAMOMEDAI HAS--SO FAR--SUCCESSFULLY ADAPTED THEIR BLOCKING TO KARASUNO'S VARIED ARSENAL OF ATTACKS.
I HOPE TO SEE KARASUNO STAY AGGRESSIVE AND KEEP BATTLING TO FIND CRACKS IN KAMOMEDAI'S DEFENSE.
THE FIRST SET OF A GAME IS A CRITICAL ONE, YES.
ULG ...!
OWWWW ...
THROB THROB THROB
"WHAT IF WE LOSE."
YOU SHOULDN'T THINK ABOUT DOWNER STUFF LIKE THAT. IT REALLY PUTS A DAMPER ON THINGS.
WHEEEW ...
*JACKET: KARASUNO HIGH VOLLEYBALL

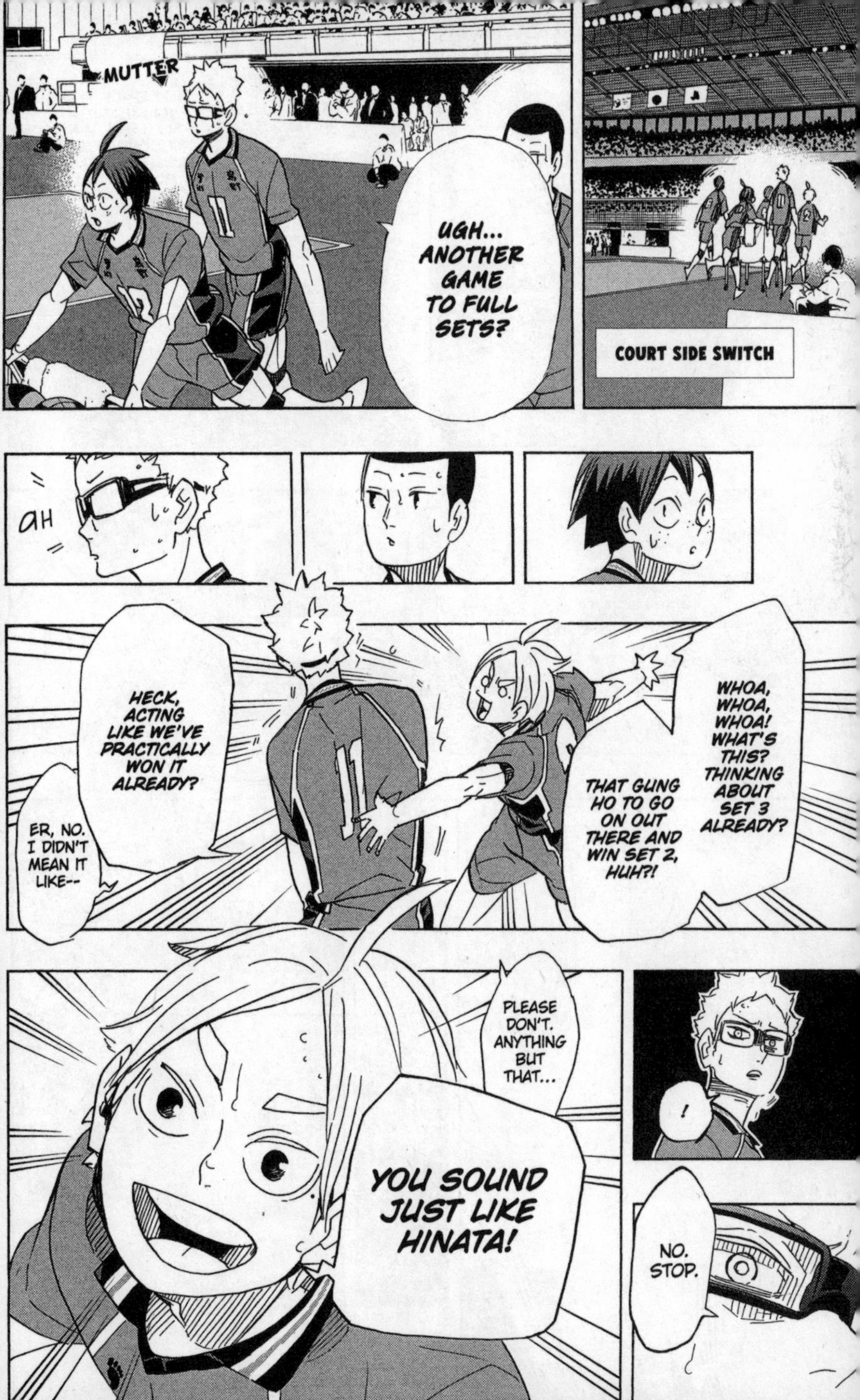
COURT SIDE SWITCH
MUTTER
UGH... ANOTHER GAME TO FULL SETS?
AH
WHOA, WHOA, WHOA! WHAT'S THIS? THINKING ABOUT SET 3 ALREADY?
THAT GUNG HO TO GO ON OUT THERE AND WIN SET 2, HUH?!
HECK, ACTING LIKE WE'VE PRACTICALLY WON IT ALREADY?
ER, NO. I DIDN'T MEAN IT LIKE--
!
NO. STOP.
PLEASE DON'T. ANYTHING BUT THAT...
YOU SOUND JUST LIKE HINATA!

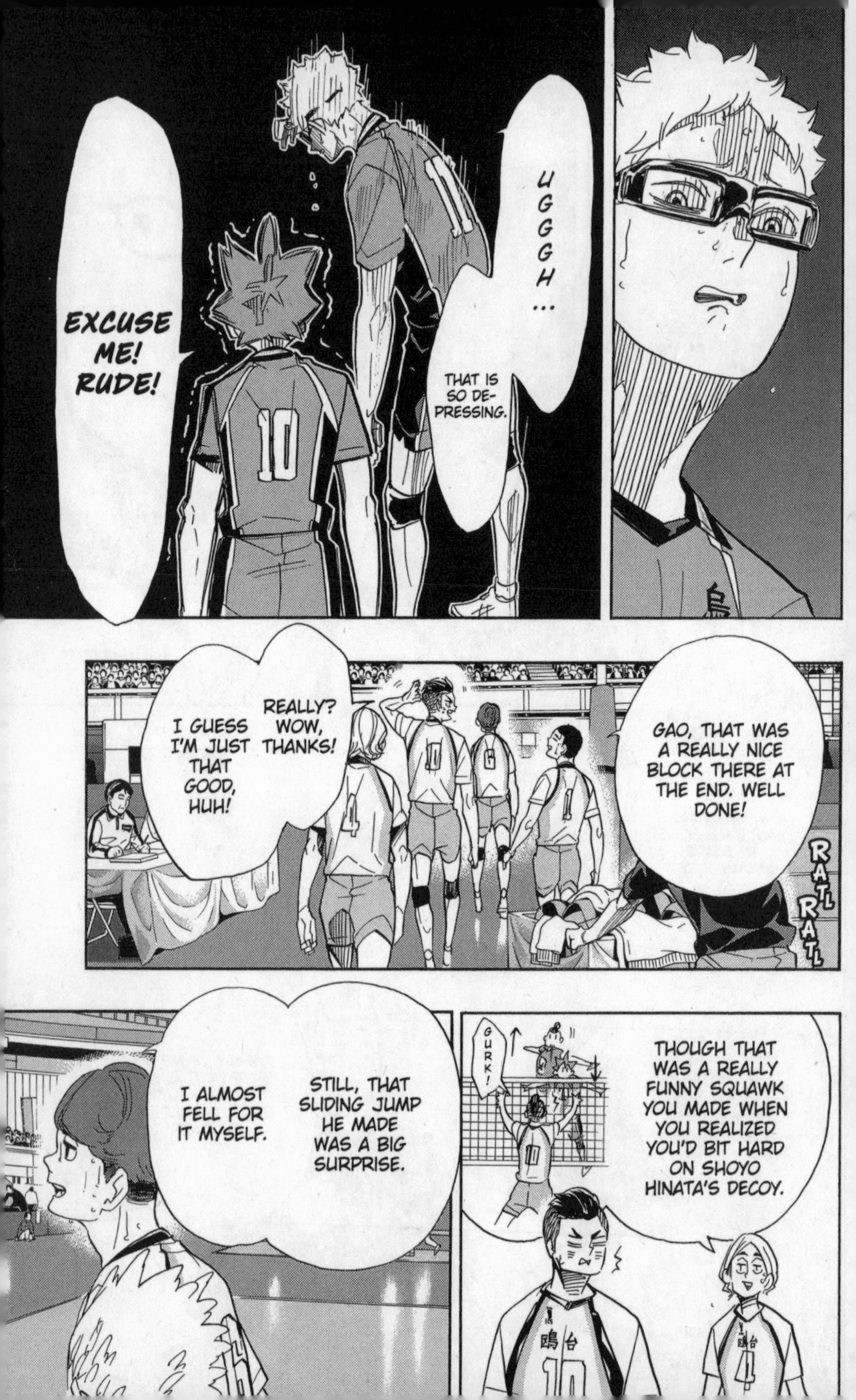
UGGGH...
THAT IS SO DE-PRESSING.
EXCUSE ME! RUDE!
GAO, THAT WAS A REALLY NICE BLOCK THERE AT THE END. WELL DONE!
RATL RATL RATL
REALLY? WOW, THANKS!
I GUESS I'M JUST THAT GOOD, HUH!
GURK!
THOUGH THAT WAS A REALLY FUNNY SQUAWK YOU MADE WHEN YOU REALIZED YOU'D BIT HARD ON SHOYO HINATA'S DECOY.
STILL, THAT SLIDING JUMP HE MADE WAS A BIG SURPRISE.
I ALMOST FELL FOR IT MYSELF.

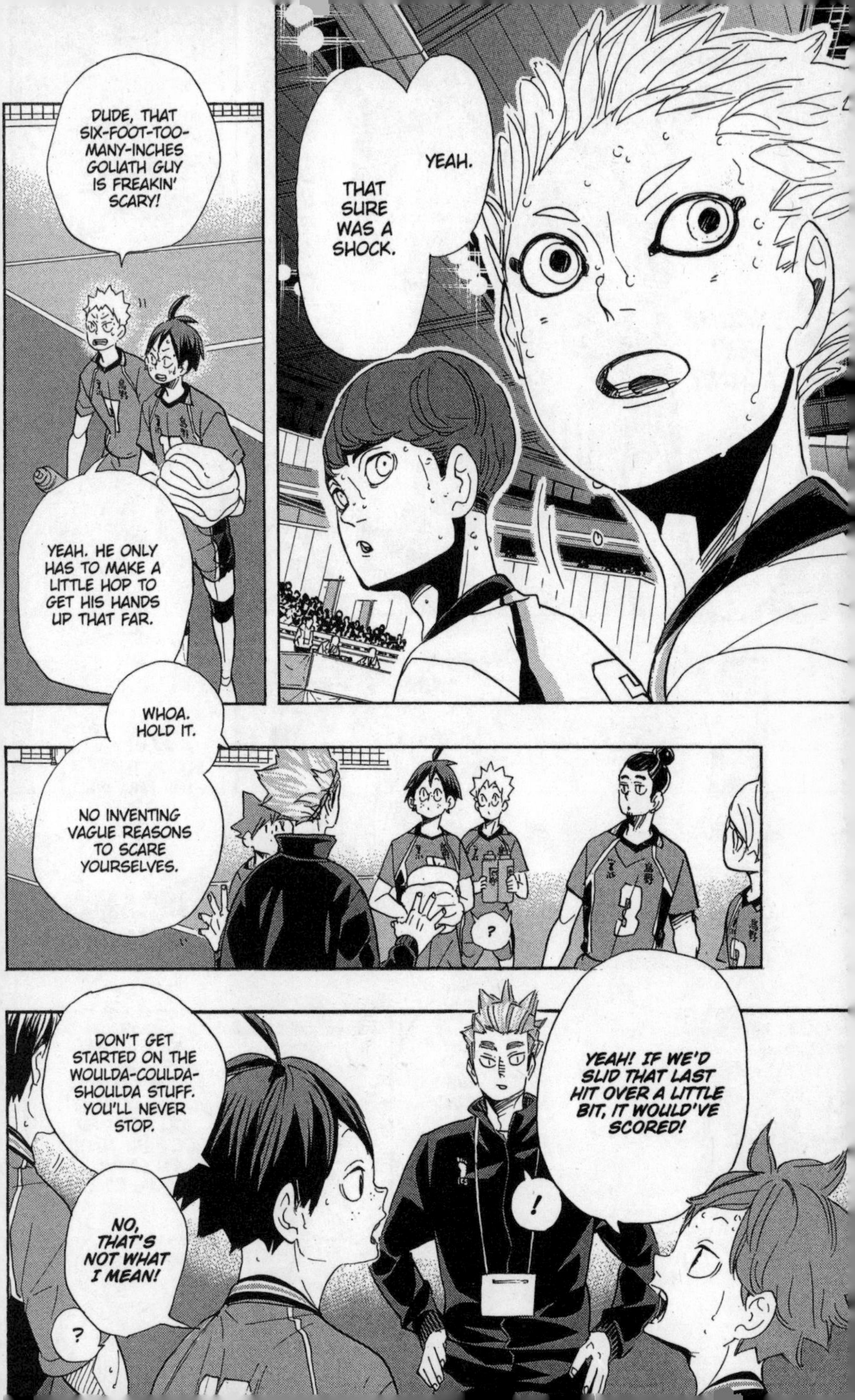
YEAH.
THAT SURE WAS A SHOCK.
DUDE, THAT SIX-FOOT-TOO-MANY-INCHES GOLIATH GUY IS FREAKIN' SCARY!
YEAH. HE ONLY HAS TO MAKE A LITTLE HOP TO GET HIS HANDS UP THAT FAR.
WHOA. HOLD IT.
NO INVENTING VAGUE REASONS TO SCARE YOURSELVES.
?
YEAH! IF WE'D SLID THAT LAST HIT OVER A LITTLE BIT, IT WOULD'VE SCORED!
!
DON'T GET STARTED ON THE WOULDA-COULDA-SHOULDA STUFF. YOU'LL NEVER STOP.
NO, THAT'S NOT WHAT I MEAN!
?

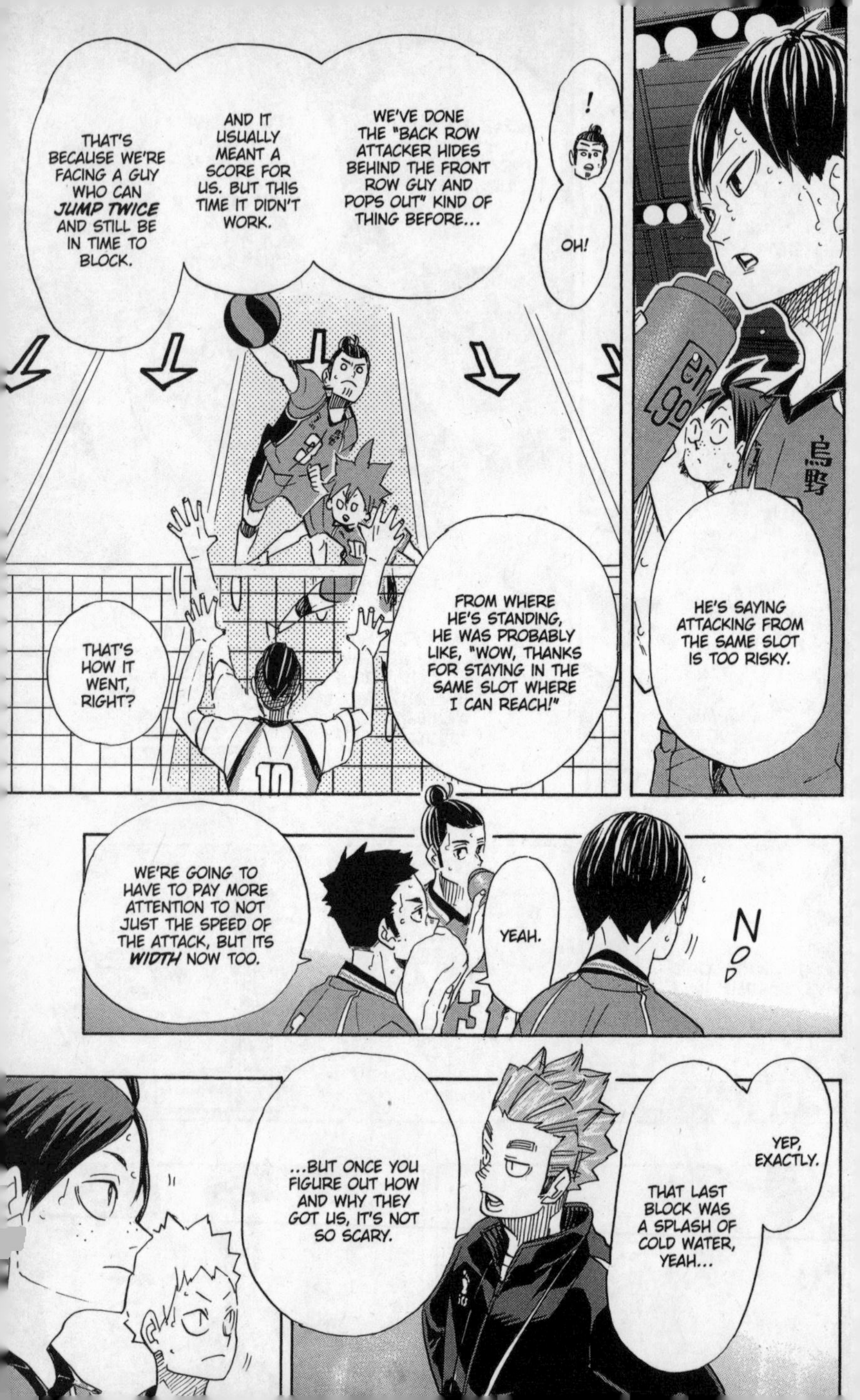
HE'S SAYING ATTACKING FROM THE SAME SLOT IS TOO RISKY.
!
OH!
WE'VE DONE THE "BACK ROW ATTACKER HIDES BEHIND THE FRONT ROW GUY AND POPS OUT" KIND OF THING BEFORE...
AND IT USUALLY MEANT A SCORE FOR US. BUT THIS TIME IT DIDN'T WORK.
THAT'S BECAUSE WE'RE FACING A GUY WHO CAN JUMP TWICE AND STILL BE IN TIME TO BLOCK.
FROM WHERE HE'S STANDING, HE WAS PROBABLY LIKE, "WOW, THANKS FOR STAYING IN THE SAME SLOT WHERE I CAN REACH!"
THAT'S HOW IT WENT, RIGHT?
NOD
YEAH.
WE'RE GOING TO HAVE TO PAY MORE ATTENTION TO NOT JUST THE SPEED OF THE ATTACK, BUT ITS WIDTH NOW TOO.
YEP, EXACTLY.
THAT LAST BLOCK WAS A SPLASH OF COLD WATER, YEAH...
...BUT ONCE YOU FIGURE OUT HOW AND WHY THEY GOT US, IT'S NOT SO SCARY.

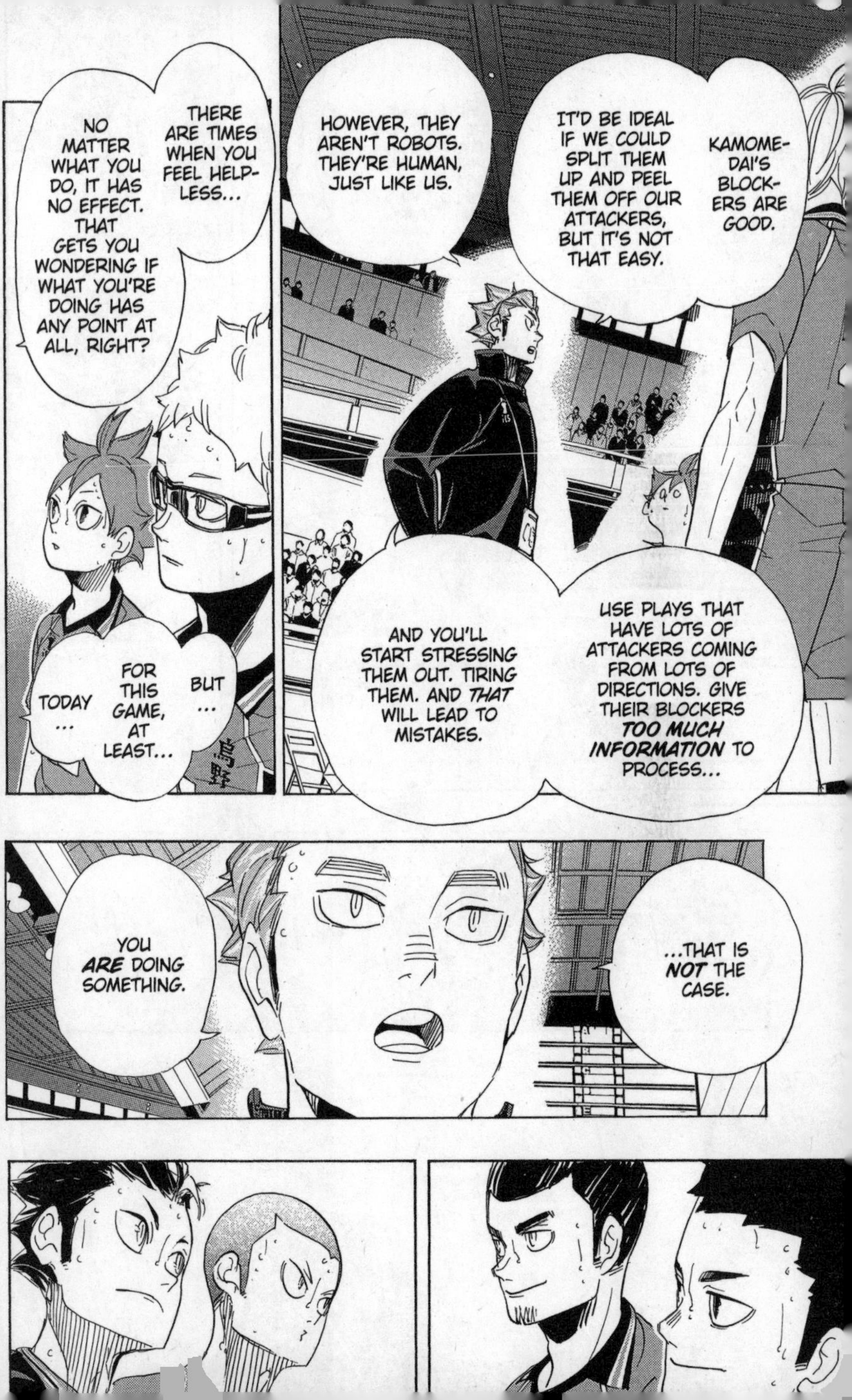
KAMOMEDAI'S BLOCKERS ARE GOOD.
IT'D BE IDEAL IF WE COULD SPLIT THEM UP AND PEEL THEM OFF OUR ATTACKERS, BUT IT'S NOT THAT EASY.
HOWEVER, THEY AREN'T ROBOTS. THEY'RE HUMAN, JUST LIKE US.
USE PLAYS THAT HAVE LOTS OF ATTACKERS COMING FROM LOTS OF DIRECTIONS. GIVE THEIR BLOCKERS TOO MUCH INFORMATION TO PROCESS...
AND YOU'LL START STRESSING THEM OUT. TIRING THEM. AND THAT WILL LEAD TO MISTAKES.
THERE ARE TIMES WHEN YOU FEEL HELPLESS...
NO MATTER WHAT YOU DO, IT HAS NO EFFECT. THAT GETS YOU WONDERING IF WHAT YOU'RE DOING HAS ANY POINT AT ALL, RIGHT?
BUT...
FOR THIS GAME, AT LEAST...
TODAY...
...THAT IS NOT THE CASE.
YOU ARE DOING SOMETHING.

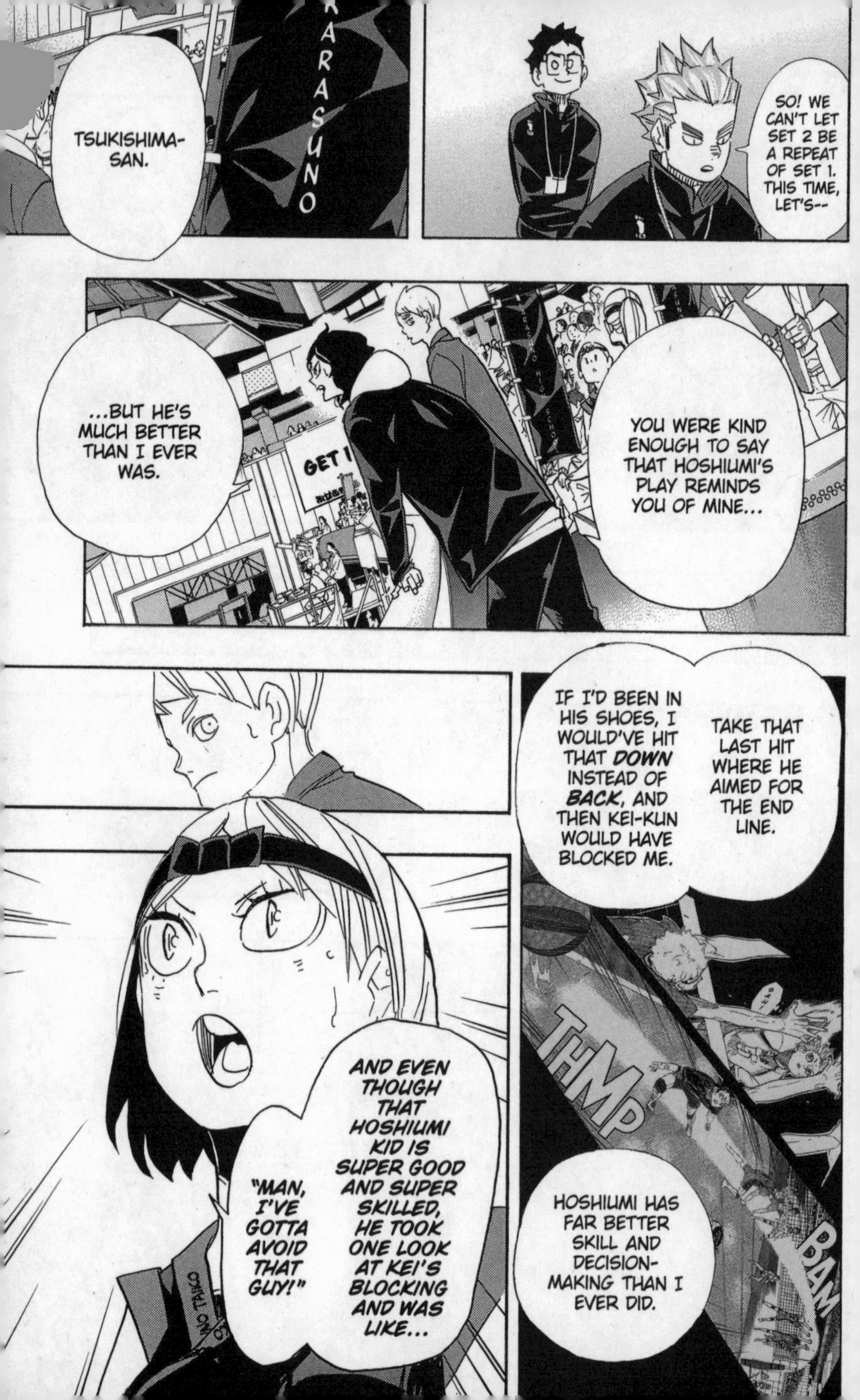
SO! WE CAN'T LET SET 2 BE A REPEAT OF SET 1. THIS TIME, LET'S--
KARASUNO
TSUKISHIMA-SAN.
YOU WERE KIND ENOUGH TO SAY THAT HOSHIUMI'S PLAY REMINDS YOU OF MINE...
...BUT HE'S MUCH BETTER THAN I EVER WAS.
TAKE THAT LAST HIT WHERE HE AIMED FOR THE END LINE.
IF I'D BEEN IN HIS SHOES, I WOULD'VE HIT THAT *DOWN* INSTEAD OF *BACK*, AND THEN KEI-KUN WOULD HAVE BLOCKED ME.
THUMP
BAM
HOSHIUMI HAS FAR BETTER SKILL AND DECISION-MAKING THAN I EVER DID.
AND EVEN THOUGH THAT HOSHIUMI KID IS SUPER GOOD AND SUPER SKILLED, HE TOOK ONE LOOK AT KEI'S BLOCKING AND WAS LIKE...
"MAN, I'VE GOTTA AVOID THAT GUY!"

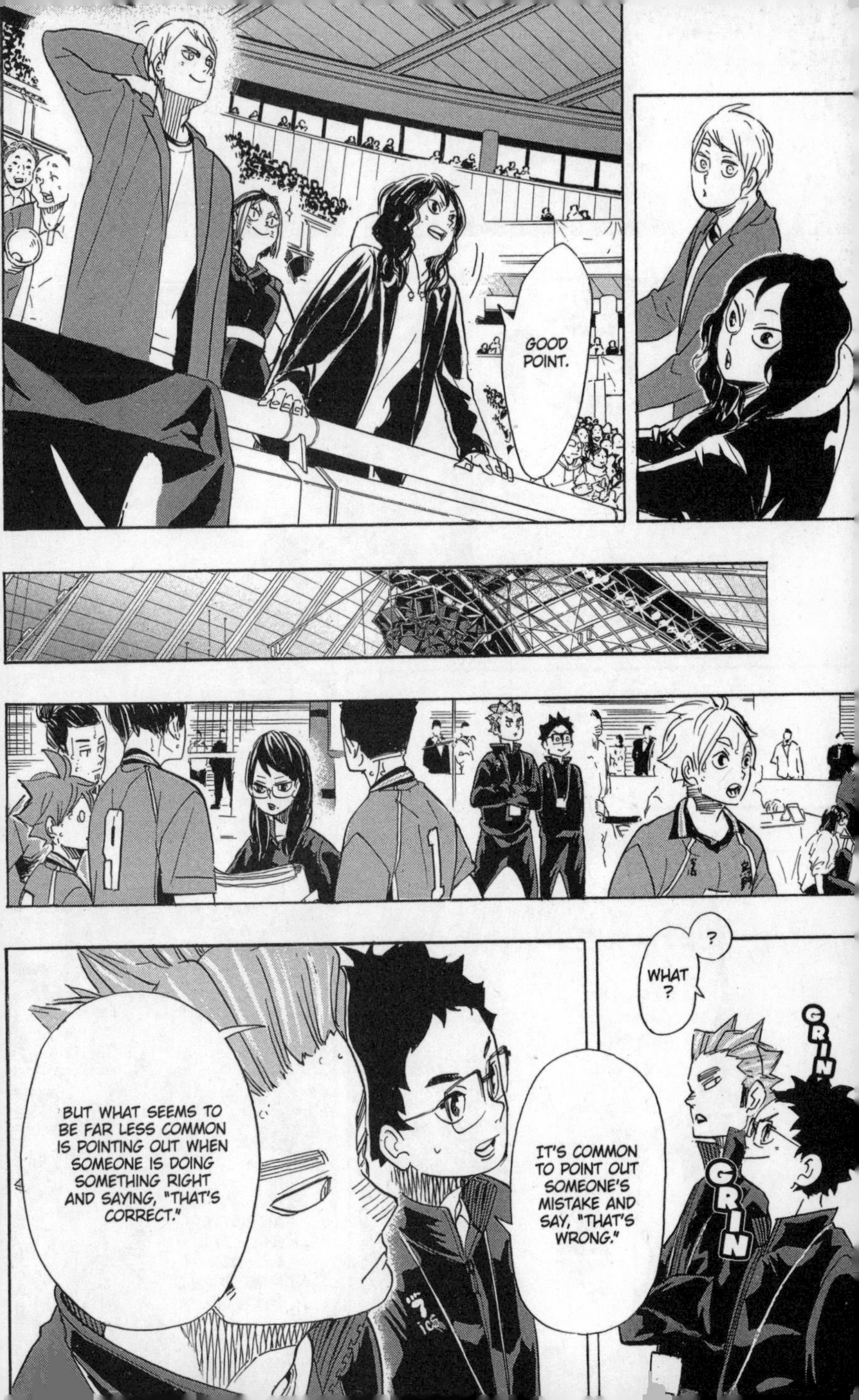
GOOD POINT.
?
WHAT ?
GRIN
GRIN
IT'S COMMON TO POINT OUT SOMEONE'S MISTAKE AND SAY, "THAT'S WRONG."
BUT WHAT SEEMS TO BE FAR LESS COMMON IS POINTING OUT WHEN SOMEONE IS DOING SOMETHING RIGHT AND SAYING, "THAT'S CORRECT."

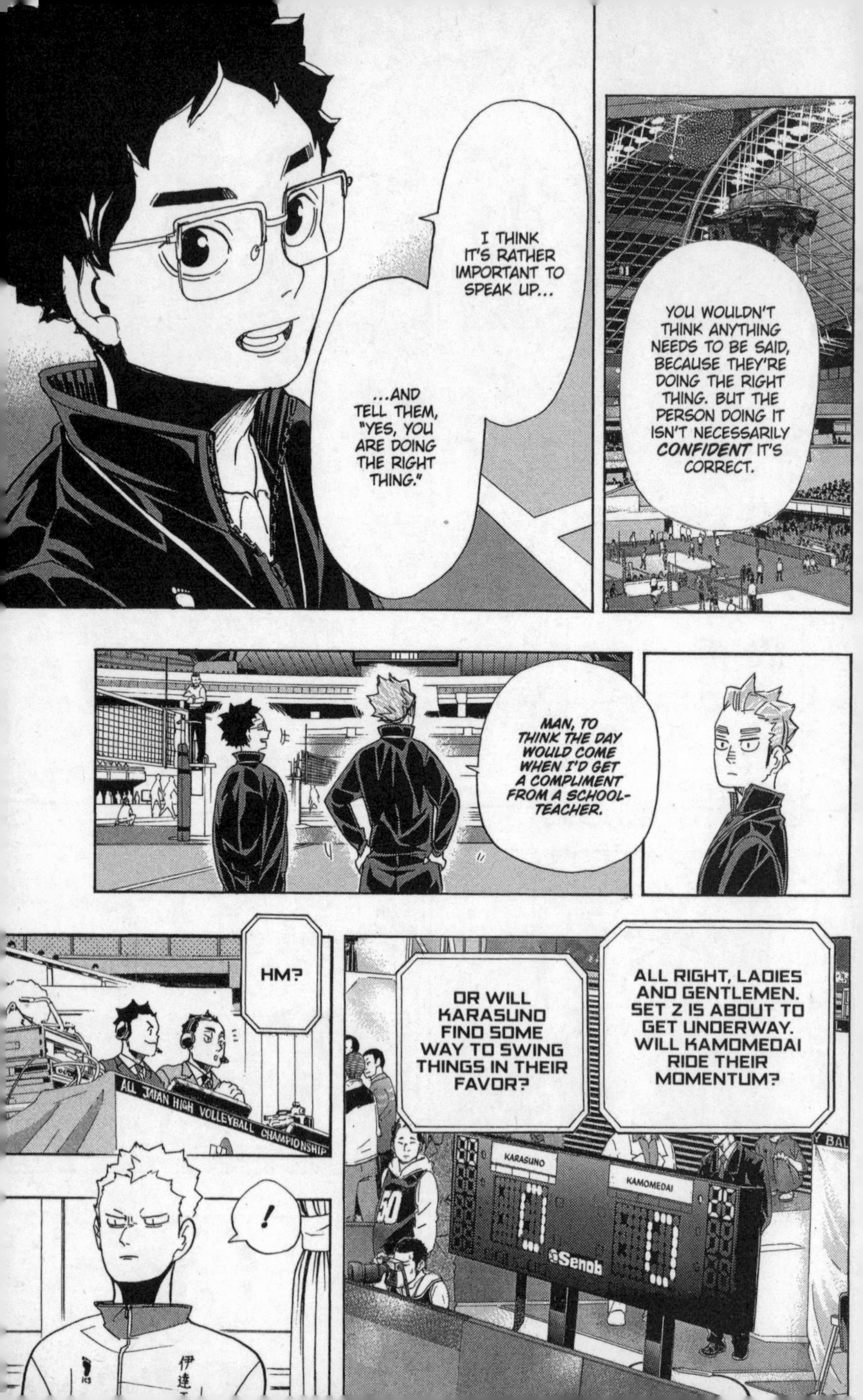
YOU WOULDN'T THINK ANYTHING NEEDS TO BE SAID, BECAUSE THEY'RE DOING THE RIGHT THING. BUT THE PERSON DOING IT ISN'T NECESSARILY *CONFIDENT* IT'S CORRECT.
I THINK IT'S RATHER IMPORTANT TO SPEAK UP...
...AND TELL THEM, "YES, YOU ARE DOING THE RIGHT THING."
MAN, TO THINK THE DAY WOULD COME WHEN I'D GET A COMPLIMENT FROM A SCHOOL-TEACHER.
ALL RIGHT, LADIES AND GENTLEMEN. SET 2 IS ABOUT TO GET UNDERWAY. WILL KAMOMEDAI RIDE THEIR MOMENTUM?
OR WILL KARASUNO FIND SOME WAY TO SWING THINGS IN THEIR FAVOR?
KARASUNO
KAMOMEDAI
Senob
HM?
ALL JAPAN HIGH VOLLEYBALL CHAMPIONSHIP
!

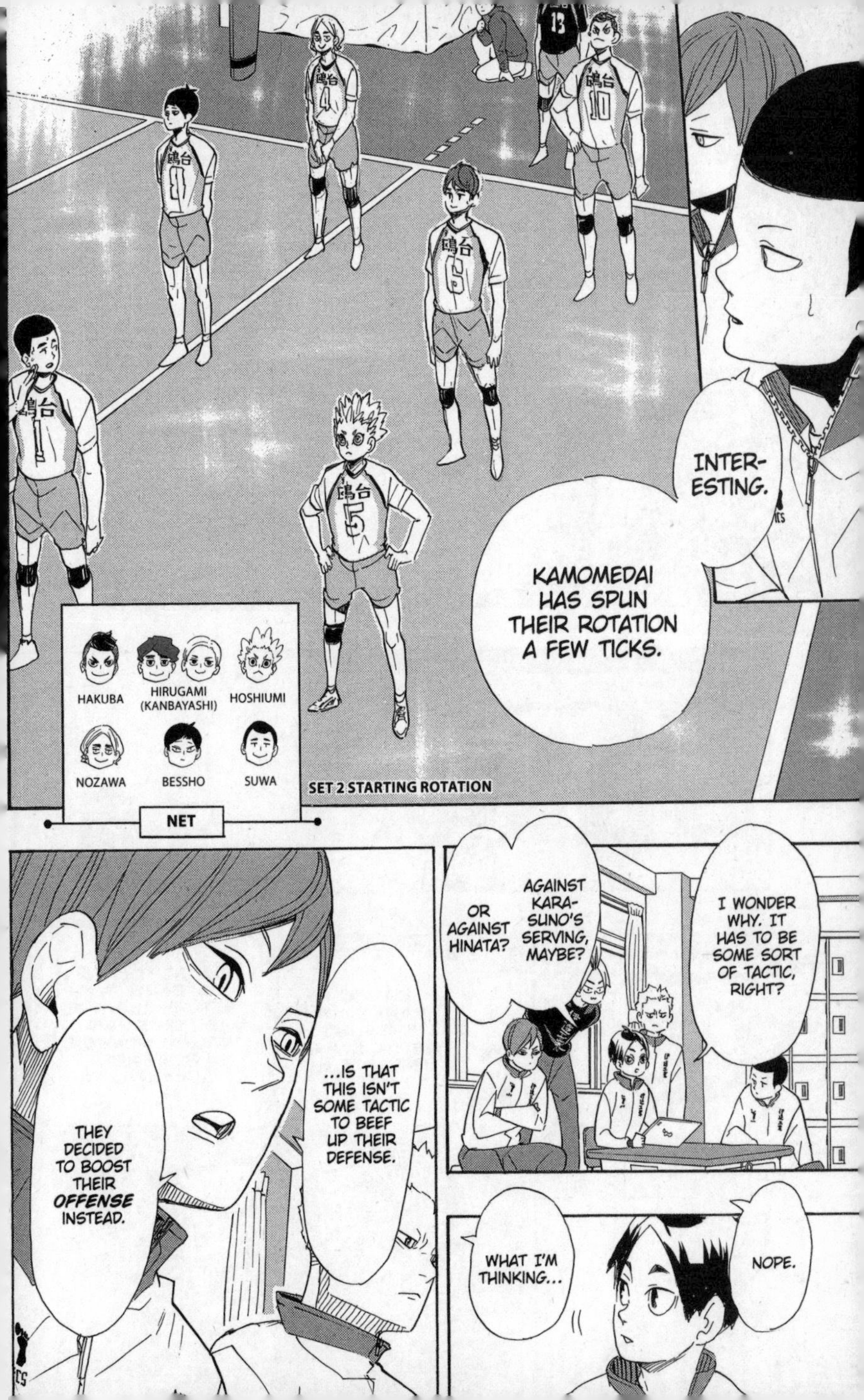
INTER-ESTING.
KAMOMEDAI HAS SPUN THEIR ROTATION A FEW TICKS.
HAKUBA
HIRUGAMI (KANBAYASHI)
HOSHIUMI
NOZAWA
BESSHO
SUWA
NET
SET 2 STARTING ROTATION
I WONDER WHY. IT HAS TO BE SOME SORT OF TACTIC, RIGHT?
AGAINST KARA-SUNO'S SERVING, MAYBE?
OR AGAINST HINATA?
NOPE.
WHAT I'M THINKING...
...IS THAT THIS ISN'T SOME TACTIC TO BEEF UP THEIR DEFENSE.
THEY DECIDED TO BOOST THEIR *OFFENSE* INSTEAD.

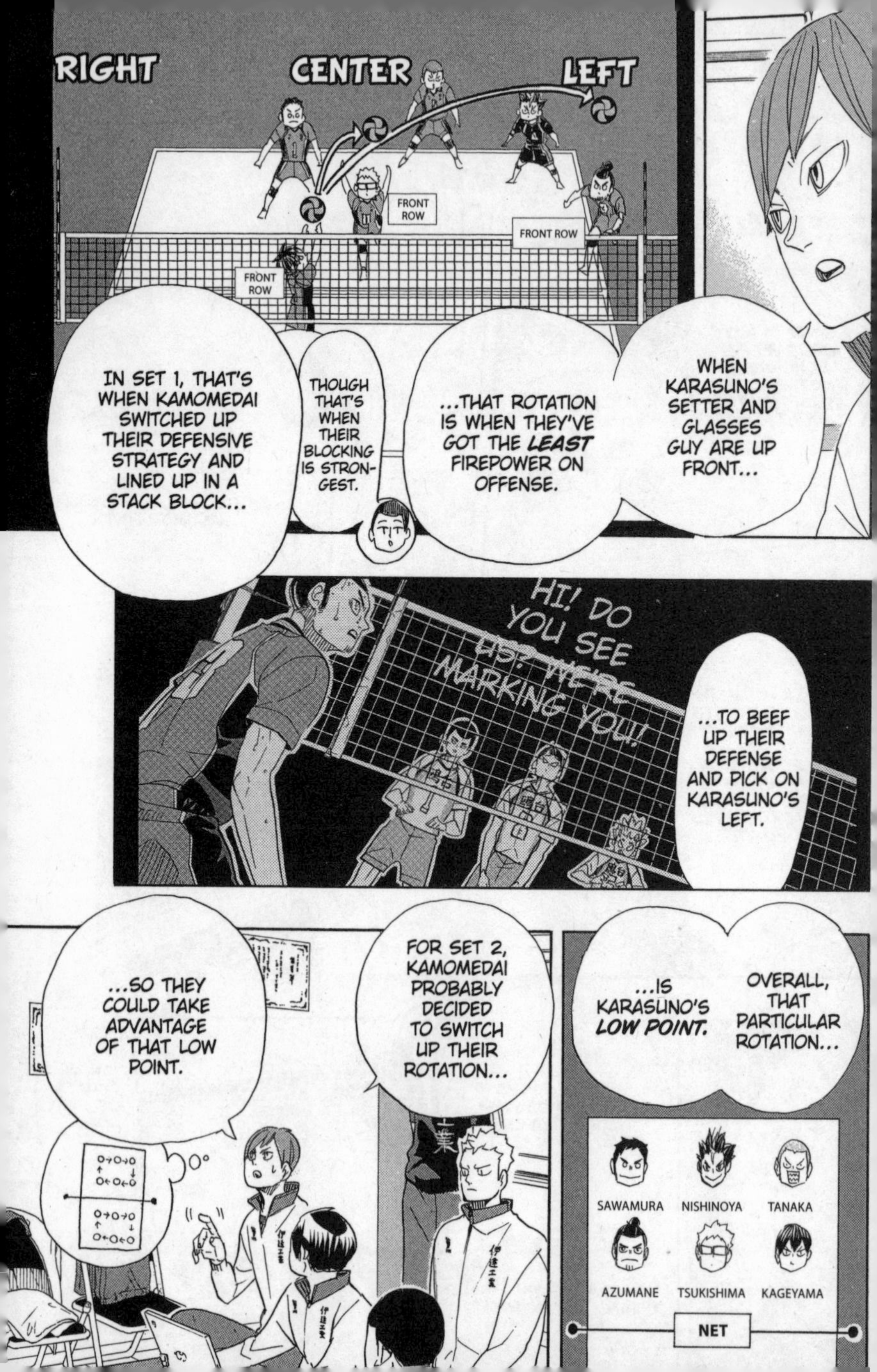
WHEN KARASUNO'S SETTER AND GLASSES GUY ARE UP FRONT...
...THAT ROTATION IS WHEN THEY'VE GOT THE *LEAST* FIREPOWER ON OFFENSE.
THOUGH THAT'S WHEN THEIR BLOCKING IS STRONGEST.
RIGHT
CENTER
LEFT
FRONT ROW
FRONT ROW
FRONT ROW
IN SET 1, THAT'S WHEN KAMOMEDAI SWITCHED UP THEIR DEFENSIVE STRATEGY AND LINED UP IN A STACK BLOCK...
HI! DO YOU SEE US? WE'RE MARKING YOU!!
...TO BEEF UP THEIR DEFENSE AND PICK ON KARASUNO'S LEFT.
OVERALL, THAT PARTICULAR ROTATION...
...IS KARASUNO'S ***LOW POINT.***
SAWAMURA
NISHINOYA
TANAKA
AZUMANE
TSUKISHIMA
KAGEYAMA
NET
FOR SET 2, KAMOMEDAI PROBABLY DECIDED TO SWITCH UP THEIR ROTATION...
...SO THEY COULD TAKE ADVANTAGE OF THAT LOW POINT.

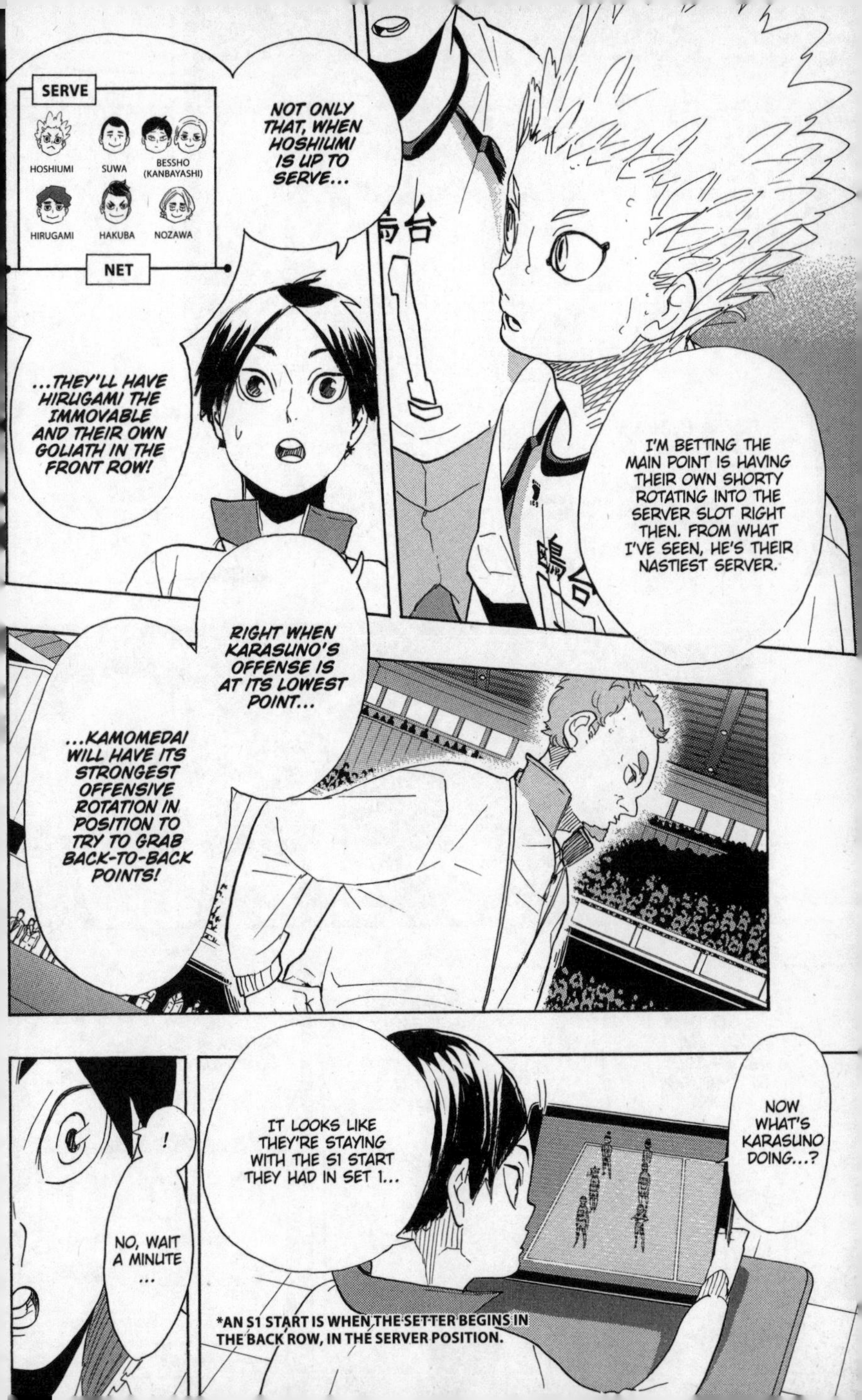
SERVE
HOSHIUMI
SUWA
BESSHO (KANBAYASHI)
HIRUGAMI
HAKUBA
NOZAWA
NET
NOT ONLY THAT, WHEN HOSHIUMI IS UP TO SERVE...
...THEY'LL HAVE HIRUGAMI THE IMMOVABLE AND THEIR OWN GOLIATH IN THE FRONT ROW!
I'M BETTING THE MAIN POINT IS HAVING THEIR OWN SHORTY ROTATING INTO THE SERVER SLOT RIGHT THEN. FROM WHAT I'VE SEEN, HE'S THEIR NASTIEST SERVER.
RIGHT WHEN KARASUNO'S OFFENSE IS AT ITS LOWEST POINT...
...KAMOMEDAI WILL HAVE ITS STRONGEST OFFENSIVE ROTATION IN POSITION TO TRY TO GRAB BACK-TO-BACK POINTS!
NOW WHAT'S KARASUNO DOING...?
IT LOOKS LIKE THEY'RE STAYING WITH THE S1 START THEY HAD IN SET 1...
!
NO, WAIT A MINUTE ...
*AN S1 START IS WHEN THE SETTER BEGINS IN THE BACK ROW, IN THE SERVER POSITION.

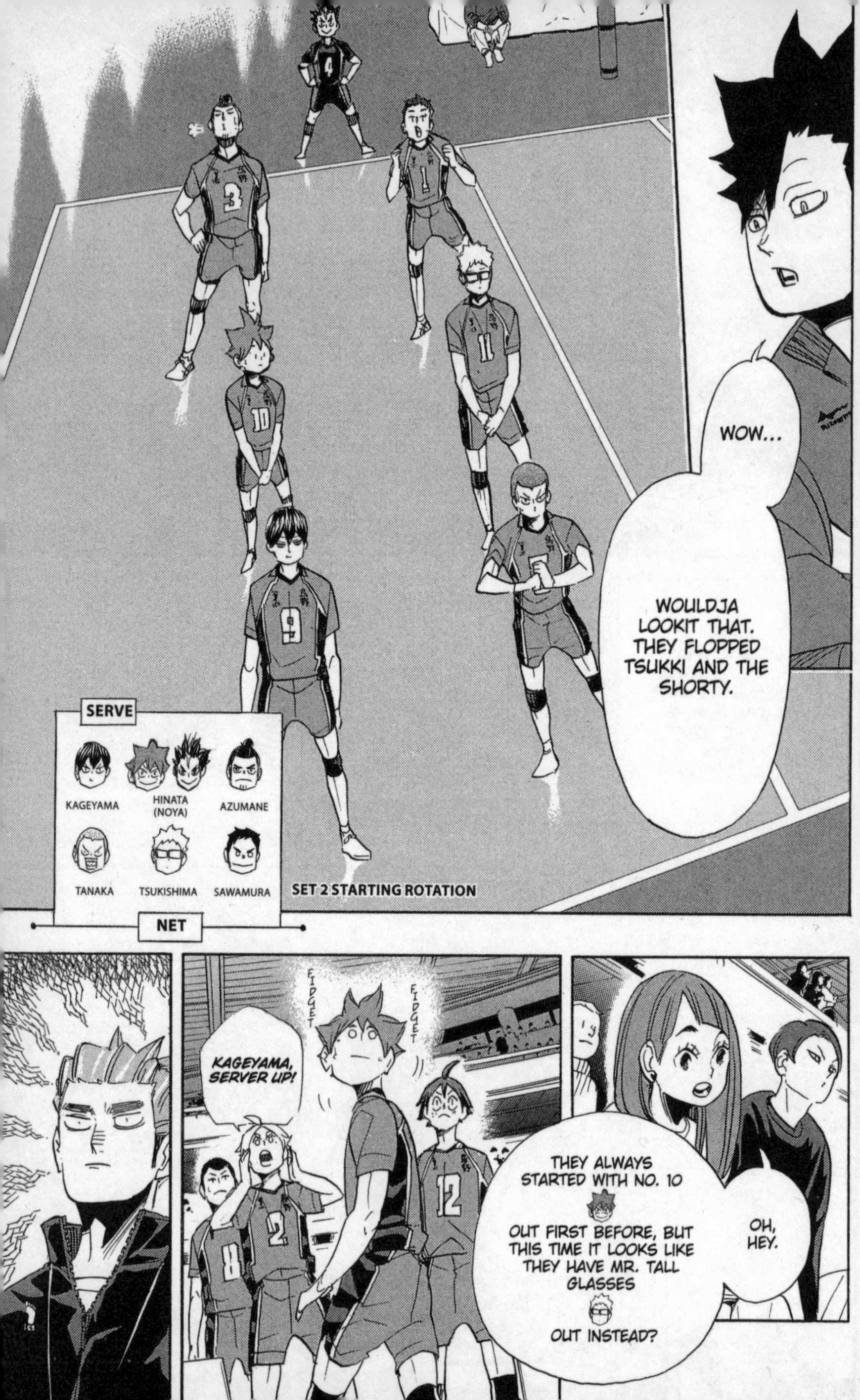
WOW...
WOULDJA LOOKIT THAT. THEY FLOPPED TSUKKI AND THE SHORTY.
SERVE
KAGEYAMA
HINATA (NOYA)
AZUMANE
TANAKA
TSUKISHIMA
SAWAMURA
NET
SET 2 STARTING ROTATION
OH, HEY.
THEY ALWAYS STARTED WITH NO. 10 OUT FIRST BEFORE, BUT THIS TIME IT LOOKS LIKE THEY HAVE MR. TALL GLASSES OUT INSTEAD?
FIDGET
FIDGET
KAGEYAMA, SERVER UP!

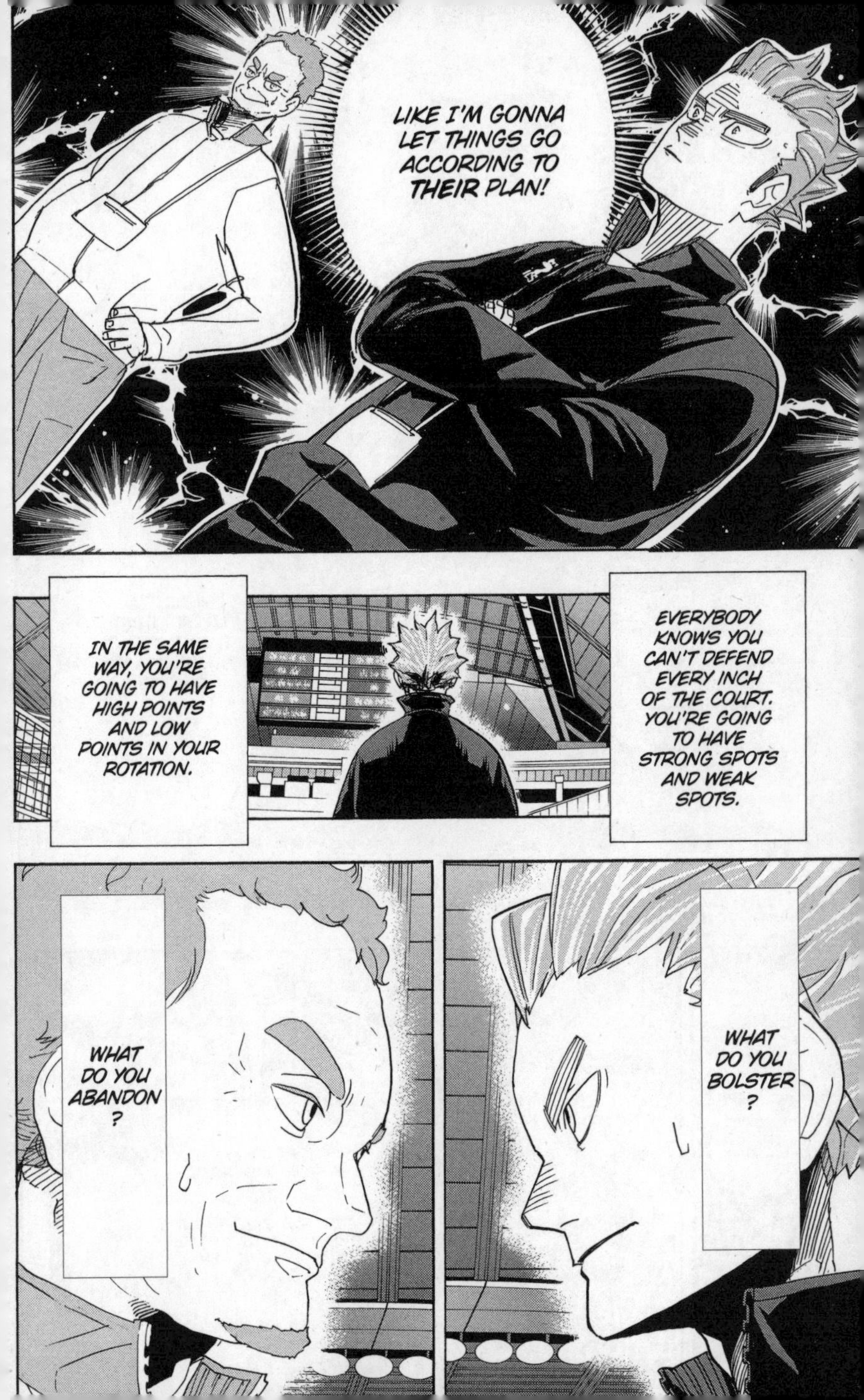
LIKE I'M GONNA LET THINGS GO ACCORDING TO THEIR PLAN!
EVERYBODY KNOWS YOU CAN'T DEFEND EVERY INCH OF THE COURT. YOU'RE GOING TO HAVE STRONG SPOTS AND WEAK SPOTS.
IN THE SAME WAY, YOU'RE GOING TO HAVE HIGH POINTS AND LOW POINTS IN YOUR ROTATION.
WHAT DO YOU BOLSTER?
WHAT DO YOU ABANDON?

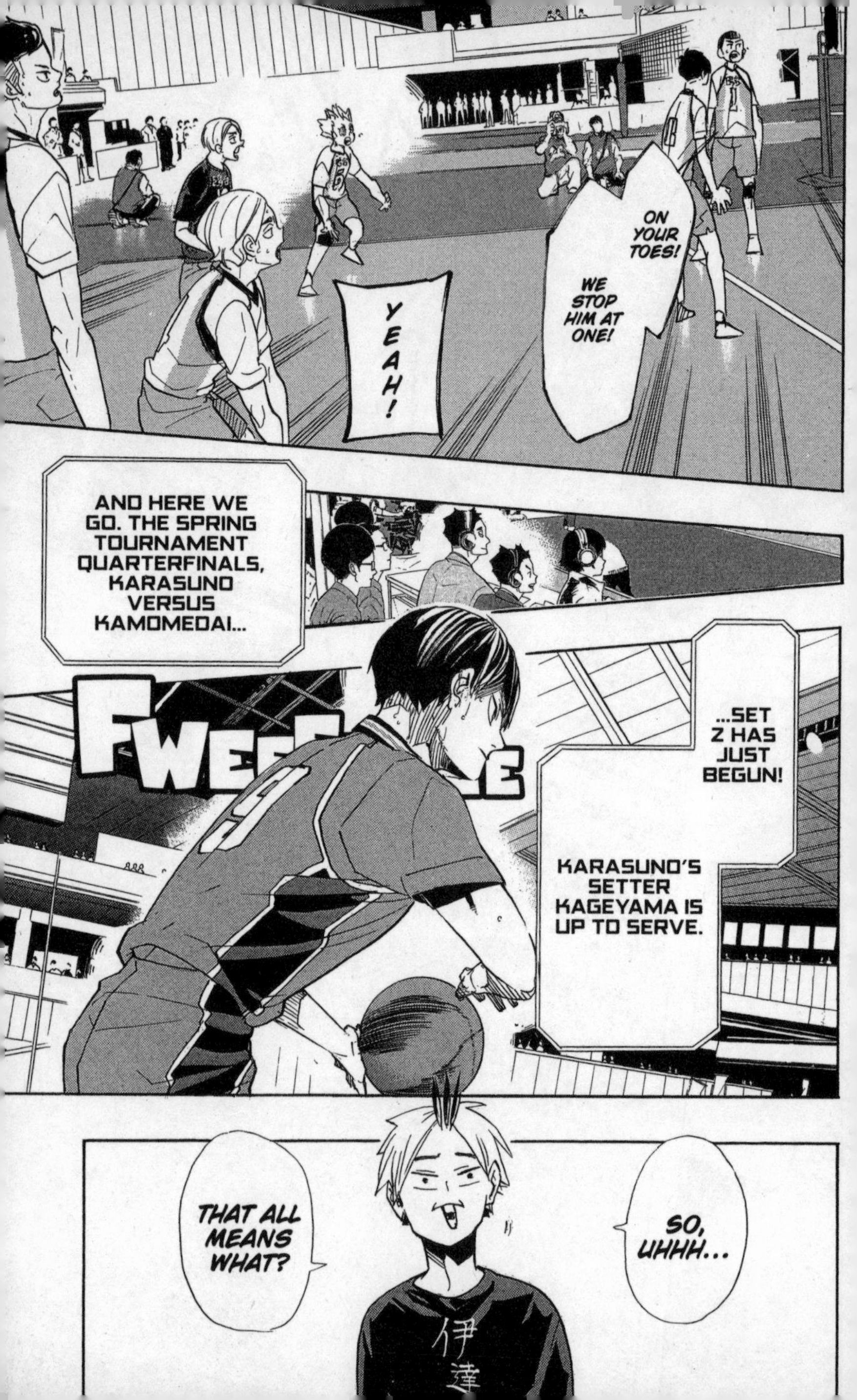
ON YOUR TOES!
WE STOP HIM AT ONE!
YEAH!
AND HERE WE GO. THE SPRING TOURNAMENT QUARTERFINALS, KARASUNO VERSUS KAMOMEDAI...
...SET 2 HAS JUST BEGUN!
KARASUNO'S SETTER KAGEYAMA IS UP TO SERVE.
SO, UHHH...
THAT ALL MEANS WHAT?

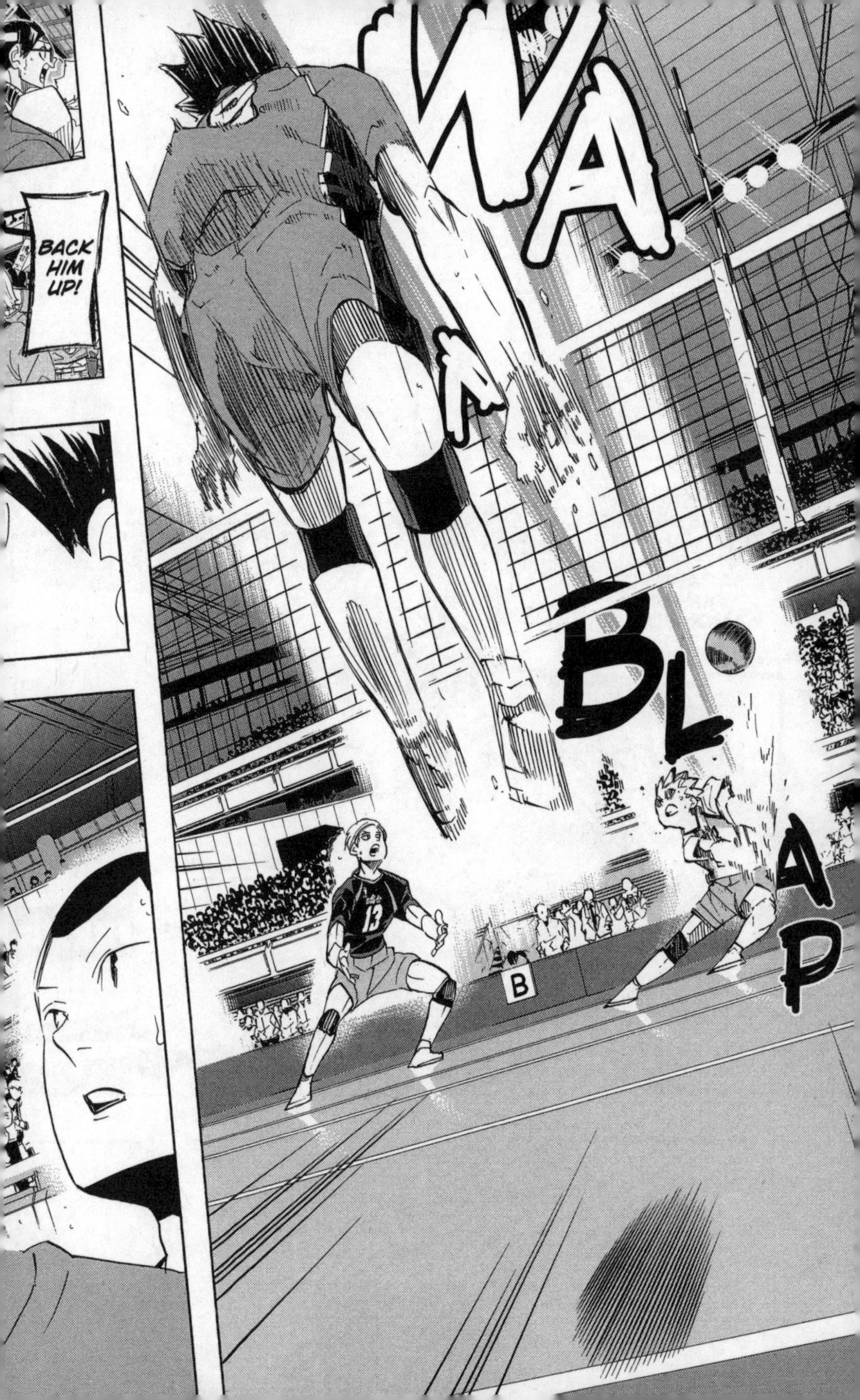
WA
BACK HIM UP!
BLAP
B
13

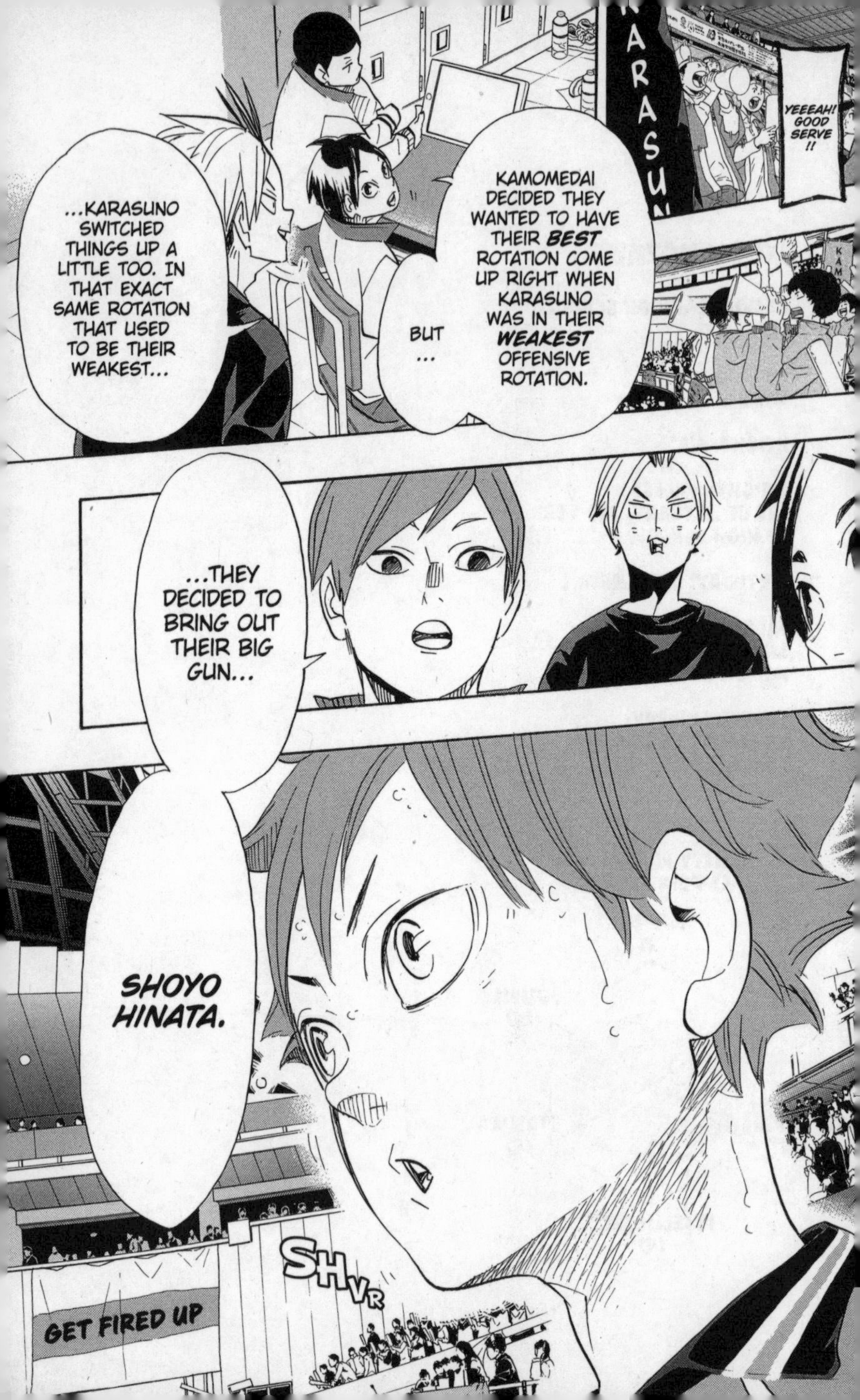
YEEEAH! GOOD SERVE !!
KAMOMEDAI DECIDED THEY WANTED TO HAVE THEIR **BEST** ROTATION COME UP RIGHT WHEN KARASUNO WAS IN THEIR ***WEAKEST*** OFFENSIVE ROTATION.
BUT ...
...KARASUNO SWITCHED THINGS UP A LITTLE TOO. IN THAT EXACT SAME ROTATION THAT USED TO BE THEIR WEAKEST...
...THEY DECIDED TO BRING OUT THEIR BIG GUN...
SHOYO HINATA.
SHVR
GET FIRED UP

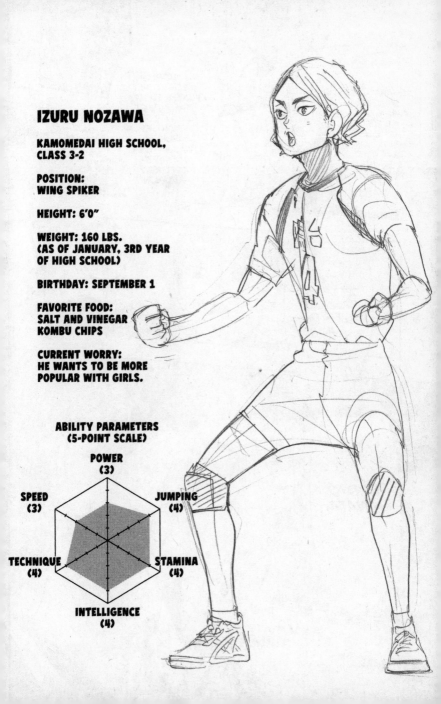

IZURU NOZAWA

KAMOMEDAI HIGH SCHOOL,
CLASS 3-2

POSITION:
WING SPIKER

HEIGHT: 6'0"

WEIGHT: 160 LBS.
(AS OF JANUARY, 3RD YEAR
OF HIGH SCHOOL)

BIRTHDAY: SEPTEMBER 1

FAVORITE FOOD:
SALT AND VINEGAR
KOMBU CHIPS

CURRENT WORRY:
HE WANTS TO BE MORE
POPULAR WITH GIRLS.

ABILITY PARAMETERS
(5-POINT SCALE)

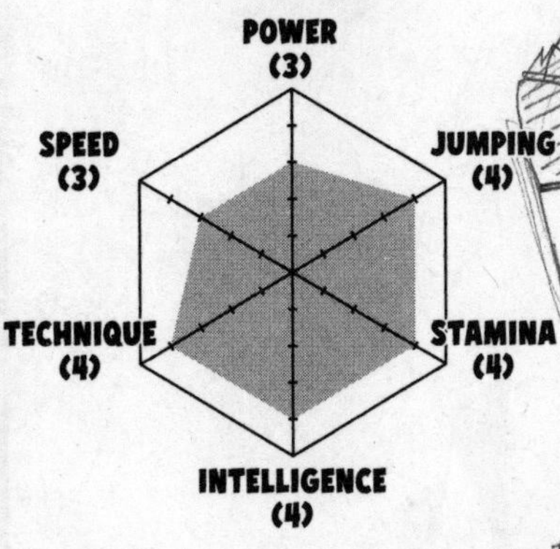
POWER (3)
JUMPING (4)
STAMINA (4)
INTELLIGENCE (4)
TECHNIQUE (4)
SPEED (3)

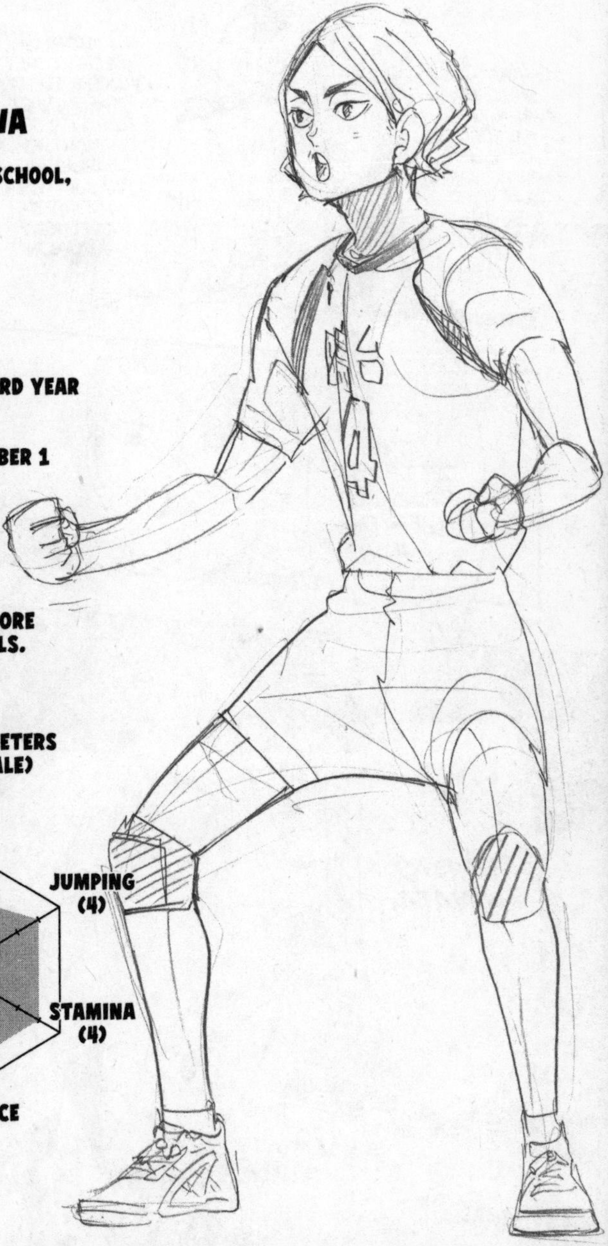

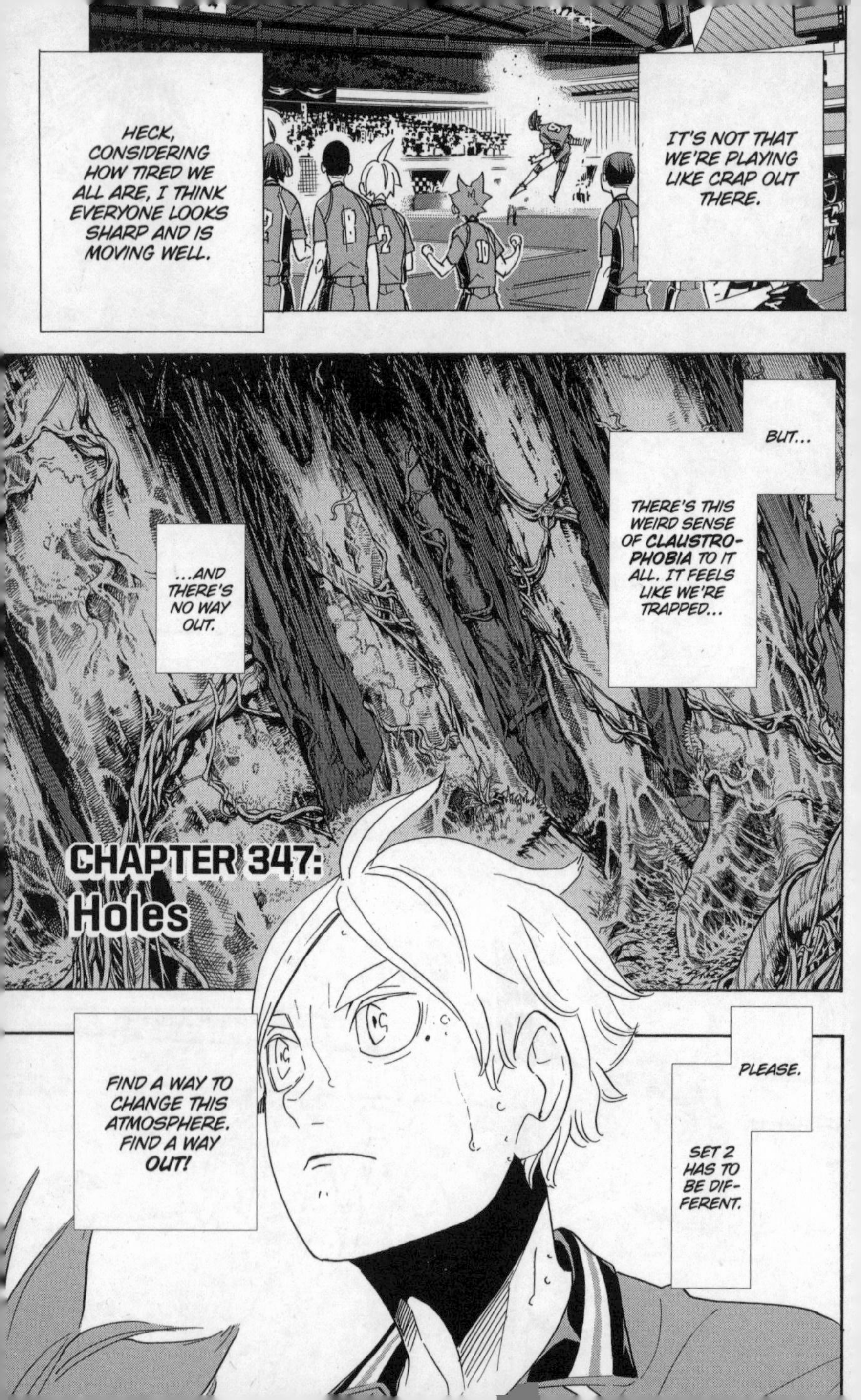
IT'S NOT THAT WE'RE PLAYING LIKE CRAP OUT THERE.
HECK, CONSIDERING HOW TIRED WE ALL ARE, I THINK EVERYONE LOOKS SHARP AND IS MOVING WELL.
BUT...
THERE'S THIS WEIRD SENSE OF CLAUSTROPHOBIA TO IT ALL. IT FEELS LIKE WE'RE TRAPPED...
...AND THERE'S NO WAY OUT.
CHAPTER 347:
Holes
PLEASE.
SET 2 HAS TO BE DIFFERENT.
FIND A WAY TO CHANGE THIS ATMOSPHERE. FIND A WAY OUT!

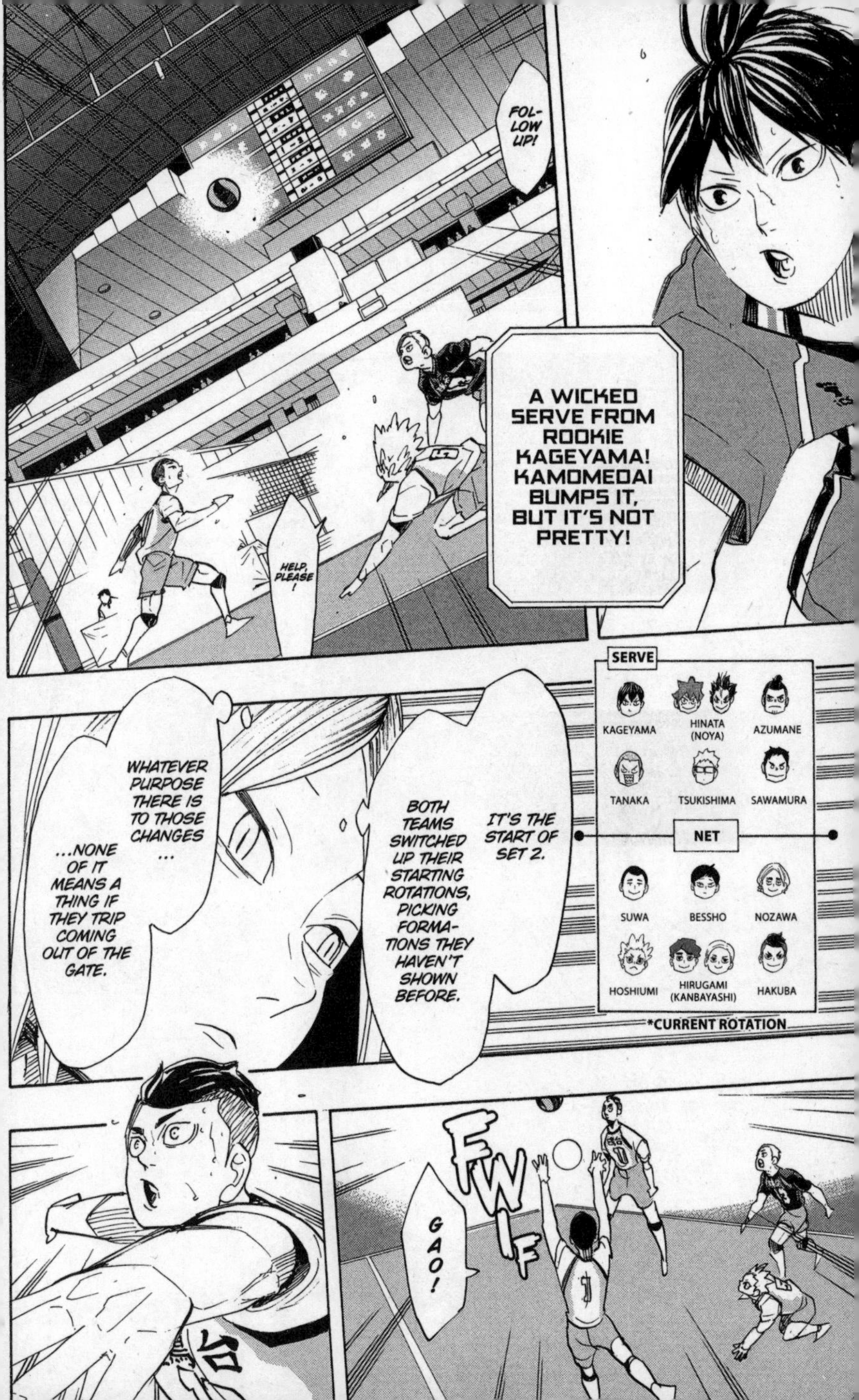
FOL-LOW UP!
A WICKED SERVE FROM ROOKIE KAGEYAMA! KAMOMEDAI BUMPS IT, BUT IT'S NOT PRETTY!
HELP, PLEASE!
SERVE
KAGEYAMA
HINATA (NOYA)
AZUMANE
TANAKA
TSUKISHIMA
SAWAMURA
NET
SUWA
BESSHO
NOZAWA
HOSHIUMI
HIRUGAMI (KANBAYASHI)
HAKUBA
*CURRENT ROTATION
IT'S THE START OF SET 2.
BOTH TEAMS SWITCHED UP THEIR STARTING ROTATIONS, PICKING FORMATIONS THEY HAVEN'T SHOWN BEFORE.
WHATEVER PURPOSE THERE IS TO THOSE CHANGES ...
...NONE OF IT MEANS A THING IF THEY TRIP COMING OUT OF THE GATE.
FWIF
GAO!

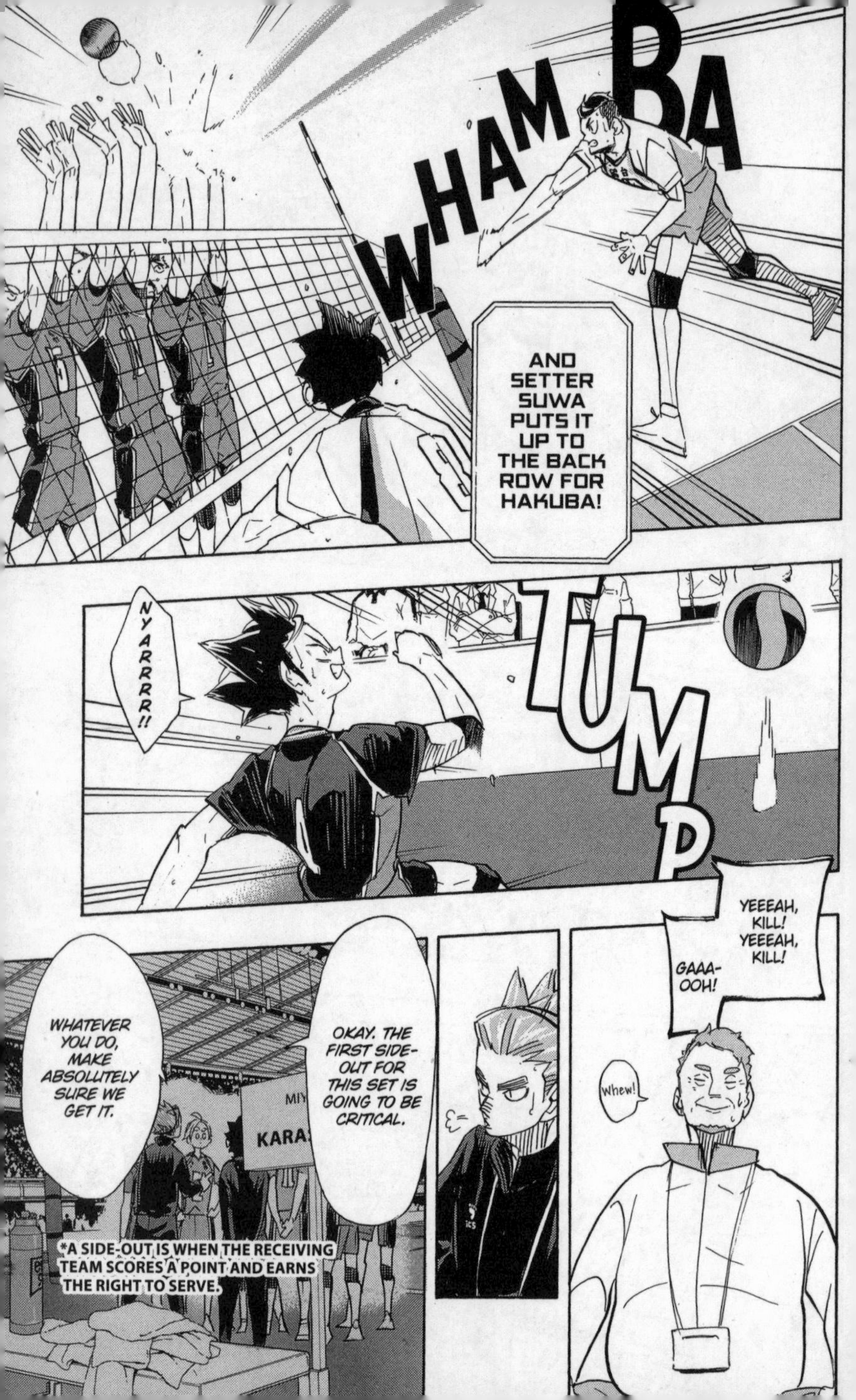
WHAM
BA
AND SETTER SUWA PUTS IT UP TO THE BACK ROW FOR HAKUBA!
TUMP
NYARRRR!!
YEEEAH, KILL! YEEEAH, KILL!
GAAA-OOH!
Whew!
OKAY. THE FIRST SIDE-OUT FOR THIS SET IS GOING TO BE CRITICAL.
WHATEVER YOU DO, MAKE ABSOLUTELY SURE WE GET IT.
*A SIDE-OUT IS WHEN THE RECEIVING TEAM SCORES A POINT AND EARNS THE RIGHT TO SERVE.

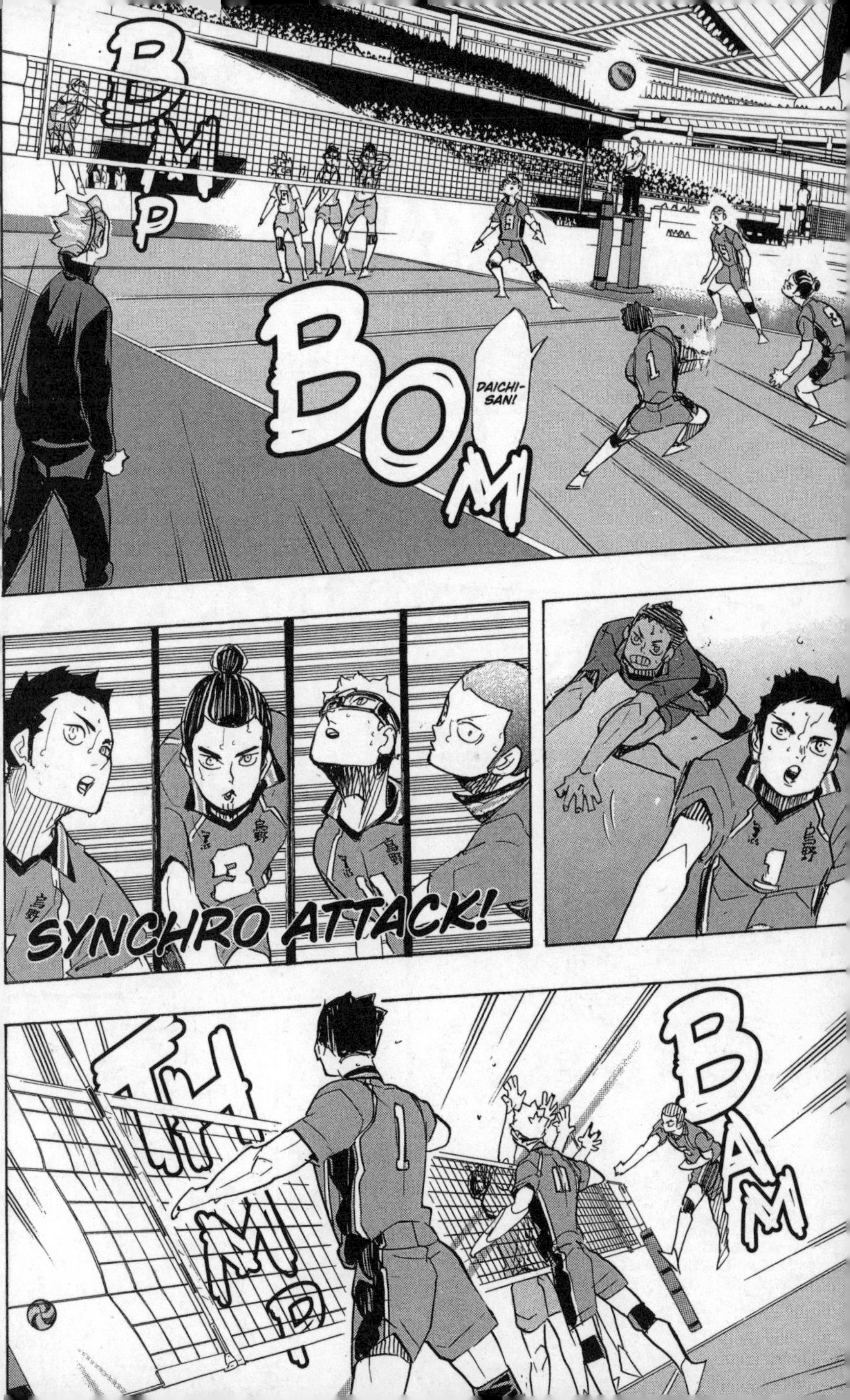
DAICHI-SAN!
BOOM
BUMP
SYNCHRO ATTACK!
BAM
THUMP

*CURRENT ROTATION

SERVE

TANAKA • KAGEYAMA • HINATA (NOYA)

TSUKISHIMA • SAWAMURA • AZUMANE

NET

HOSHIUMI • HAKUBA • BESSHO

HIRUGAMI (KANBAYASHI) • SUWA • NOZAWA

YES!

KARASUNO	KAMOMEDAI
1	1

THAT WAS NOT A CLEAN SET IN ANY SENSE, BUT HOSHIUMI STILL HIT IT WITH ALL HE HAD AND MADE IT COUNT!

SORRY!

SHAKE IT OFF!

KARASUNO	KAMOMEDAI
1	2

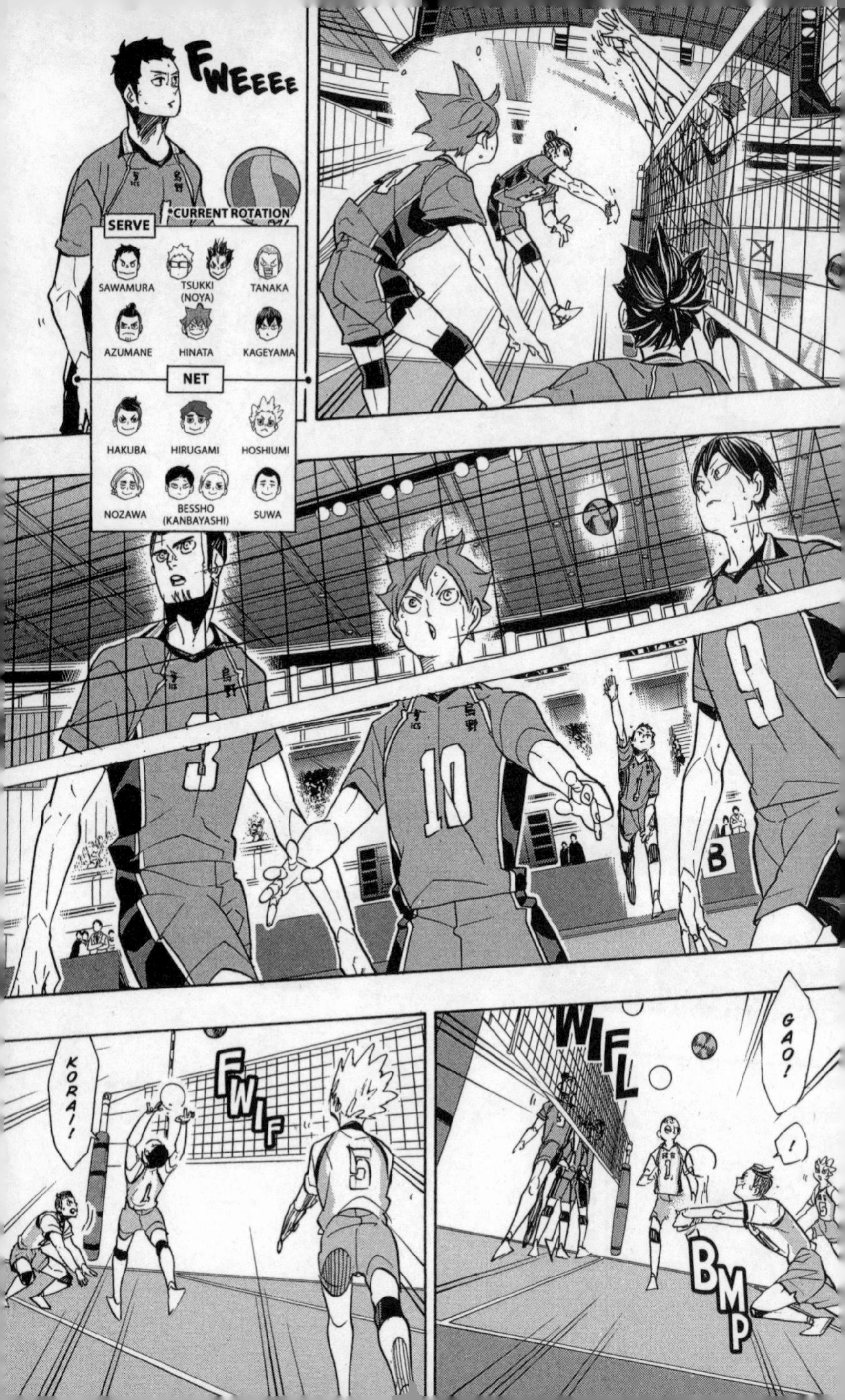
FWEEEE
*CURRENT ROTATION
SERVE
SAWAMURA
TSUKKI (NOYA)
TANAKA
AZUMANE
HINATA
KAGEYAMA
NET
HAKUBA
HIRUGAMI
HOSHIUMI
NOZAWA
BESSHO (KANBAYASHI)
SUWA
WIFL
GAO!
!
BMP
KORAI!
FWIF

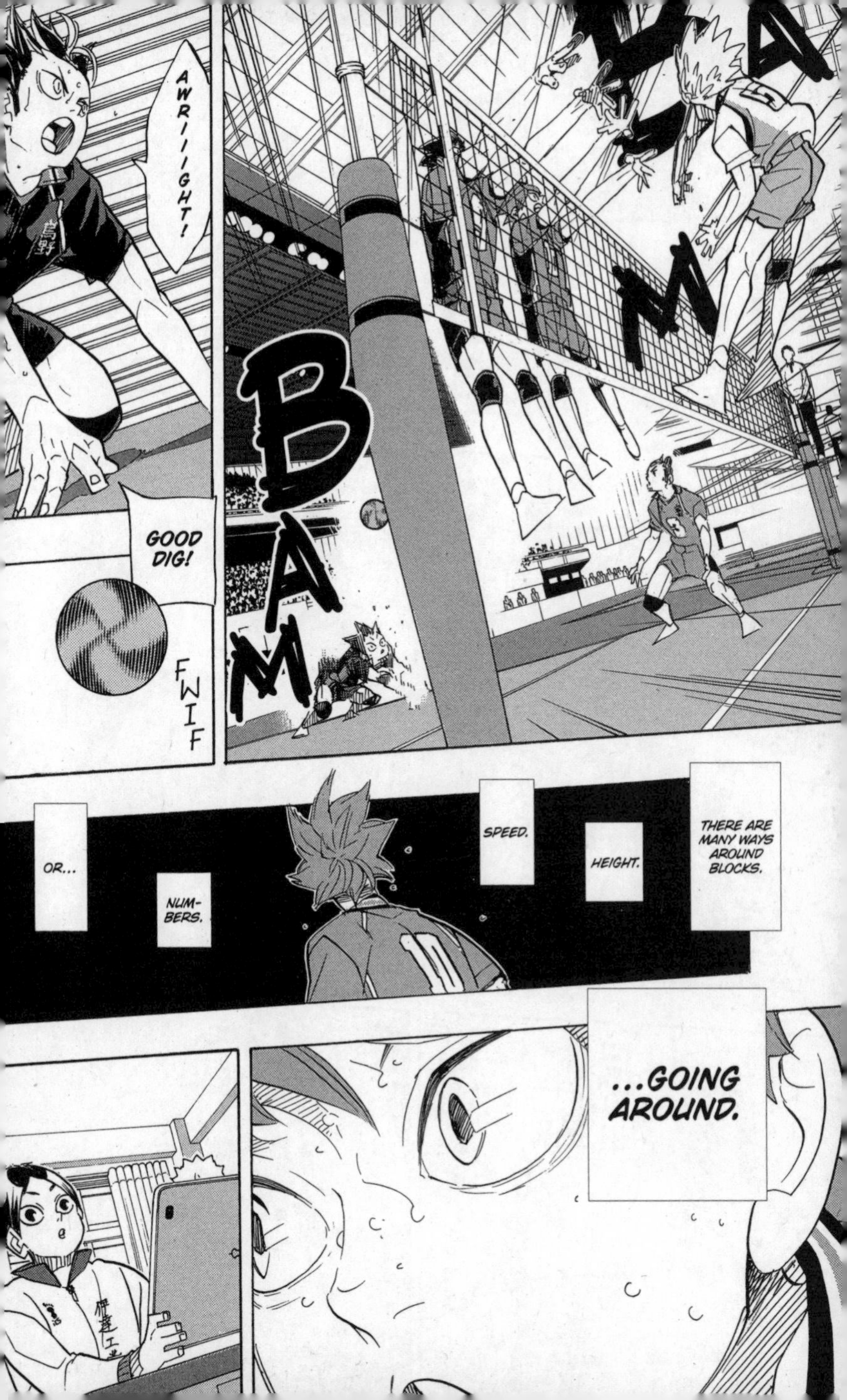
BAM
AWRIIIGHT!
GOOD DIG!
FWIF
THERE ARE MANY WAYS AROUND BLOCKS.
HEIGHT.
SPEED.
NUMBERS.
OR...
...GOING AROUND.

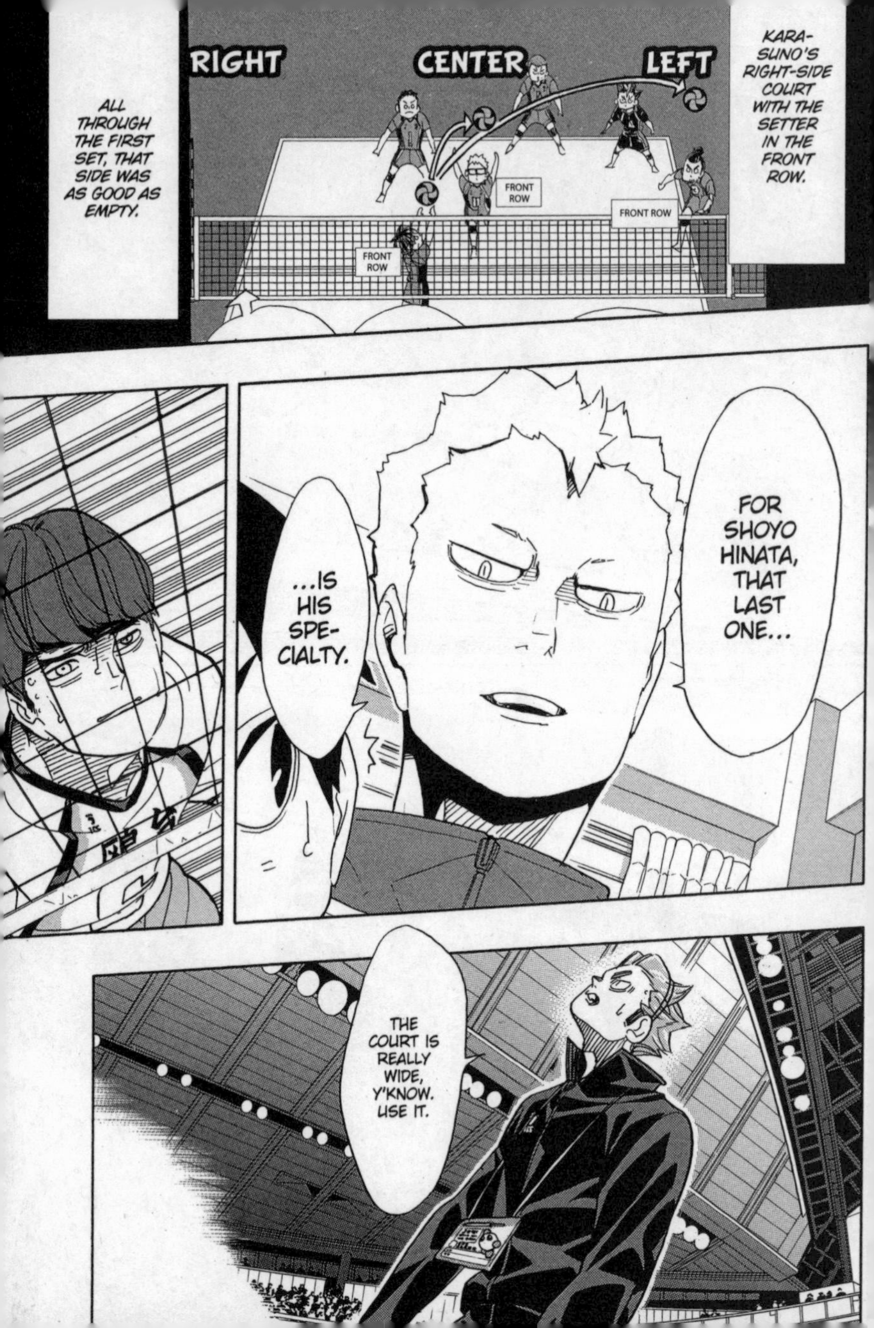
KARA-SUNO'S RIGHT-SIDE COURT WITH THE SETTER IN THE FRONT ROW.
LEFT
CENTER
RIGHT
FRONT ROW
FRONT ROW
FRONT ROW
ALL THROUGH THE FIRST SET, THAT SIDE WAS AS GOOD AS EMPTY.
FOR SHOYO HINATA, THAT LAST ONE...
...IS HIS SPECIALTY.
THE COURT IS REALLY WIDE, Y'KNOW. USE IT.

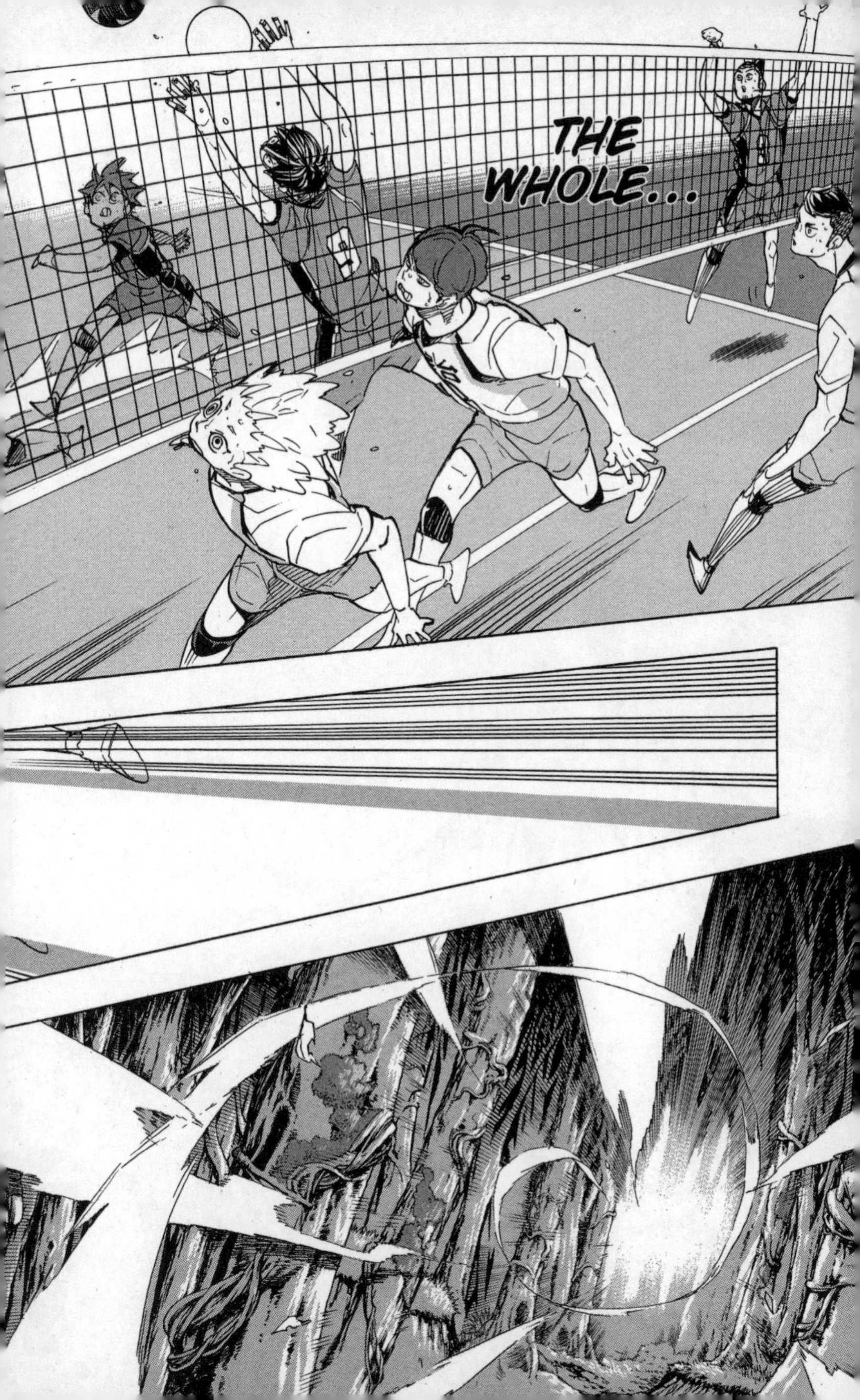
THE WHOLE...

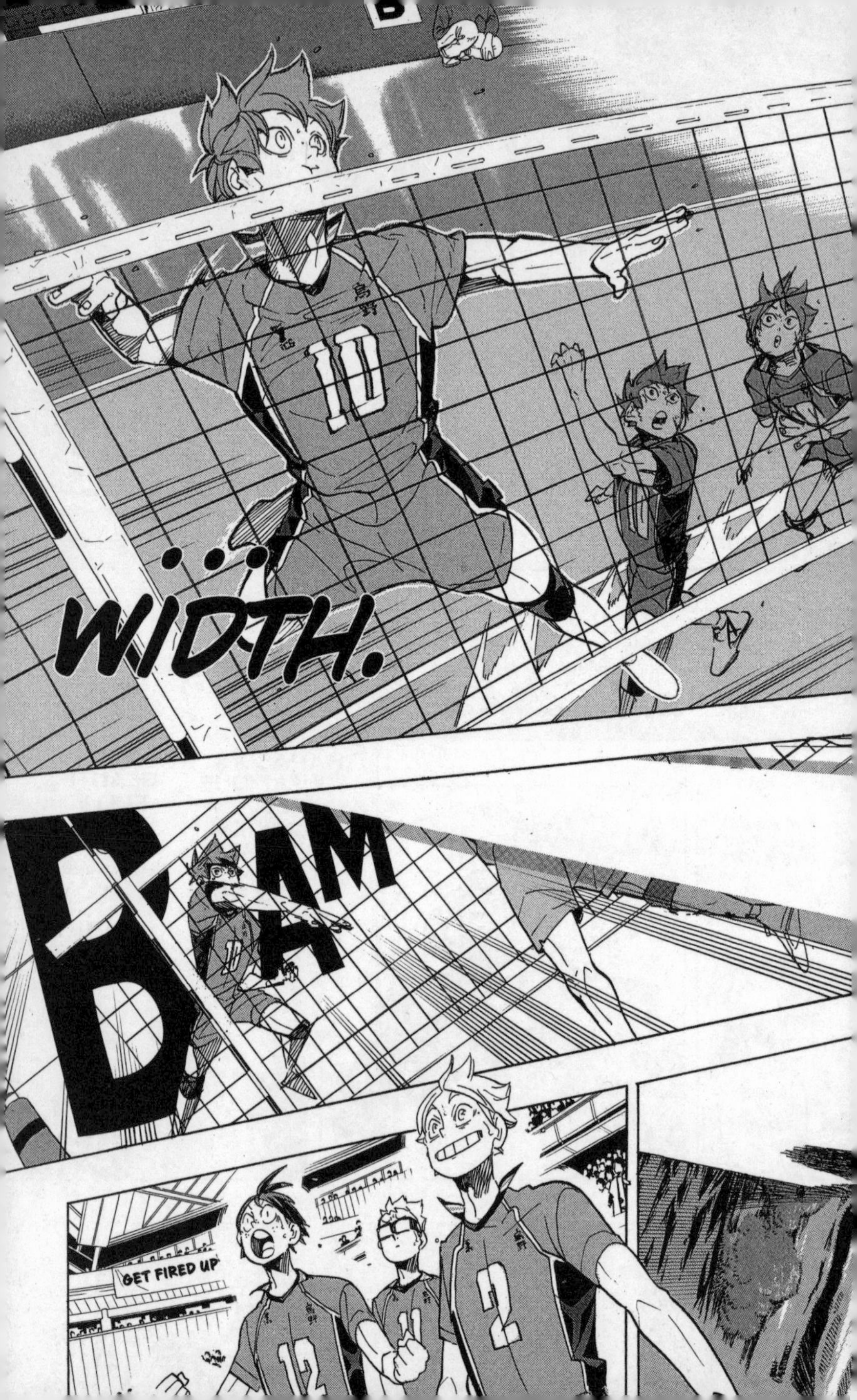

...WIDTH.
BAM
GET FIRED UP

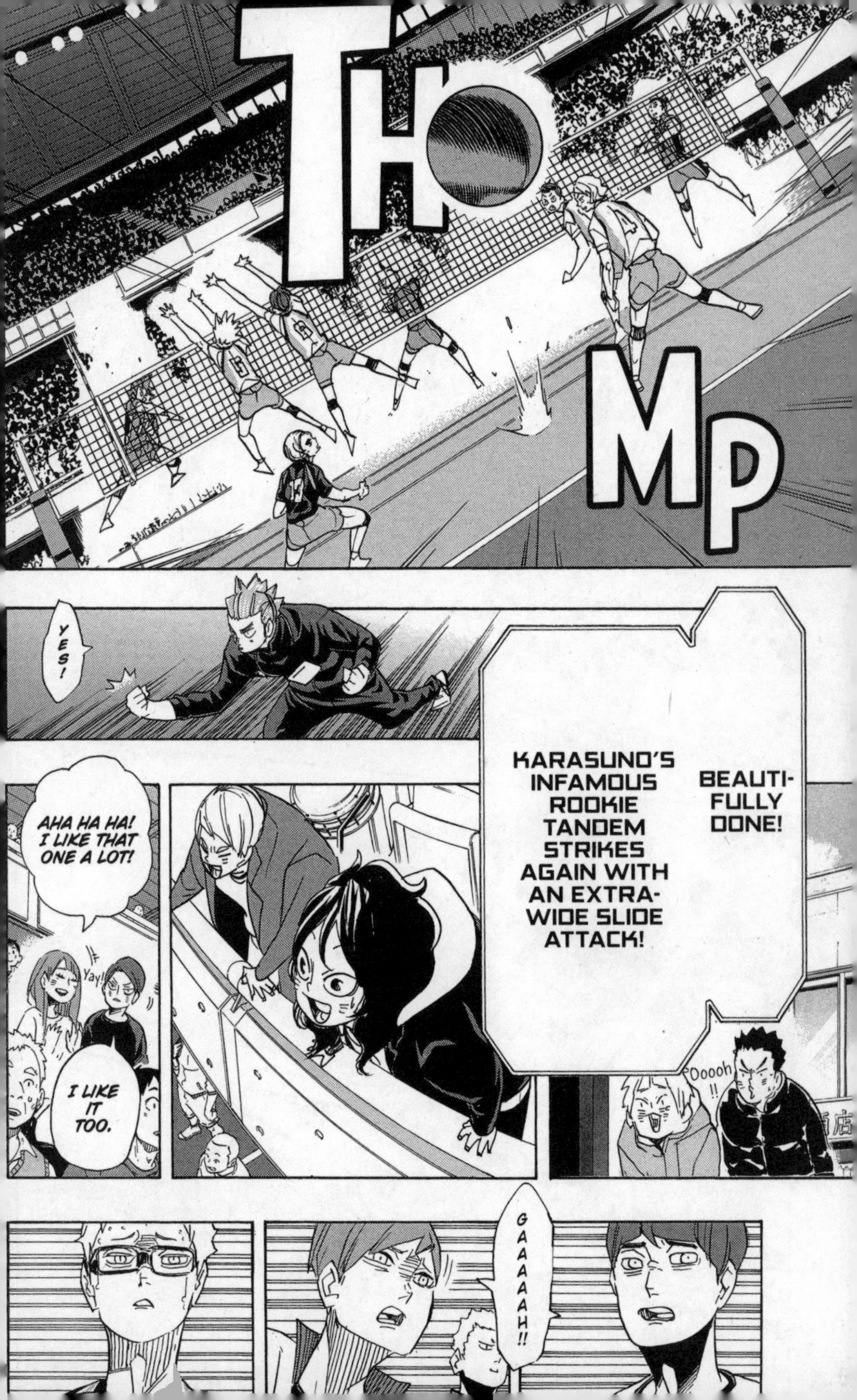
THOMP
YES!
KARASUNO'S INFAMOUS ROOKIE TANDEM STRIKES AGAIN WITH AN EXTRA-WIDE SLIDE ATTACK!
BEAUTIFULLY DONE!
Ooooh!!
AHA HA HA! I LIKE THAT ONE A LOT!
Yay!
I LIKE IT TOO.
GAAAAAAH!!

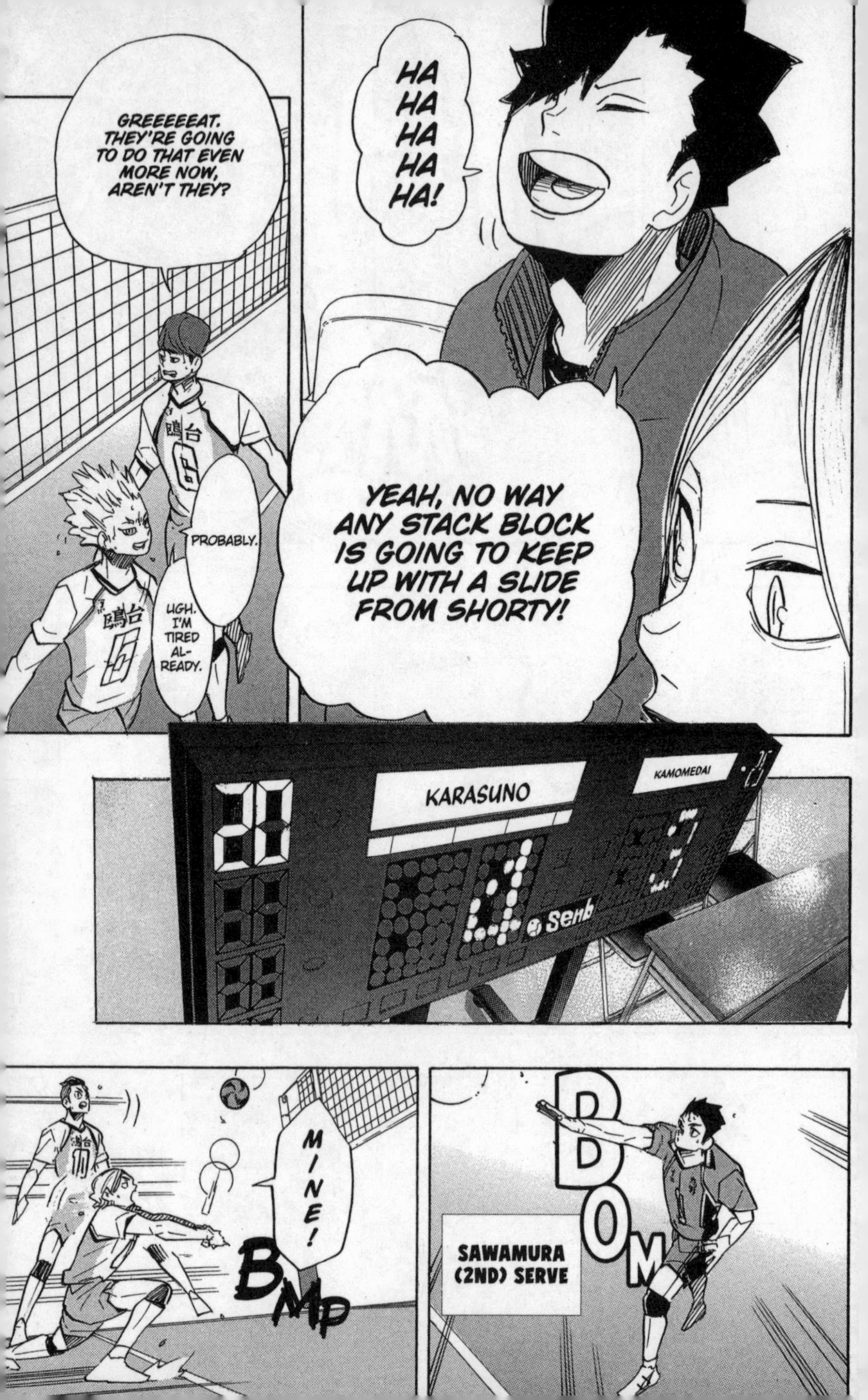
HA HA HA HA HA!
YEAH, NO WAY ANY STACK BLOCK IS GOING TO KEEP UP WITH A SLIDE FROM SHORTY!
GREEEEEAT. THEY'RE GOING TO DO THAT EVEN MORE NOW, AREN'T THEY?
PROBABLY.
UGH. I'M TIRED AL-READY.
KARASUNO
KAMOMEDAI
Senb
BDOM
SAWAMURA (2ND) SERVE
MINE!
BMP

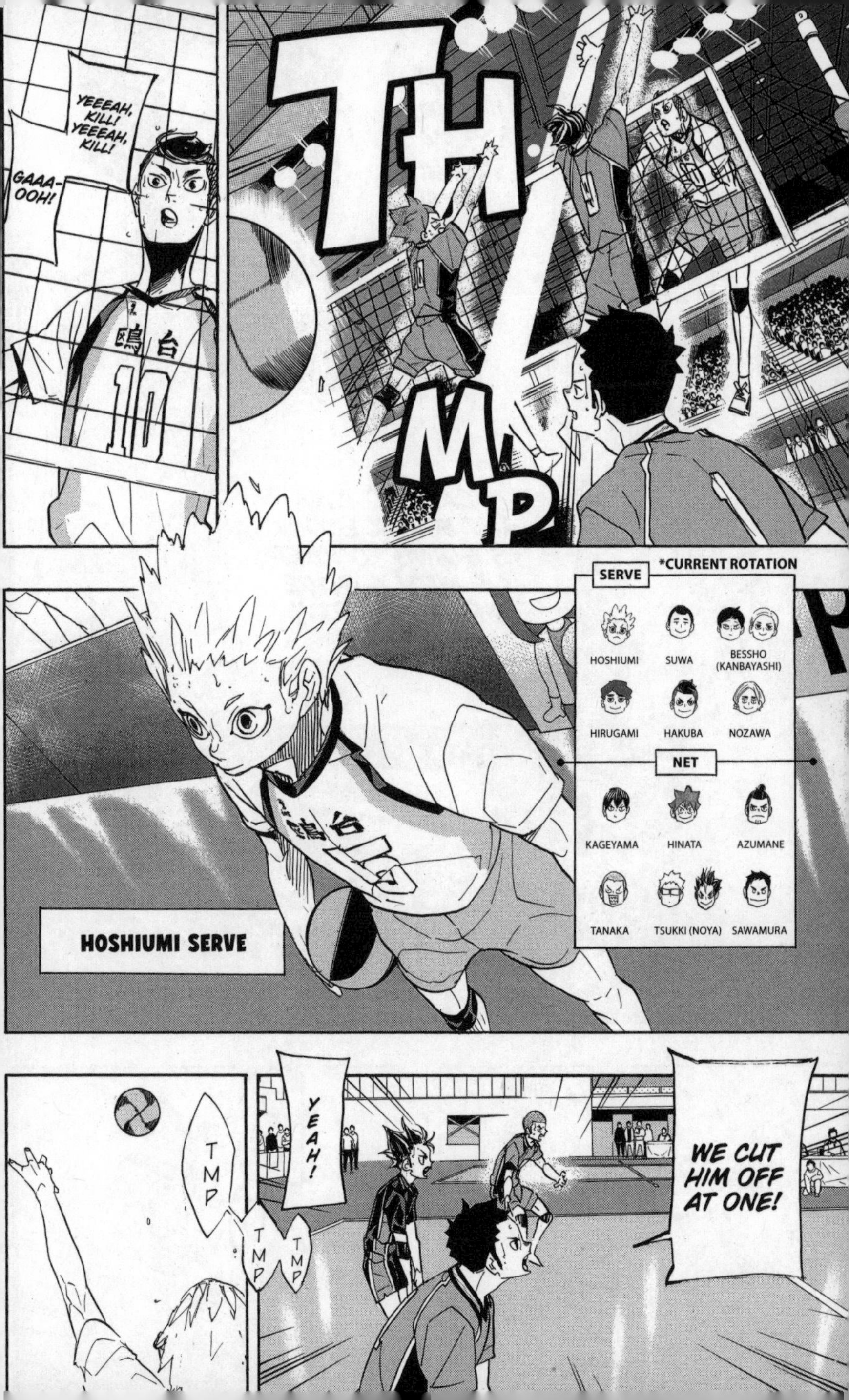
THMP
YEEEAH, KILL! YEEEAH, KILL!
GAAA-OOH!
*CURRENT ROTATION
SERVE
HOSHIUMI
SUWA
BESSHO (KANBAYASHI)
HIRUGAMI
HAKUBA
NOZAWA
NET
KAGEYAMA
HINATA
AZUMANE
TANAKA
TSUKKI (NOYA)
SAWAMURA
HOSHIUMI SERVE
WE CUT HIM OFF AT ONE!
YEAH!
TMP
TMP
TMP
TMP

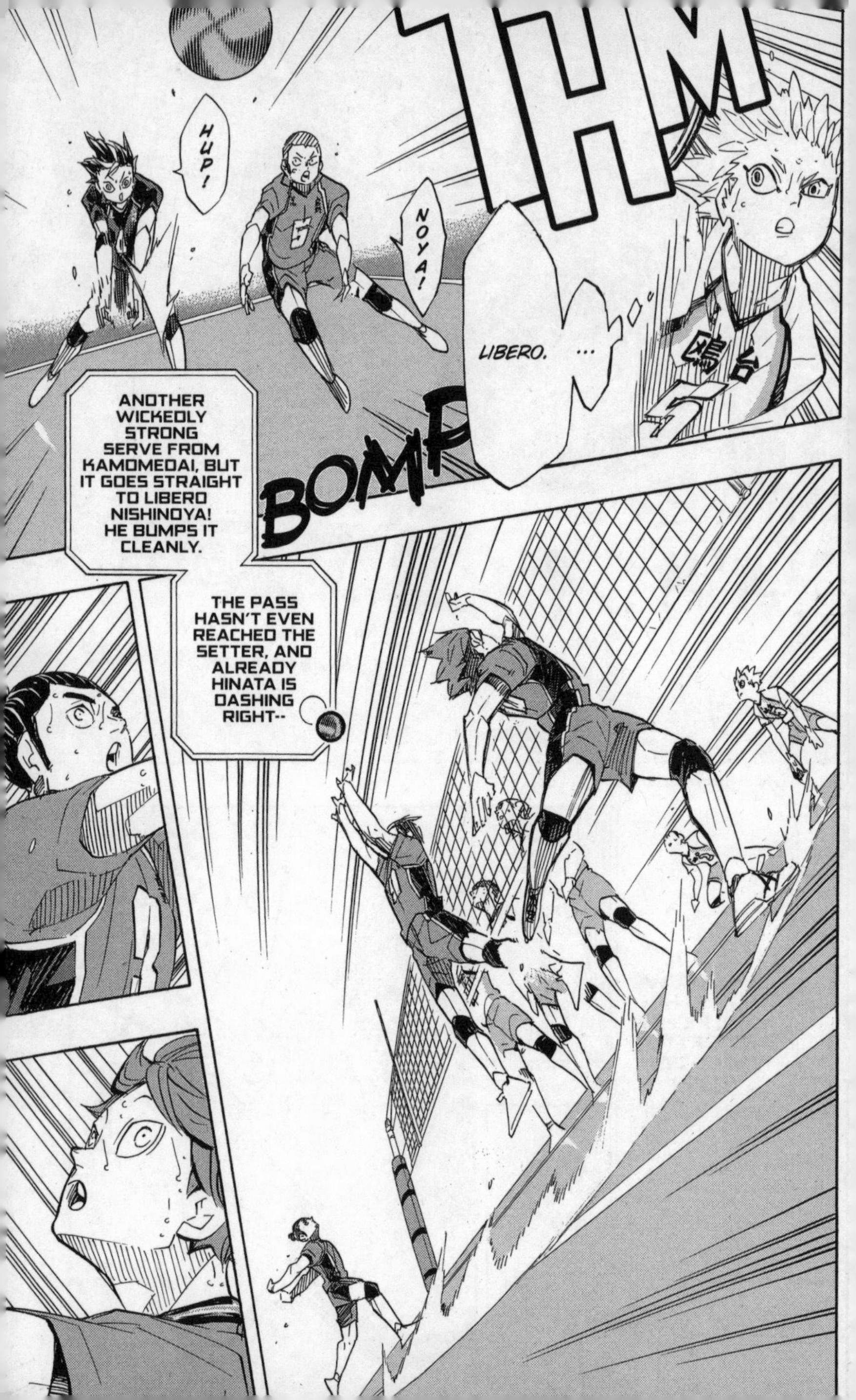
THM
LIBERO. ...
NOYA!
HUP!
BOMP
ANOTHER WICKEDLY STRONG SERVE FROM KAMOMEDAI, BUT IT GOES STRAIGHT TO LIBERO NISHINOYA! HE BUMPS IT CLEANLY.
THE PASS HASN'T EVEN REACHED THE SETTER, AND ALREADY HINATA IS DASHING RIGHT--

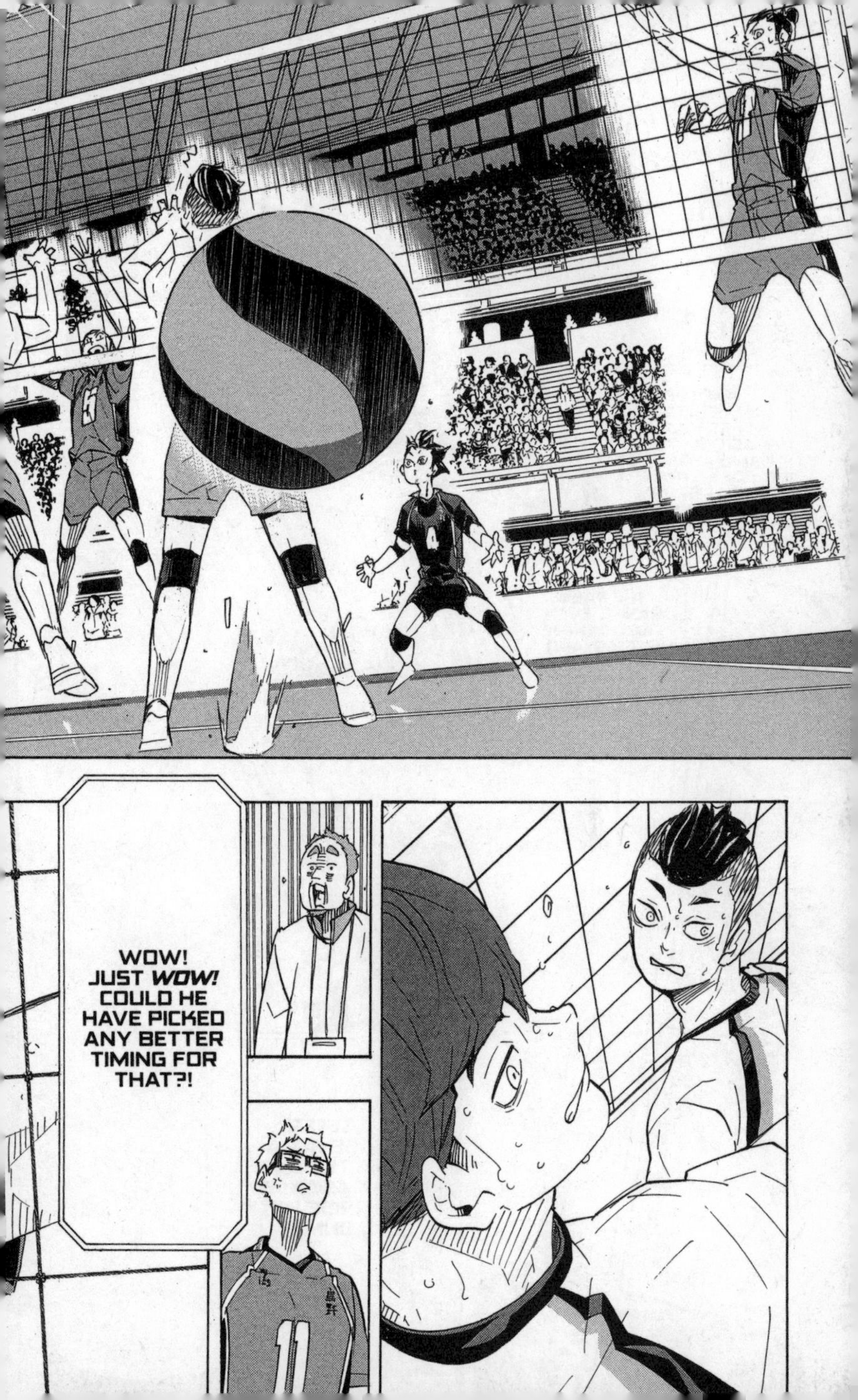
WOW! JUST WOW! COULD HE HAVE PICKED ANY BETTER TIMING FOR THAT?!

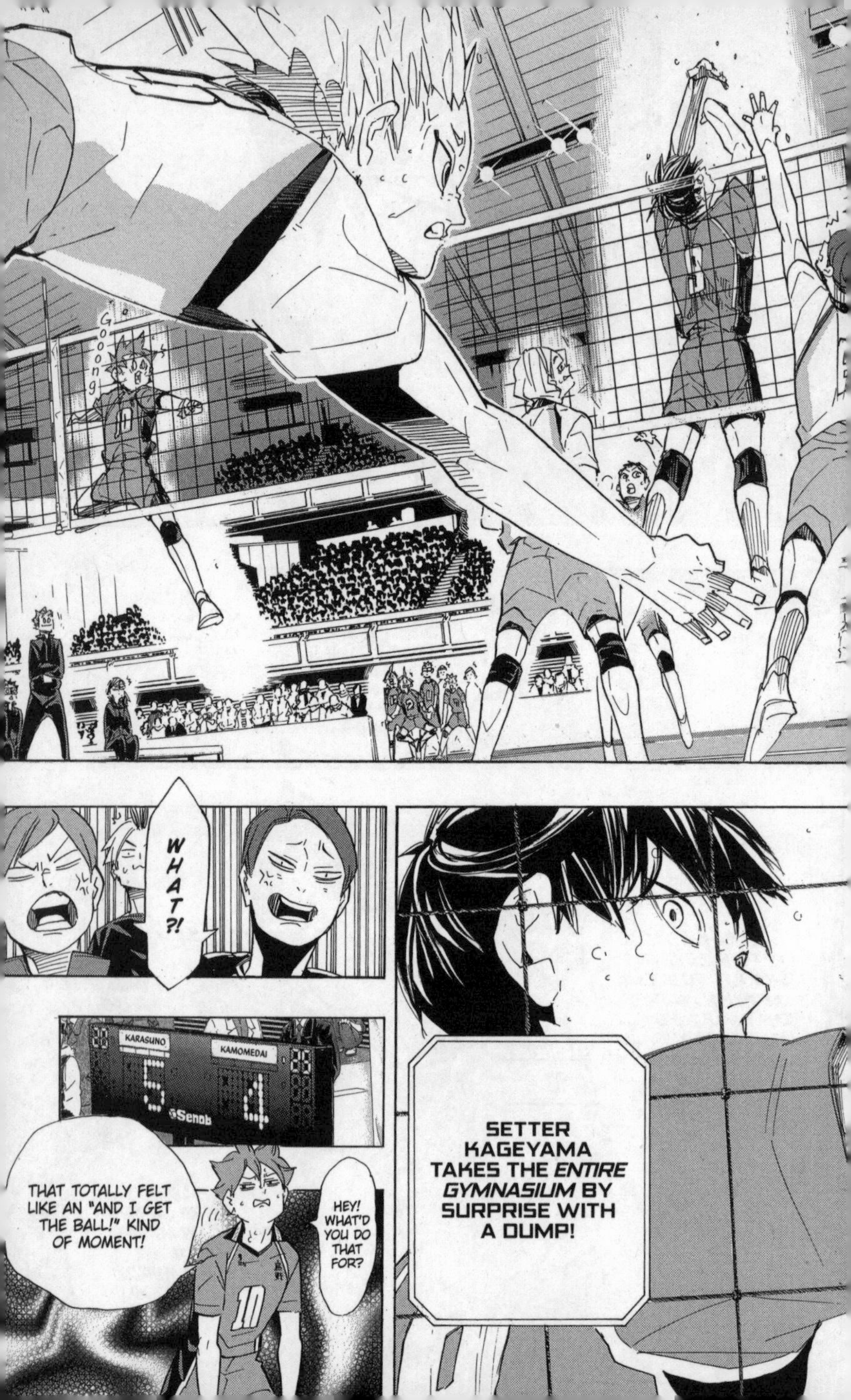
Goooong
SETTER KAGEYAMA TAKES THE *ENTIRE GYMNASIUM* BY SURPRISE WITH A DUMP!
WHAT?!
KARASUNO
KAMOMEDAI
HEY! WHAT'D YOU DO THAT FOR?
THAT TOTALLY FELT LIKE AN "AND I GET THE BALL!" KIND OF MOMENT!

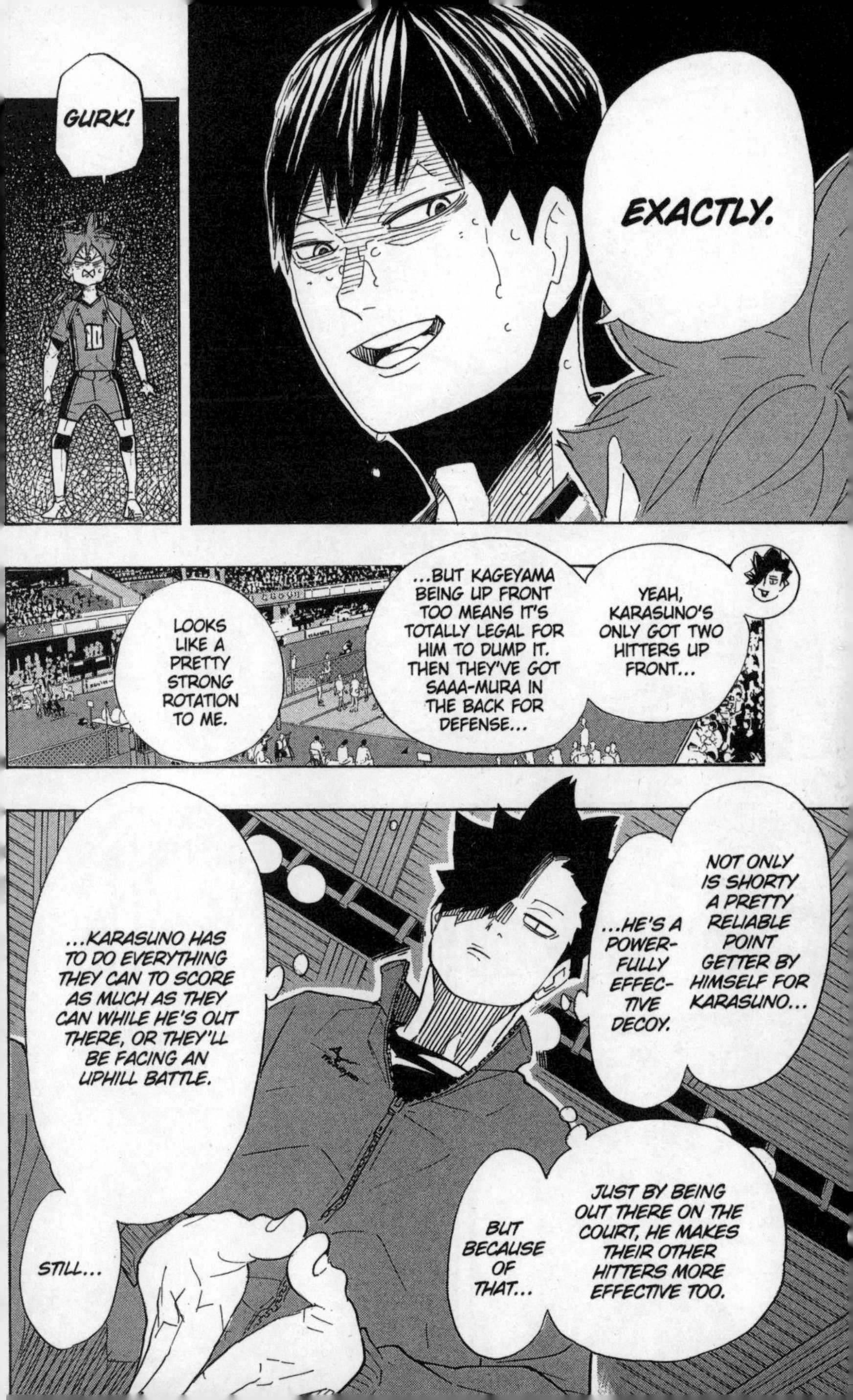
EXACTLY.
GURK!
YEAH, KARASUNO'S ONLY GOT TWO HITTERS UP FRONT...
...BUT KAGEYAMA BEING UP FRONT TOO MEANS IT'S TOTALLY LEGAL FOR HIM TO DUMP IT. THEN THEY'VE GOT SAAA-MURA IN THE BACK FOR DEFENSE...
LOOKS LIKE A PRETTY STRONG ROTATION TO ME.
NOT ONLY IS SHORTY A PRETTY RELIABLE POINT GETTER BY HIMSELF FOR KARASUNO...
...HE'S A POWER-FULLY EFFEC-TIVE DECOY.
JUST BY BEING OUT THERE ON THE COURT, HE MAKES THEIR OTHER HITTERS MORE EFFECTIVE TOO.
BUT BECAUSE OF THAT...
...KARASUNO HAS TO DO EVERYTHING THEY CAN TO SCORE AS MUCH AS THEY CAN WHILE HE'S OUT THERE, OR THEY'LL BE FACING AN UPHILL BATTLE.
STILL...

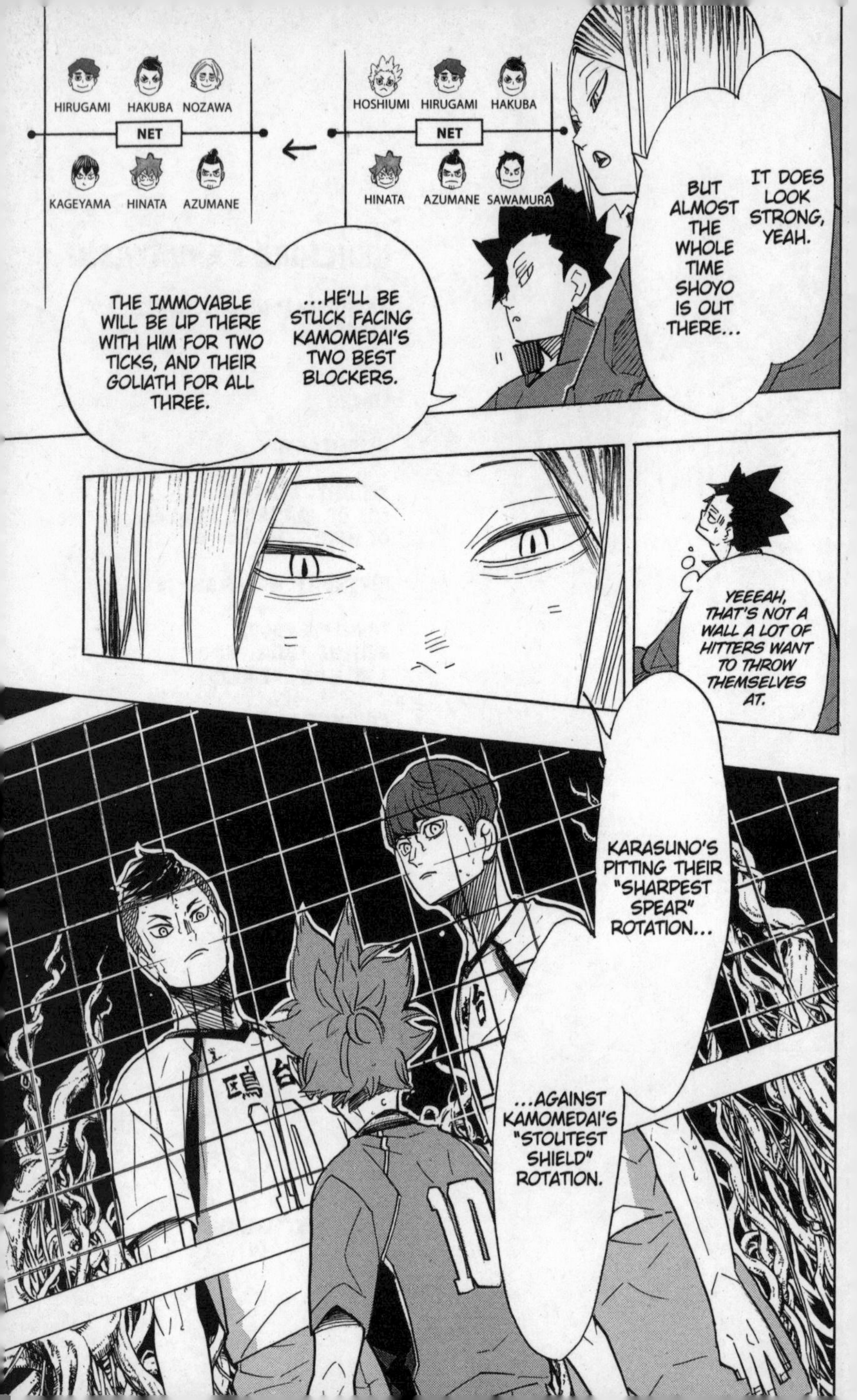
IT DOES LOOK STRONG, YEAH.
BUT ALMOST THE WHOLE TIME SHOYO IS OUT THERE...
HOSHIUMI HIRUGAMI HAKUBA
NET
HINATA AZUMANE SAWAMURA
HIRUGAMI HAKUBA NOZAWA
NET
KAGEYAMA HINATA AZUMANE
...HE'LL BE STUCK FACING KAMOMEDAI'S TWO BEST BLOCKERS.
THE IMMOVABLE WILL BE UP THERE WITH HIM FOR TWO TICKS, AND THEIR GOLIATH FOR ALL THREE.
YEEEAH, THAT'S NOT A WALL A LOT OF HITTERS WANT TO THROW THEMSELVES AT.
KARASUNO'S PITTING THEIR "SHARPEST SPEAR" ROTATION...
...AGAINST KAMOMEDAI'S "STOUTEST SHIELD" ROTATION.

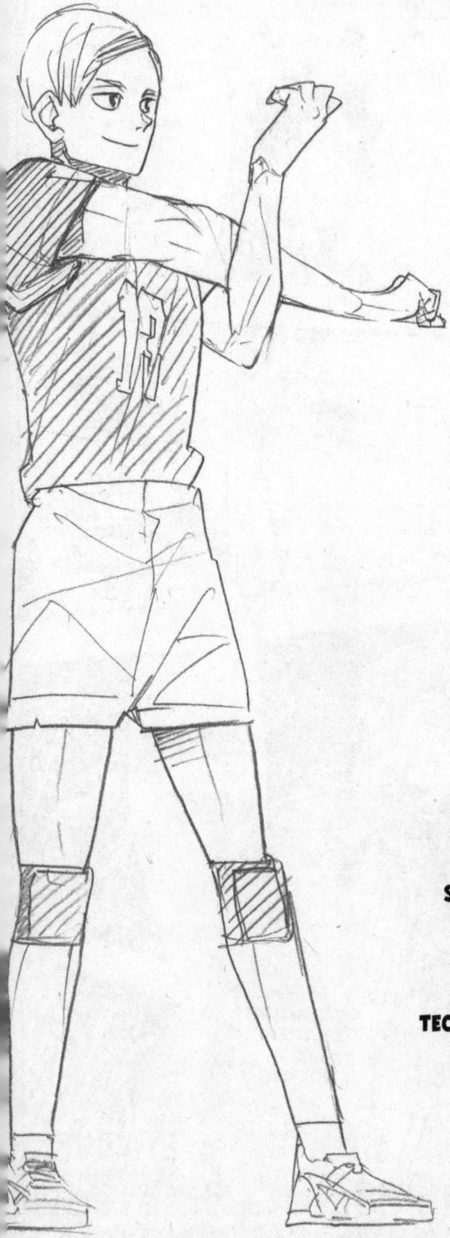

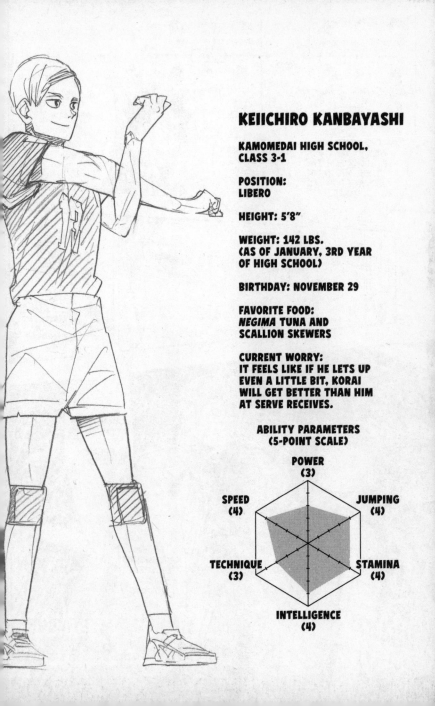

KEIICHIRO KANBAYASHI

KAMOMEDAI HIGH SCHOOL, CLASS 3-1

POSITION:
LIBERO

HEIGHT: 5'8"

WEIGHT: 142 LBS.
(AS OF JANUARY, 3RD YEAR OF HIGH SCHOOL)

BIRTHDAY: NOVEMBER 29

FAVORITE FOOD:
***NEGIMA* TUNA AND SCALLION SKEWERS**

CURRENT WORRY:
IT FEELS LIKE IF HE LETS UP EVEN A LITTLE BIT, KORAI WILL GET BETTER THAN HIM AT SERVE RECEIVES.

ABILITY PARAMETERS
(5-POINT SCALE)

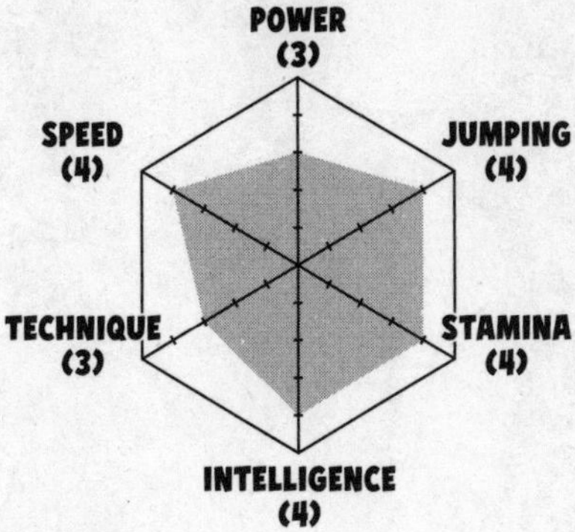
POWER
(3)
JUMPING
(4)
STAMINA
(4)
INTELLIGENCE
(4)
TECHNIQUE
(3)
SPEED
(4)

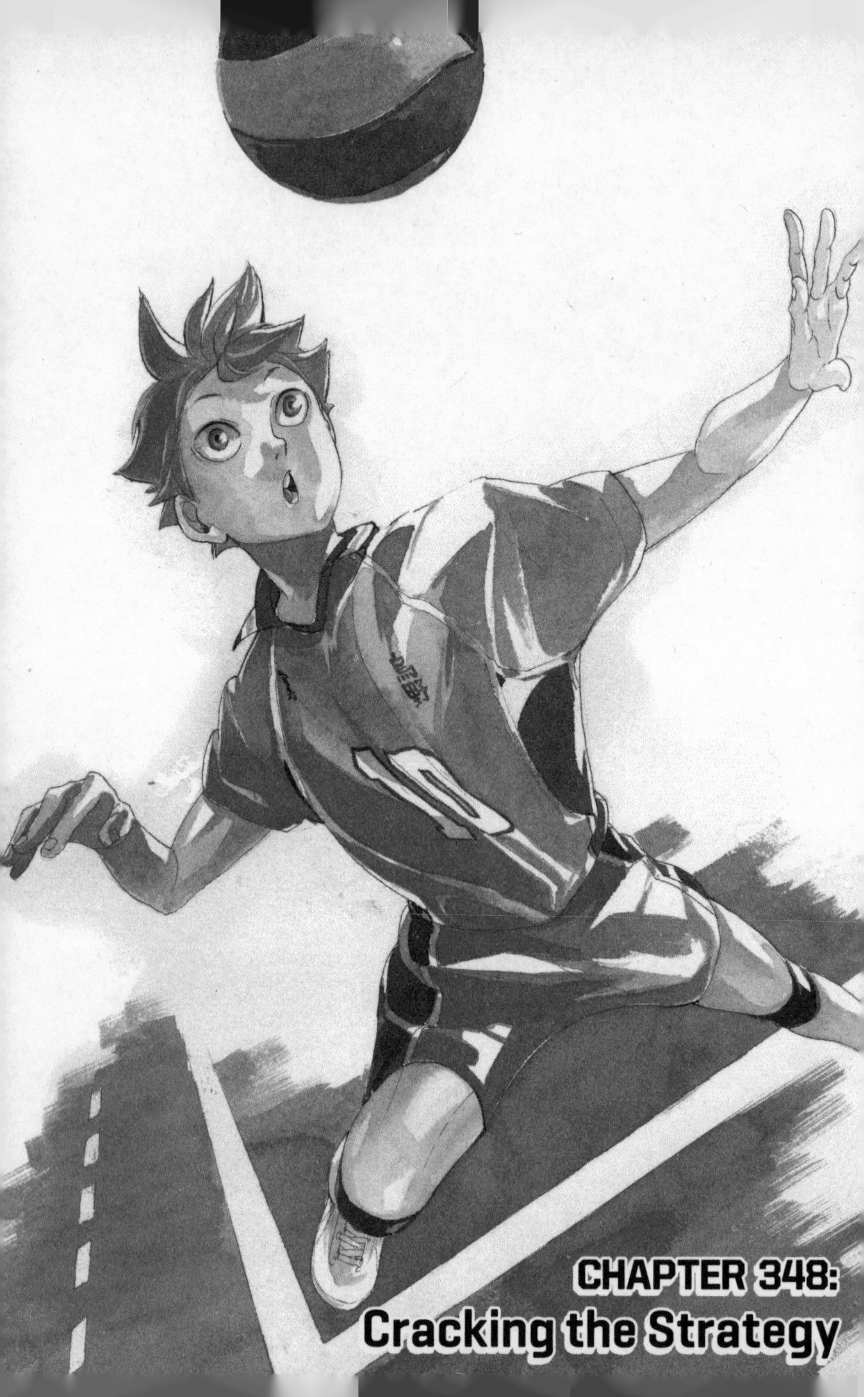
CHAPTER 348:
Cracking the Strategy

HAIKYU!!

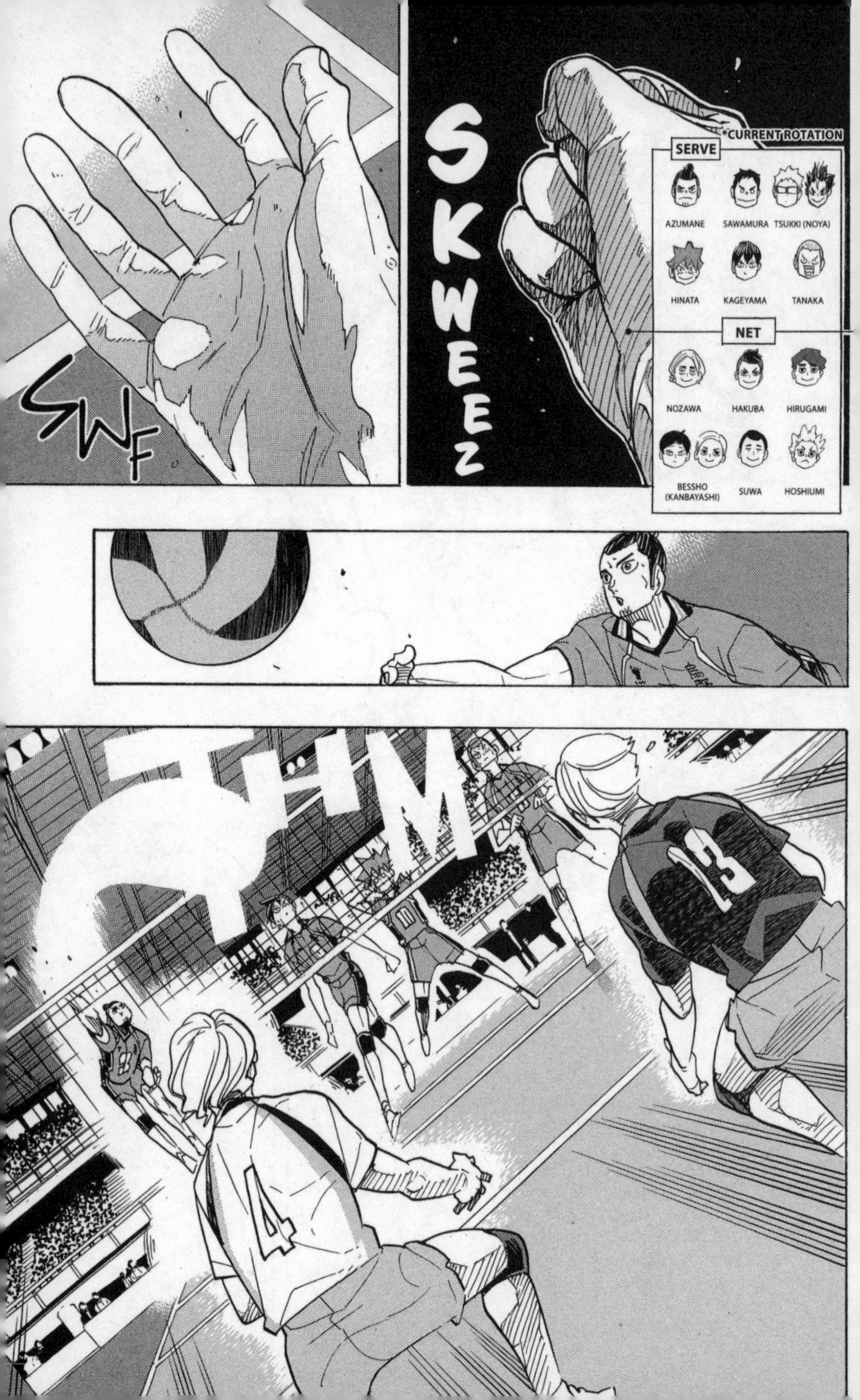
SKWEEZ
*CURRENT ROTATION
SERVE
AZUMANE
SAWAMURA
TSUKKI (NOYA)
HINATA
KAGEYAMA
TANAKA
NET
NOZAWA
HAKUBA
HIRUGAMI
BESSHO (KANBAYASHI)
SUWA
HOSHIUMI
SWF

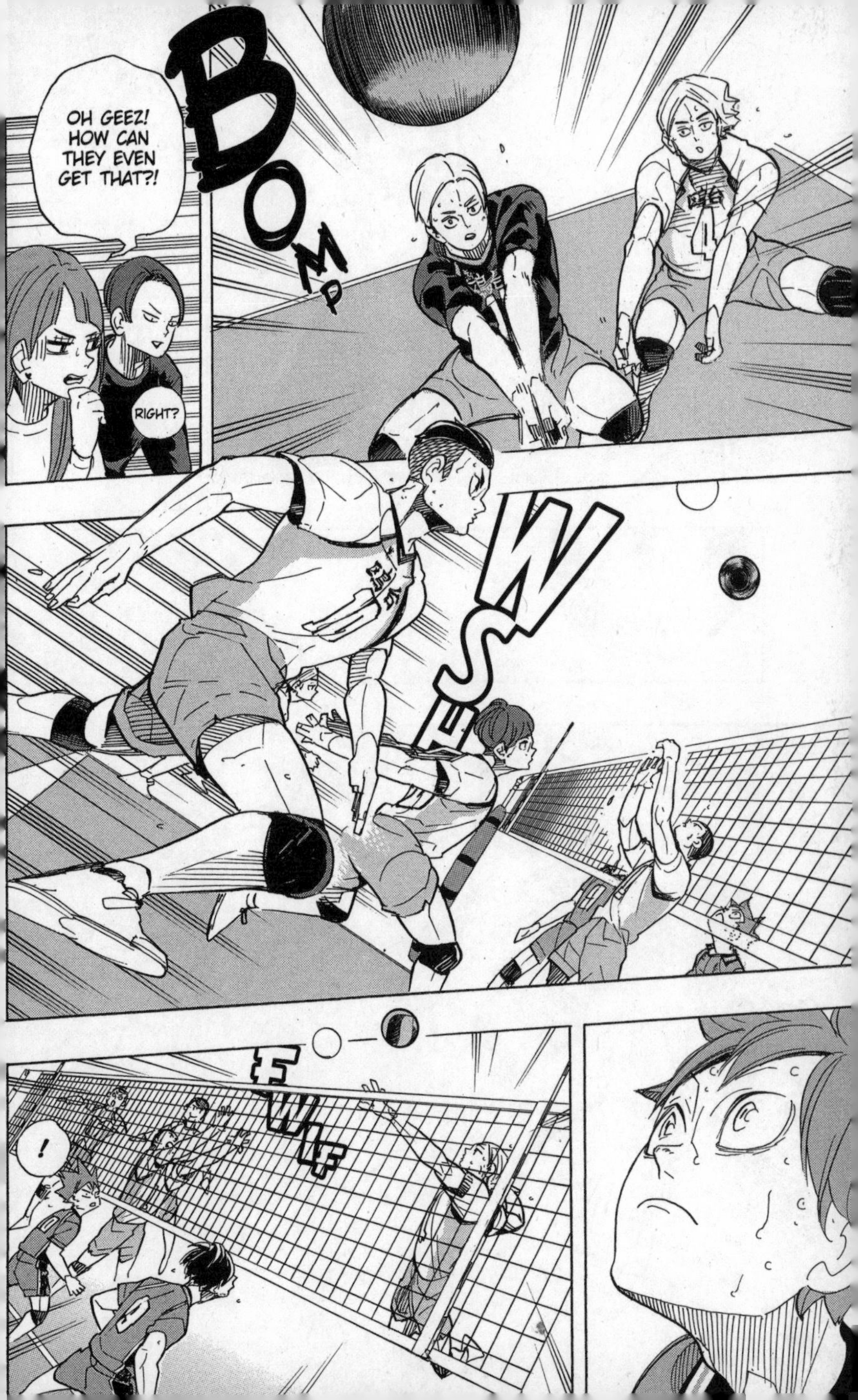
BOMP
OH GEEZ! HOW CAN THEY EVEN GET THAT?!
RIGHT?
!

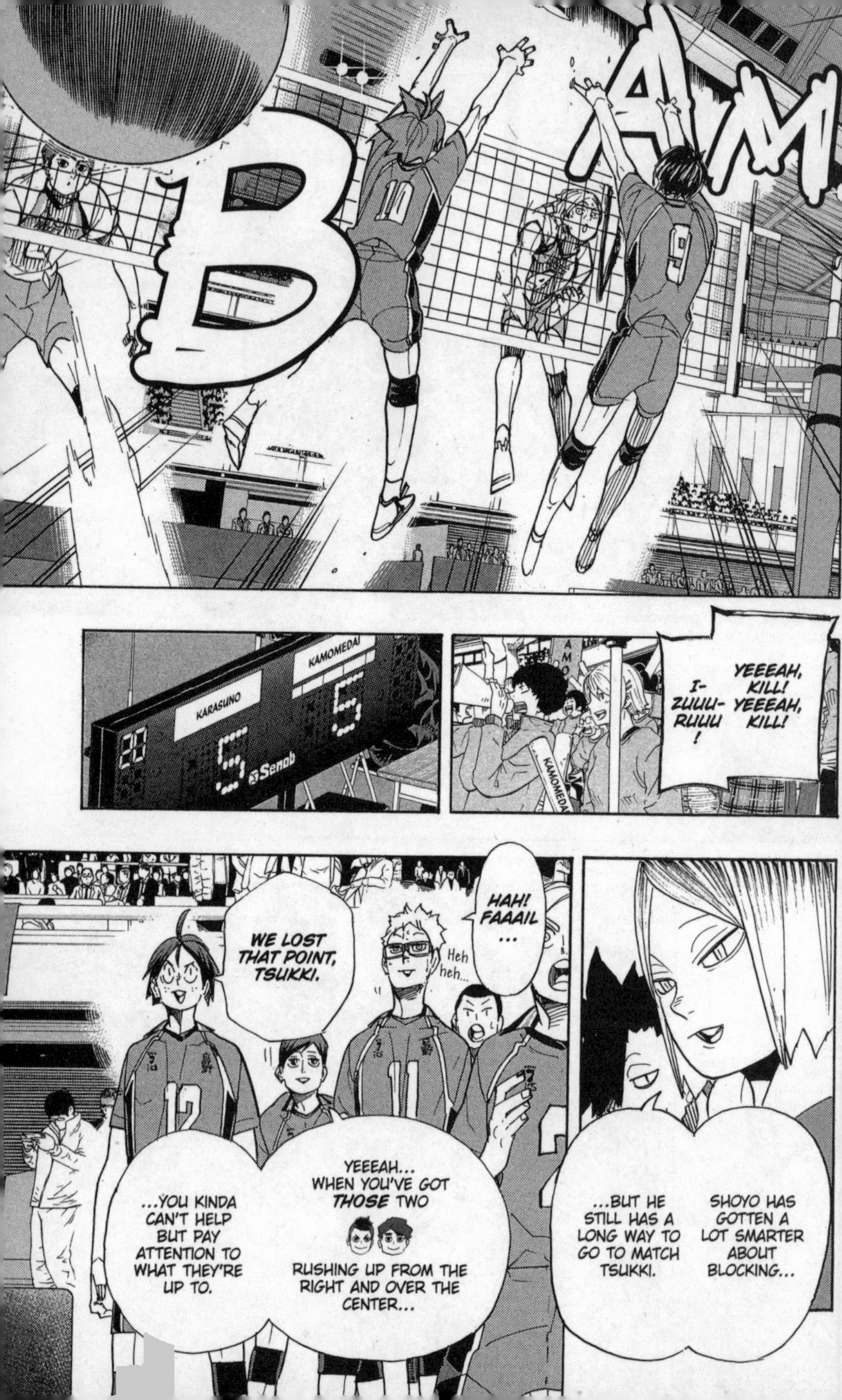
BAM
YEEEAH, KILL! YEEEAH, KILL!
I-ZUUU-RUUU!
KAMOMEDAI
KARASUNO
KAMOMEDAI
SHOYO HAS GOTTEN A LOT SMARTER ABOUT BLOCKING...
...BUT HE STILL HAS A LONG WAY TO GO TO MATCH TSUKKI.
HAH! FAAAIL...
Heh heh...
WE LOST THAT POINT, TSUKKI.
YEEEAH... WHEN YOU'VE GOT THOSE TWO RUSHING UP FROM THE RIGHT AND OVER THE CENTER...
...YOU KINDA CAN'T HELP BUT PAY ATTENTION TO WHAT THEY'RE UP TO.

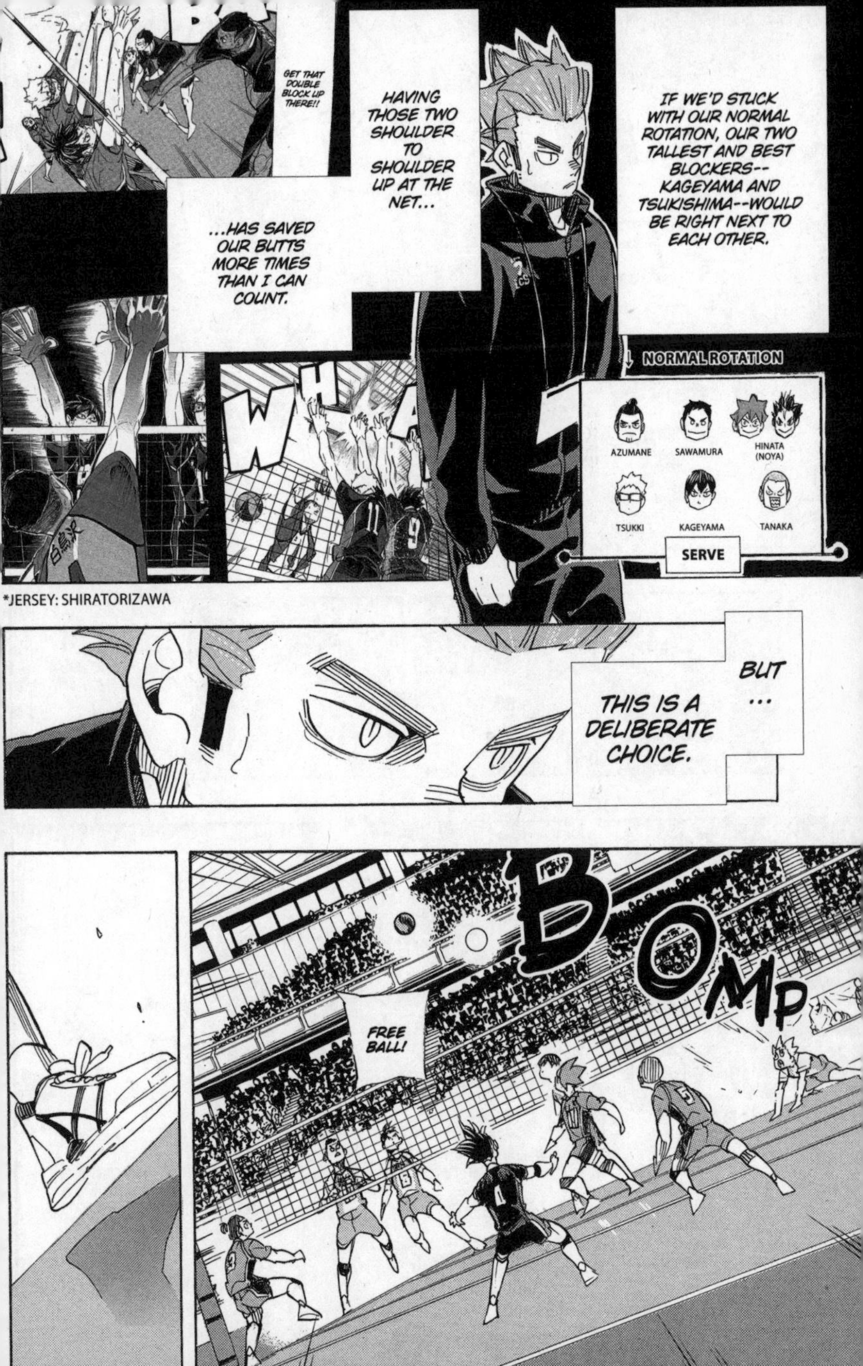
IF WE'D STUCK WITH OUR NORMAL ROTATION, OUR TWO TALLEST AND BEST BLOCKERS--KAGEYAMA AND TSUKISHIMA--WOULD BE RIGHT NEXT TO EACH OTHER.
NORMAL ROTATION
AZUMANE
SAWAMURA
HINATA (NOYA)
TSUKKI
KAGEYAMA
TANAKA
SERVE
HAVING THOSE TWO SHOULDER TO SHOULDER UP AT THE NET...
...HAS SAVED OUR BUTTS MORE TIMES THAN I CAN COUNT.
GET THAT DOUBLE BLOCK UP THERE!!
WHA
BUT...
THIS IS A DELIBERATE CHOICE.
BOMP
FREE BALL!
*JERSEY: SHIRATORIZAWA

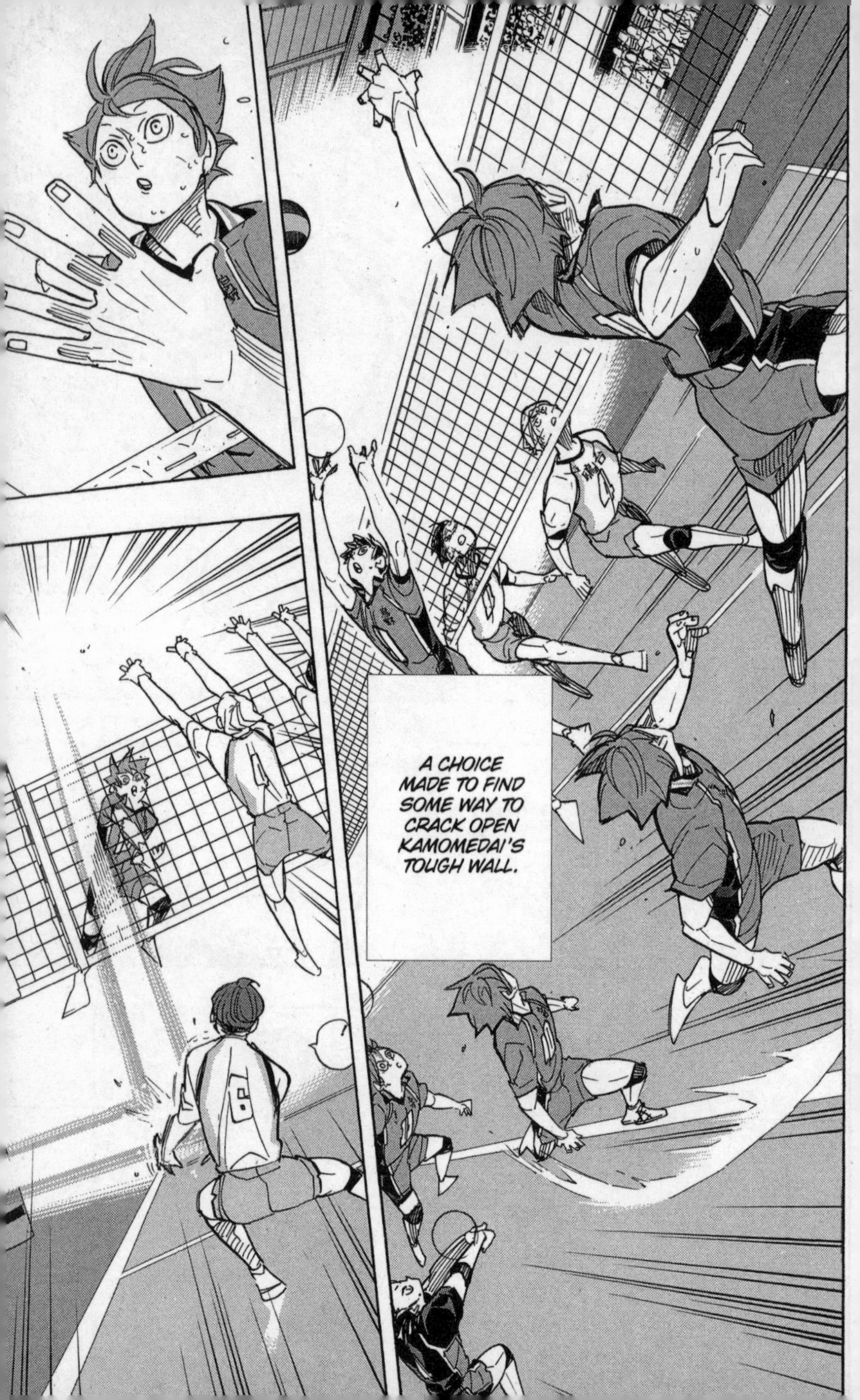
A CHOICE MADE TO FIND SOME WAY TO CRACK OPEN KAMOMEDAI'S TOUGH WALL.

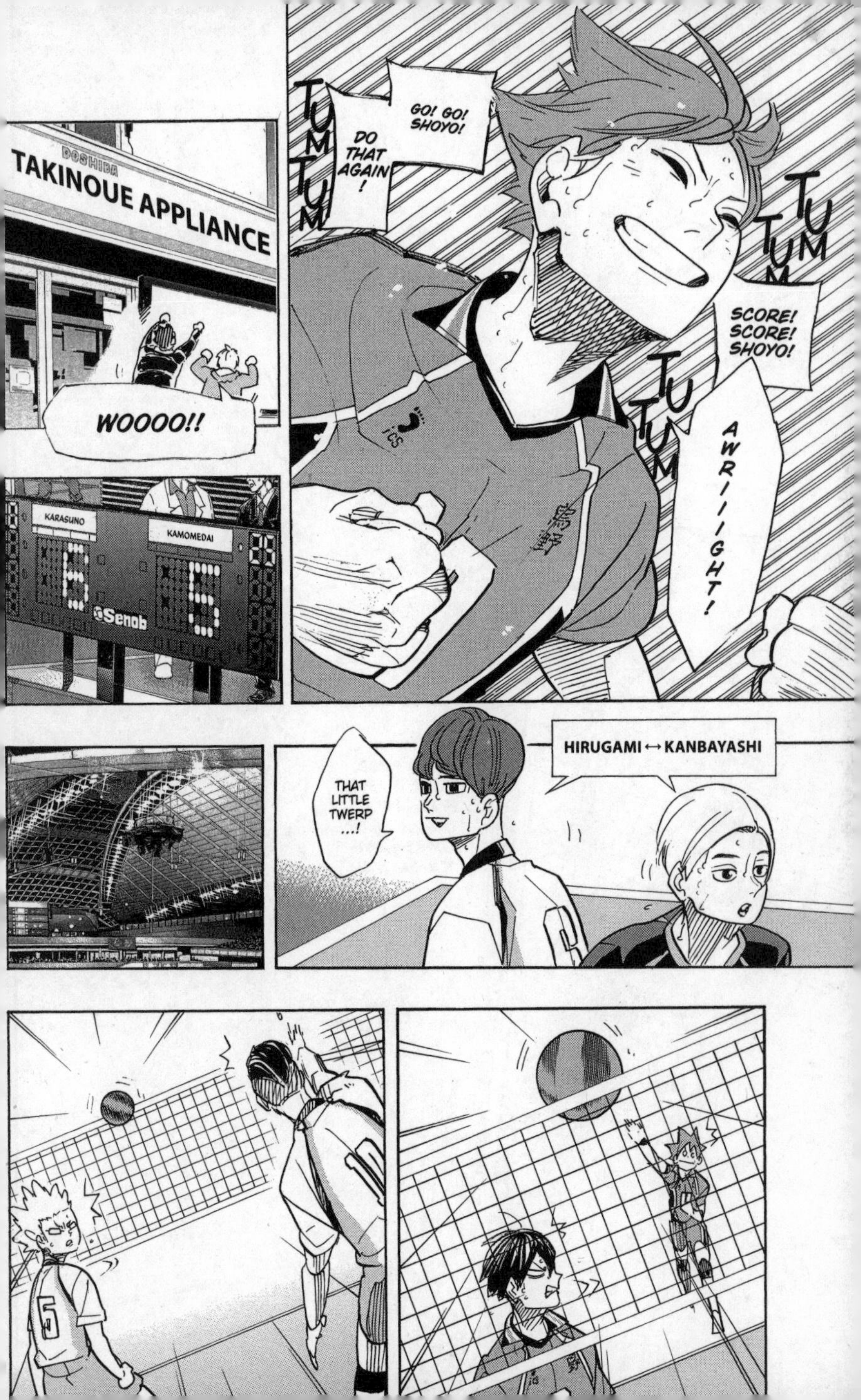
TU TUM
SCORE! SCORE! SHOYO!
TU TU TUM
AWRIIIGHT!
GO! GO! SHOYO!
DO THAT AGAIN!
TUM TUM
DOSHIBA
TAKINOUE APPLIANCE
WOOOO!!
KARASUNO
KAMOMEDAI
Senob
HIRUGAMI ↔ KANBAYASHI
THAT LITTLE TWERP ...!

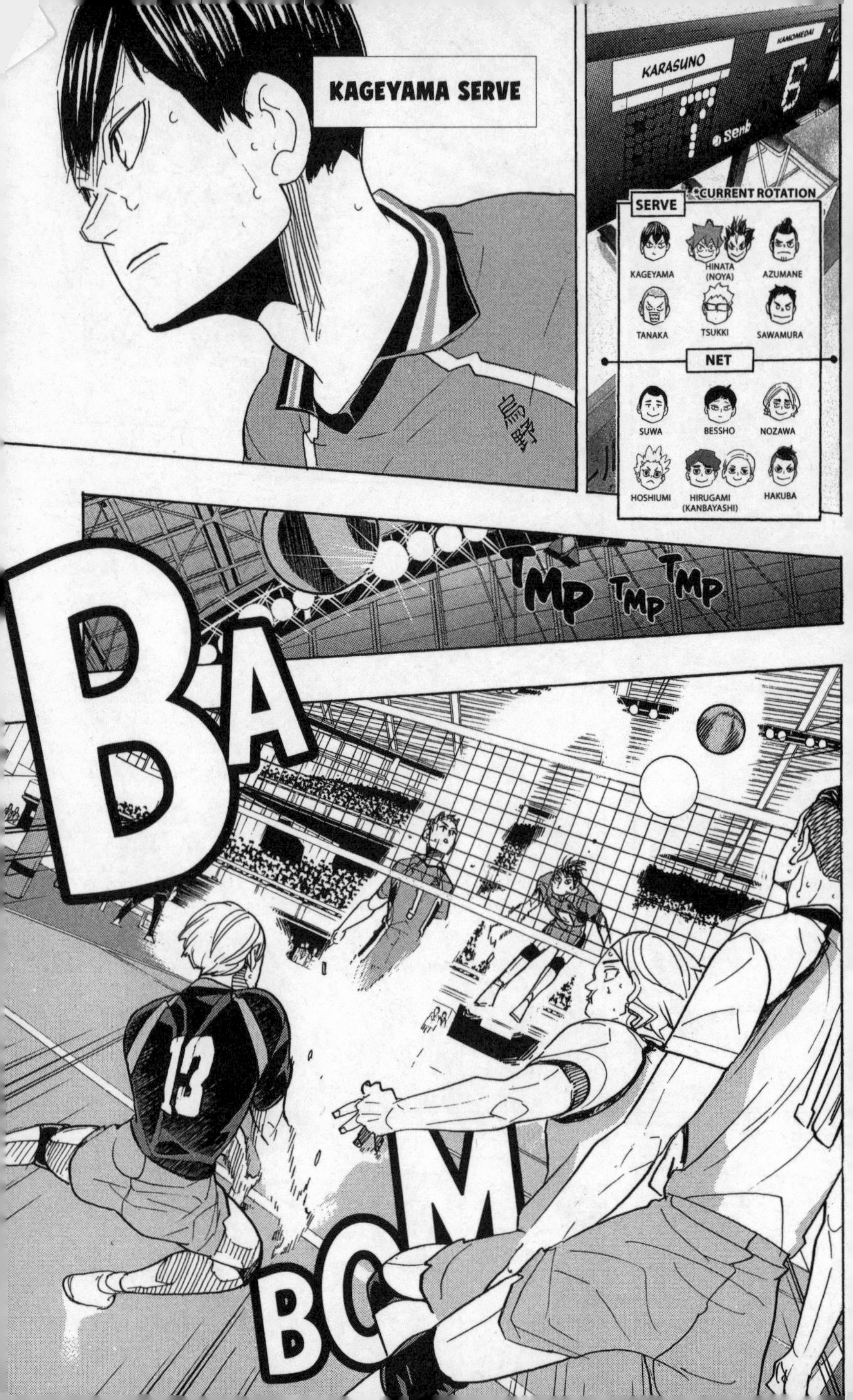
KARASUNO
KAMOMEDAI
7
6
CURRENT ROTATION
SERVE
KAGEYAMA
HINATA (NOYA)
AZUMANE
TANAKA
TSUKKI
SAWAMURA
NET
SUWA
BESSHO
NOZAWA
HOSHIUMI
HIRUGAMI (KANBAYASHI)
HAKUBA
KAGEYAMA SERVE
TMP TMP TMP
BA
BOM

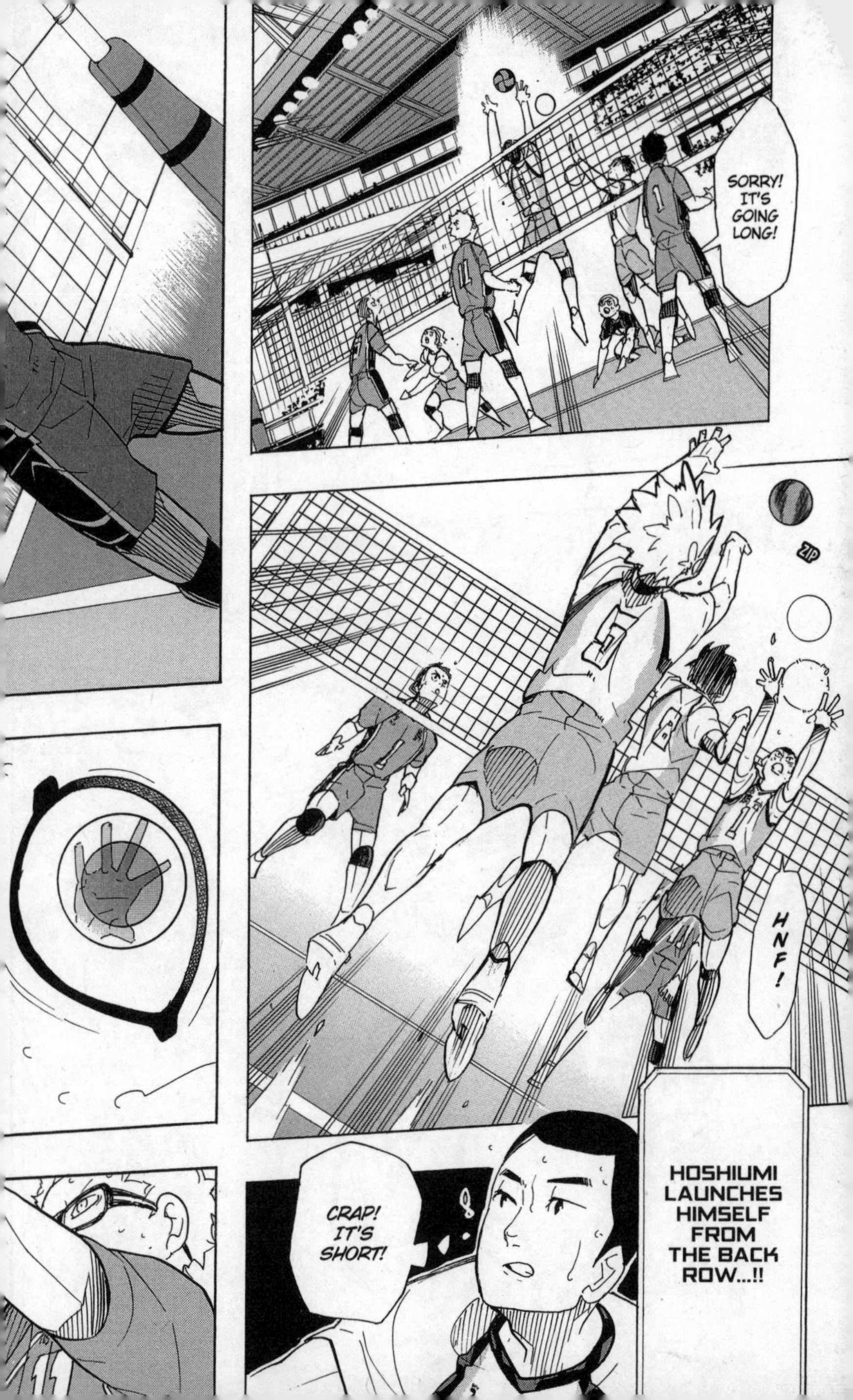
SORRY! IT'S GOING LONG!
ZIP
HNF!
HOSHIUMI LAUNCHES HIMSELF FROM THE BACK ROW...!!
CRAP! IT'S SHORT!

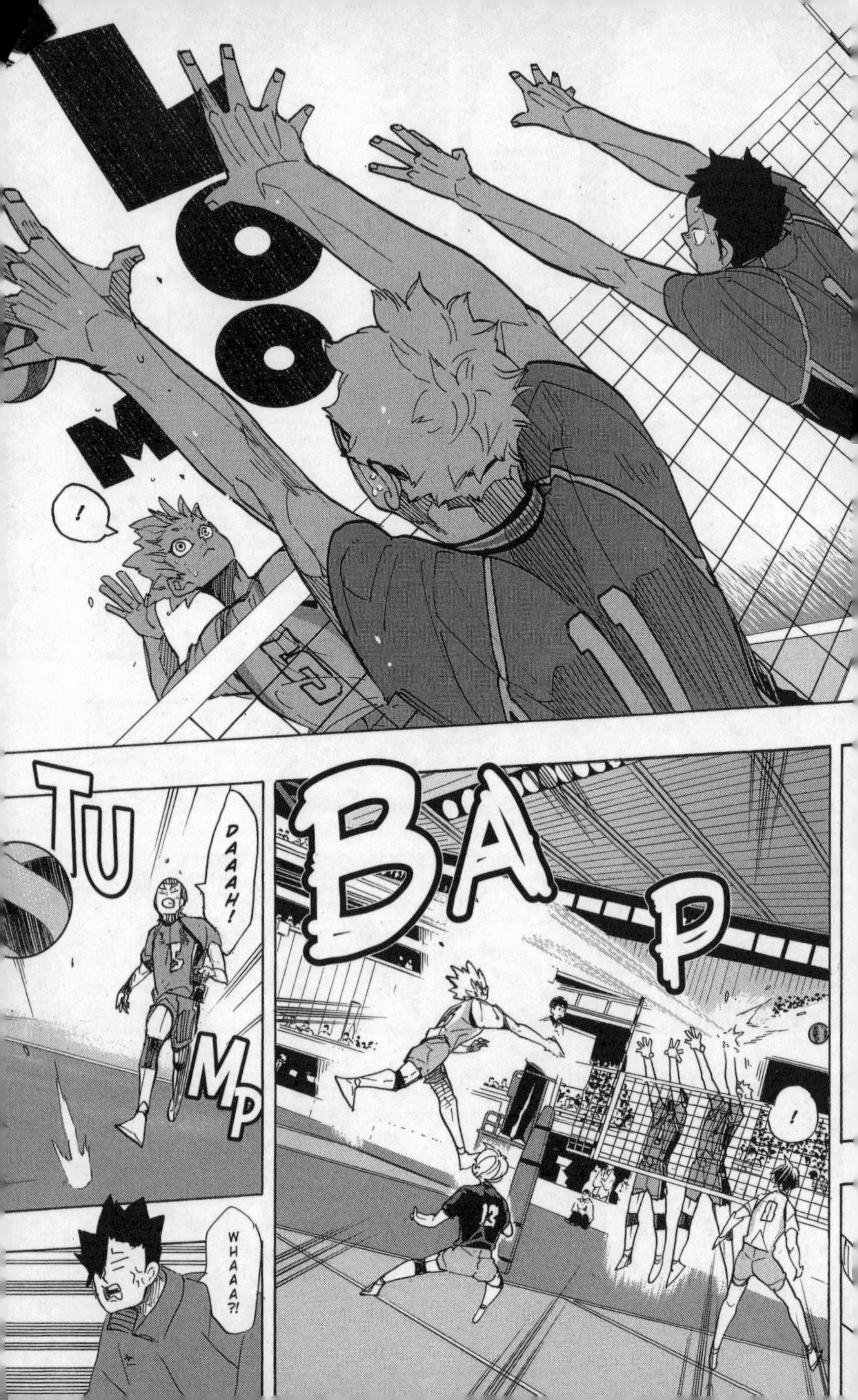

OOM
!
BAP
!
TUMP
DAAAAH!
WHAAAA?!

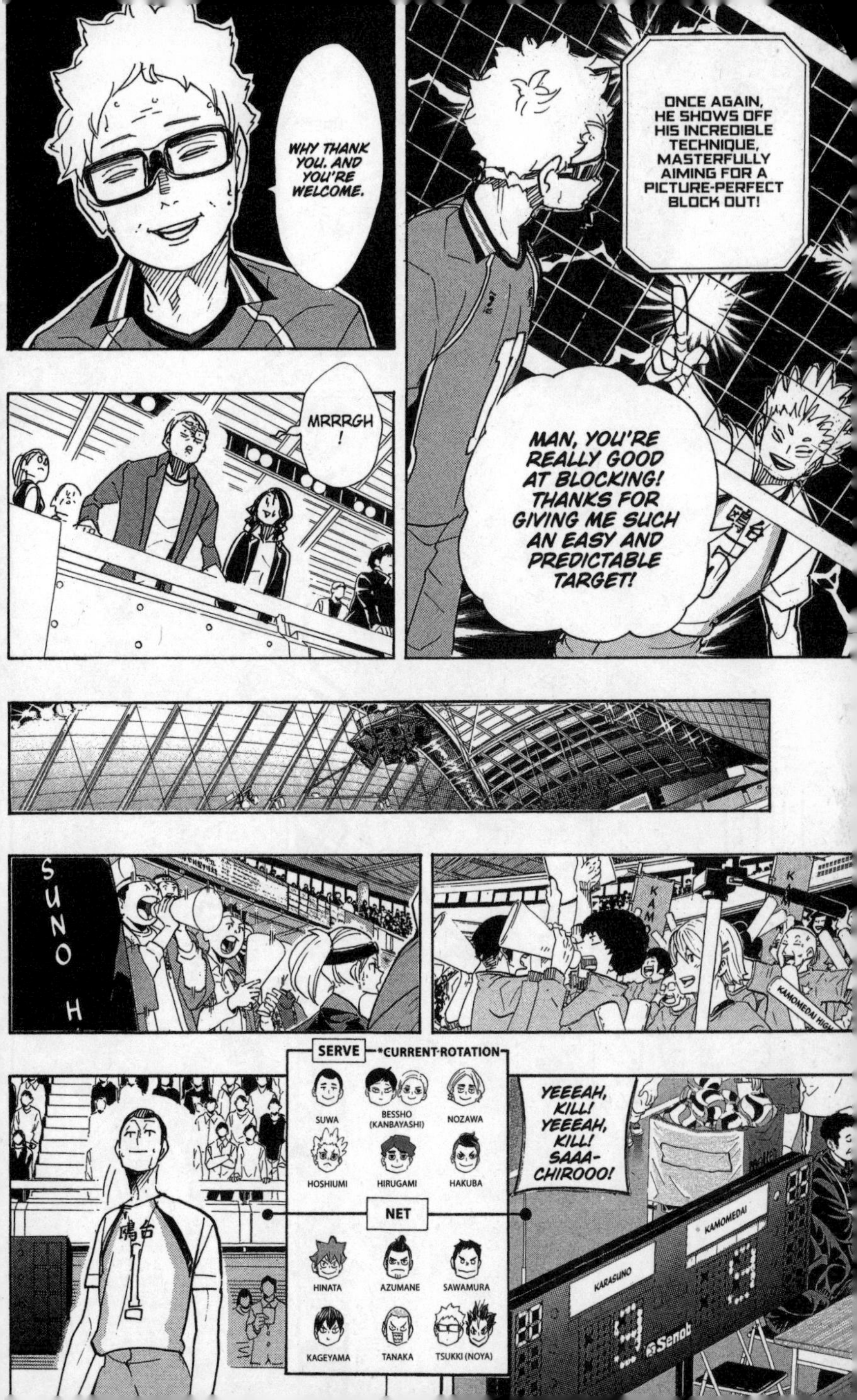
ONCE AGAIN, HE SHOWS OFF HIS INCREDIBLE TECHNIQUE, MASTERFULLY AIMING FOR A PICTURE-PERFECT BLOCK OUT!
MAN, YOU'RE REALLY GOOD AT BLOCKING! THANKS FOR GIVING ME SUCH AN EASY AND PREDICTABLE TARGET!
WHY THANK YOU. AND YOU'RE WELCOME.
MRRRGH!
KAM
KAMOMEDAI HIGH
SUNO H
YEEEAH, KILL! YEEEAH, KILL! SAAA-CHIROOO!
KAMOMEDAI
KARASUNO
Senob
SERVE
*CURRENT ROTATION
SUWA
BESSHO (KANBAYASHI)
NOZAWA
HOSHIUMI
HIRUGAMI
HAKUBA
NET
HINATA
AZUMANE
SAWAMURA
KAGEYAMA
TANAKA
TSUKKI (NOYA)

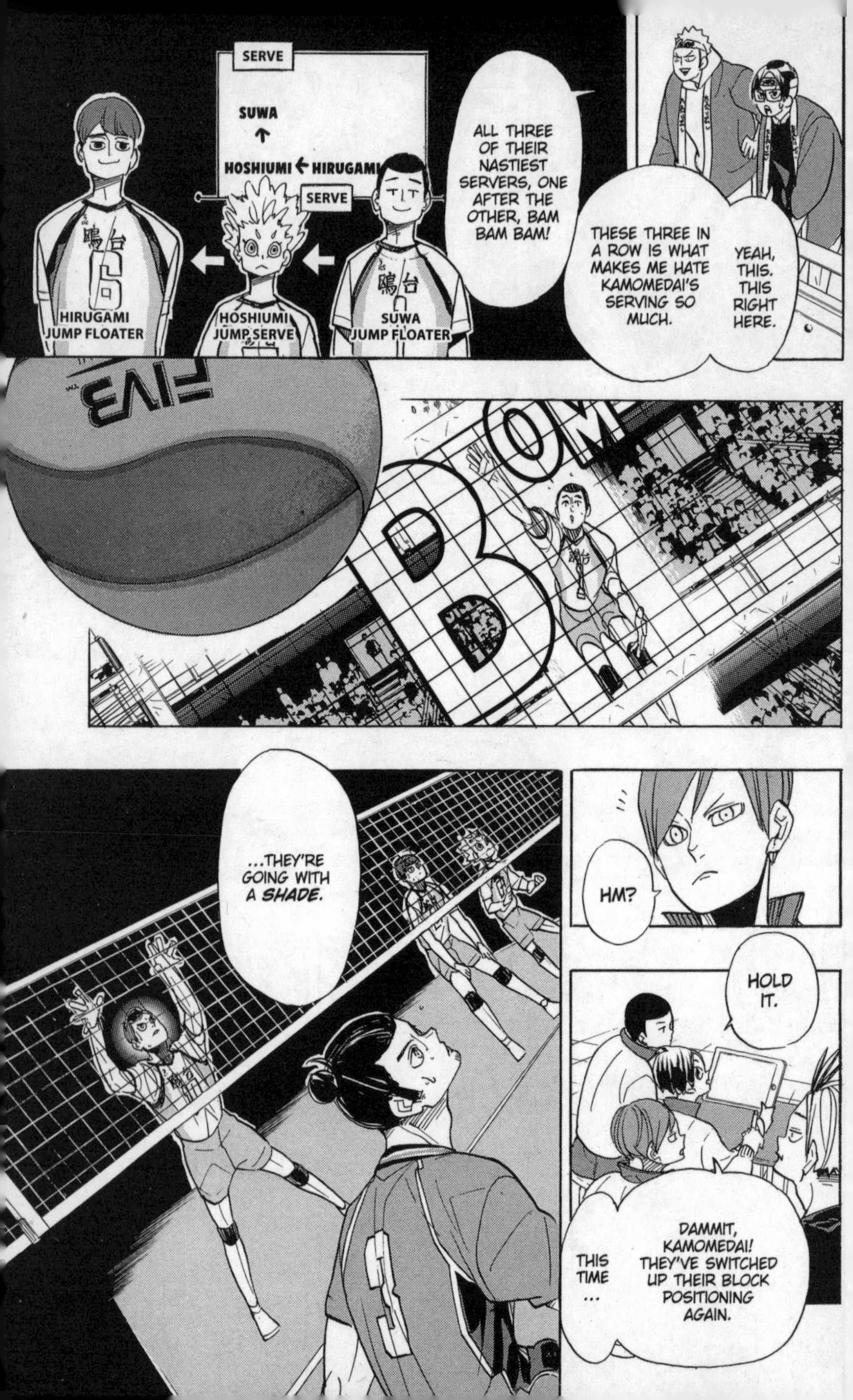
YEAH, THIS. THIS RIGHT HERE.
THESE THREE IN A ROW IS WHAT MAKES ME HATE KAMOMEDAI'S SERVING SO MUCH.
ALL THREE OF THEIR NASTIEST SERVERS, ONE AFTER THE OTHER, BAM BAM BAM!
SERVE
SUWA
HOSHIUMI ← HIRUGAMI
SERVE
SUWA JUMP FLOATER
HOSHIUMI JUMP SERVE
HIRUGAMI JUMP FLOATER
HM?
HOLD IT.
DAMMIT, KAMOMEDAI! THEY'VE SWITCHED UP THEIR BLOCK POSITIONING AGAIN.
THIS TIME ...
...THEY'RE GOING WITH A *SHADE.*

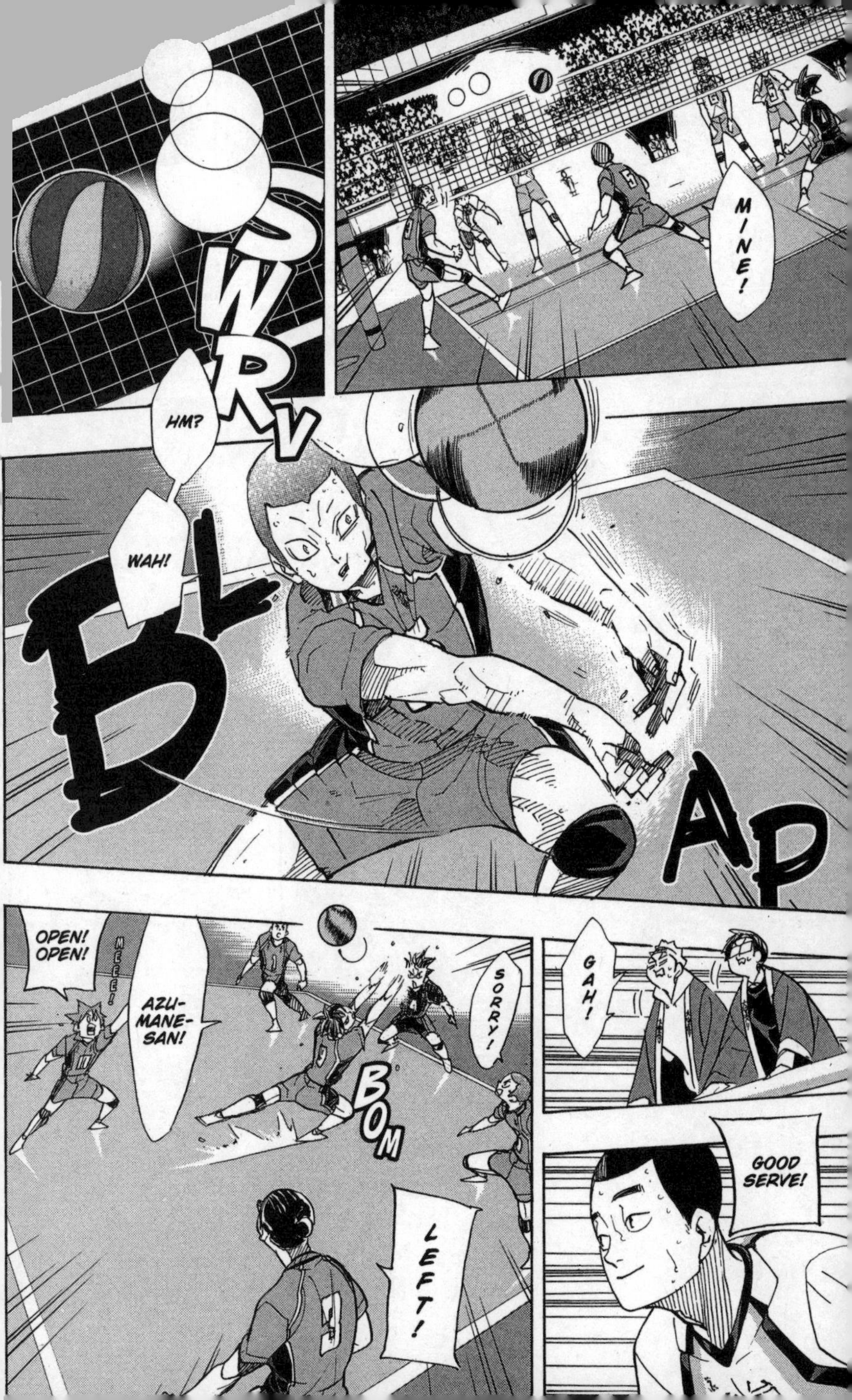
MINE!
SWRV
HM?
WAH!
BLAP
GAH!
GOOD SERVE!
SORRY!
AZUMANE-SAN!
MEEE!
OPEN! OPEN!
BOM
LEFT!

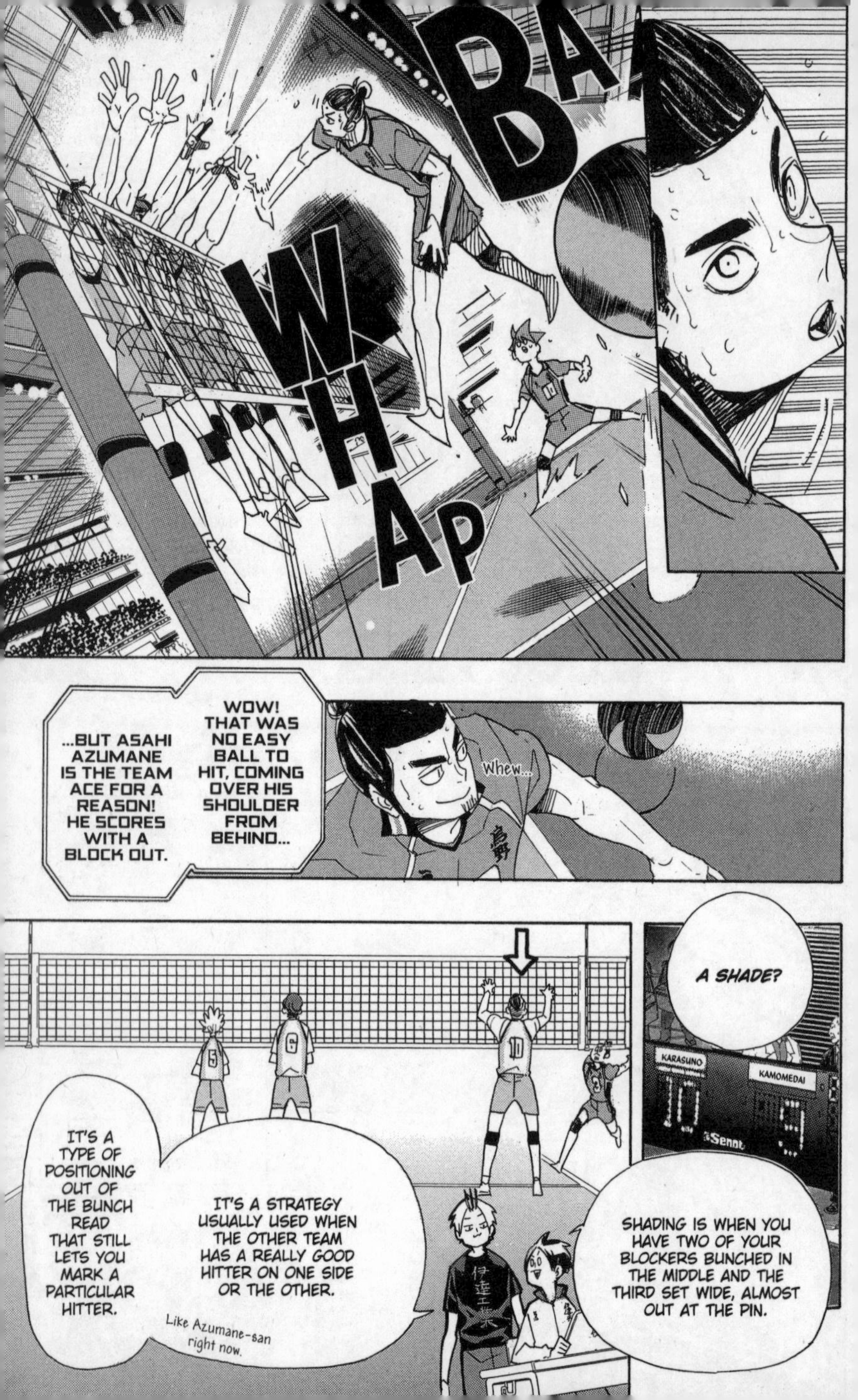
BA
WHAP
Whew...
WOW! THAT WAS NO EASY BALL TO HIT, COMING OVER HIS SHOULDER FROM BEHIND...
...BUT ASAHI AZUMANE IS THE TEAM ACE FOR A REASON! HE SCORES WITH A BLOCK OUT.
A SHADE?
KARASUNO
KAMOMEDAI
SHADING IS WHEN YOU HAVE TWO OF YOUR BLOCKERS BUNCHED IN THE MIDDLE AND THE THIRD SET WIDE, ALMOST OUT AT THE PIN.
IT'S A STRATEGY USUALLY USED WHEN THE OTHER TEAM HAS A REALLY GOOD HITTER ON ONE SIDE OR THE OTHER.
IT'S A TYPE OF POSITIONING OUT OF THE BUNCH READ THAT STILL LETS YOU MARK A PARTICULAR HITTER.
Like Azumane-san right now.

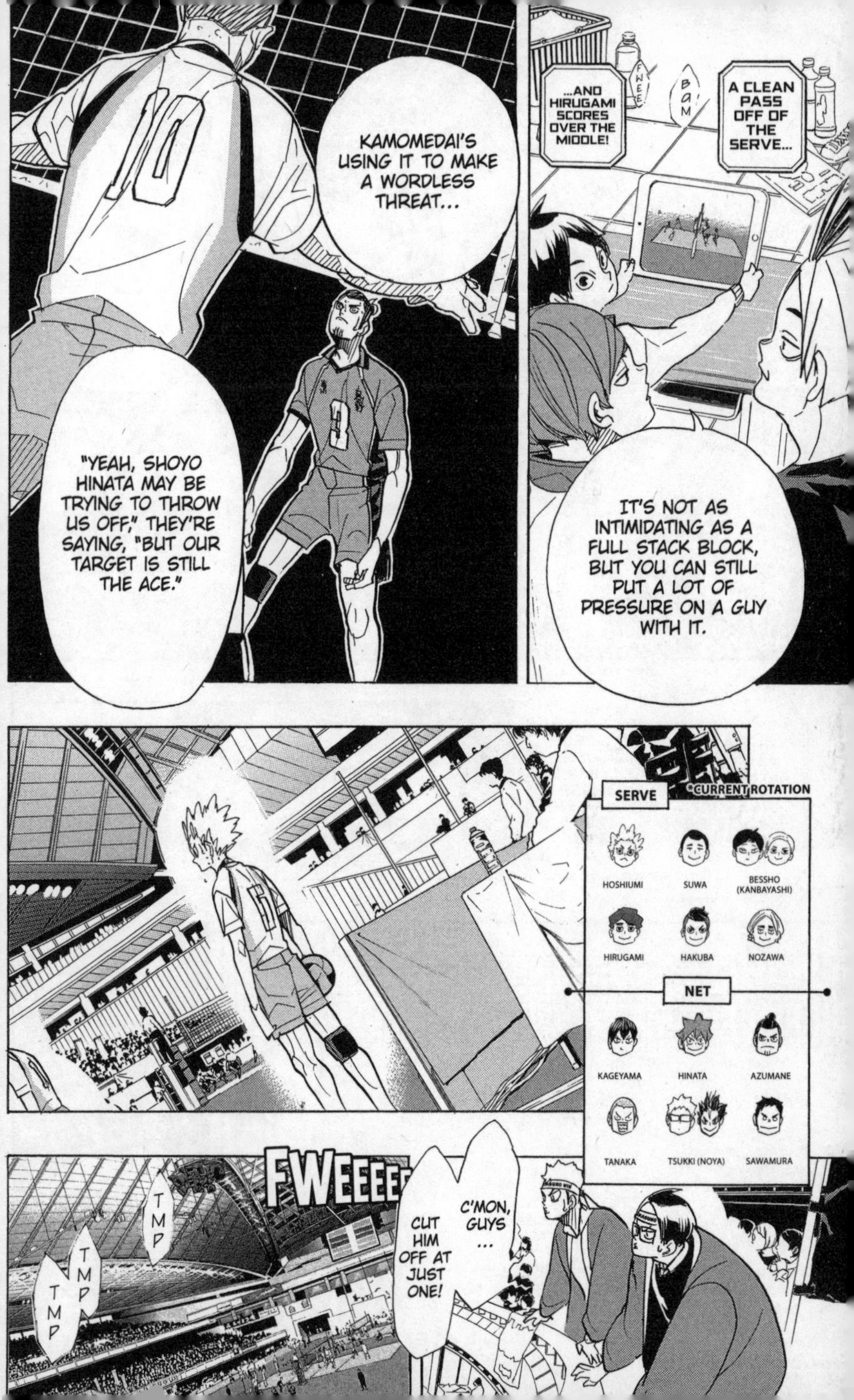
A CLEAN PASS OFF OF THE SERVE...
FWEE
BAM
...AND HIRUGAMI SCORES OVER THE MIDDLE!
IT'S NOT AS INTIMIDATING AS A FULL STACK BLOCK, BUT YOU CAN STILL PUT A LOT OF PRESSURE ON A GUY WITH IT.
KAMOMEDAI'S USING IT TO MAKE A WORDLESS THREAT...
"YEAH, SHOYO HINATA MAY BE TRYING TO THROW US OFF," THEY'RE SAYING, "BUT OUR TARGET IS STILL THE ACE."
*CURRENT ROTATION
SERVE
HOSHIUMI
SUWA
BESSHO (KANBAYASHI)
HIRUGAMI
HAKUBA
NOZAWA
NET
KAGEYAMA
HINATA
AZUMANE
TANAKA
TSUKKI (NOYA)
SAWAMURA
FWEEEEE
C'MON, GUYS...
CUT HIM OFF AT JUST ONE!
TMP
TMP
TMP

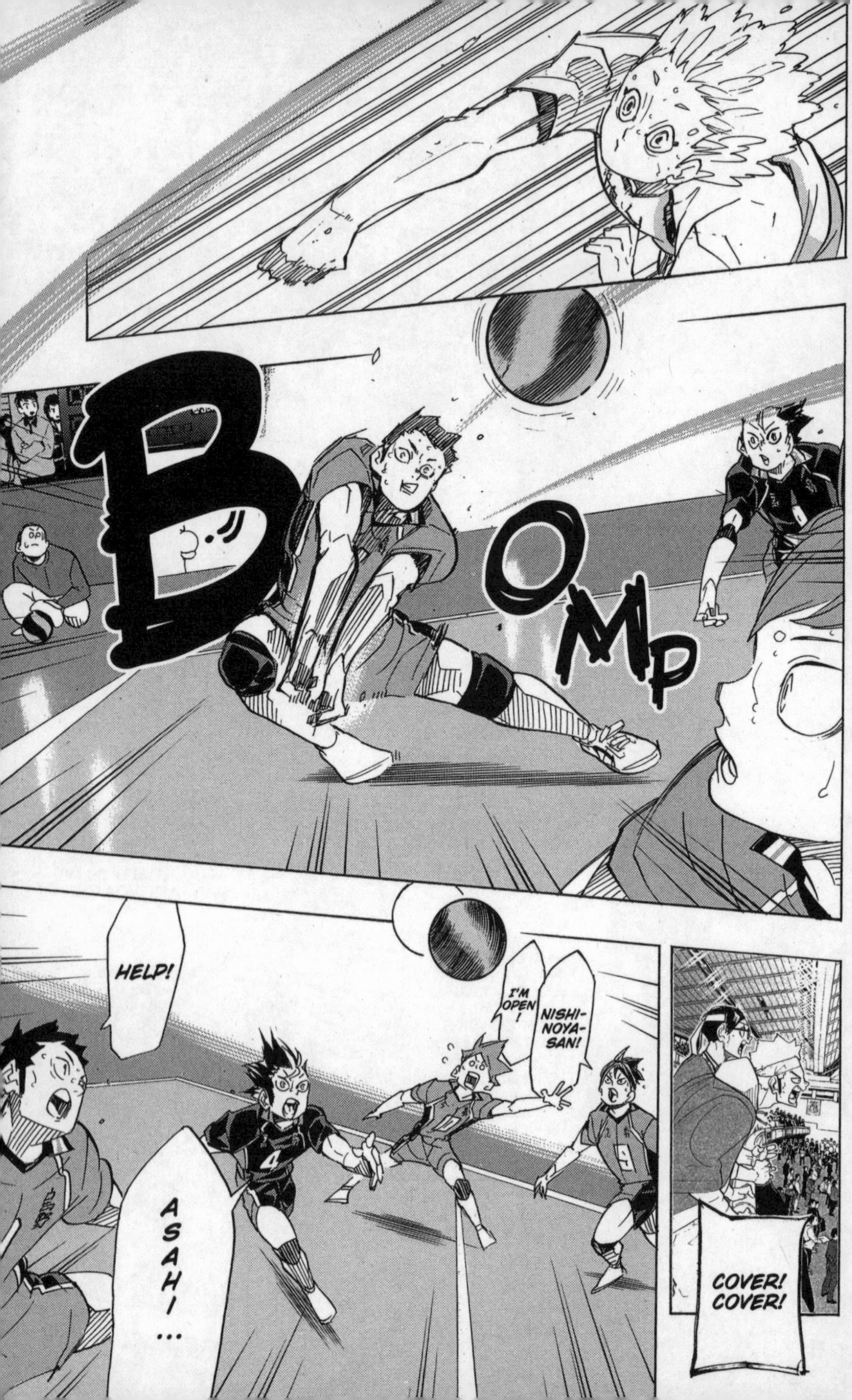
BOOMP
COVER! COVER!
NISHI-NOYA-SAN!
I'M OPEN!
HELP!
ASAHI...

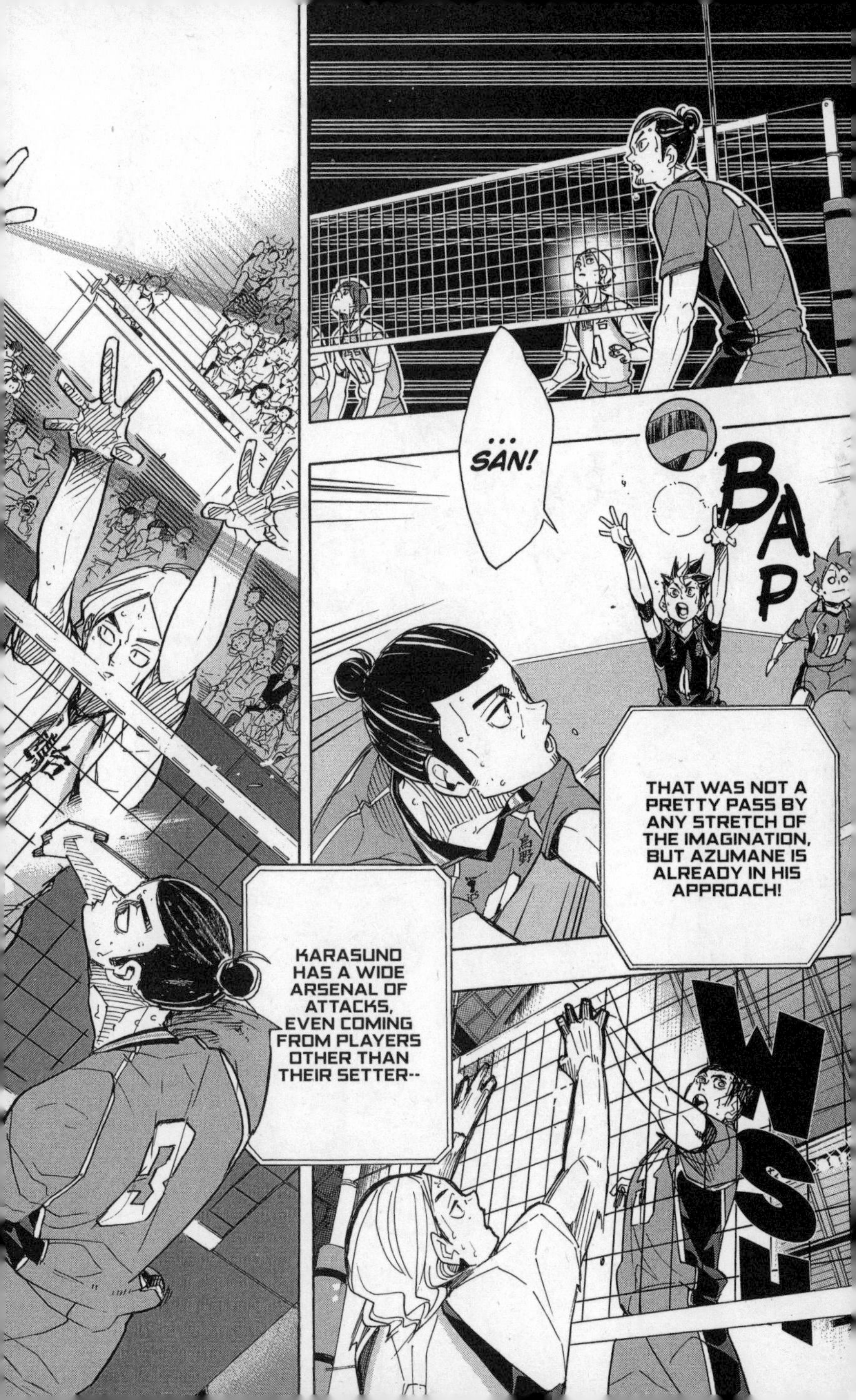
...SAN!
BAP
THAT WAS NOT A PRETTY PASS BY ANY STRETCH OF THE IMAGINATION, BUT AZUMANE IS ALREADY IN HIS APPROACH!
KARASUNO HAS A WIDE ARSENAL OF ATTACKS, EVEN COMING FROM PLAYERS OTHER THAN THEIR SETTER--
WSH

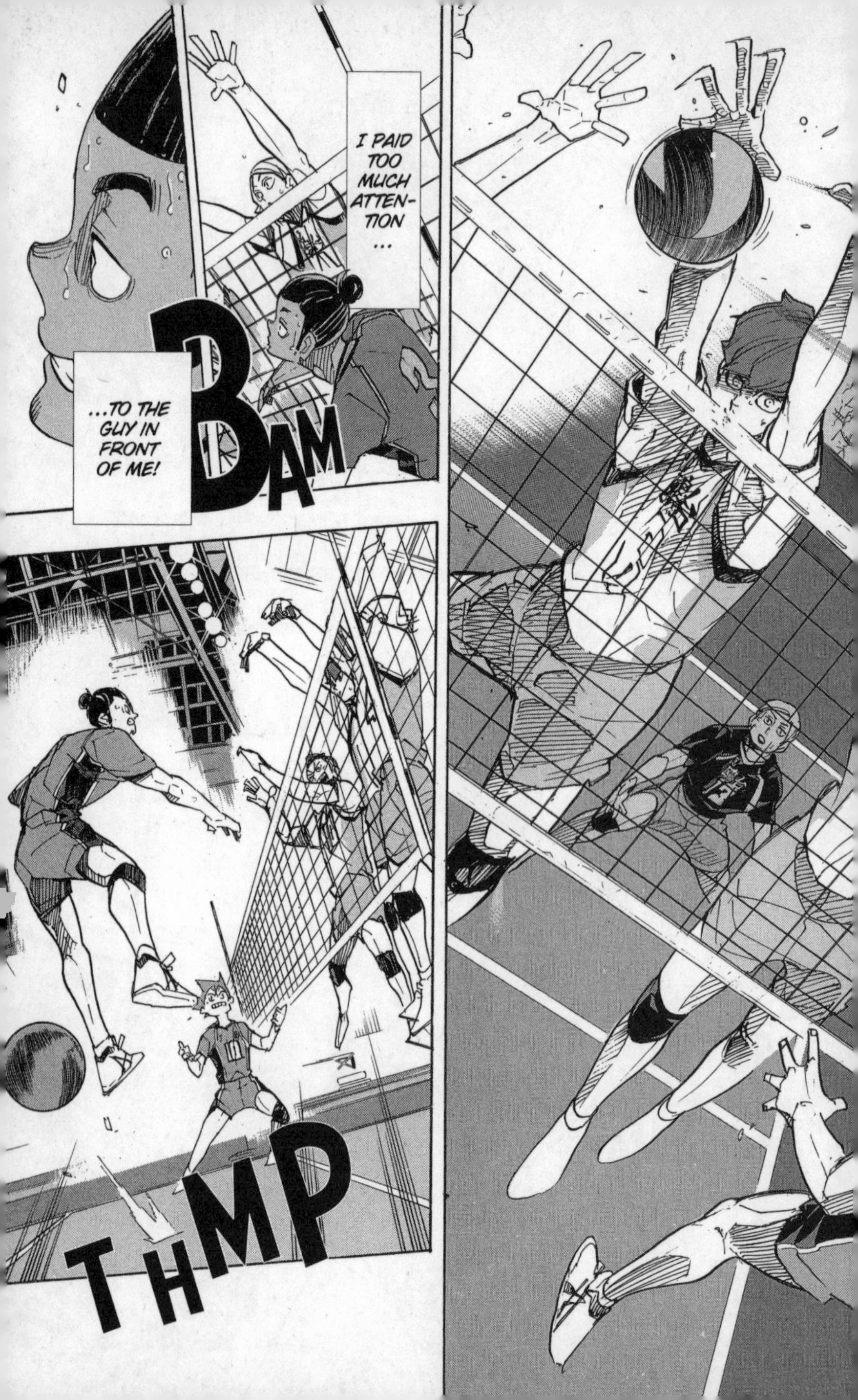
I PAID TOO MUCH ATTENTION ...
...TO THE GUY IN FRONT OF ME!
BAM
THMP

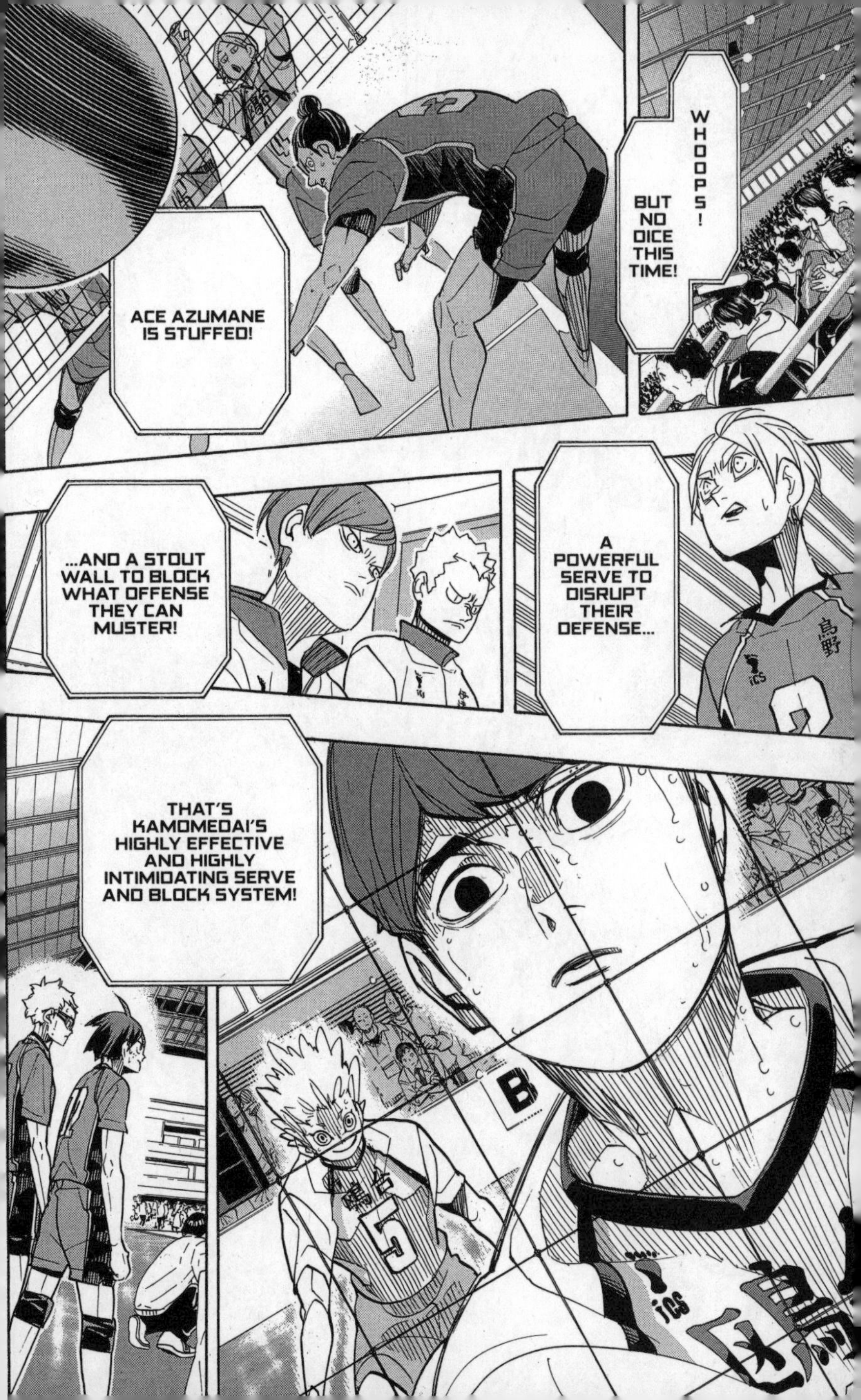
WHOOPS!
BUT NO DICE THIS TIME!
ACE AZUMANE IS STUFFED!
A POWERFUL SERVE TO DISRUPT THEIR DEFENSE...
...AND A STOUT WALL TO BLOCK WHAT OFFENSE THEY CAN MUSTER!
THAT'S KAMOMEDAI'S HIGHLY EFFECTIVE AND HIGHLY INTIMIDATING SERVE AND BLOCK SYSTEM!

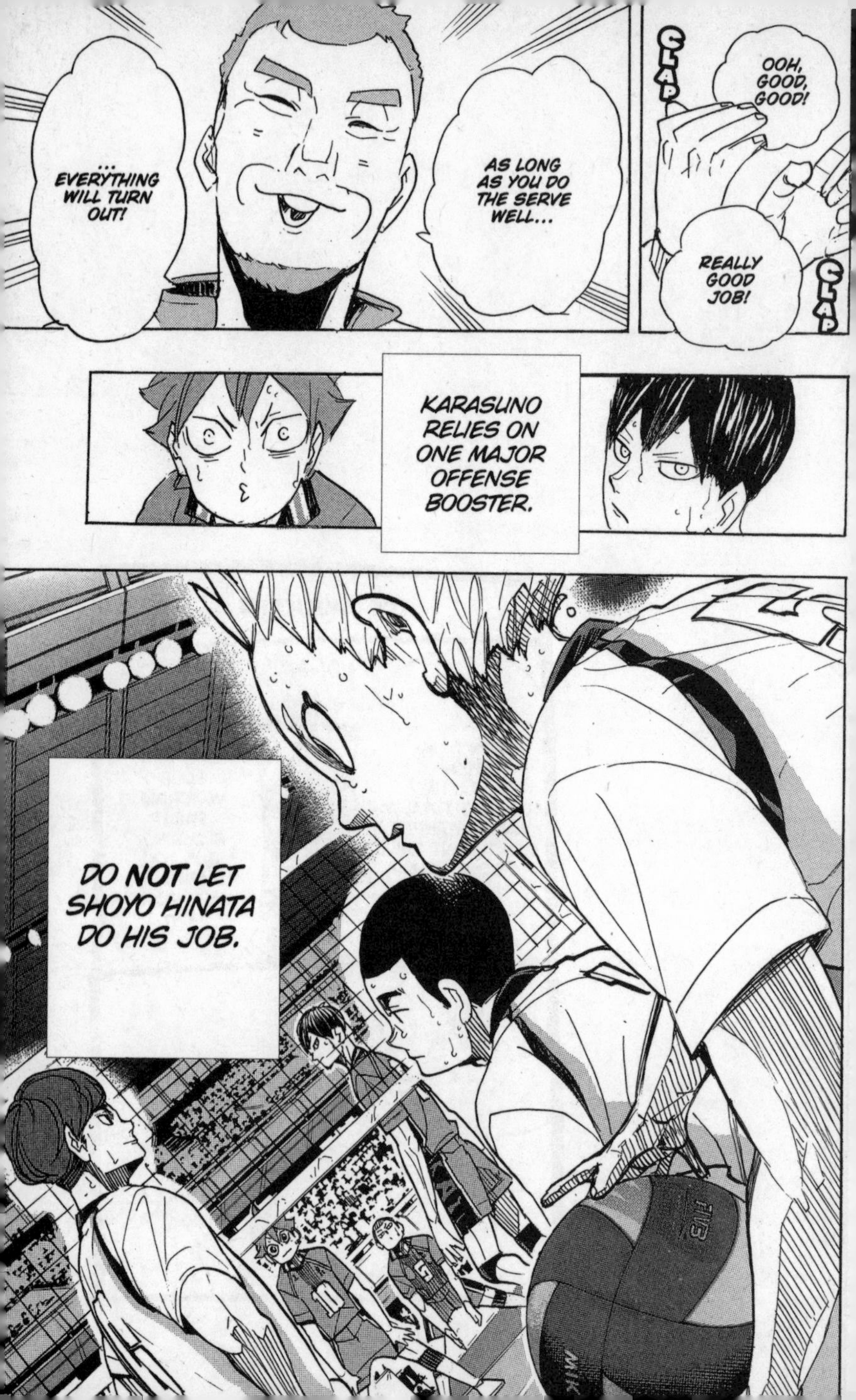
OOH, GOOD, GOOD!
CLAP
REALLY GOOD JOB!
CLAP
AS LONG AS YOU DO THE SERVE WELL...
...EVERYTHING WILL TURN OUT!
KARASUNO RELIES ON ONE MAJOR OFFENSE BOOSTER.
DO NOT LET SHOYO HINATA DO HIS JOB.

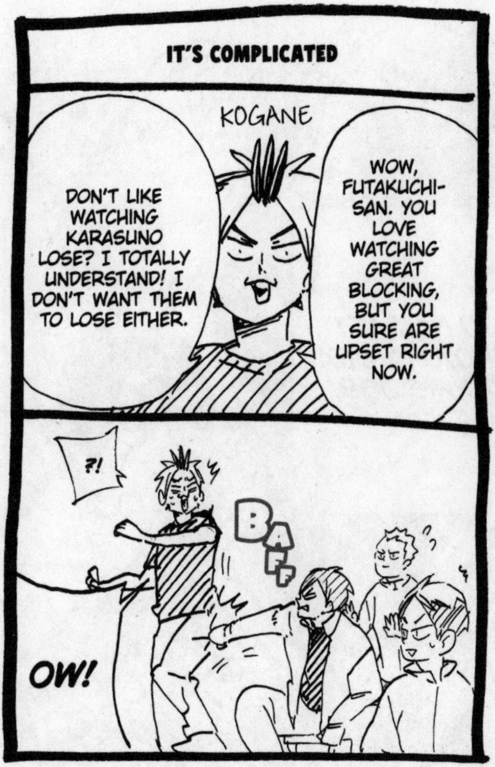
IT'S COMPLICATED
WOW, FUTAKUCHI-SAN. YOU LOVE WATCHING GREAT BLOCKING, BUT YOU SURE ARE UPSET RIGHT NOW.
KOGANE
DON'T LIKE WATCHING KARASUNO LOSE? I TOTALLY UNDERSTAND! I DON'T WANT THEM TO LOSE EITHER.
BAFF
?!
OW!

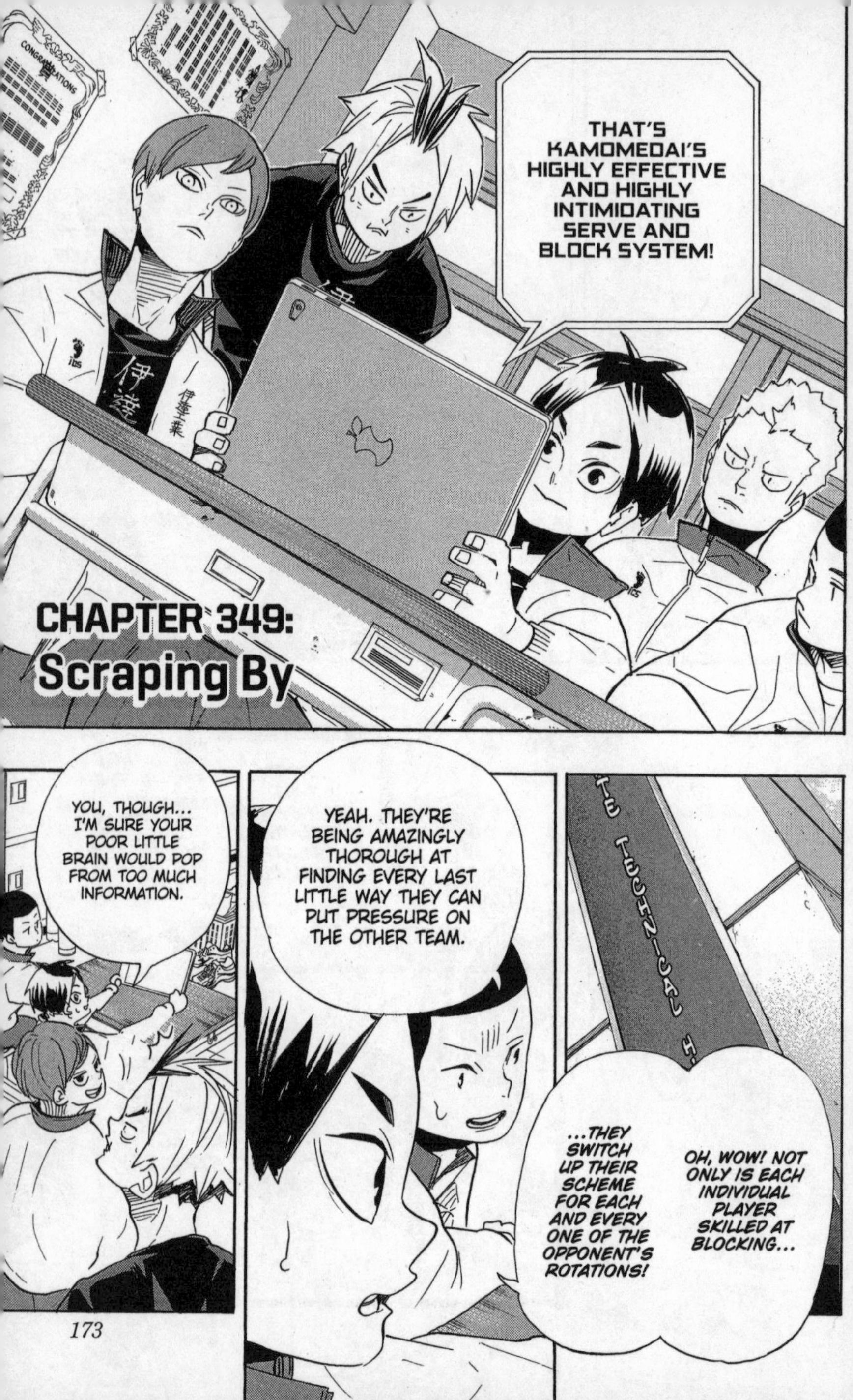
THAT'S KAMOMEDAI'S HIGHLY EFFECTIVE AND HIGHLY INTIMIDATING SERVE AND BLOCK SYSTEM!
CHAPTER 349:
Scraping By
OH, WOW! NOT ONLY IS EACH INDIVIDUAL PLAYER SKILLED AT BLOCKING...
...THEY SWITCH UP THEIR SCHEME FOR EACH AND EVERY ONE OF THE OPPONENT'S ROTATIONS!
YEAH. THEY'RE BEING AMAZINGLY THOROUGH AT FINDING EVERY LAST LITTLE WAY THEY CAN PUT PRESSURE ON THE OTHER TEAM.
YOU, THOUGH... I'M SURE YOUR POOR LITTLE BRAIN WOULD POP FROM TOO MUCH INFORMATION.

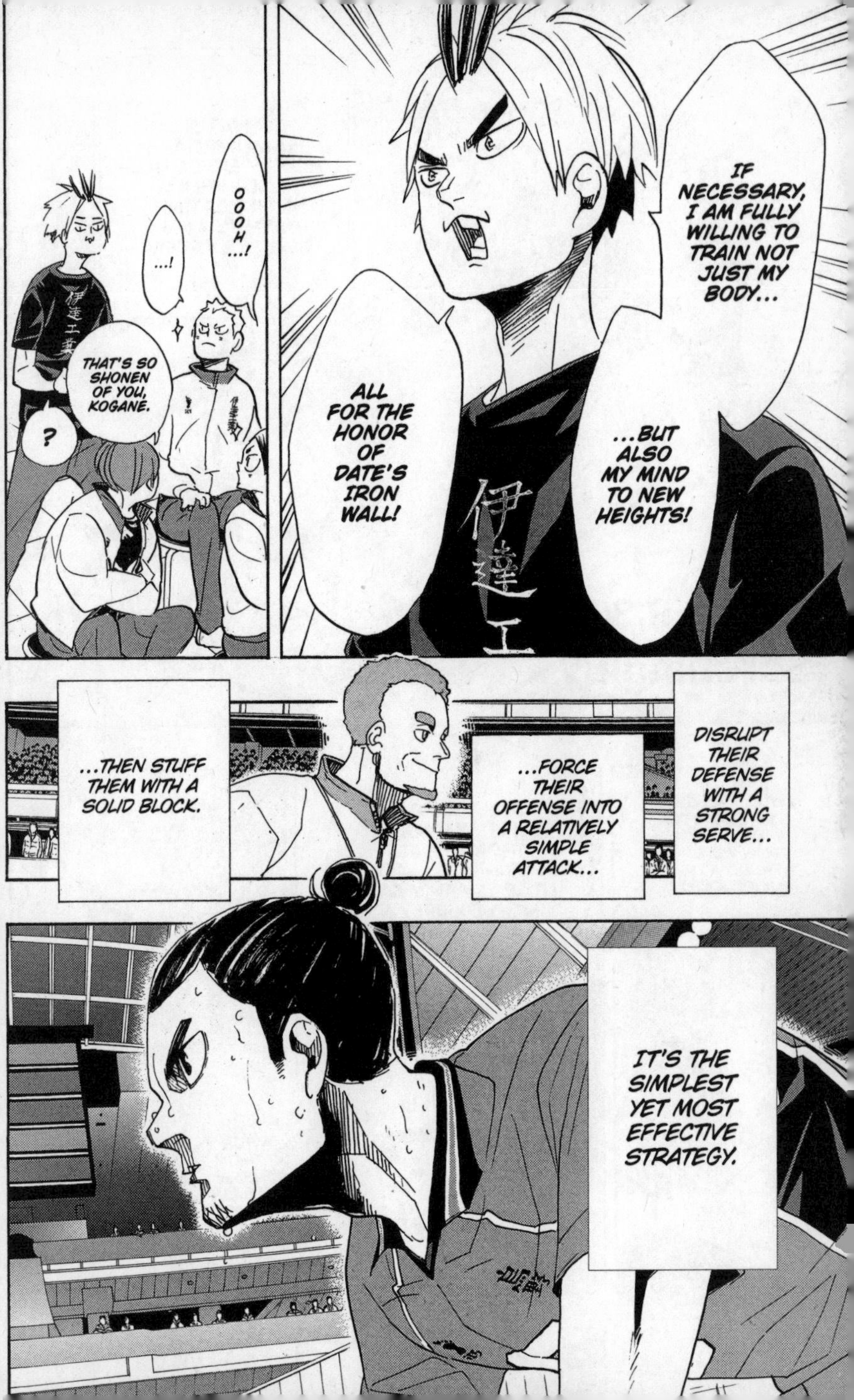
IF NECESSARY, I AM FULLY WILLING TO TRAIN NOT JUST MY BODY...
...BUT ALSO MY MIND TO NEW HEIGHTS!
ALL FOR THE HONOR OF DATE'S IRON WALL!
OOOH...!
...!
THAT'S SO SHONEN OF YOU, KOGANE.
?
DISRUPT THEIR DEFENSE WITH A STRONG SERVE...
...FORCE THEIR OFFENSE INTO A RELATIVELY SIMPLE ATTACK...
...THEN STUFF THEM WITH A SOLID BLOCK.
IT'S THE SIMPLEST YET MOST EFFECTIVE STRATEGY.

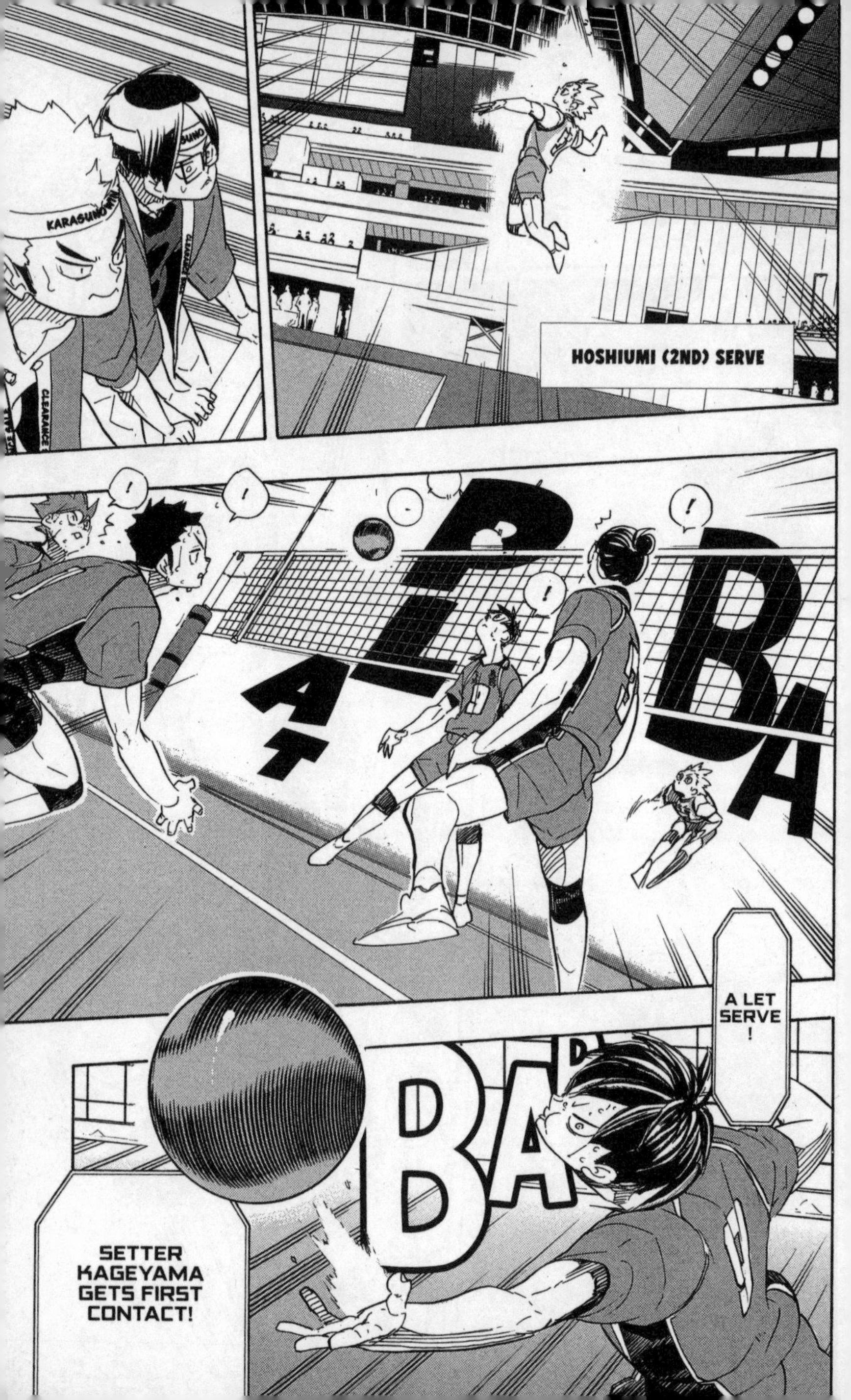
HOSHIUMI (2ND) SERVE
KARASUNO
!
!
!
!
PAT
BA
A LET SERVE!
BA
SETTER KAGEYAMA GETS FIRST CONTACT!

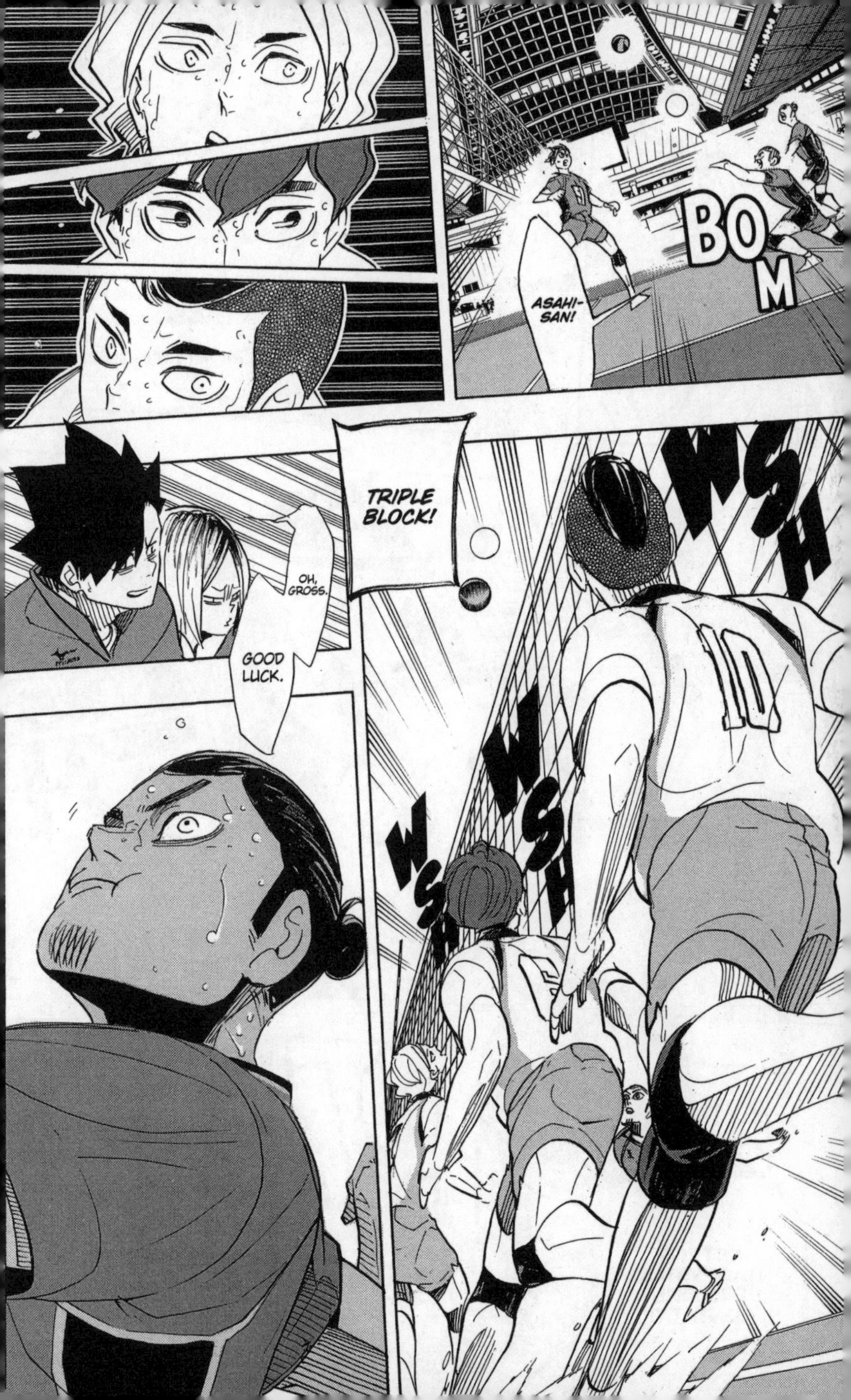
ASAHI-SAN!
BOM
TRIPLE BLOCK!
WSH
WSH
WSH
OH, GROSS.
GOOD LUCK.

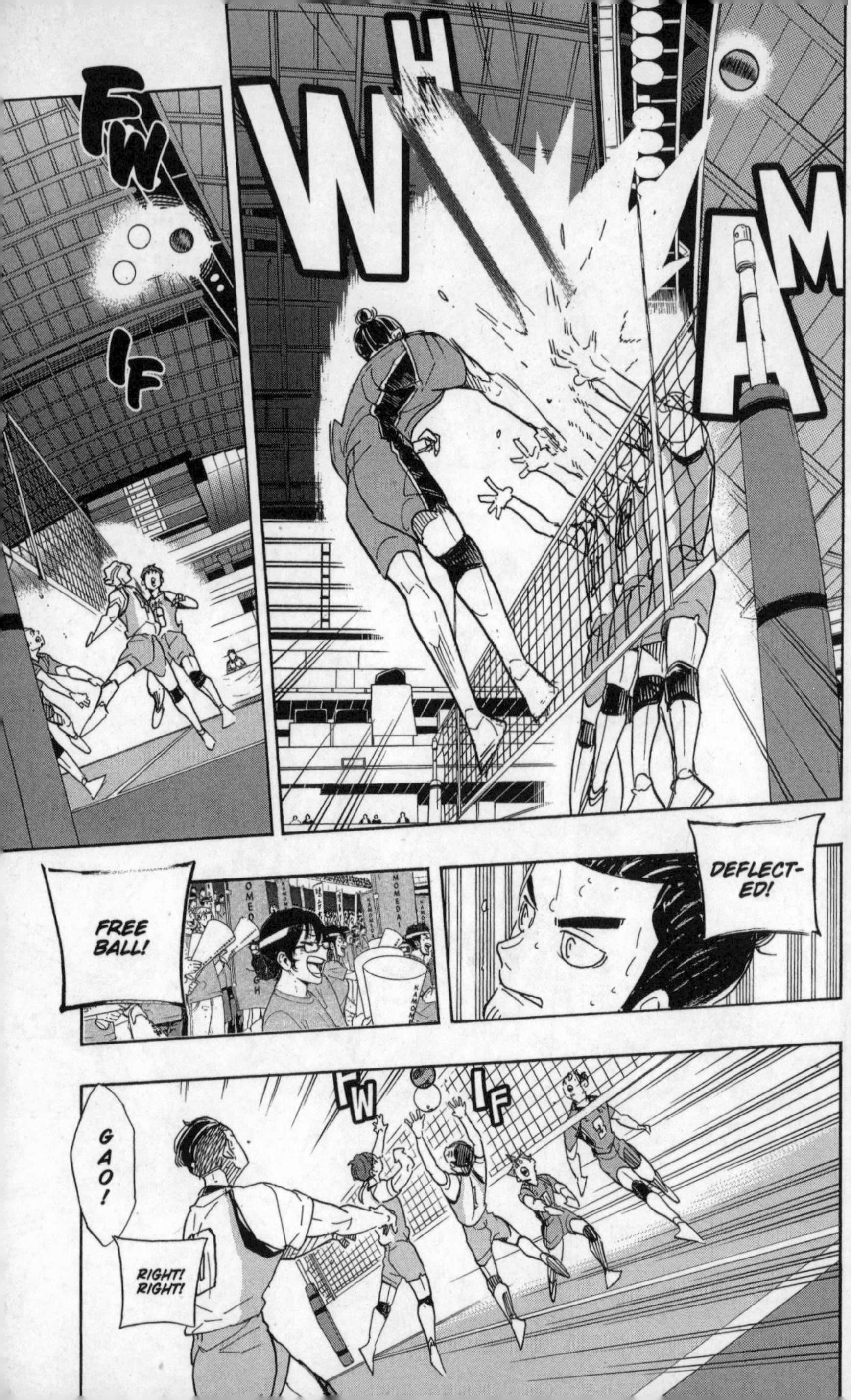
WHAM
FWIF
DEFLECTED!
FREE BALL!
FWIF
GAO!
RIGHT! RIGHT!

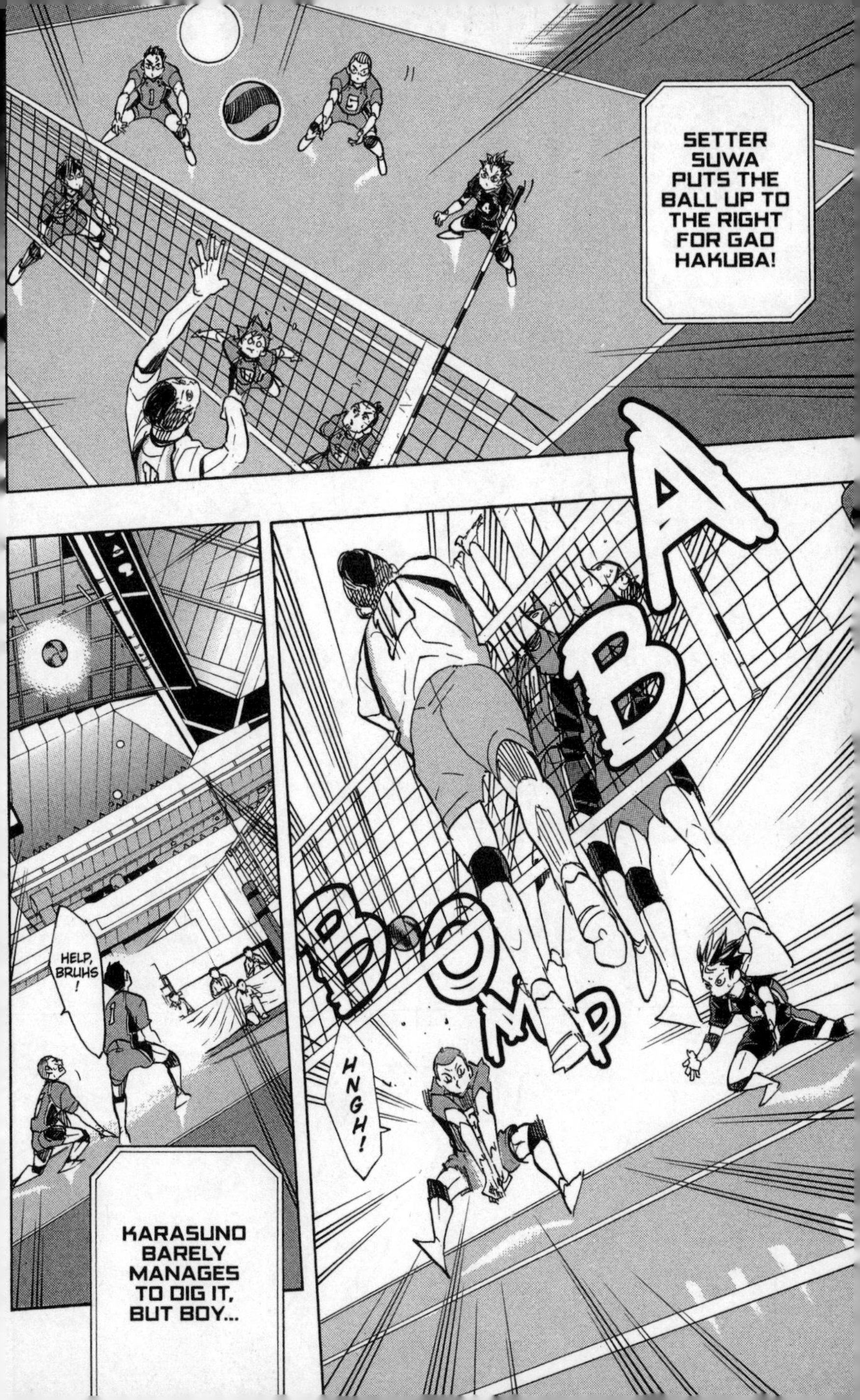
SETTER SUWA PUTS THE BALL UP TO THE RIGHT FOR GAO HAKUBA!
BOMP
HNGH!
HELP, BRUHS!
KARASUNO BARELY MANAGES TO DIG IT, BUT BOY...

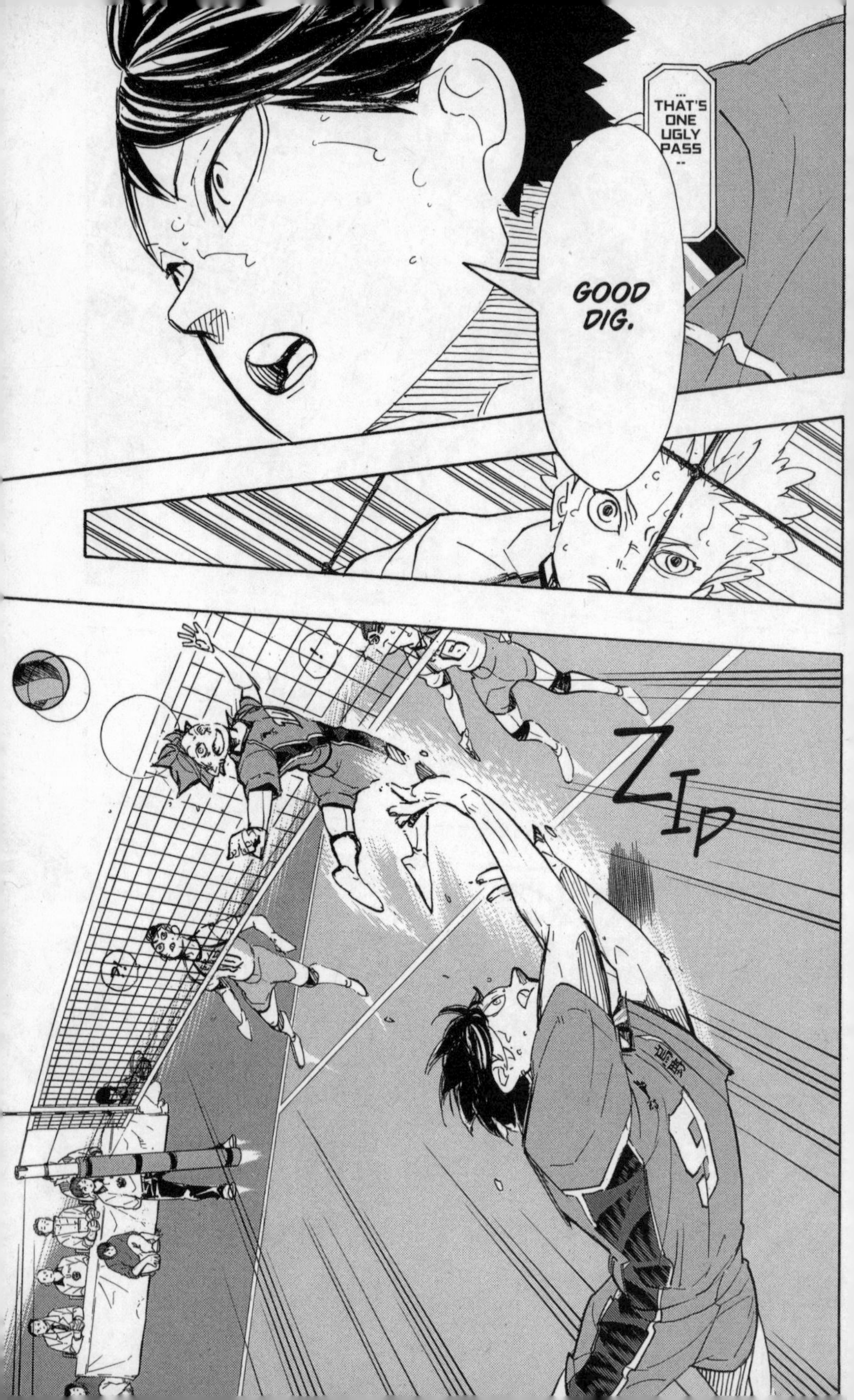
...THAT'S ONE UGLY PASS --
GOOD DIG.
ZIP

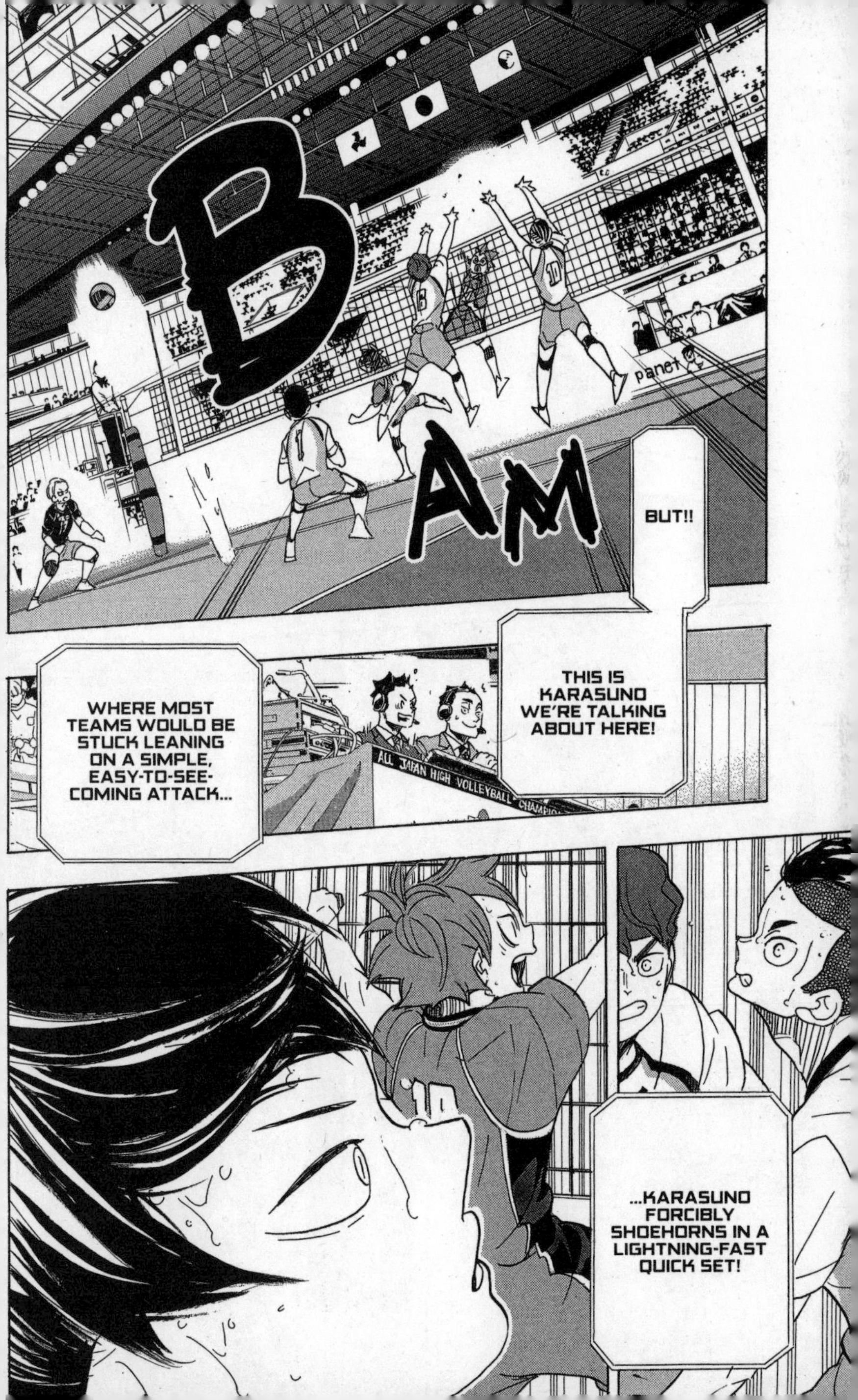
BAM
panet
BUT!!
THIS IS KARASUNO WE'RE TALKING ABOUT HERE!
WHERE MOST TEAMS WOULD BE STUCK LEANING ON A SIMPLE, EASY-TO-SEE-COMING ATTACK...
...KARASUNO FORCIBLY SHOEHORNS IN A LIGHTNING-FAST QUICK SET!

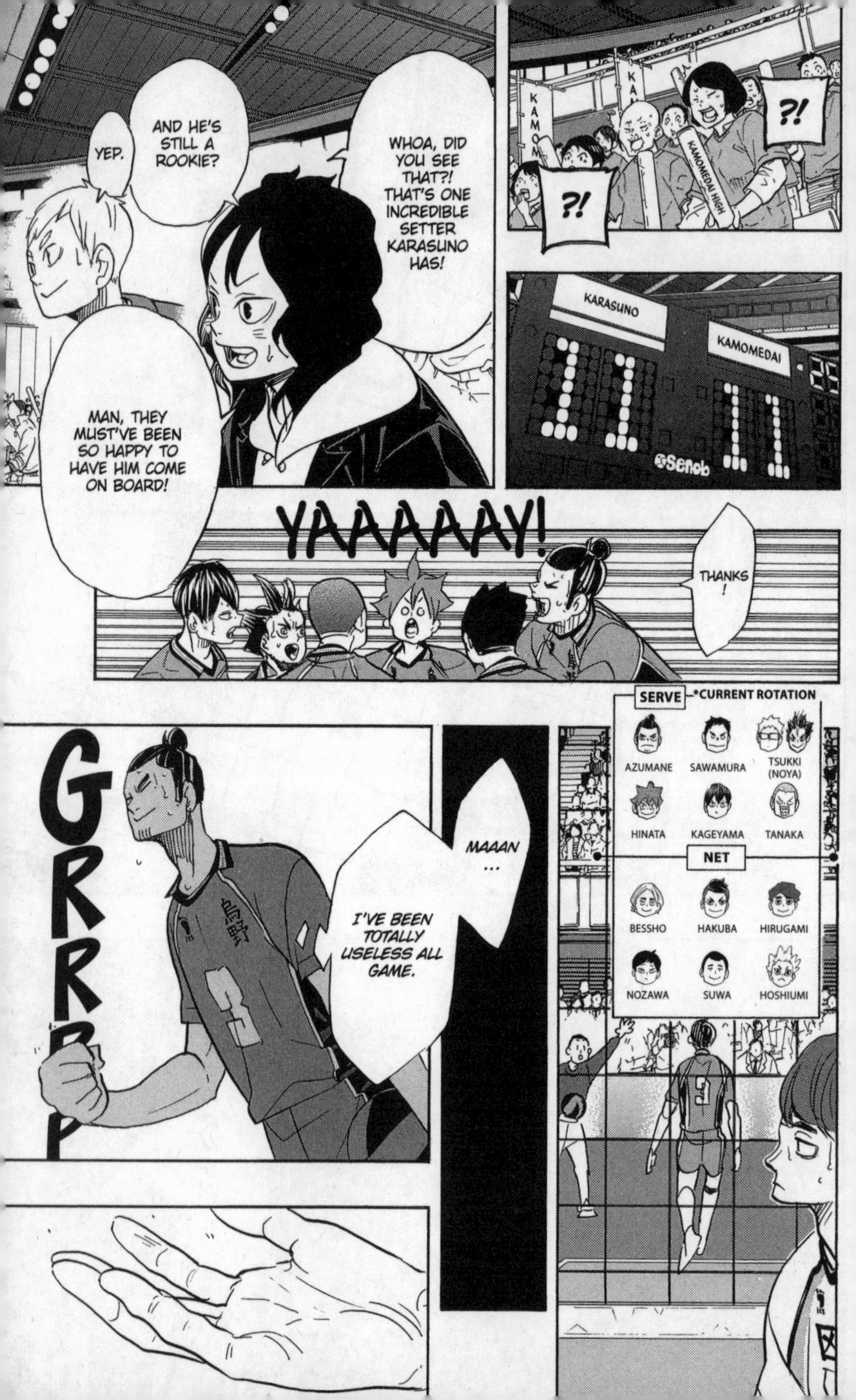
?!
?!
KAMOMEDAI HIGH
KARASUNO
KAMOMEDAI
Senob
WHOA, DID YOU SEE THAT?! THAT'S ONE INCREDIBLE SETTER KARASUNO HAS!
AND HE'S STILL A ROOKIE?
YEP.
MAN, THEY MUST'VE BEEN SO HAPPY TO HAVE HIM COME ON BOARD!
YAAAAAY!
THANKS!
SERVE
*CURRENT ROTATION
AZUMANE
SAWAMURA
TSUKKI (NOYA)
HINATA
KAGEYAMA
TANAKA
NET
BESSHO
HAKUBA
HIRUGAMI
NOZAWA
SUWA
HOSHIUMI
MAAAN...
I'VE BEEN TOTALLY USELESS ALL GAME.
GRRR

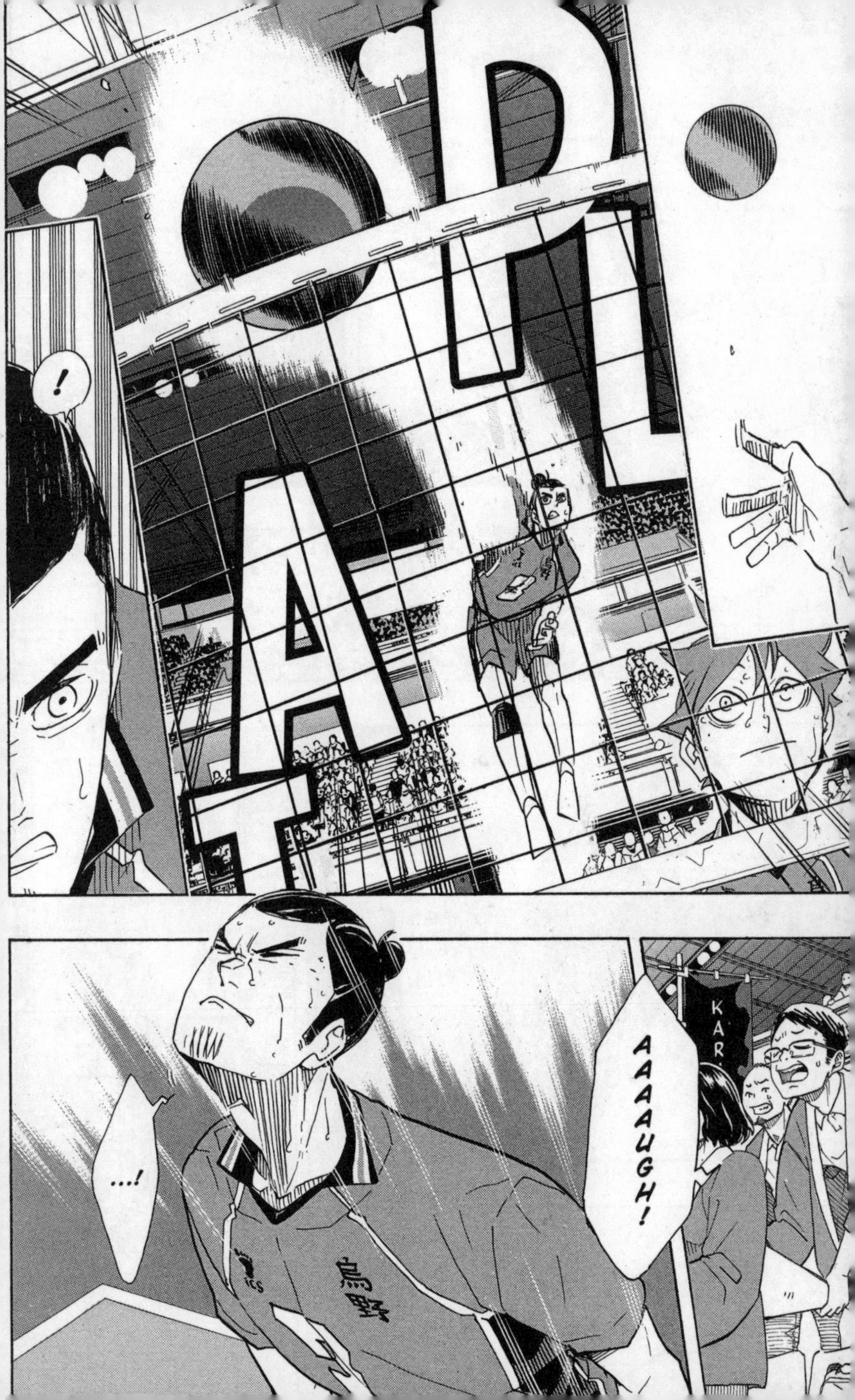

!
AAAAUGH!
...!
KAR

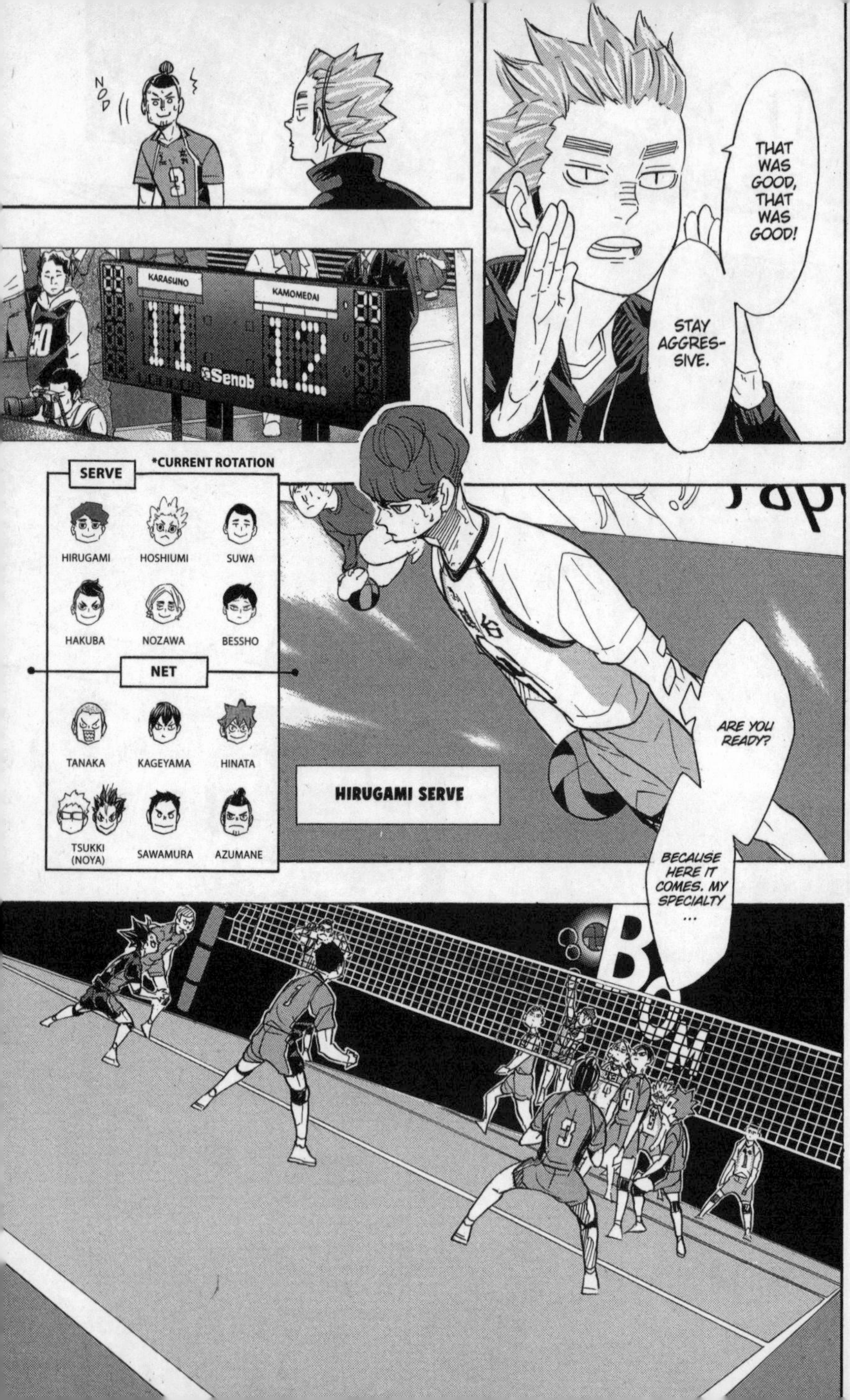
THAT WAS GOOD, THAT WAS GOOD!
STAY AGGRES-SIVE.
NOD
KARASUNO
11
KAMOMEDAI
12
Senob
ARE YOU READY?
BECAUSE HERE IT COMES. MY SPECIALTY ...
HIRUGAMI SERVE
*CURRENT ROTATION
SERVE
HIRUGAMI
HOSHIUMI
SUWA
HAKUBA
NOZAWA
BESSHO
NET
TANAKA
KAGEYAMA
HINATA
TSUKKI (NOYA)
SAWAMURA
AZUMANE

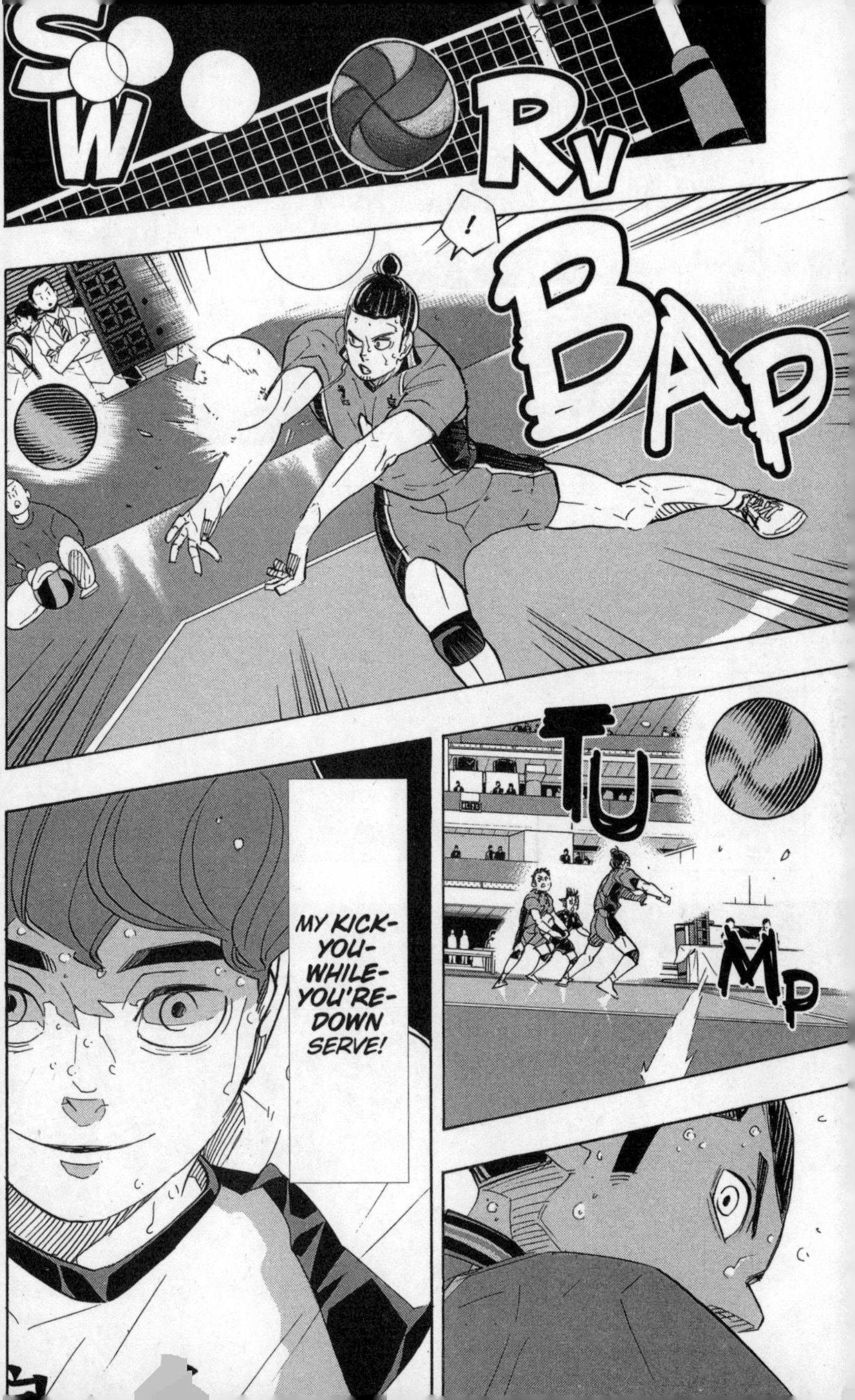
SWORV
!
BAP
TUMP
MY KICK-YOU-WHILE-YOU'RE-DOWN SERVE!

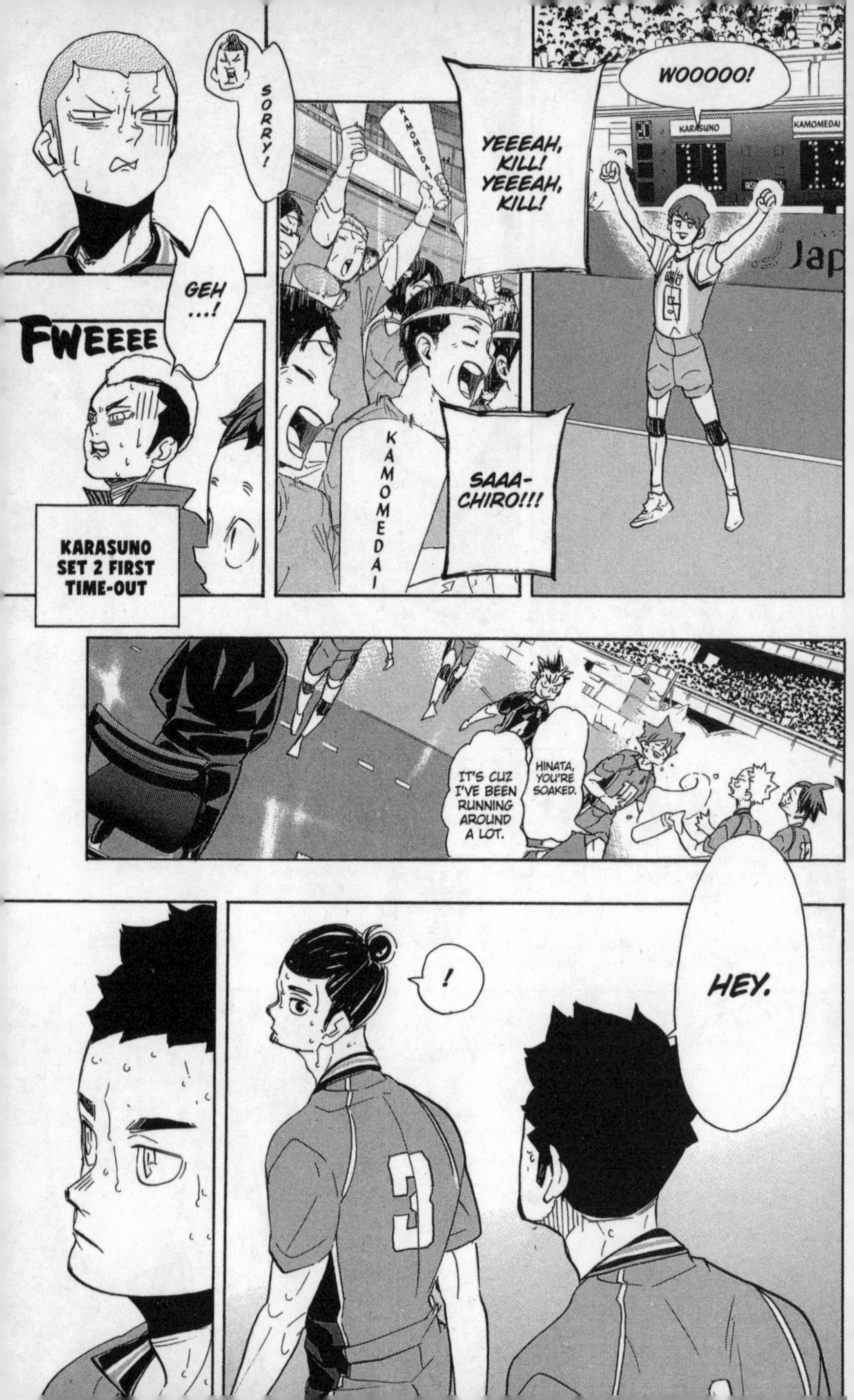
WOOOOO!
KARASUNO
KAMOMEDAI
YEEEAH, KILL! YEEEAH, KILL!
KAMOMEDAI
KAMOMEDAI
SAAA-CHIRO!!!
SORRY!
GEH ...!
FWEEEE
KARASUNO SET 2 FIRST TIME-OUT
HINATA, YOU'RE SOAKED.
IT'S CUZ I'VE BEEN RUNNING AROUND A LOT.
HEY.
!

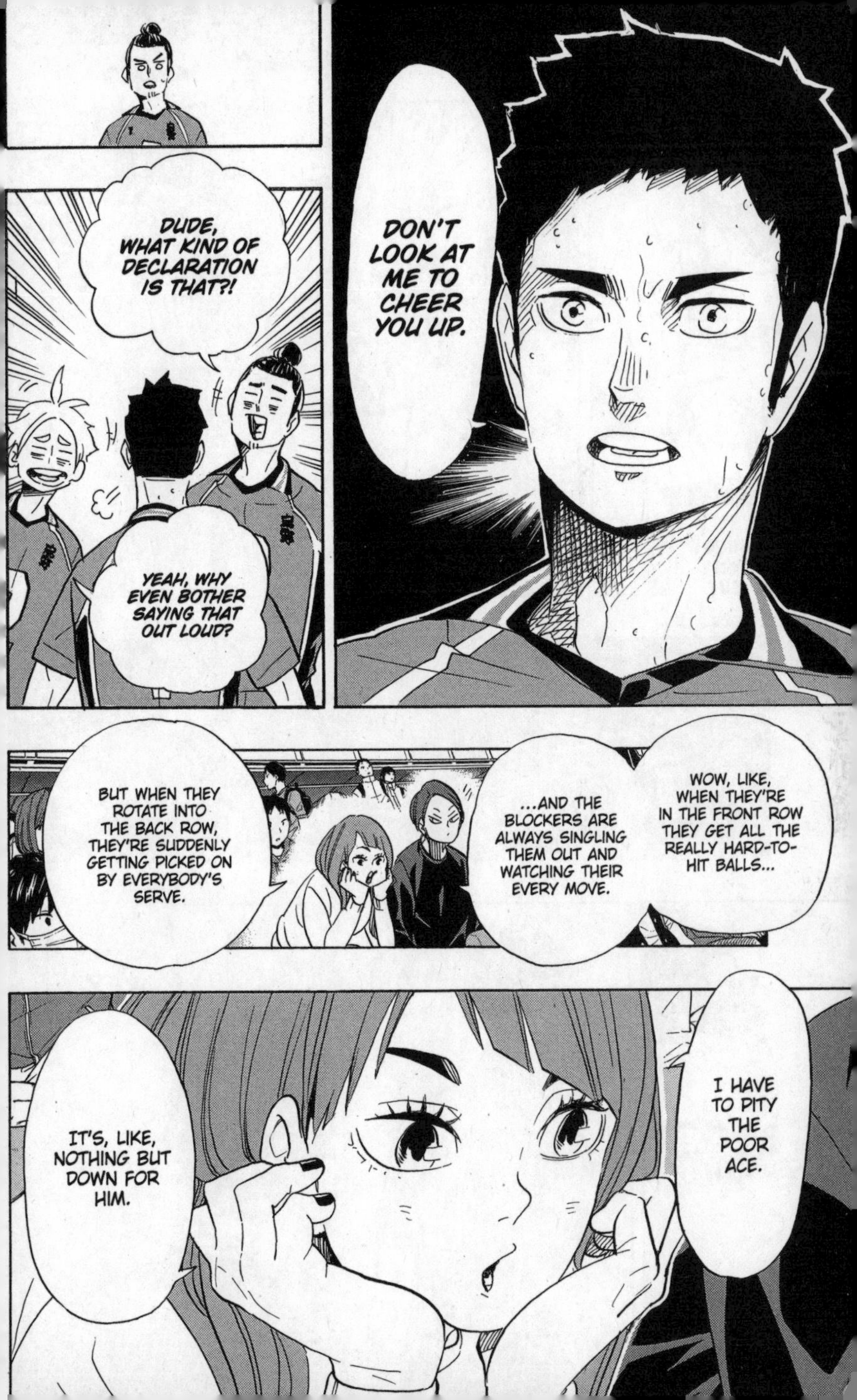
DON'T LOOK AT ME TO CHEER YOU UP.
DUDE, WHAT KIND OF DECLARATION IS THAT?!
YEAH, WHY EVEN BOTHER SAYING THAT OUT LOUD?
WOW, LIKE, WHEN THEY'RE IN THE FRONT ROW THEY GET ALL THE REALLY HARD-TO-HIT BALLS...
...AND THE BLOCKERS ARE ALWAYS SINGLING THEM OUT AND WATCHING THEIR EVERY MOVE.
BUT WHEN THEY ROTATE INTO THE BACK ROW, THEY'RE SUDDENLY GETTING PICKED ON BY EVERYBODY'S SERVE.
I HAVE TO PITY THE POOR ACE.
IT'S, LIKE, NOTHING BUT DOWN FOR HIM.

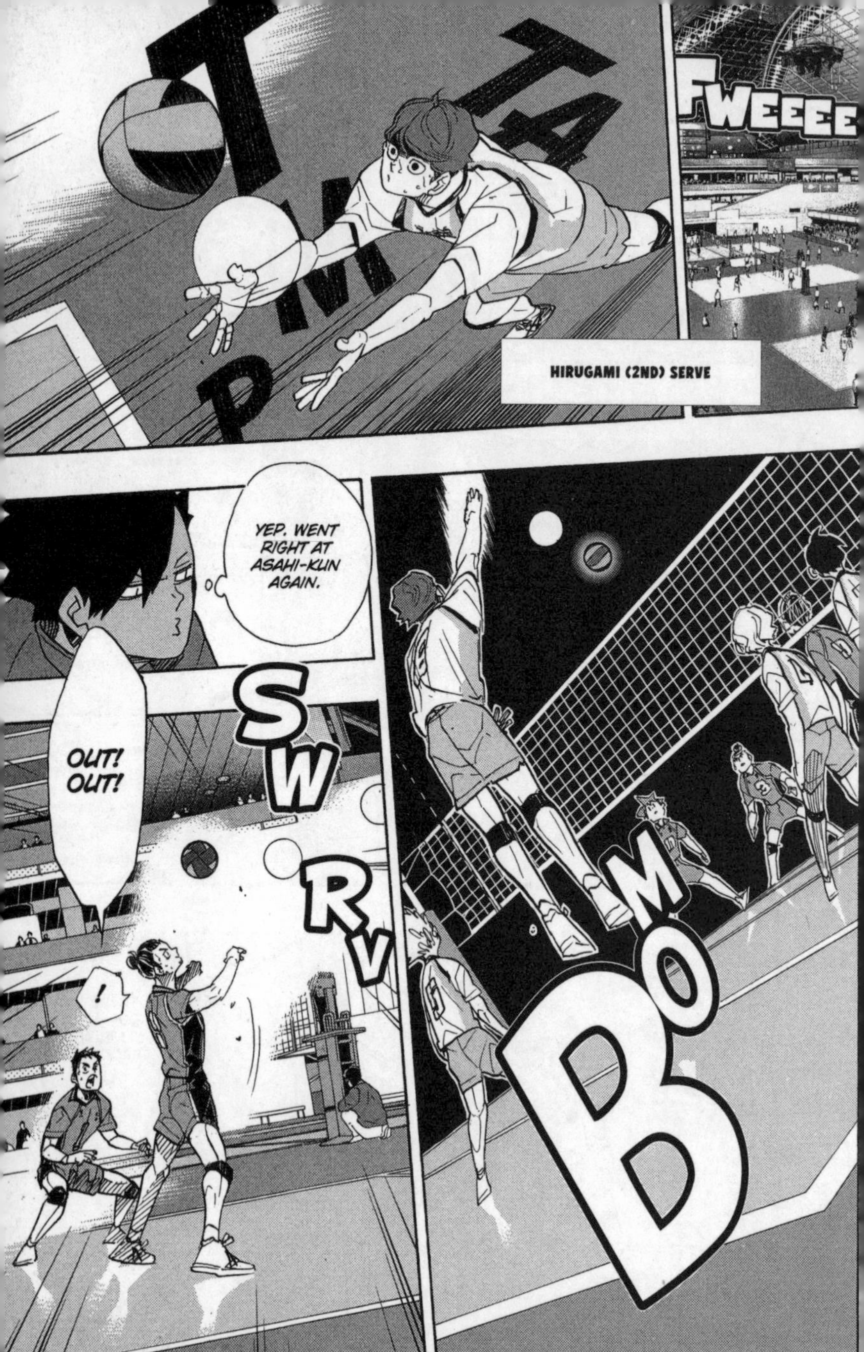
FWEEEE
HIRUGAMI (2ND) SERVE
TAMP
BOOM
YEP. WENT RIGHT AT ASAHI-KUN AGAIN.
SWRV
OUT! OUT!
!

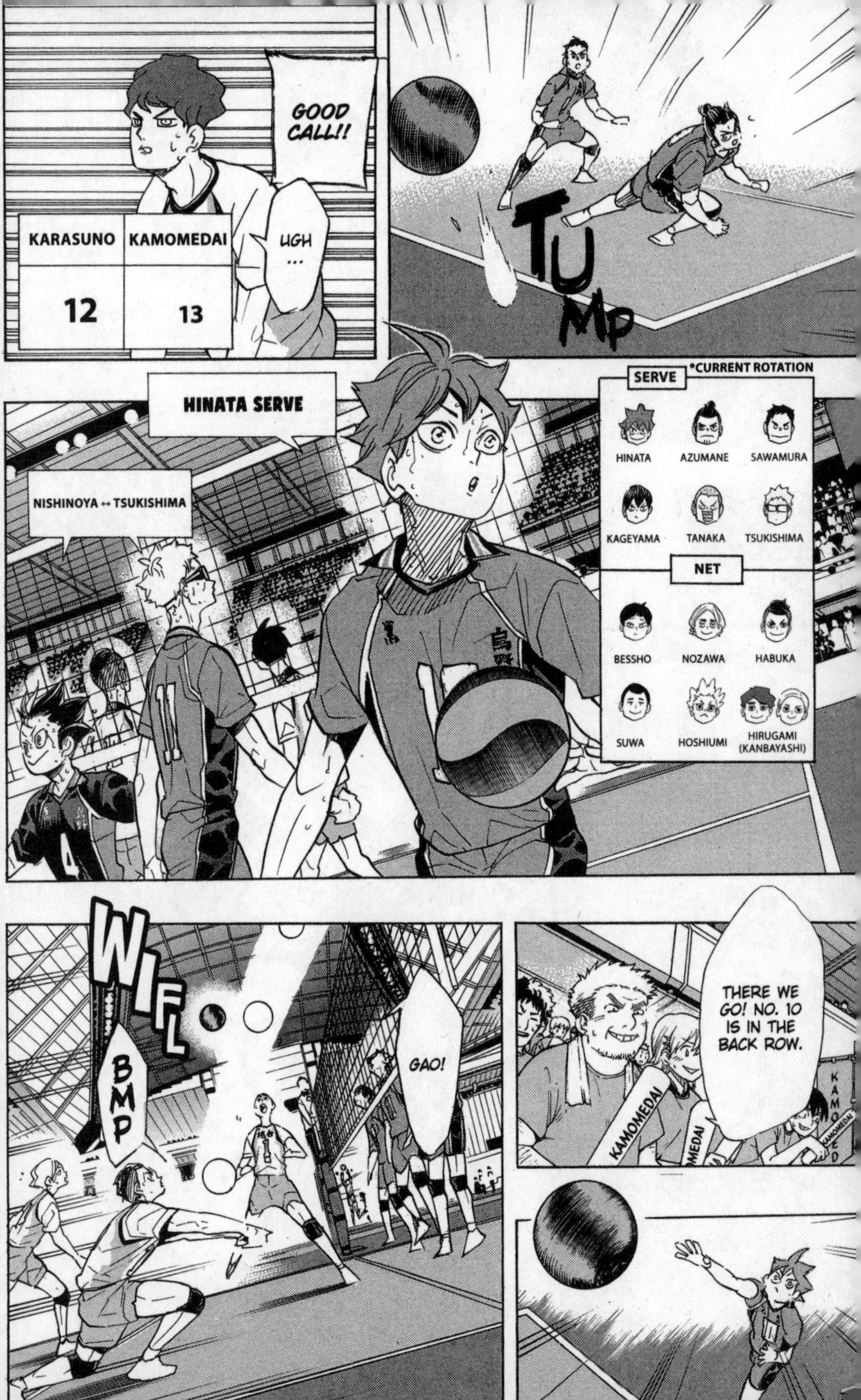
TUMP
GOOD CALL!!
UGH...
KARASUNO 12
KAMOMEDAI 13
*CURRENT ROTATION
SERVE
HINATA
AZUMANE
SAWAMURA
KAGEYAMA
TANAKA
TSUKISHIMA
NET
BESSHO
NOZAWA
HABUKA
SUWA
HOSHIUMI
HIRUGAMI (KANBAYASHI)
HINATA SERVE
NISHINOYA ↔ TSUKISHIMA
THERE WE GO! NO. 10 IS IN THE BACK ROW.
KAMOMEDAI
KAMOMEDAI
KAMOMEDAI
GAO!
WIFL
BMP

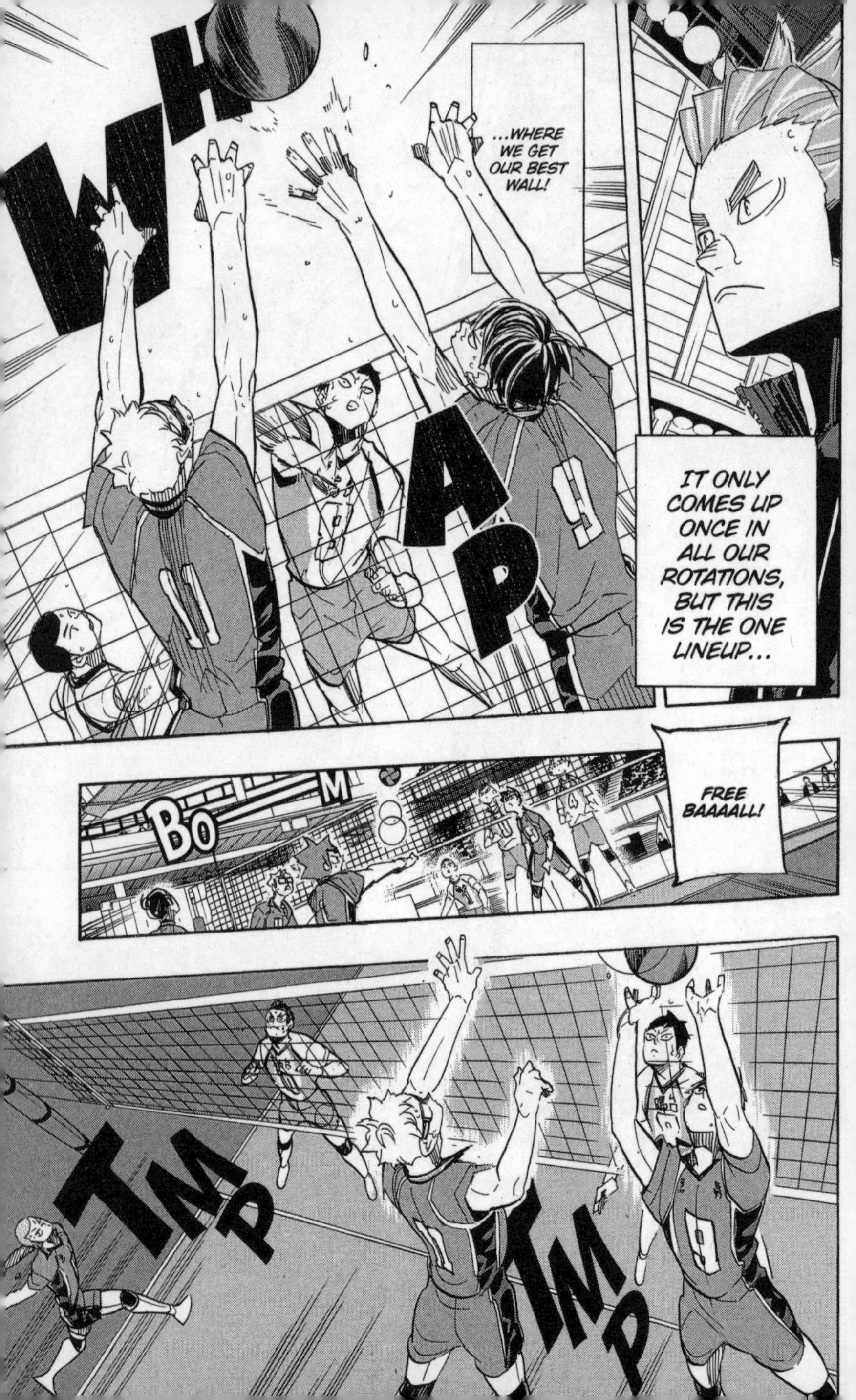
IT ONLY COMES UP ONCE IN ALL OUR ROTATIONS, BUT THIS IS THE ONE LINEUP...
...WHERE WE GET OUR BEST WALL!
WHAP
FREE BAAAALL!
BoM
TMP
TMP

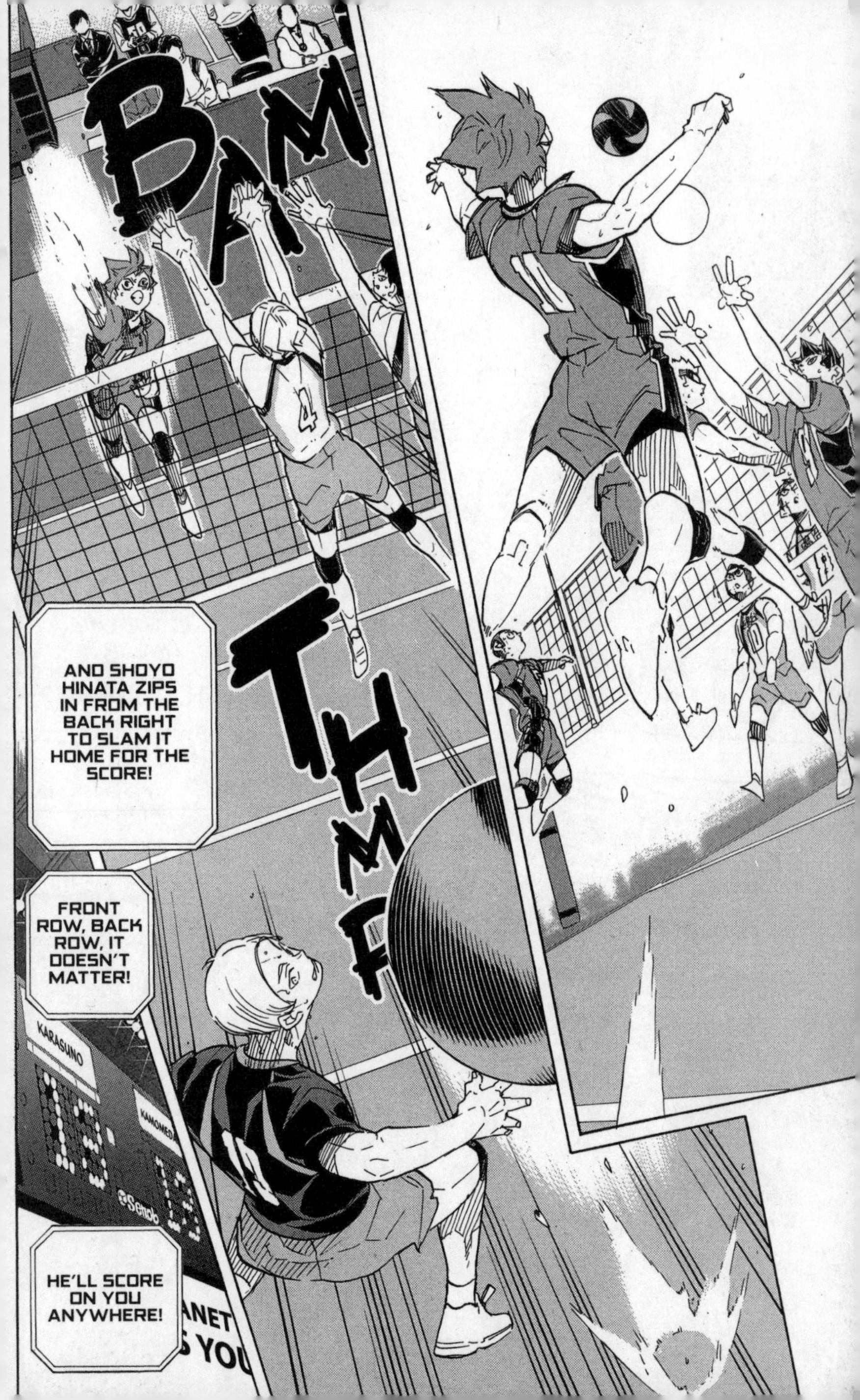
BAM
AND SHOYO HINATA ZIPS IN FROM THE BACK RIGHT TO SLAM IT HOME FOR THE SCORE!
THUMP
FRONT ROW, BACK ROW, IT DOESN'T MATTER!
HE'LL SCORE ON YOU ANYWHERE!
KARASUNO

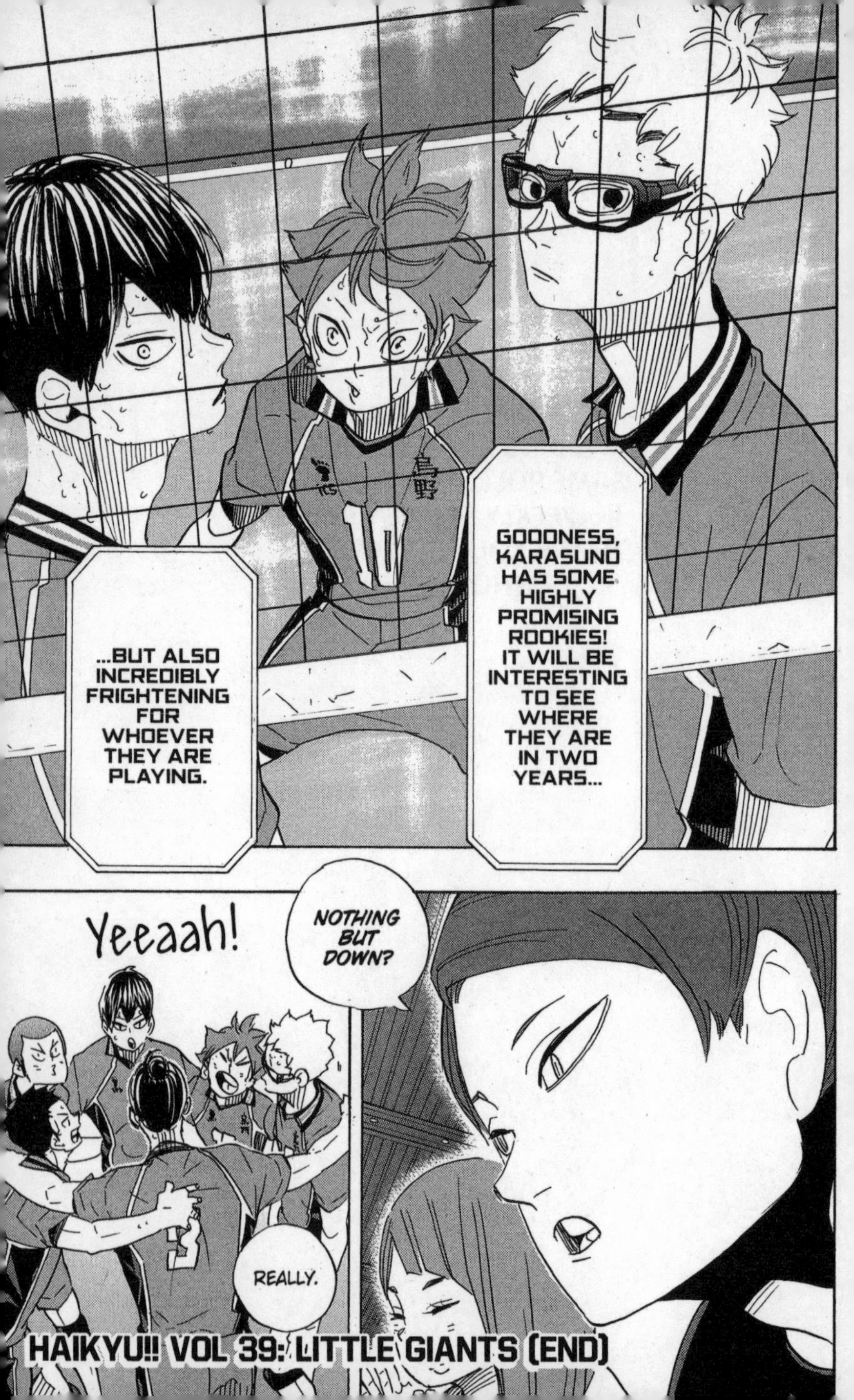
GOODNESS, KARASUNO HAS SOME HIGHLY PROMISING ROOKIES! IT WILL BE INTERESTING TO SEE WHERE THEY ARE IN TWO YEARS...
...BUT ALSO INCREDIBLY FRIGHTENING FOR WHOEVER THEY ARE PLAYING.
NOTHING BUT DOWN?
Yeeaah!
REALLY.
HAIKYU!! VOL 39: LITTLE GIANTS (END)

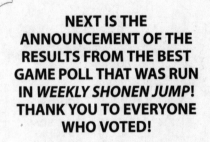

NEXT IS THE ANNOUNCEMENT OF THE RESULTS FROM THE BEST GAME POLL THAT WAS RUN IN *WEEKLY SHONEN JUMP*! THANK YOU TO EVERYONE WHO VOTED!

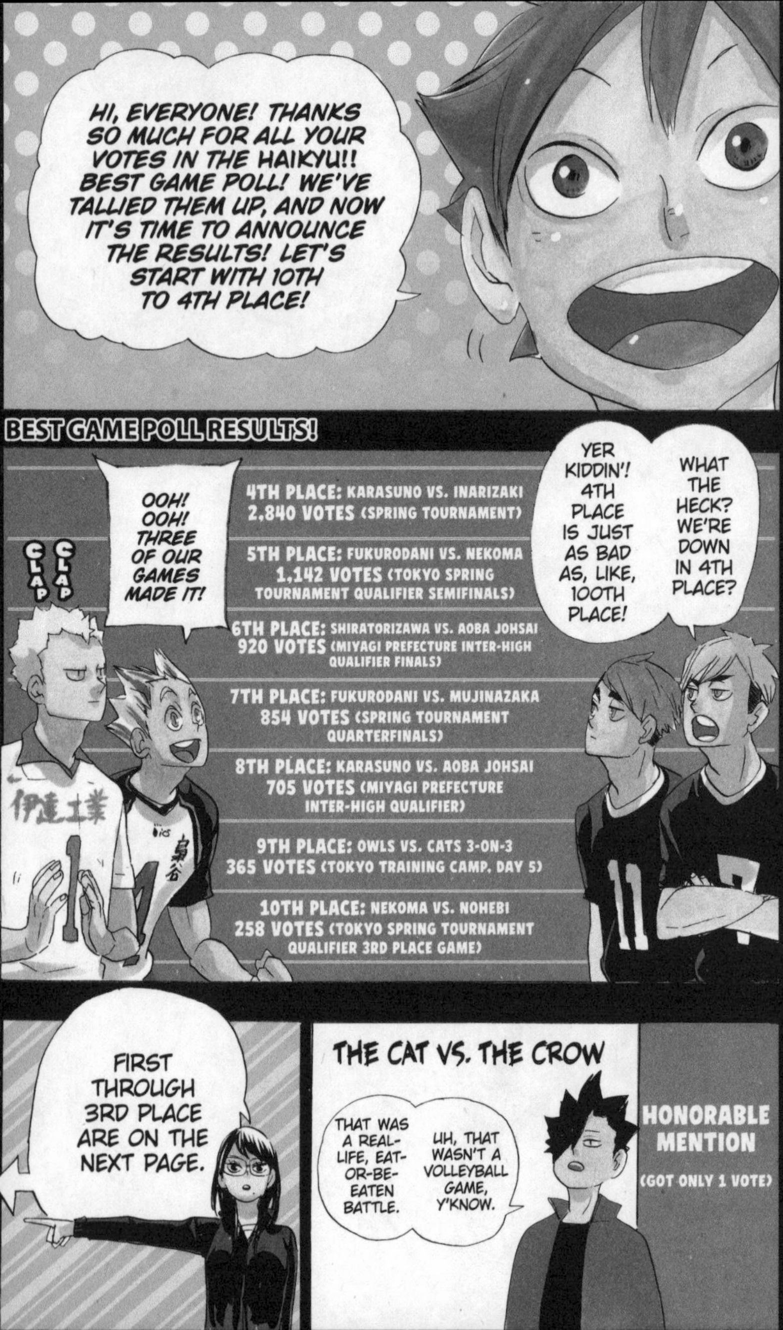
HI, EVERYONE! THANKS SO MUCH FOR ALL YOUR VOTES IN THE HAIKYU!! BEST GAME POLL! WE'VE TALLIED THEM UP, AND NOW IT'S TIME TO ANNOUNCE THE RESULTS! LET'S START WITH 10TH TO 4TH PLACE!
BEST GAME POLL RESULTS!
WHAT THE HECK? WE'RE DOWN IN 4TH PLACE?
YER KIDDIN'! 4TH PLACE IS JUST AS BAD AS, LIKE, 100TH PLACE!
4TH PLACE: KARASUNO VS. INARIZAKI 2,840 VOTES (SPRING TOURNAMENT)
5TH PLACE: FUKURODANI VS. NEKOMA 1,142 VOTES (TOKYO SPRING TOURNAMENT QUALIFIER SEMIFINALS)
6TH PLACE: SHIRATORIZAWA VS. AOBA JOHSAI 920 VOTES (MIYAGI PREFECTURE INTER-HIGH QUALIFIER FINALS)
7TH PLACE: FUKURODANI VS. MUJINAZAKA 854 VOTES (SPRING TOURNAMENT QUARTERFINALS)
8TH PLACE: KARASUNO VS. AOBA JOHSAI 705 VOTES (MIYAGI PREFECTURE INTER-HIGH QUALIFIER)
9TH PLACE: OWLS VS. CATS 3-ON-3 365 VOTES (TOKYO TRAINING CAMP, DAY 5)
10TH PLACE: NEKOMA VS. NOHEBI 258 VOTES (TOKYO SPRING TOURNAMENT QUALIFIER 3RD PLACE GAME)
OOH! OOH! THREE OF OUR GAMES MADE IT!
CLAP CLAP
HONORABLE MENTION
(GOT ONLY 1 VOTE)
THE CAT VS. THE CROW
UH, THAT WASN'T A VOLLEYBALL GAME, Y'KNOW.
THAT WAS A REAL-LIFE, EAT-OR-BE-EATEN BATTLE.
FIRST THROUGH 3RD PLACE ARE ON THE NEXT PAGE.

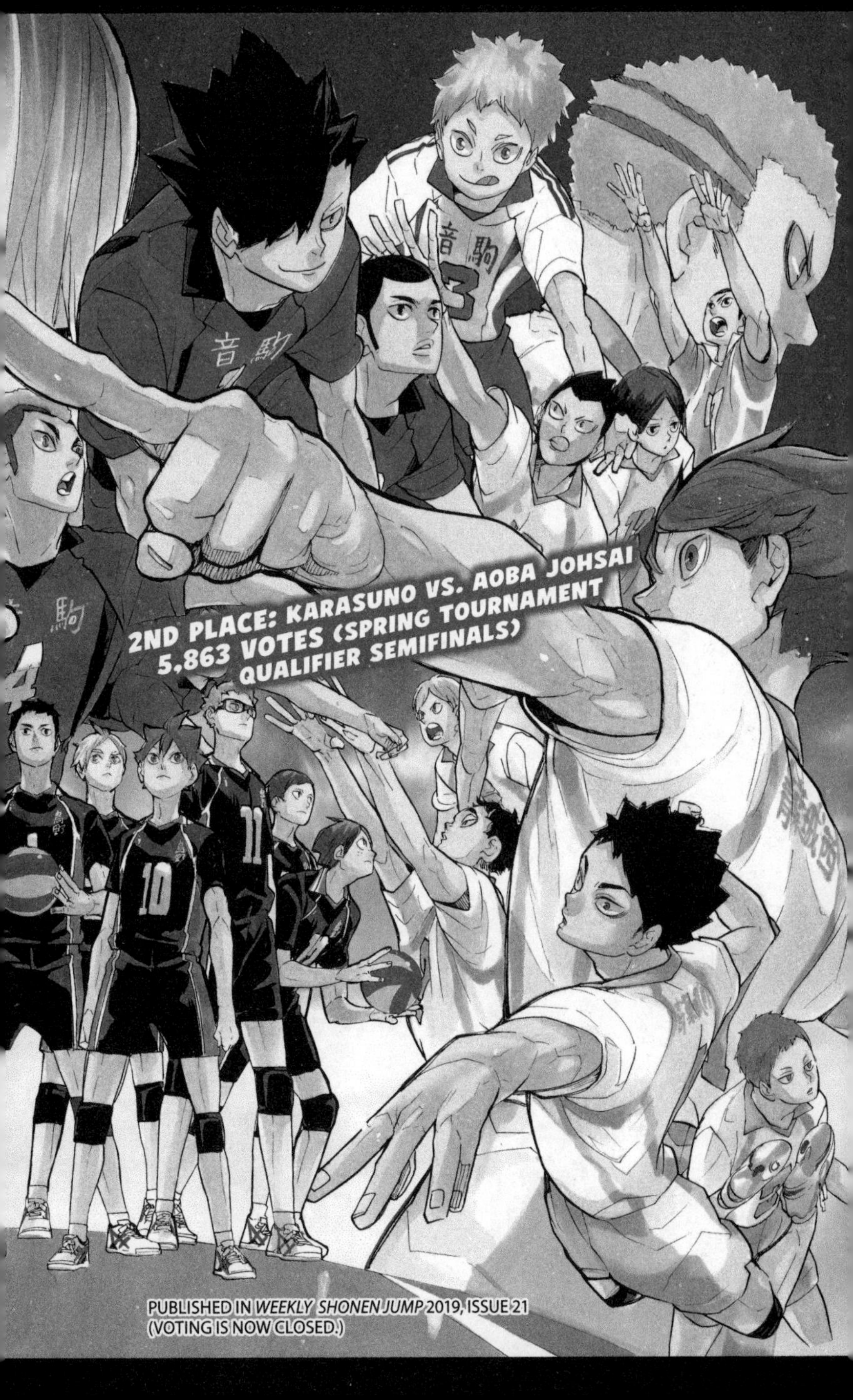
2ND PLACE: KARASUNO VS. AOBA JOHSAI
5,863 VOTES (SPRING TOURNAMENT
QUALIFIER SEMIFINALS)

PUBLISHED IN *WEEKLY SHONEN JUMP* 2019, ISSUE 21
(VOTING IS NOW CLOSED.)

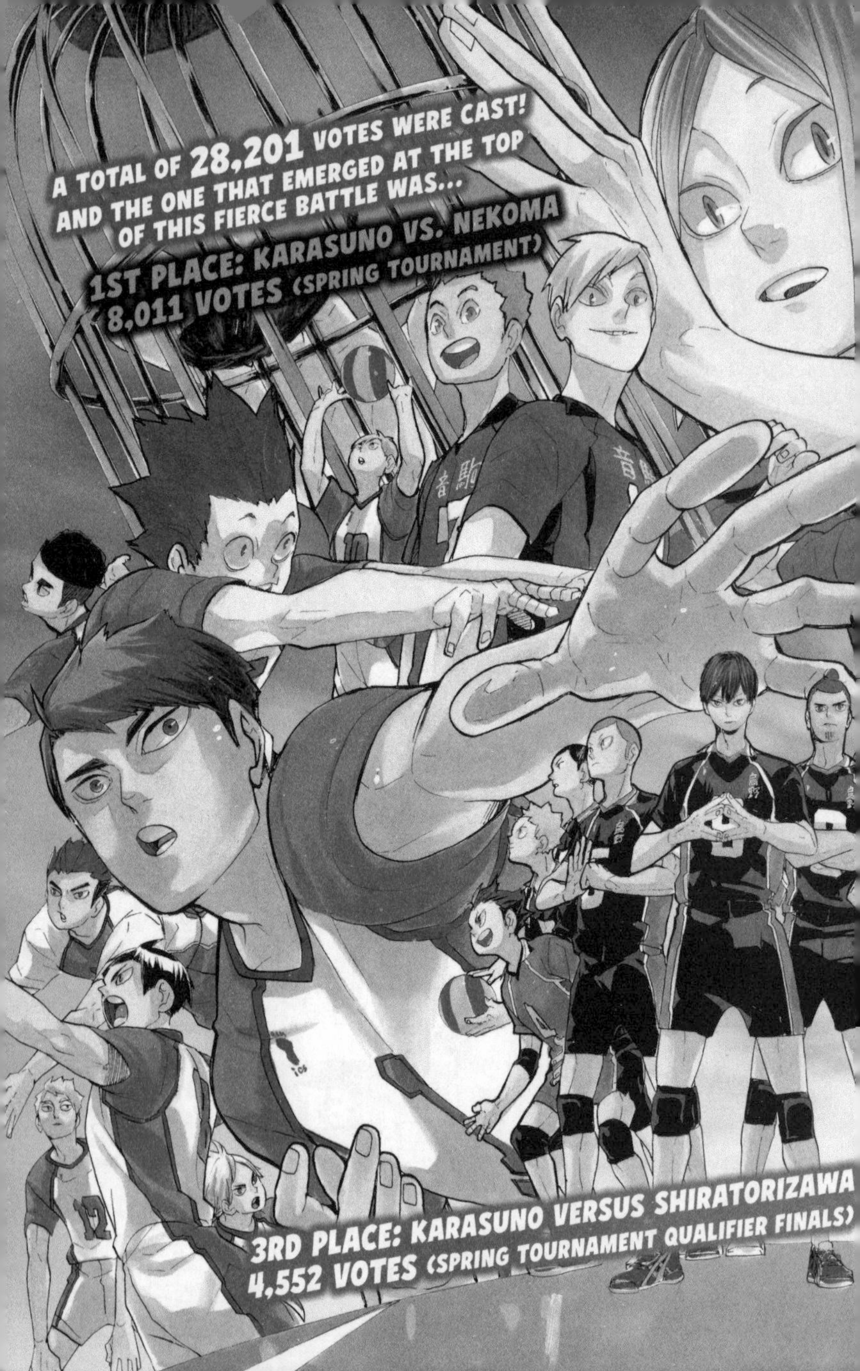
A TOTAL OF 28,201 VOTES WERE CAST!
AND THE ONE THAT EMERGED AT THE TOP
OF THIS FIERCE BATTLE WAS...
1ST PLACE: KARASUNO VS. NEKOMA
8,011 VOTES (SPRING TOURNAMENT)
3RD PLACE: KARASUNO VERSUS SHIRATORIZAWA
4,552 VOTES (SPRING TOURNAMENT QUALIFIER FINALS)

HAIKYU!! BEST GAME

4TH PLACE AND DOWN

POPULARITY POLL

RESULTS!!

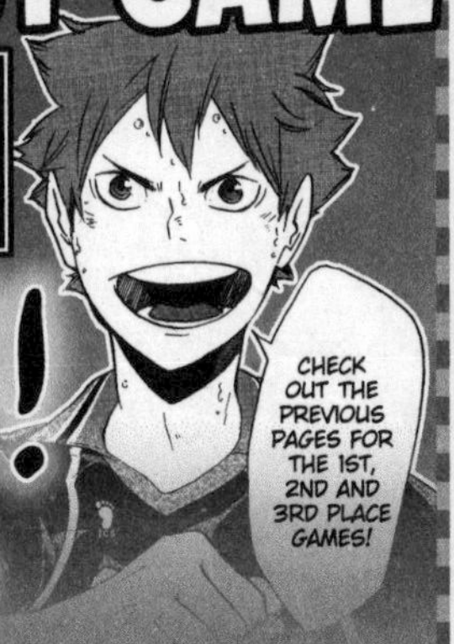
CHECK OUT THE PREVIOUS PAGES FOR THE 1ST, 2ND AND 3RD PLACE GAMES!

WE ASKED FOR READERS' VOTES IN *WEEKLY SHONEN JUMP* 2019, ISSUE 12, AND GOT A WHOPPING 28,201 RESPONSES! LET'S SEE HOW EVERYTHING SHOOK OUT!

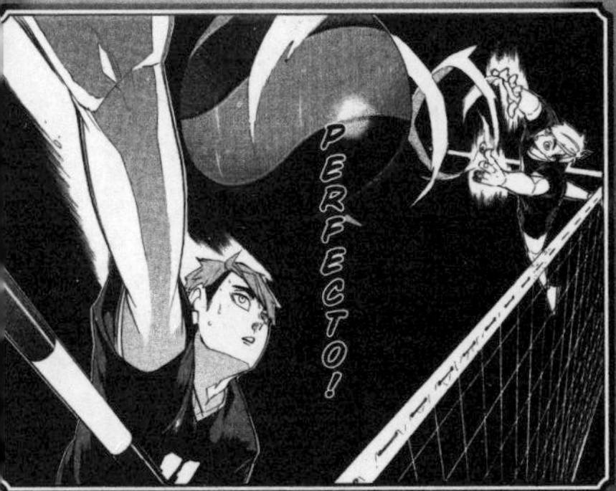
PERFECTO!

4TH

KARASUNO VS. INARIZAKI
(SPRING TOURNAMENT, ROUND 2)

2,840 VOTES

KARASUNO HAS IT ROUGH AGAINST THE MIYA TWINS' FREAK QUICK, BUT THEIR SPEED WINS IN THE END.

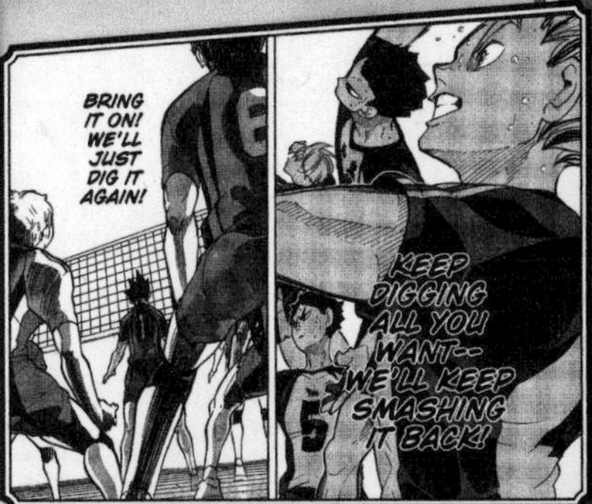
KEEP DIGGING ALL YOU WANT-- WE'LL KEEP SMASHING IT BACK!
BRING IT ON! WE'LL JUST DIG IT AGAIN!

5TH

FUKURODANI VS. NEKOMA
(TOKYO SPRING TOURNAMENT QUALIFIER SEMIFINALS)

1,142 VOTES

NEKOMA IS TENACIOUS ON DEFENSE, AND BOKUTO ISN'T IN TOP FORM! BUT AKAASHI'S SKILL GIVES FUKURODANI THE WIN.

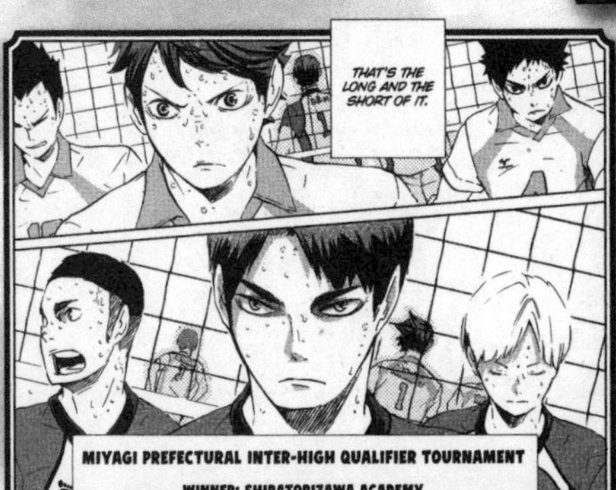
THAT'S THE LONG AND THE SHORT OF IT.
MIYAGI PREFECTURAL INTER-HIGH QUALIFIER TOURNAMENT
WINNER: SHIRATORIZAWA ACADEMY

6TH

SHIRATORIZAWA VS. AOBA JOHSAI

(MIYAGI PREFECTURE INTER-HIGH QUALIFIER FINALS)

920 VOTES

AOBA JOHSAI IS HIGHLY COMPETENT OVERALL, BUT USHIWAKA IS JUST TOO OVERWHELMINGLY GOOD…

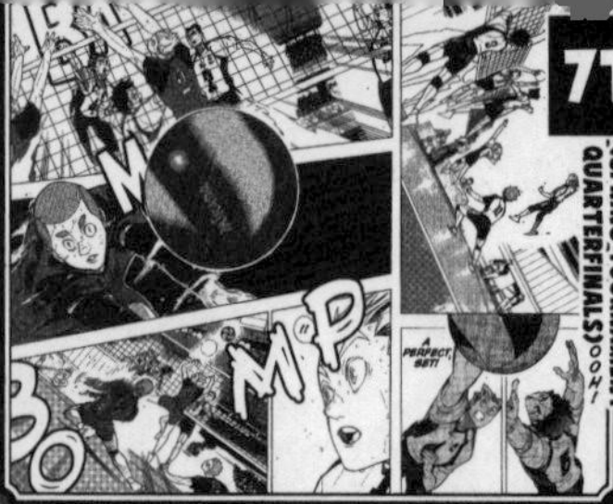
A PERFECT SET!

7TH

FUKURODANI VS. MUJINAZAKA (SPRING TOURNAMENT QUARTERFINALS)

854 VOTES

IT'S A BATTLE OF ACES BETWEEN FUKURODANI'S BOKUTO AND MUJINAZAKA'S KIRYU. BOKUTO, PLAYING HIS BEST EVER, GETS THE WIN.

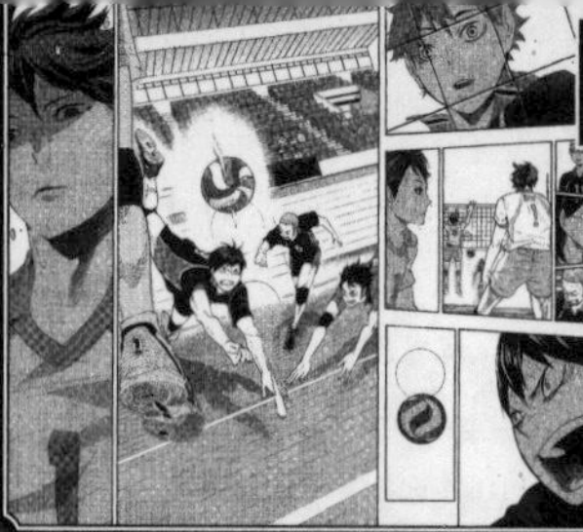

8TH

KARASUNO VS. AOBA JOHSAI (MIYAGI PREFECTURE INTER-HIGH QUALIFIER)

705 VOTES

HINATA AND KAGEYAMA'S FREAK QUICK IS TRIPLE-BLOCKED BY AOBA JOHSAI, ELIMINATING KARASUNO FROM THE TOURNAMENT...

9TH

OWLS VS. CATS 3-ON-3 (TOKYO TRAINING CAMP, DAY 5)

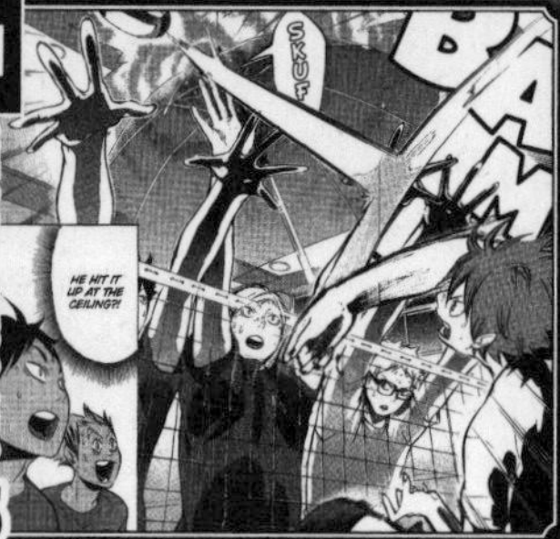
SKUF
HE HIT IT UP AT THE CEILING?!

365 VOTES

THIS IS WHERE BOKUTO AND HINATA BECOME MASTER AND DISCIPLE, AND HINATA LEARNS WAYS TO ATTACK OTHER THAN A QUICK SET.

10TH

NEKOMA VS. NOHEBI (TOKYO SPRING TOURNAMENT QUALIFIER 3RD PLACE GAME)

258 VOTES

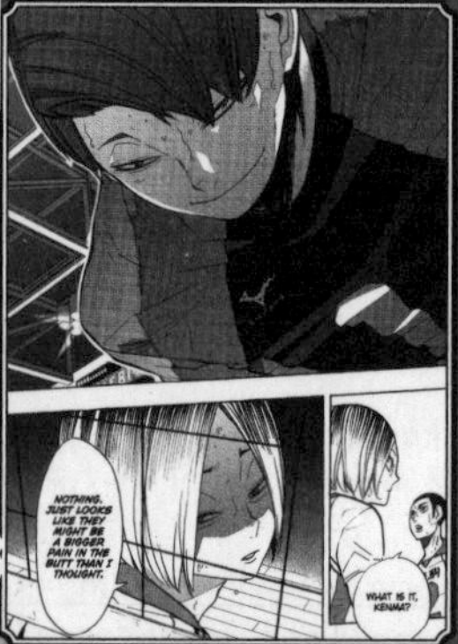
WHAT IS IT, KENMA?
NOTHING. JUST LOOKS LIKE THEY MIGHT BE A BIGGER PAIN IN THE BUTT THAN I THOUGHT.

NEKOMA WINS BY RESISTING NOHEBI'S ATTEMPTS TO MAKE THEM IMPLODE.

- **11TH** DATE TECH vs. AOBA JOHSAI (SPRING TOURNEY QUALIFIER).....212 VOTES
- **12TH** KARASUNO vs. FUKURODANI (TOKYO TRAINING CAMP, LAST DAY)
  YOUTH CAMP POSITION SHUFFLE.....185 VOTES
- **14TH** KITAGAWA DAIICHI VS YUKIGAOKA.....173 VOTES
- **15TH** KARASUNO vs. NEKOMA (PRACTICE GAME).....165 VOTES
- **16TH** KARASUNO vs. MUNICIPAL TEAM.....163 VOTES
- **17TH** KARASUNO vs. WAKUTANI MINAMI
  (SPRING TOURNEY QUALIFIER).....140 VOTES
- **18TH** INTRA-TEAM 3-ON-3
  KARASUNO vs. DATE TECH (PRACTICE GAME).....135 VOTES
- **19TH** KARASUNO vs. TOKONAMI (INTER-HIGH PRELIMS).....133 VOTES
- **20TH** KARASUNO vs. TOKONAMI (INTER-HIGH PRELIMS).....133 VOTES
- **21ST** OWLS vs. CATS 3-ON-3 (TOKYO TRAINING CAMP DAY 3).....125 VOTES
- **22ND** KARASUNO vs. DATE TECH (INTER-HIGH PRELIMS).....110 VOTES
- **23RD** NEKOMA vs. SARUKAWA TECH (SPRING TOURNEY DAY 2).....98 VOTES
- **24TH** ROOKIE TEAM vs. SHIRATORIZAWA 3RD YEARS
  (ROOKIE CAMP DAY 1).....88 VOTES
- **25TH** READERS' CHOICE TEAM vs. AUTHOR'S CHOICE TEAM...80 VOTES
- **26TH** ROOKIE TEAM vs. SHIRATORIZAWA 3RD YEARS
  (ROOKIE CAMP DAY 2).....79 VOTES
- **27TH** KARASUNO vs. NEKOMA (TOKYO TRAINING CAMP, DAY 3)
  SHIRATORIZAWA vs. INARIZAKI.....71 VOTES
- **29TH** KARASUNO vs. AOBA JOHSAI (PRACTICE GAME)
  KARASUNO vs. JOHZENJI (SPRING TOURNEY PRELIMS).....50 VOTES
- **31ST** FUKURODANI vs. ITACHIYAMA
  (TOKYO SPRING TOURNEY QUALIFIER FINALS).....45 VOTES
- **32ND** KITAGAWA DAIICHI vs. SHIRATORIZAWA MIDDLE SCHOOL
  (PRACTICE GAME).....30 VOTES
- **33RD** SHIRABU'S FLASHBACK OF OIKAWA & IWAIZUMI'S GAME
  (CH. 165).....24 VOTES
- **34TH** SHIRATORIZAWA vs. OUGI MINAMI (FLASHBACK).....17 VOTES
- **35TH** NEKOMA vs. FUKURODANI (TOKYO TRAINING CAMP DAY 2)
  KARASUNO vs. TSUBAKIHARA (SPRING TOURNEY ROUND 1).....10 VOTES
- **37TH** NEKOMA vs. FUKURODANI (TOKYO TRAINING CAMP DAY 2)
  KARASUNO vs. OUGI MINAMI (SPRING TOURNEY PRELIMS).....9 VOTES
- **39TH** KARASUNO GIRLS vs. SHIRATO GIRLS (INTER-HIGH PRELIMS)....8 VOTES
- **40TH** KARASUNO vs. NEKOMA (TOKYO TRAINING CAMP DAY 2)
  FUKURODANI vs. EIWA (SPRING TOURNEY ROUND 1).....7 VOTES
- **42ND** KARASUNO vs. FUKURODANI (TOKYO TRAINING CAMP DAY 3).....6 VOTES
- **43RD** KARASUNO vs. FUKURODANI (TOKYO TRAINING CAMP DAY 1)
  NEKOMA vs. KIYOKAWA (SPRING TOURNEY ROUND 1).....5 VOTES
- **45TH** AOBA JOHSAI vs OMISAKI (INTER-HIGH PRELIMS)
  KARASUNO vs. FUKURODANI (TOKYO TRAINING CAMP DAY 1)
  FUKURODANI vs. MATSUYAMA NISHI (SPRING TOURNEY ROUND 3)
  TSUKISHIMA & GOSHIKI vs. KUNIMI & HYAKUZAWA
  (ROOKIE CAMP, CH. 217).....4 VOTES
- **49TH** KARASUNO vs. UBUGAWA (TOKYO TRAINING CAMP DAY 2)
  KARASUNO vs. KAKUGAWA (SPRING TOURNEY PRELIMS)
  SHIRATORIZAWA vs. HAKUSUIKAN (SPRING TOURNEY QUALIFIER)
  HYAKUZAWA & KUROISHI vs. KUNIMI & NAGAMATSU
  (ROOKIE CAMP, CH. 217).....3 VOTES
- **53RD** NEKOMA vs. TSUKINOKIZAWA (PRACTICE GAME)
  NEKOMA vs. UBUGAWA (TOKYO TRAINING CAMP DAY 1)
  KARASUNO vs. UBUGAWA (TOKYO TRAINING CAMP DAY 2)
  SHINZEN vs. UBUGAWA (TOKYO TRAINING CAMP DAY 1)
  AOBA JOHSAI 3RD YEARS POST
  SPRING TOURNEY QUALIFIER GAME (VOL. 17 BONUS STORY)...2 VOTES
- **58TH** ALL OTHERS
  (14 GAMES RECEIVED ONE VOTE, FOR A TOTAL OF 14 VOTES)

EDITOR'S NOTES

The English edition of Haikyu!! maintains the honorifics used in the original Japanese version. For those of you who are new to these terms, here's a brief explanation to help with your reading experience!

When saying someone's name in Japanese, a suffix is often attached to indicate how familiar the speaker is with the person. Some are more polite and respectful, while others are endearing.

1. **-kun** is often used for young men or boys, usually someone you are familiar with.

2. **-chan** is used for young children and can be used as a term of endearment.

3. **-san** is used for someone you respect or are not close to, or to be polite.

4. **Senpai** is used for someone who is older than you or in a higher position or grade in school.

5. **Kohai** is used for someone who is younger than you or in a lower position or grade in school.

6. **Sensei** means teacher.

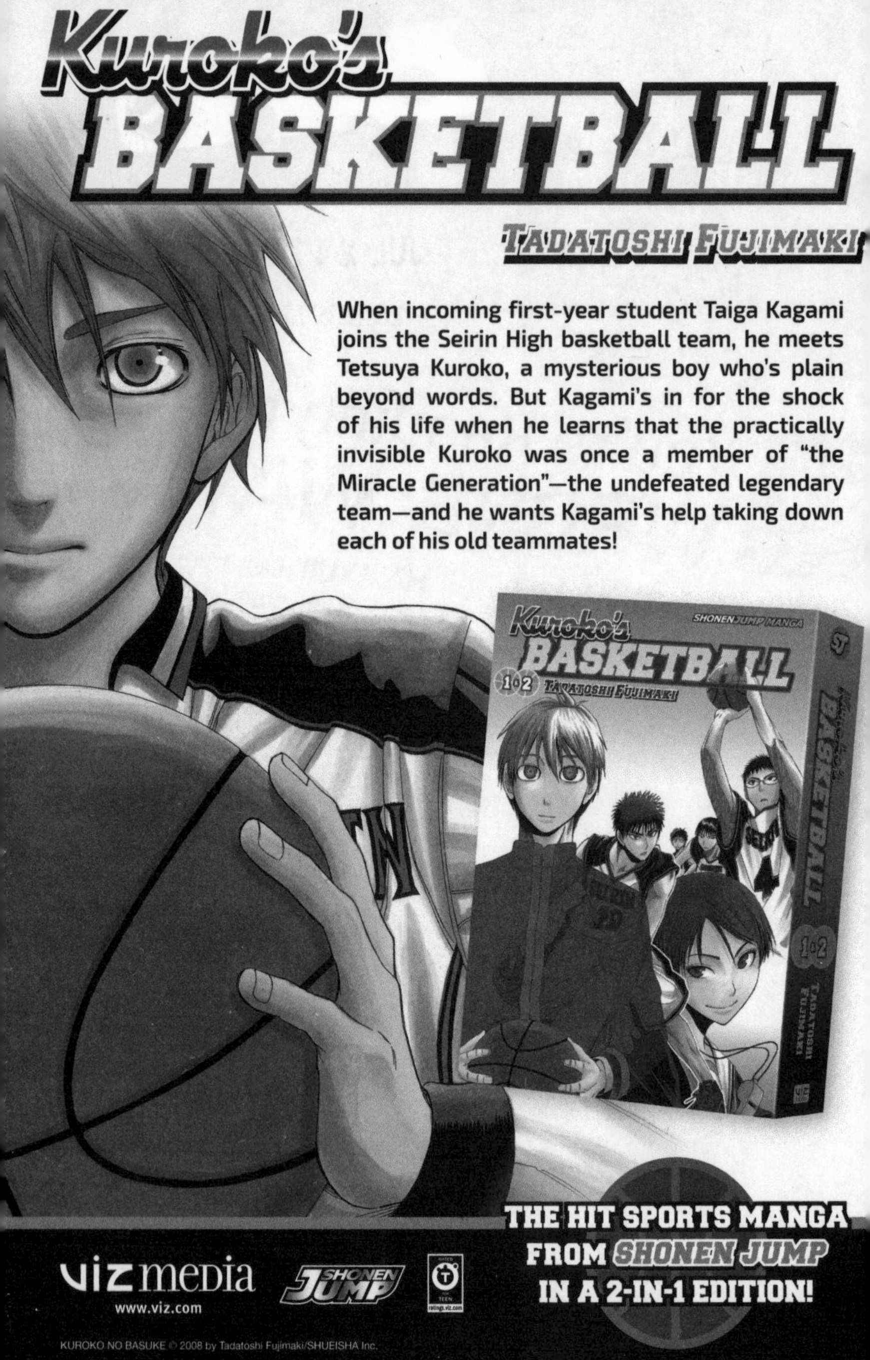
Kuroko's
BASKETBALL
TADATOSHI FUJIMAKI
When incoming first-year student Taiga Kagami joins the Seirin High basketball team, he meets Tetsuya Kuroko, a mysterious boy who's plain beyond words. But Kagami's in for the shock of his life when he learns that the practically invisible Kuroko was once a member of "the Miracle Generation"—the undefeated legendary team—and he wants Kagami's help taking down each of his old teammates!
SHONEN JUMP MANGA
Kuroko's
BASKETBALL
1•2
TADATOSHI FUJIMAKI
THE HIT SPORTS MANGA
FROM SHONEN JUMP
IN A 2-IN-1 EDITION!
viz media
www.viz.com
SHONEN JUMP
ratings.viz.com

You're Reading the WRONG WAY!

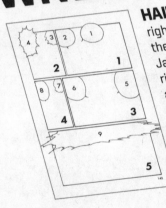

HAIKYU!! reads from right to left, starting in the upper-right corner. Japanese is read from right to left, meaning that action, sound effects and word-balloon order are completely reversed from English order.